ORGANIZATION THEORY

Sara Miller McCune founded SAGE Publishing in 1965 to support the dissemination of usable knowledge and educate a global community. SAGE publishes more than 1000 journals and over 800 new books each year, spanning a wide range of subject areas. Our growing selection of library products includes archives, data, case studies and video. SAGE remains majority owned by our founder and after her lifetime will become owned by a charitable trust that secures the company's continued independence.

Los Angeles | London | New Delhi | Singapore | Washington DC | Melbourne

ORGANIZATION
THEORY
Management & Leadership Analysis

Jesper Blomberg

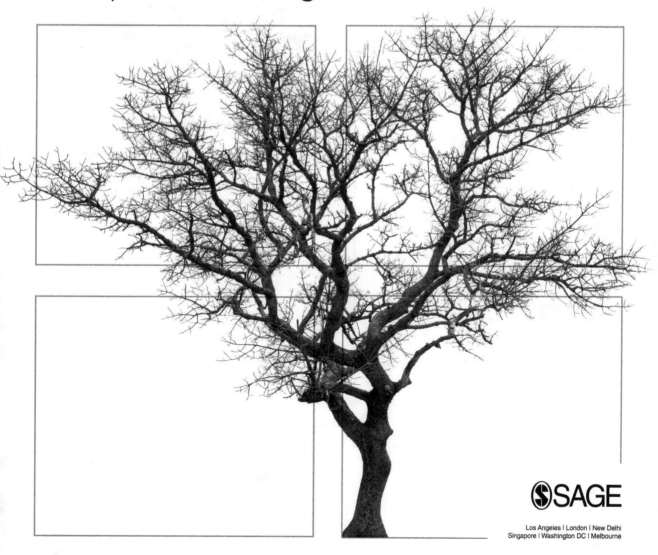

$SAGE

Los Angeles | London | New Delhi
Singapore | Washington DC | Melbourne

Los Angeles | London | New Delhi
Singapore | Washington DC | Melbourne

SAGE Publications Ltd
1 Oliver's Yard
55 City Road
London EC1Y 1SP

SAGE Publications Inc.
2455 Teller Road
Thousand Oaks, California 91320

SAGE Publications India Pvt Ltd
B 1/I 1 Mohan Cooperative Industrial Area
Mathura Road
New Delhi 110 044

SAGE Publications Asia-Pacific Pte Ltd
3 Church Street
#10-04 Samsung Hub
Singapore 049483

Editor: Ruth Stitt
Assistant editor: Jessica Moran
Assistant editor, digital: Sunita Patel
Production editor: Sarah Cooke
Copyeditor: Sharon Cawood
Proofreader: Katie Forsythe
Indexer: Silvia Benvenuto
Marketing manager: Abigail Sparks
Cover design: Francis Kenney
Typeset by: Cenveo Publisher Services

First published 2020

Library of Congress Control Number: 2019957496

British Library Cataloguing in Publication data

A catalogue record for this book is available from
the British Library

ISBN 978-1-5297-1313-8
ISBN 978-1-5297-1312-1 (pbk)

Contents

Extended Contents

List of Figures and Tables

Figures

Tables

About the Author

Jesper Blomberg is Associate Professor at the Stockholm School of Economics, where he also earned his PhD. His current research includes project management, with both an instrumental and critical stance, organizational analysis of the finance sector, as well as sustainable leadership and resilient organizing. Blomberg has published several books and articles covering organization and management theory, project management and organizational finance. He is also an appreciated lecturer both by graduate students and executive education participants and by professionals and managers.

Online Resources

Head online to **https://study.sagepub.com/blomberg** to access a range of online resources that will aid study and support teaching. *Organization Theory: Management and Leadership Analysis* is accompanied by:

For lecturers

- **PowerPoint slides**, featuring tables and figures from each chapter, which can be adapted and edited to suit your own teaching needs.
- An **Instructor's Manual**, providing ideas and inspiration for seminars and tutorials.
- A **Testbank** to help instructors assess students' progress and understanding.
- A **Resource Pack** to easily upload all the lecturer and student resources into your university's online learning platform (i.e. Blackboard or Moodle), and customise the content to suit your teaching needs.

For students

- **Video** links providing further insights into the key concepts discussed in the book.

1

An Introduction to Organization Theory, Management and Leadership Analysis

Organization theory, management and leadership analysis can be described in a variety of ways: as descriptions of activities in companies and organizations, as research orientations consisting of many different theories, as histories of ideas regarding different types of organization and management methods, as a number of metaphors for human interaction, and so on. Organization theory, management, and leadership analysis can also be described in a variety of styles: as a practical guide with normative advice for how to manage, organize and lead, or as a complex body of theoretical investigations. In this book, models and theoretical frameworks are the focus, rather than the practices of managing, organizing and leading. However, this does not mean that 'reality' can be ignored, or even consigned to a fuzzy background. On the contrary – through the presented theoretical frameworks and analytical models, reality will emerge, albeit in a more problematized and critically reviewed form. The practices of managing, organizing and leading will therefore become clearer than if they were presented on their own.

Organization theory, management and leadership analysis offer tools to analyze not only business and professional organizations, but almost any kind of social grouping. Everything, from the most unnoticed, trivial encounter between two people to major societal historical trends, can be analyzed with the tools offered in this book. The primary purpose of such analysis is not an intellectual or academic exercise, but to increase understanding for what we do, from very small interactions to society at large. A better understanding of what we do opens up more alternative possible actions. We increase our understanding of others, of what works well and of what doesn't. Most importantly, it gives us the knowledge and power to address real problems with practical working solutions. Thus, with the organizational, management and leadership theories described in this book, we can create better human relations, better organizations, and become better organizational members, professionals, change agents, managers and leaders working toward a better world for all of us.

In this first chapter, we jump straight into a quite abstract reasoning of why the combination of 'theoretical pluralism', 're-framing' and 'multi-frame analysis' is the most useful way of analyzing any organizational, management and leadership phenomena. Multi-frame analysis is compared with 'free thinking' and 'single-frame analysis'. It is concluded that multi-frame analysis creates a deeper and more useful understanding. The description of multi-frame analysis ends with a short presentation of the four basic theoretical frameworks that structure the content of the book.

Before we present the benefits of reflective and critical analysis with the help of different theoretical frameworks, some sort of unproblematized description of reality must be given some space. What more specific 'organizational phenomena' are the many analytical tools supposed to help us understand better? What practical aspects and activities can we understand in different, more fruitful ways, given the deeper analytical knowledge that management and organizational theory can offer us? In order to answer these questions, we start this chapter by putting the many models and theoretical frameworks on hold. This makes it slightly easier for us to construct a short and unproblematized picture of what kind of subject organizational analysis is, what organizations are and what organizing is, what organizing processes consist of and what it is we do when we manage, organize and lead.

The empirical material of organizational analysis

An organization (or, more correctly, 'organizational processes') can consist of anything from a couple of people who do something together, for example build a fence or try to reduce street violence among young people, to activities in large multinational companies that include tens of thousands of people and shipments of goods and financial transactions across several continents, have close collaboration with political institutions and handle huge sums of money. It can range from non-profit organizations to virtual 'communities', with the goal of stopping environmental pollution or creating an international caliphate. Basically, everything we do involves some kind of organizing or some form of organization. We grow up, we study, we work, we travel, we fall ill, we get well, we grow older and we die, all within the setting of organizations. But why is it like this? Why do organizations exist? What do they consist of? And how can we influence, organize, manage and lead them?

Just as a manufacturing company, for example, has usually organized its business into a number of specialized functions, such as purchasing, product development, manufacturing, marketing, accounting and management, educational business economics programs have been specialized into a number of subject areas. Thus, you study accounting, finance, marketing, strategy, operations and other subjects, as part of most business economics programs. Organizational theory can thus be seen as a specialized discipline among others. But it can also be said to differ from the others, partly because its practical function differs from that of other subjects.

In order for a group of people to succeed in building a fence or for a large company to be successful, the work of different people and the activities of different functions must be connected in some way. If I cut planks that are too short for the intended fence, or if you do not understand how my cut planks should be put together, or if a marketing department markets a product that the production department cannot manufacture, then the organization will not work. Organization theory is about how an activity can be divided into several, more specialized activities and how these activities can be combined, integrated or coordinated to form some kind of value-adding process. It does not matter how talented a number of specialists are, how innovative product developers are, how efficient a production department is, or how effective a marketing strategy is, if the different specialist functions do not work reasonably well together. Organization theory therefore differs from other functions, in that it combines them, so to speak, both through their theoretical models and in practice – the reality.

Set in a business context, the central position and weight of the subject of management and organization theory can be illustrated by Figure 1.1. Organization theory can be said to discuss not only how different functions are coordinated, but also how they can and should be coordinated.

Figure 1.1 Organization as a central and cohesive function

However, this is a substantial simplification. In order for an activity to be coordinated, it must also be divided and specialized into different sub-activities. Organization theory is as much about division of labor as about coordination of labor. But even that description is a substantial simplification. The question of what constitutes an organization receives different answers, depending on which theoretical framework the answer is based on. Organizations comprise several and qualitatively different basic theoretical assumptions that can be clustered into a number of consistent frameworks. These frameworks are very important to understand in order to be able to perform proper management analysis. Thus, the content of this book is structured into four basic theoretical frameworks. We return to these frameworks and their different answers at the end of this chapter, and in the next.

Even on a less problematized and less theoretical level, organization is both a more comprehensive and more fundamental phenomenon than Figure 1.1 shows. As mentioned earlier, we also organize ourselves in smaller and more informal contexts (see examples in Figure 1.2). Whether we build a fence in our free time, play games, cook together, do sports or just hang out online or in real life, we relate to each other and can be said to be organizing ourselves. We can definitely understand better what happens in the most trivial social contexts by analyzing them with organization theory. How do we divide tasks up into small groups when we work on a project as part of a course in, say, management? How do we coordinate the same work? How do we make decisions? Who has the most influence, and why? Do we all let everyone speak? Why? Why not? These and similar questions can be answered with the help of organizational analysis. But also, major social phenomena, historical trends, industrial sectors and institutional structures can be understood and analyzed using management and organizational theory.

The many models, theories and concepts in the book have been selected based on the criterion that, if properly applied, they will be able to provide concrete and action-based new knowledge about organization and leadership in practical contexts and situations. Correctly applied, these models will create new insights into appropriate ways of acting in real-world, practical contexts and situations. Well-conducted analyses, based on the many models and the four frameworks in the book, can create better understanding, decisions and actions. This applies to everything from informal organization in small groups, our friendship circles, social media, the formal organizations and companies we often work in, to major, overarching social issues.

After this brief initial description of the empirical subject of organizational analysis, it is time to address its theoretical basis or, more accurately, its theoretical bases. One idea that forms the basis of organizational analysis comes from the concepts of theoretical pluralism, re-framing and multi-frame analysis (explained below). Another, though closely related, theoretical basis is the formulation of four distinct and partly contradictory fundamental theoretical frameworks. In the remainder of this first chapter, we explain why theoretical pluralism/multi-frame analysis is a better starting point for organizational, management and leadership analysis than 'free thinking' and

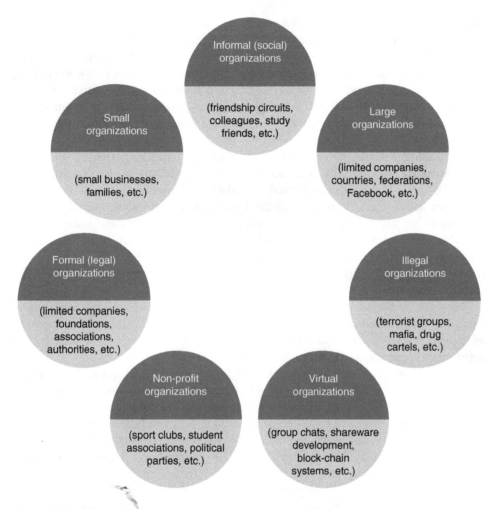

Figure 1.2   **Some examples of categories of organizations**

'single-frame analysis'. The chapter concludes with an initial presentation of the four theoretical frameworks.

Critical thinking, theoretical pluralism and multi-frame analysis

It is often said that critical thinking is an important skill among citizens and leaders in a democratic society. Also, in business practice and management contexts, the ideal of the 'reflective practitioner' is widespread (Schön 1983). A critical thinker or a reflective practitioner is usually conceptualized as an individual person, not getting stuck in old trains of thought, but having the ability to discover and interpret new information and to think and act creatively. There are many sayings expressing this conception: 'think outside the box' and 'leave your comfort zone' are perhaps the most well-known. It has also been suggested that successful, educated and smart people are actually worse at reflective and critical thinking than people in general (Argyris 1991). It is argued that this makes them less fitting as leaders and change agents of organizations that need to be responsive, flexible and innovative.

The assumption that successful management and leadership create flexible, fast and innovative organizations, is usually taken for granted. We seldom review it critically. This means that we often overlook other fundamental functions required in all organizations, namely stabilizing, disciplining and controlling human behavior. In order to say an organization exists, it must lock in resources and stabilize activities. This is one of several possible fundamental definitions of an organization. If an organization reacted to everything, it would lose the ability to invest, develop and create added value. Instead, it would be reduced to a reactive, passive, dissolved, chaotic organism.

But what do we actually mean by reflection? What do we mean by critical thinking? And why is it important? Organization theory, as described in this book, provides an explicit answer to these questions – an answer that also relates to the content and structure of organization theory itself.

We can view any object or phenomenon from very different perspectives. Everything, from a simple drawing to a complex organizational process, can be interpreted qualitatively differently. Such different interpretations are usually a consequence of the fact that they are based on different underlying perspectives or frameworks. Each framework will highlight some aspects and hide others. There is no framework that can show us everything. Thus, a key strength of organizational analysis is the use of different, complementary and partly contradicting theoretical frameworks. Figure 1.3 is deliberately drawn to be interpreted as qualitatively different things. For example, it can be interpreted as a three-dimensional cube or as an umbrella from above. The interpretation depends on who you are, what past experiences you have in life and the context you are in. For example, at a lecture at the Swedish military high command, most participants saw the figure as an army tent from above.

It cannot be argued that a cube, an umbrella or a tent is the correct or true interpretation. These interpretations are equally reasonable, and they are caused by different, equally reasonable interpretative frames. From a military perspective, the army tent is a very reasonable interpretation; and, based on a geometric perspective, the cube is reasonable. Neither can the different interpretations be combined into some kind of true synthesis, for example a 'cubic umbrella'. Instead, we have to accept a simultaneous presence of several, equally true interpretations. In other words, we can accept *theoretical pluralism*.

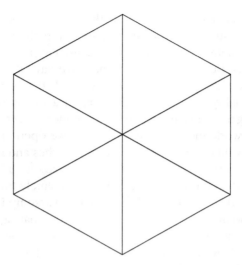

Figure 1.3   **What is this? A cube, an umbrella or perhaps an army tent from above?**

An additional point concerning Figure 1.3 is that we first see the figure, or the 'phenomenon', as something, regardless of whether this something happens to be an umbrella, a tent or a cube. After that, using theory, we can begin to examine and dissect the figure/phenomenon into smaller elements – that is, analyze it. Based on one theory, for example, the figure consists of nine (or 12) straight lines of certain specific lengths, with angles relative to each other. According to another theory, it consists of light hitting a paper surface, which in turn reflects different quantities of light, which is then perceived by our eyes, which in turn sends signals. Now it starts getting slightly complicated because light is not only composed of matter but also of wavelengths. The scientific answer depends on which scientific theory you apply.

However, this is not a physics book, nor a chapter on the human eye and brain. More important, in this context, is that, according to a third theory, the figure is an artifact whose meaning and significance are produced by or negotiated between its users, in this case the author of this text, the text itself and its readers. Depending on how this interaction and negotiation develop, the figure takes on different meanings. Suddenly, we face a more natural science (physical and biological) versus a social science (semiotic and literary critical) interpretation of the figure. With the help of theory, we can problematize and go beyond the obvious and seemingly true interpretations that we so easily make in our everyday thinking. Different theoretical frameworks reveal different aspects, and no aspect needs to be truer than the other. Again, it is about theoretical pluralism.

When we consider something, such as a figure in a textbook or on a company's website, we do not see it primarily as some advanced physical phenomenon or as a semiotic language game, we see it as a figure, a company or something else more or less obvious. In everyday life as well as in working life, we take most phenomena for granted. We rarely ask ourselves what an organization really is, or why organizations exist, and we do not analyze seemingly trivial everyday phenomena with the aid of theoretical frameworks. But we can if we want, if we have the necessary knowledge about how the appropriate analytical tools are used. If we pose these and other, similar, seemingly trivial questions, as well as master a variety of analytical tools and frameworks, we will gain a greater, deeper and broader insight into the organizations we encounter in our work and in our spare time. If we open up our thinking to new types of insights, we will be more open to new approaches and new ways to influence these organizations, and thus our own and other people's lives.

There is no established knowledge mass that is absolutely true. There is no science that cannot be criticized for its more or less unfounded assumptions. There is no management theory, economic theory or organization theory that can legitimately claim to have a higher truth content than all other similar theories. The fact that organization theory is characterized by theoretical pluralism should therefore be seen as something positive rather than as a shortcoming. Within a number of other economic and business disciplines, the subject is presented as *one* coherent theory. Organization theory textbooks are often more honest, as they actually reflect the theoretical diversity that characterizes the subject area. In this way, organization theory is also more challenging. It does not only require the student to mechanically perform model- and theory-based analyses, but also requires that the student perform this type of analysis based on different, and in many cases, conflicting theories. Gaining an ability to see phenomena from a variety of perspectives – to learn how to conduct *re-framing* and *multi-frame analysis* – is one of the cornerstones of research-based 'academic', 'scientific' organizational analysis. It is also one of the cornerstones of this book. It is not enough to completely master a number of models. It is also necessary to understand the basic assumptions of these models, and, when required, to abandon them in favor of models based on other, sometimes completely contradictory assumptions.[1]

However, *multi-frame analysis* and theoretical *re-framing* do not have to conflict with the ability to showcase the use of individual concrete analysis tools. On the contrary, the ability to use analytical models based on different fundamental frameworks can support and give multi-frame analysis a helping hand. Being able to talk unhindered about basic assumptions and various frameworks is not enough to fully master organizational analysis. It is also necessary to apply the frameworks in the form of analysis of concrete organizational phenomena. Organization theory therefore has two fundamental, mutually supportive functions or purposes:

1. to offer specific analytical tools in the form of models and concepts which can be applied to analyze and increase understanding of any organizational phenomena
2. to offer several, internally coherent and partly contradictory fundamental theoretical frameworks that, when applied in analysis, replace, complement or re-frame common-sense thinking.

Multi-frame analysis can both deepen knowledge about and provide an ability to critically review the analyzed phenomena. It can also serve as a tool to critically review the individual analytical models and the analyses and conclusions produced using them.

In short, management, organizational and leadership theory offers models and tools that make it easier for us to think and act in and around organizations in new ways. We understand more and better. We can increase our tolerance and our control. We can increase our freedom of action and make our organizations better.

Three types of critical thinking

As organizational theory consists of several, partly contradictory, theories, re-framing and multi-frame analysis are one way of looking at critical thinking and help us, in part, to answer the question of what critical thinking is. To explain the benefits of this specific version of critical thinking (by re-framing and multi-frame analysis), it can be compared with two other ways of looking at critical thinking: thinking freely and technical single-frame analysis. We take a look at these three types of critical thinking below.

Thinking freely

'To think freely is great', the saying goes. Thinking freely is trying to think outside of one's normal lines of thought, without any real systematic approach. Some people may be perceived as being better at coming up with new ideas or solving problems in a creative way, and these people appear to be better at free thinking than others. There is nothing 'wrong' with free thinking – on the contrary, it can be 'great' – but it's not obviously the most effective way to try and understand organization. Free thinking involves a number of problems. Among others, it can be difficult to know how free it actually is.

All our thinking is, among other things, a product of our previous experiences. Even a person's freest thoughts derive to a high degree from that thinking person. If we see something, we can only see this something as something we can imagine ourselves. The thoughts, perspectives and possible interpretations are always limited by our own experience, our own knowledge, creativity and imagination. We all have a limited amount of experience, and therefore there is a limit even for our most daring, unusual and different thoughts. Critically reviewing something, for example trying to understand the causes of an organizational problem, let's say high staff turnover, means that the solutions are limited by our previous experiences. To be really critical, you must also criticize these experiences of your own, that is, yourself. Self-criticism is difficult, especially without external help. Theory offers such outside assistance, and

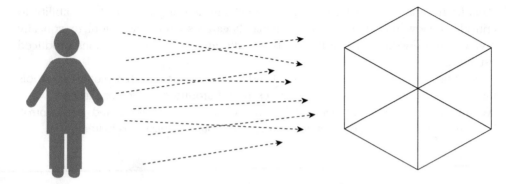

Figure 1.4   Analysis by 'free thinking'

without analytical help, for example from organizational theory, a critical review of, for example, 'high staff turnover' becomes difficult. We may be able to deal with, and possibly even lower, the high staff turnover in all sorts of ways, but with the help of theory, we can come much further, something we will soon illustrate.

Our practical experiences are, to a high degree, stored in our mind as being taken-for-granted, implicit assumptions, values and ideas. We often refer to these assumptions and ideas as 'common sense'. They do not offer coherent logical systems or explicit theoretical assumptions. Perhaps our common sense includes theoretical pluralism, perhaps not. Because it is not systematically described, we cannot know. All we know is that it comes from ourselves and our experiences. This is illustrated by the arrows in Figure 1.4, which are overlapping and dotted, that is to say unclear.

In summary, free thinking can be a relatively inefficient way of thinking critically and analyzing organizational phenomena. It is not as free as it may seem, and it is unclear as it is not based on conscious assumptions or systematic systems.

Technical single-frame analysis

A common way of trying to do the almost impossible, that is, change our ingrained ways of thinking, our common sense and behavior patterns, is to enlist external help, in the case of technical single-frame analysis, from a more formalized theory. Such theory is based on other people's experiences and is often formulated, more or less, as coherent logical systems. Even theory is based on assumptions that can be more or less substantiated, but, unlike everyday thinking, common sense and personal experiences, the assumptions are usually explicitly formulated and thus easier to review. The greater the distance between the formal theory we use and its basic assumptions, our own common sense and own experiences, the greater the potential of the theory to challenge the analyst's thinking. Or expressed slightly differently: the greater the

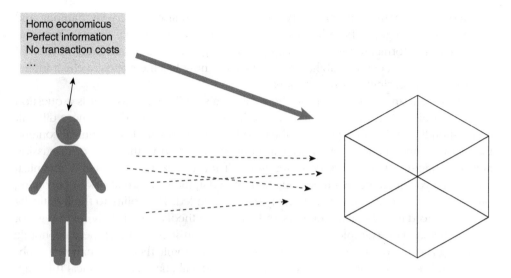

Figure 1.5   Technical analysis – analysis with the aid of theory

distance between our own everyday thinking and the more formal theory, the higher the potential of the analysis to show a phenomenon in new light.

Figure 1.5 shows how theory offers an alternative starting point for analysis. The distance between the analyst's everyday thinking (in the red person's head) and the more formal theory (the grey box) can enable interpretations of the phenomenon from a new point of view. In addition, the theory contains a number of basic assumptions (in the grey box). They indicate that this theory is a very traditional economic theory based on an assumption of the rational, utility-maximizing human being, *homo economicus.*

But even technical single-frame analysis, i.e. analysis with the aid of one particular theory, can be problematic. For example, what theory is chosen is crucial to how much it can challenge the analyst to think critically. We all tend to seek supportive information, which means that we often choose a theory that we like. This is often because the theory has much in common with our common sense, our everyday thinking and the implicit assumptions we already make. The distance between formal theory and our own everyday theories therefore becomes unnecessarily small. Thus, the reflection, the critical review, will also be unnecessarily small. As a student or leader, we often choose to specialize in subjects that we like, and since we often like what is similar to us, the possibility of learning a higher degree of re-framing has already been exacerbated.

It will be even worse if we then study this theory in detail and for an extended time, without studying other, contradictory theories in similar detail. With longer and more intimate contact with a formal theory, the tendency is that our everyday thinking and common sense begin to be influenced by and resemble the formal theory. Our common sense and formal theory increasingly merge together, and the original function of the theory – to broaden our ability to understand – now has the opposite effect in that we become increasingly narrow-minded.

The content and structure of the theory itself also influence this. If it is a question of a technically advanced formal theory, perhaps highly quantified, it is more difficult to question the basic assumptions of the theory. In theories with less technical content, the theory's fundamental assumptions are often more vivid in the form of discussion and self-criticism. If you have educated yourself for a long time in a highly technical theory that you liked the first time you encountered it, there is a great risk of becoming one with the theory and hence extremely narrow-minded. The ability to think critically is then reduced to unfamiliar contexts and where the theory you usually rely on is not applied before. For example, if you are working in a business setting where economic reasoning is commonplace, and you use advanced economic theory to analyze a problem, there is a risk of it leading to the opposite of critical analysis and critical thinking, albeit in the form of technically dazzling analysis.

In Figure 1.6, the economically everyday-thinking person has chosen a theoretical area that, from the beginning, was relatively similar to their own everyday thinking, that is, a classic economic theory. As this person has also carried out detailed studies in this field of theory, its everyday thinking has also been influenced by and become increasingly similar to the studied theory. As this theory is also technologically

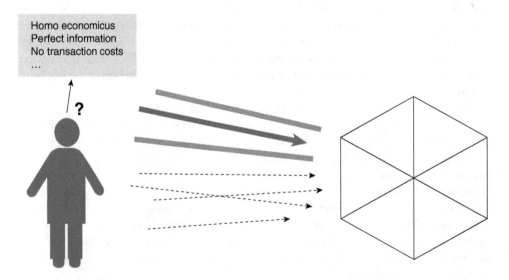

Homo economicus
Perfect information
No transaction costs
...

Figure 1.6   If the distance between analysts and theory decreases, the risk of narrow-mindedness increases

advanced, it does not include much self-criticism regarding its basic assumptions. The highly technical theory thus constitutes an obstacle to re-framing (illustrated by the thick grey lines in the figure). The overall effect is that the theory, instead of implying reflection and criticism of the person's everyday thinking, leads to narrow-minded, one-dimensional analysis.

Theoretical pluralism and multi-frame analysis

The solution provided by organization theory to the problems outlined above is to encompass many theories, some of them partly contradictory. This makes it difficult or impossible for a person who perceives and analyzes a phenomenon to make their everyday thinking and their 'common sense' merge with a theory. The different theoretical frameworks act as criticism both of the everyday thinking of people and of each other. A person may feel more connected with one of the frameworks, but the theoretical pluralism of organization theory implies a critical review of this framework as well.

In this book, four more or less logically coherent fundamental theories or frameworks (see Figure 1.7) are presented. If they are used properly in the analysis of a real organizational phenomenon, they will complement and contradict each other.

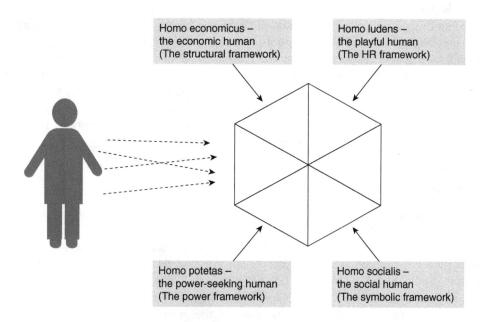

Figure 1.7   Four different assumptions about human nature and four different theoretical frameworks

An organizational analysis using the four frameworks includes both technical analysis and multi-frame analysis. Technical analyses based on several more or less formalized models are complemented by the fact that the models derive from different frames of references with partly contradictory fundamental assumptions.

If we want to be able to analyze organizational phenomena and problems as well as possible, we should also put extra energy into the frameworks that we initially dislike or find most difficult to apply. If we are attracted to, for example, the structural framework, we should put extra energy into an analysis from, for example, the power framework. If we do the opposite, i.e. concentrate our analysis on the frame of reference we like and are familiar with, we risk the same problems arising as in a one-dimensional, more technical analysis, i.e. the analysis creates narrow-mindedness rather than critical analysis and reflection. It is thus important to be able to analyze organization from several frameworks, preferably all four, i.e. to go full circle, as in Figure 1.7.

Four frameworks on management, organization and leadership

The book describes four fundamental theoretical frameworks, as well as a number of models that are included within them. Each framework is presented in two chapters. The first describes the more basic models of the framework and the other describes the more in-depth models. The description of each fundamental perspective begins with a brief historical description of how the current frame of reference has evolved from research and organizational practice. This is followed by a description of a number of analytical models and how these can be used in the analysis of concrete organizational phenomena. Finally, the strengths and weaknesses of the framework are described. However, to create a preliminary picture of organization theory as a whole, the four frameworks are briefly introduced here.

Two modern organizational frameworks

The first two frameworks described in the book, *the structural framework* (Chapters 2 and 3) and *the HR framework* (Chapters 4 and 5), are very topical and established in business and organizational practice. For example, if you ask a business executive what their organization looks like, you usually get answers that describe how the business is structured, what processes they have 'set' and how they treat employees. These two frameworks are also the two oldest in the organization research field and can be termed 'modern', not in the sense that they are the most fashionable or trendy today but because they are examples of 'modernist' thinking. They are relatively easy to use in the analysis of organizational phenomena and problems, and if the analyses are performed correctly, they lead to specific normative conclusions as to whether we have organized appropriately or whether we should re-organize the business into some other, better way. Organizations are seen from these frameworks largely as instruments that can be used to achieve formulated goals, such as the efficient production of goods and services.

The structural framework

An organizational analysis based on a structural framework answers the question of whether we have chosen to formalize and structure organizational processes in an appropriate manner. Do the current structure and the formalized processes support the organization's strategy, its environment and operations, or should it be restructured to allow it to be able to conduct operations more efficiently? The structural framework has a close link to traditional economic theory and views the human being as a rational maximizer of material wealth (*homo economicus*). Within the structural framework, there are a variety of models for formalizing, specializing and coordinating activities, that is, how organizations can and should be structured to be as efficient as possible (see Figure 1.8).

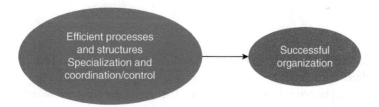

Figure 1.8   A successful organization according to the structural framework

The HR framework

An organizational analysis based on the HR framework (HR as in *human resources* or *human relations*) is more about how the needs of the organization and the employees fit together (see Figure 1.9). If they do not fit together, the work organization

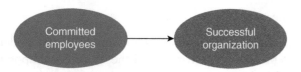

Figure 1.9   A successful organization according to the HR perspective

and/or employee policy should be changed to better meet employees' needs. Employ-ees are assumed to naturally like to work, just as children like to play, given that they are allowed to work/play (*homo ludens*). If employees are given interesting work tasks, they will become motivated to work hard. According to the HR framework, motivated employees are a prerequisite for efficient operations. If a particular structure or design of a process is in conflict with employees' needs for, for example, influence, self-determination or stimulating tasks, it does not matter whether the structure or process is right from the point of view of a structural framework. Both the structural and HR frameworks are about what leads to successful organizations, but they have different and partially contradictory recipes.

Two contemporary organizational frameworks

The last two fundamental frameworks described in this book, *the power framework* (Chapters 6 and 7) and *the symbolic framework* (Chapters 8 and 9), can be said to be more contemporary. They emerged as distinct frameworks within organization theory after the structural and HR frameworks were developed. They can be seen both as a criticism of and as a complement to these other frameworks.

The power framework

Within a power framework, all organizational processes, goals and solutions, are prod-ucts of political processes between actors with different and conflicting interests. There are neither targets nor efficiency measures that benefit everyone. What is efficient for some is less efficient for others. Conflicts, power struggles and political processes are daily occurrences and cannot be made to disappear, using either optimal structures, correctly set processes or satisfied human needs. The framework assumes that human beings are always striving to increase their powers (*homo potestas*). The power frame-work consists of different ways of mapping and analyzing the political landscape, which, according to this perspective, characterizes all organizations and their sur-roundings (see Figure 1.10). Through such an analysis, different, more or less 'smart' power strategies can be applied to promote certain interests at the expense of other interests and stakeholders.

The symbolic framework

The symbolic framework can be seen as a criticism of the two modernist frameworks (the structural and the HR frameworks) and the more contemporary power frame-work. The structural and HR frameworks can be said to be romantic or naive in their

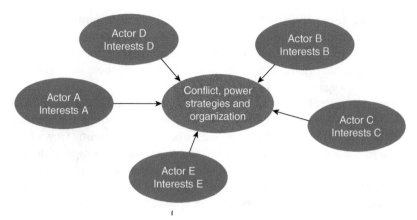

Figure 1.10   A power framework on organizational phenomena

belief in efficiency and in their ability to organize in a way that benefits everyone, that is, in the assumption of overall rationality or harmony. The power framework can be said to be cynical in its view of the human being as not just a will-driven but also a power-seeking creature (*homo potestas*). The power framework can be said to immunize against power blindness, but, if it is not complemented by other perspectives, it can also lead to power hypersensitivity. The risk of a unilateral utilization of the power framework is that opportunities for rational and common solutions tend to be underestimated.

Within a symbolic framework, the human being is neither rational, selfish, caring, nor power-driven. The human being is rather what the social context makes her into (*homo socialis*). Given a certain cultural context, the human being can become a thoroughbred bureaucrat, an enthusiastic team player, a strong-willed entrepreneur, a power animal or perhaps a bit of everything – or something else entirely. The symbolic framework's basic assumption of the human being is that she seeks meaning, that is, to understand an infinitely complex, changing and uncertain world. By creating culture together with, and/or against, others, the complexity can be simplified and may make the world understandable, meaningful and manageable. However, the specific content of such a culture can vary from context to context. For example, a company can be said to recreate a specific corporate culture, while another is characterized by a rather different one. In addition, each department within a company can have its specific character, and different professions can be in conflict with each other. National or regional identities are another way of looking at symbolism and culture.

Organizational analysis based on a symbolic frame is about understanding how symbols express, create and recreate meaning and organizational culture, for example through symbolic leadership, and what effects symbols and culture may conceivably have. Does organizational culture coordinate people's actions and/or does it exacerbate any attempts to implement change? Do certain symbols primarily fulfill the function of legitimizing the organization's operations by making them look good, or do the symbols affect the organization's activities more directly?

On a more basic level, the symbolic frame can be said to be the basis for the entire organization theory. The idea of multi-frame analysis and the strength of theoretical pluralism itself are an expression of the symbolic frame's more relativistic view of the human being and organization. Artifacts in the form of, for example, an organizational chart, a formalized process, a factory or balance sheet, mean different things and are interpreted differently in different cultural contexts (see Figure 1.11). Depending on these interpretations, management, organization and leadership will be conducted in different ways.

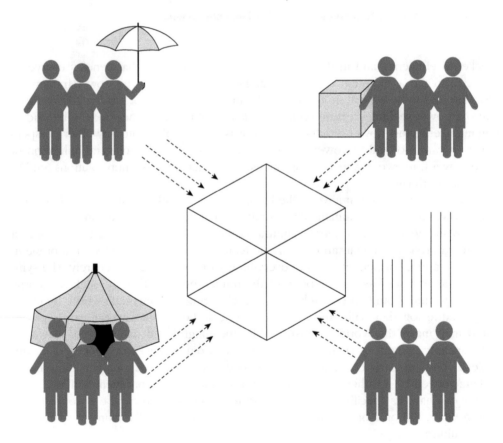

Figure 1.11   A symbolic framework on organizational phenomena

Note: Within different cultures, the same phenomenon is perceived entirely differently.

A fifth framework?

In academic textbooks, organization theory is usually presented in the form of a number of clear theoretical perspectives. Sometimes they are categorized a little differently than they are here, as an author may advocate a particular thesis and try to synthesize these perspectives into a single theoretical framework. In some books, the power framework is omitted or integrated into the others, while others focus on a single framework.[2] There are also those who divide up organizational theory into a relatively large number of 'metaphors'.[3]

However, as this book is intended as a concise introduction to organizational theory, it cannot cover everything. For example, organizational research includes more pronounced *critical social theory*, which can be said to be driven by more emancipatory or radical-critical knowledge interests, rather than explanatory and regulatory ones. Instead of merely describing how organizations work, an attempt is made to create knowledge about how they *could* work – not necessarily to become more efficient, in the traditional sense, but to make society better, expose injustice, help weak actors or show how minorities are systematically segregated and act under worse conditions than strong, favored groups or majorities. In such, even more critical, organizational analysis, concepts such as class, social background, gender, ethnicity, diversity and intersectionality are important.

This type of analysis could be presented as a fifth framework. Such a framework could then be said to encompass all the previous four frameworks but with a sharper and more critical ambition. However, within the format of this book, there is no scope for doing justice to this extensive part of organization theory. However, in the book's in-depth chapters on the power and symbolic frameworks respectively (Chapters 7 and 9), a number of theories are described which can be referred to as being more critical. These theories are key to understanding the full scope of organizational analysis. They are very important in themselves as analytical tools, but they also link to another, larger and more critical world of organizational analysis.

However, the division into four frameworks made here (see Figure 1.12) is not unique to this particular book. The division is rather a variation on how Bolman and Deal (2013) divide organization theory. Here, however, the frameworks and their fundamental assumptions are even more pronounced in order to facilitate multi-frame analysis. The big difference between Bolman and Deal's presentation and this book is the content of the different frameworks. Instead of long descriptions and heroic explanations of mainly American white men and senior executives, this book contains more analytical models as well as descriptions of how these can be applied in theory-driven and action-based management, organizational and leadership analysis.

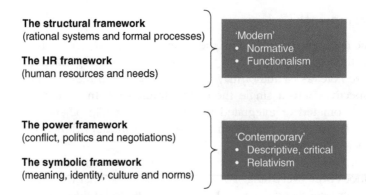

The structural framework
(rational systems and formal processes)

The HR framework
(human resources and needs)

'Modern'
• Normative
• Functionalism

The power framework
(conflict, politics and negotiations)

The symbolic framework
(meaning, identity, culture and norms)

'Contemporary'
• Descriptive, critical
• Relativism

Figure 1.12   Four fundamental theoretical frameworks

A toolbox of analytical devices

Even if we ignore the above reasoning about multi-frame analysis, critical reflection and theoretical pluralism, there is much to be found in management, organizational and leadership analysis. The many analytical models can be seen as tools with different functions that are appropriate for different situations. This book then becomes a toolbox – just open the various compartments and choose a suitable tool for the task at hand. Interpreting it like this, the four frameworks become four main compartments. The function of the frameworks will then be toned down – it will be more about finding the right department in the toolbox rather than acquiring a better ability to think critically with the aid of multi-frame analysis. This type of interpretation is of course completely legitimate, but it also means that the potential of organizational analysis is not fully utilized.

Although the toolbox metaphor provides a simplified view of organizational analysis, it can be seen as a good start to the journey into the subject. How to approach organizational analysis is very much a matter of taste. Either you start, as in this chapter, focusing on fundamental theoretical frameworks, or you begin by choosing and rejecting more pragmatically from among all the analytical models described in this book. In the latter case, it will automatically be a more empirically driven analysis. First, you identify a 'problem', and then you select a few sensible tools. However, as the example below shows, defining something as a problem requires a perspective, a framework. And maybe, what is seen as a problem from one framework, might be perceived as a non-problem or even a solution from another.

An apparently straightforward example

It was mentioned briefly above that the phenomenon of 'high staff turnover' can be understood with the aid of organizational analysis. With *the structural framework's* focus on the human being as an economically benefit-maximizing individual, an analysis of high staff turnover can lead to the conclusion that staff are not receiving adequate wages for their efforts. They therefore choose to work in any other organization that offers higher pay. Possible solutions would be to offer higher or more performance-oriented pay. It may also be a matter of poorly structured processes. By clarifying the specialized roles each individual has, or should have, one can make it easier for the employee to do their work successfully.

From an *HR framework* perspective, the issue of motivating employees is important, but this does not necessarily happen by means of pay, clear processes or well-defined roles. On the contrary, the solution may be to re-frame the tasks themselves so that they become more challenging and stimulating. Perhaps operations can be organized with less specialization but with increased self-management in teams that communicate and formulate common strategies and goals.

From a *power framework* perspective, it is perhaps more about how management can strengthen its position of power vis-à-vis the employees. Possible solutions can be individual rewards, increased control, trying to make employees less valuable by transforming their skills into structural capital, or building alliances with trade union representatives. But, from a power framework perspective – as well as from a *symbolic framework* perspective – high staff turnover can also be good for an organization's success. It may be cheaper to exploit the employees for a few years, then replace them, than allow them to develop so that they want to stay. At the same time, it may be important to set goals and formally work towards lowering the high staff turnover, but on a more symbolic level. An organization that exploits its staff may appear illegitimate and may therefore find it difficult to recruit new staff, sell its products or finance its investments. One solution may be to set goals and formally work towards reduced staff turnover, but without ever succeeding in doing so.

That which from one perspective can be seen as a problem can therefore be seen as a solution from another. The value of the different analytical models therefore increases if they are based on different fundamental assumptions, i.e. belong to different, complementary and partly contradictory frameworks of organizational theory.

Strategy, operation management, leadership and related subjects

Another issue relevant to the selection of the analytical models included in this book is what subject or discipline they belong to or derive from. Or, put another way: where should the boundary be drawn between more general management and organizational analysis and analysis that is usually considered as belonging to other disciplines such as strategy formulation, operation management, entrepreneurship or leadership? This book represents a tolerant view of what is included or not included in organization theory. There is no reason to deselect those analytical models that fit well into an organizational analysis, and in any of the four frameworks, solely on the basis that, in other texts and contexts, they are considered to belong to another subject. The purpose here is to assist the reader with the most useful models for organizational analysis, regardless of where these models originate. Therefore, the following chapters contain models that, in other courses and programs, should be defined as belonging to strategic management, organizational behavior, talent management, operation management, change management, entrepreneurship, project management, industrial marketing or some other, related subject area.

Leadership theory and analysis lie within an Anglo-Saxon tradition, regarded as both a research field and a study subject separate from management and organization theory. The typical Anglo-Saxon mainstream leadership textbook has a very different structure and quite different content to textbooks in organization theory. In a Scandinavian and, to some extent, European tradition, leadership is viewed as an integral part of management and organization theory. One common formulation about leadership in Scandinavia is that leadership is the application of organization theory in practice. This does not exclude many of the leadership concepts and models developed in the Anglo-Saxon tradition, but they are often included and placed side by side with more organizational and managerial concepts and models. Within this Scandinavian tradition, leadership has 'always' been viewed as relational, distributed, organizational, as a process, and not necessarily defined as something to do with 'shared goals' (the latter corresponding to one of the four frameworks in this book). This book is firmly rooted in this Scandinavian view of leadership. Leadership models are incorporated in all four fundamental theoretical frameworks, which might surprise the reader not used to this.

How to use this book

As noted in the preface to the book, this text is consciously relatively deficient in empirical illustrations and examples and can therefore appear to be abstract. One reason for this is that the best empirical material to apply all the models and frameworks to in your analysis is your own experience. Everyone has the experience of various organizational settings. Everything from informal organizational processes in the most mundane, everyday situations, to the formal reorganization efforts of large corporations, can work as empirical material in applying the models and frameworks presented here. But for the student, the less experienced employee, manager or leader, this can still be problematic. There might be a need for less personal and more ready-packaged material to practice your organizational analysis on.

Using Chapter 10 for examples

It is warmly recommended that those readers who desire more concrete examples of how the many models may be used, jump to Chapter 10, the last chapter of the book, at any time. Chapter 10 describes a company with, in many ways, a typical organizational problem, which is then analyzed on the basis of each of the four theoretical frameworks. It is perfectly possible to alternate between reading about different models in the following chapters, and to read about how they are applied to one and the same phenomenon in Chapter 10.

The fact that the book is designed in this way is partly due to the ambition to keep the length short, but there are also many other benefits. Different readers have different needs for empirical illustration. For example, many leaders already have so much experience of real problems, dilemmas and successes that they can easily apply the described models without using Chapter 10.

Another important motive for concentrating most of the application of theory in the last chapter is that this text can serve as a kind of reference book. This is an important function for both the less experienced student and the senior manager. In the description of models and theoretical perspectives, the reader should know that what is actually written there are academically based and structured analytical tools and nothing else. Neither less relevant theoretical digressions nor irrelevant empirical examples should, so to speak, dilute or make it more difficult to find the most relevant analytical tools.

A third motive is theoretical. The power of multi-frame analysis is best communicated by gathering all the analytical applications in one place. For example, when the analyses from the structural framework and the HR framework stand side by side, it is much easier to understand the similarities and differences between these frameworks, compared with if these analyses appeared in different places in the book. Gathering up the applications of all four frameworks up to Chapter 10 means that both differences and similarities between the frameworks appear much more clearly. But, as has been said, feel free to use the analyses in Chapter 10 wherever you find yourself in the other chapters.

Reading Chapters 2–9

The four basic theoretical frameworks are presented in two chapters each. In each framework's first chapter, the more basic and 'mainstream' models and concepts are described. These are the very tools and models that you usually find in other management textbooks and sometimes also in more practical management literature. Each framework's second chapter consists of more advanced theory – either in the form of more fundamental social theory, results from more contemporary research and/or important theories that for different reasons have been excluded from most texts on management. Despite the more advanced content in these second chapters, the presentations are straightforward, accessible and geared towards how to apply theory in everyday organizational life. The book is written to be read in the order the chapters are presented, but you can also apply other strategies. As a reader, you can choose to only focus on the more basic chapters for your first read. You could stop there and still have learned a lot of new tools for analyzing management, organization and leadership processes; or you can view it as a first step and then read the more advanced chapters.

Enough with prefaces, provisos and instructions. It is high time to deliver, that is, to describe the frameworks and all their different analytical models.

Videos

Don't forget to watch the video to discover more about the key concepts in this chapter: **https://study.sagepub.com/blomberg**

Notes

1   For a relatively accessible, original and well-written introduction to the scientifically philo-
    sophical position which the form of 're-framing', 'multi-frame analysis' or 'aspect seeing'
    described here is based on, see Asplund (1983).
2   *Organisation från grunden [Organization from the ground up]* (Forssell & Ivarsson Wester-
    berg 2007) provides a basic and detailed description of the structural perspective, but very
    little or nothing is said about the other perspectives.
3   A good book with a description of a large number of perspectives, is *Images of organization*
    (Morgan 1986). Morgan describes seven different metaphors that can be used to analyze
    organizations. All these metaphors cannot be said to be established within the subject area;
    however, the large number also risks fragmenting established and relatively coherent perspectives.

2

Structures, Formalized Processes and Rational Decisions – The Basics of the Structural Framework

What company is this?

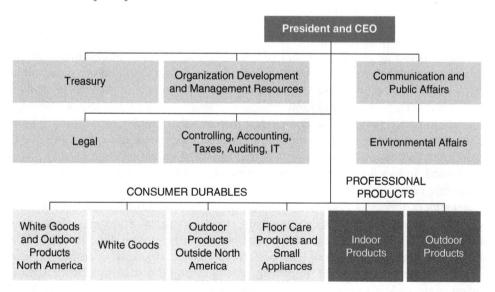

Figure 2.1   A large corporation's formal organizational structure

No, it's not one of the global white goods corporations that is shown in Figure 2.1 above. It is possibly the formal organizational structure of one of them as it appeared a number of years ago. It is, rather, a diagram depicting a common way of describing organizations, in this case the Swedish-based global white goods producer Electrolux. We recognize this way of describing organizations so well that we mix up the description with what it intends to describe, without too much thought. The reason why we are able to quickly accept the structural image as a good description of a corporation (in this case Electrolux) is that the structural framework is such an integral part of our everyday knowledge of and thinking about organizations.

The structural framework is the oldest and most established of the four frameworks. Organizational research has been conducted based on the basic assumptions of the framework since the late 1800s, and extensive structural organizational research is still carried out today. Within areas such as strategy and operations management, this type of research predominates. Even in business administration, i.e. among managers and management consultants, for example, the structural framework is still dominant. When managers say 'organization', they are often referring to formally structured organizational processes.

The historical roots of the structural framework

Ever since its inception 100–150 years ago, the structural framework has had one foot anchored firmly in academic social science research and the other, equally firmly, in organizational practice. During the second half of the 19th century, many new-age capitalist companies had grown so large that they became difficult to manage and control. These successful (and wealthy) capitalists needed methods and models that could create order in the companies' increasingly complex activities and more control over the increasing number of employees. Help came from the more practically oriented organizational analysts of the day, some of whom were, just like today, celebrated and well-paid management gurus. One of the more well-known is the American engineer and consultant Frederick W. Taylor (1856–1915). His scientific management theory – also called Taylorism – was concerned with how to depersonalize employee knowledge, build up structural capital and design formalized processes. These formalized processes consisted of very precise descriptions of how highly specialized tasks should be performed (Taylor 1911). As a result, employees could not 'get away with' informally putting a limit on their workload, without being noticed. Management obtained new instruments to control and exploit 'its' labor force. At the same time, the French mining engineer and author Henri Fayol (1841–1925) developed 14 principles to ensure efficient management, which complemented Taylor's scientific management principles (Fayol 1916/2008). Taylor and

Fayol's principles provided practical, applicable guidance for how to design and lead efficient organizations.

Taylor and Fayol were both engineers and employed a relatively simple problem-solving approach, which still characterizes much of the structural framework. However, there was, and still is, a more social, problematizing and theoretical foundation for structural organizational analysis. This can be said to be derived from sociologists such as Karl Marx, Max Weber and Émile Durkheim. An integral contribution made to organizational analysis is undoubtedly Weber's account of what he thought was the most efficient form of organization – the formal-rational bureaucracy.

What the German sociologist, economics historian and economist Max Weber (1864–1920) and his contemporaries were interested in was understanding the rise and development of industrialized Western society. Weber (1924/1983, 1924/1987) described this development as a rationalization in which efficiency and rationality gradually replaced tradition and customs. In Weber's world, however, formal organizations were not something that would benefit only the owner, management or any other category of individual, but also society as a whole. It was therefore important that organizations were protected from special interests (including capital owners) and that goals were set within the framework of democratic processes. Weber said that a capitalist and democratic society was far superior to a communist one but that the capitalists' interest in returns should not be above the will of the people and democratically developed goals. All formal organizations, regardless of whether they take the form of nation states or large corporations, were to pursue goals as rationally and efficiently as possible. According to Weber, excessive influence from a particular group, be it employees or owners, could hinder efficiency and rationally conducted activities. Weber's formal-rational bureaucracy is characterized by the following principles:

1. an established division of labor among staff
2. coordination via an authority and responsibility hierarchy
3. generally valid rules that determine different work tasks and rewards
4. a clear distinction between personal and official property and responsibility
5. recruitment and promotion of staff on the basis of formal qualifications
6. full employment and established career paths
7. a full-time job with a sufficient wage to live on.

Taylor, Weber and their contemporaries defined the very basics of the structural framework, as well as the more sociological strand developed in the advanced theory of social organizing. Much of the more advanced thought was downplayed as other aspects were added on, when the more current structural framework of organization theory developed. Much of the 'add-ons' will be covered in this and the following chapter, while some of the more advanced theory will show up in later parts of the book.

The basic assumptions of the structural framework

The more practical and academic knowledge interests that underpinned the structural framework eventually merged into one basic organizational theory. The historical interest in the sociological and social science waned, as did the problematization of democratic goal-formulation processes and special interests. Instead, the focus turned to a relatively unproblematized concept of efficiency, where overall goals and interests remained unstated, yet firmly anchored in corporate management and capital ownership. The basic assumptions of the structural framework are formulated in Weber's description of formal-rational bureaucracy to a great extent, but can be developed somewhat to better fit the extensive structural research that has been pursued since then.

The basic assumptions of the structural frame can thus be formulated as follows:

1. Organizations exist because they are efficient tools to achieve established goals.
2. Well-advanced division of labor/specialization leads to efficiency.
3. Coordination is best achieved through vertical hierarchical control ('top down') and formalized processes/structures.
4. People are motivated to work through material rewards (pay), clear, formalized work descriptions (information/rules) and control.
5. Optimal processes and structures are rationally designed based on objective/ material conditions – by studying and analyzing facts, efficient organizations can be designed.
6. Inefficiency arises due to incorrectly or ambiguously designed processes and structures and is addressed by means of restructuring.

Given these basic assumptions, a number of key concepts form the basis of the structural framework. The three most basic concepts are efficiency, division of labor and coordination. We go through each of these below.

Efficiency

Although the structural framework can be said to be characterized by analytical models with strong explanatory and normative power, rather than problematizing interpretations, there are obviously problematizations of key concepts. The most central of these concepts is efficiency. With the framework's strong focus on efficiency, a number of different efficiency concepts have been developed.

Efficiency (*internal efficiency*) is the measure of the amount of resources needed to achieve something, such as how many working hours, or how much money, are needed to make a car. If it takes 17 hours to manufacture a car, the organization is less efficient if it takes 19 hours to manufacture the same car (all other factors being equal). A focus on internal efficiency can also be described as production orientation, in contrast to market orientation.

Effectiveness (external efficiency) is about how many resources are needed to produce something that is in demand. Effectiveness thus includes (internal) efficiency, but adds demand, that is, a market aspect. It does not matter how many hours it takes to make a car if there is no one willing to buy it. It is better to manufacture a car that is in demand in 20 hours, than to manufacture a car that is not in demand in 17. If efficiency is to do something right, effectiveness is to do the right thing.

The concept of *system efficiency* can be said to include both efficiency and effectiveness but adds a time or change dimension. It is thus a measure of how quickly and efficiently activities can be adjusted if/when demand changes. The crucial aspect is that it doesn't matter whether a car can be manufactured in as few hours as possible, if this manufacturing is difficult to adjust when demand changes. It may be better to manufacture a car in demand in 20 hours than in 17 hours if, in the first case, production can be adjusted quickly and smoothly to manufacture another type of car when demand changes.

The most recently developed efficiency concept is *flow efficiency*. It can be seen as a development of the above but where the time factor is emphasized further. Flow efficiency is defined as the ratio between valued-adding time (i.e. the time spent actively working towards the completion of a task) and lead time (that is, the time it takes from an order being placed to it being delivered to the customer). Thus, this concept includes both efficiency and effectiveness but adds the time factor in relation to both needs/market and delivery/production. More on this can be found in the section on Lean in Chapter 3.

If we stick to the car example, we may say that Ford's great success in the first decade of the 20th century was due to a strong focus on internal efficiency. The cost of manufacturing a Ford Model T (the first practical, affordable car for the general public that was mass-produced on assembly lines) dropped radically during its 10-year success story. However, this focus on internal efficiency was driving Ford, the world's most profitable company, towards bankruptcy because its competitor, General Motors (GM), was more effective (external efficiency). Once the large, newly rich American masses had bought their first car, they wanted something nicer and different. With its different brands and variations, GM offered a wider range of car models than Ford. Fifty years later, however, the Japanese car industry, and in particular Toyota, showed that it was better at adjusting production than the US car industry. Instead of optimizing the manufacture of a range of variants of basically the same car construction, Japanese car manufacturers worked according to more dynamic principles that required lower investment in machines, and production was thus easier to adjust. In an industry characterized by customers who were not satisfied with variations on the same theme, but instead wanted station wagons one year, a mini-van the next, an SUV the next, and then wanted to buy an alternative-fuel vehicle, the capacity to adjust was perhaps the most important factor. The fact that Toyota could also push down its manufacturing costs more than its European and American competitors can be explained by its dynamic and continuous efforts to increase its flow efficiency.

These different concepts of efficiency point to a major organizational problem: how to organize in order to maximize efficiency in both the short and long terms. On the one hand, the fewer resources invested in developing future products and processes, the more you can gain in the short term. On the other hand, the more resources you invest in future products and processes, the better the organization is equipped for the future. However, it is important to distinguish between efficiency and *profitability*. Profitability is primarily about the distribution of added value created, while efficiency is more about how the production of goods and services is organized. But how should efficient organizations be structured according to this structural framework? This question leads us to the other two key concepts of the structural framework: *division of labor* and *specialization*.

Division of labor

In order to organize efficiently, the work involved in the production of goods and services should, as far as possible, be divided up, i.e. broken down, into different activities. What is possible is limited by a variety of circumstances, which we will soon return to. However, it should be noted that it is not only possible to divide labor in terms of degree, but also in different qualitative ways – based on a number of different principles. We discuss each in turn below.

Division of labor based on function

The functional organization is considered the first developed form of organization, as it was developed well before modern organizational theory. In the organization of the Roman Empire's armies, the construction of Ancient Egypt's pyramids, indeed, as far back in time as we can say something about human organization, division of labor by function has been a recurring principle.

Although functional organization has been supplemented and, to some extent, replaced by other work division principles, it is generally always possible to find elements of functional organization in present-day organizations as well. The main motive for dividing up an activity into different functions is that they require different knowledge and skill-sets. An expert on purchasing does not have the same skills as an expert on manufacturing or financing. The purely functional organization has different departments for, for example, purchasing, production, product development, marketing and sales. These functions are placed side by side in an organizational structure and together form the organization's internal value chain. Above this can be found a formal organizational hierarchy with management at the top, assisted by support staff (see Figure 2.2).

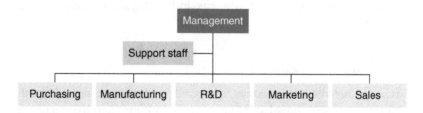

Figure 2.2   A typical/simple function-based organization

Division of labor based on product

Organizations whose offerings include several goods and services that differ in terms of product and production technology often create organizational units for the different products or product groups. For example, a company that sells both personal computers, large integrated customized IT systems to multinational companies, and strategy and management consultancy services can divide labor in its organization on the basis of these quite different offerings.

Division of labor based on customer and market

Different customers may have different needs regarding different goods and services, but also the ways these are marketed and distributed might need to be different. For example, one computer could be marketed and distributed in completely different ways: to companies purchasing computers for their employees, to people purchasing a computer for personal use and to students, who have a different range of requirements. But even the product itself and its manufacturing can be organized differently. For example, washing machines look different in the USA to those in Europe. In the USA, top-loaded machines are used to wash quickly, while in Europe the preferred machine is front-loaded and washes more slowly and gently. Washing machine manufacturers can try to change these consumer behaviors in order to achieve greater economies of scale, but, if this is difficult, it is better to divide labor for product design and manufacturing instead, based on different types of customers.

Division of labor based on location

Division of labor based on location is often combined with the principle of labor division based on the customer, as in the washing machine example above: on two different continents, different types of washing machine are in demand. Different locations also have different conditions for efficient production. For example, in areas with many highly educated people, 'knowledge-intensive' activities (like in consulting and advisory business) are appropriate, whereas, in low-wage areas, it is more efficient to conduct more manual, 'work-intensive' activities.

Division of labor based on time

Several types of activities are suitable for organizing based on time. Regardless of the demand for, for example, bread and tomatoes, agriculture often has a more or less logical organization of time: sow, manage and harvest. Even though modern technology has made and is still making a lot of industrial agriculture less dependent on weather, daily and seasonal rhythms still play a major role in how labor is divided in agricultural production over time. Another example is the police. Different crimes have different seasonal cycles and are committed at different times of the day. For example, more police are out on the streets on Friday and Saturday nights, and more administrative follow-up work is conducted at the beginning of the week.

Division of labor based on process

In a way, the principle of dividing labor based on process has become more common, replacing the more traditional functional principle. At the same time, the difference between process and function can be problematic. The basic idea behind division by function is that it is based on logical steps in a value-creating chain or process: purchasing, product development, manufacturing, marketing and distribution. The basic idea behind division of labor on process is that the work should follow a flow of gradually adding value to the product or service. We return to the issue of whether or not a reorganization from function to process is real or mostly a change in how to describe the same organization in the chapters on the symbolic framework. However, there can be real differences. In the service sector, for example, the work can be set up so that a customer meets a single service provider throughout the process (for example, in the form of a personal banker or family doctor). This contrasts with the customer meeting different people at different stages (like one doctor for testing, another for diagnosis and a third for treatment). The same applies to the manufacturing industry, where the work is often organized on the basis of processes and flows of material, information, financial capital, and so on, and not on different resources, such as purchasers, machines or warehouses. To take the example of a car factory, you can really see the process of flowing material when a car gradually evolves with its movement through the factory. We look at this in more detail when we discuss lean and flow efficiency in the next chapter.

Division of labor based on projects

Project organization, according to the structural framework, means delimiting resources in time and space to reach a specific goal. Each project is allocated the resources needed to achieve the goals for that particular project. Dividing labor based on projects is often combined with other labor division principles. For example, in a functionally divided organization, cross-functional groups can be formed that carry out activities to which the otherwise functionally divided organization is not suited. A project group can, for instance, be formed to develop a new product, a new manufacturing process or something else that requires resources from several functions. Labor in project groups can also be more permanently divided and combined with labor division based on, for example, function. Then a 'matrix organization' emerges in which employees and other resources are both divided and coordinated by two different management structures, in this example by both project managers and function managers. Both project management and matrix organization constitute extensive areas of knowledge within the structural perspective and are therefore treated in separate sections (matrix organization later in this chapter and project management towards the end of the next).

Coordination

The more labor-divided or specialized an activity is, the higher the requirements for coordination. Coordination takes place using the same processes, rules and structures designed for operational labor division. However, language usage has changed over the years when talking about efficient organizations based on a structural framework. Sixty years ago, it was said that well-developed bureaucracy was the key to success. Thirty years ago, clear structures were said to be the key to success. Today, instead, we speak of 'setting the processes'. However, it is the same model behind the reasoning, and the basic principle is the same: that hierarchical, vertical coordination or 'top-down' control determines what is being done, when and by whom.

From a structural perspective, it is always efficient to have specialized activities as much as possible, as well as to coordinate the specialized working tasks with formalized rules, processes and physical structures. Designing tasks, structures and processes should also be done from the top. The fact that top management has both the most responsibility and the most influence is a rational and logical consequence of the fact that, according to the structural framework, the ideal organization not only consists of a bureaucratic system but also constitutes a meritocratic system, that is, the higher up in the hierarchy you go, the more qualified and skilled are the people involved in organization and leadership. The right person in the right place is thus the same as recruitment and career paths being governed by formally established qualifications and skills, rather than favoritism, personal relationships or other criteria that are not primarily about how well duties can be performed.

Although, within a structural framework, you should always strive for maximum specialization, the clearest possible processes and the development of formal control structures, sometimes specialization and hierarchical or vertical coordination are not always the most appropriate. In these cases, you can supplement or replace hierarchical vertical coordination with horizontal coordination. There are thus two basic strategies for how to coordinate and control labor-divided activities, vertically or horizontally, and we look at each in more depth below.

Vertical coordination and control

Vertical coordination is about the higher, hierarchical levels defining and controlling what the lower levels do. Vertical coordination and control can take place in different ways. For example, it may be a manager giving a direct order to their subordinates, who is in *direct control*. Vertical control may also consist of the organization's management designing formal rules and structures that those subordinates on lower levels are expected to follow. This *bureaucratic control* can range from detailed employment contracts and job descriptions to formalized process instructions and incentive structures in the form of payroll systems. It may also include instructions on how service personnel should address their clients, on consultant companies' 'up-or-out' policies (if you do not show a specified level of performance within a specified timeframe or before you reach a specified age, you will be asked to leave the company) or on financial institutions' risk-management systems. An important part of such structural or *bureaucratic control* is the design of physical structures, such as the workplace and work technology. Such structures set limits to what actions it is possible to take. The conveyor belt is perhaps the most famous example of a highly controlled, physically designed workplace.

Horizontal coordination and control

When, for different reasons (more about these in subsequent paragraphs), it is not possible or appropriate to coordinate an organization vertically, it can be coordinated horizontally instead. Horizontal coordination and control, in principle, mean that people on the same hierarchical level interact with each other and decide what to do together, without giving a higher-level manager more right of determination. Horizontal coordination can consist of face-to-face interaction in, for example, cross-functional project groups and teams. If these groups are made more permanent, so-called 'matrix structures' (see final section in this chapter) are obtained, combining coordination in two dimensions. Horizontal coordination may also consist of different networks that span multiple functions or units that are labor-divided according to other principles. These networks may, but need not, be supported by information technology and are sometimes referred to as knowledge management systems (cf. Nonaka and Takeuchi's (1995) model for knowledge dissemination in organizations in Chapter 5). There may also be special coordination roles that, instead of exercising vertical control, have the task of disseminating information among employees and units on the same hierarchical level. An example of such a horizontal coordination role is 'runners', who, in large merchant banks, run between different units or 'desks' specializing in different types of securities trading, and disseminate information between them.

An initial simple model

If an organization is stable in terms of production methods, material use and customer demand, it is rational to break it down into as many small, specialized tasks as possible. According to the structural framework, it is also efficient to coordinate these with job descriptions and rule systems that are as specific as possible. However, in other situations, similarly detailed processes and structures cannot or should not be developed, nor should the activity be steered using vertical control alone.

In an organization that is characterized by great uncertainty, for example due to a changing market, new competing manufacturing technologies, changing legislation or simply highly technically complex products, it can be a complete waste of resources to design detailed processes and complex organizational structures. For example, if production has to be readjusted, perhaps because people want to buy small hybrids or electric cars instead of large, gas-guzzling SUVs, then it would not have been a good investment to build a large specialized production plant for large gasoline engines. Neither is it smart to plan in detail and structure the work of developing a product, the physical appearance of which is not known, for example, the advanced development of software that will be used in next-generation spacecraft in 15 years. In these cases, the organization includes so much uncertainty that the work can and should not be broken into small specialized tasks and coordinated by means of vertical structural control. Instead, problems have to be solved as and when they occur, and the work should be carried out more flexibly by qualified teams. Coordination should then take place horizontally, through interaction and communication between employees on the same level. This reasoning leads to a simple, one-dimensional model that can be used to analyze the efficiency of an organization (see Figure 2.3).

Using this particularly simple but practical model involves asking two questions:

1. To what extent is our current organization characterized by specialization and vertical coordination? That is, where on the scale of the model *are* we?
2. To what extent is our organization, including its environment, characterized by stability and predictability versus changeability and uncertainty? That is, where in the model *should* we be?

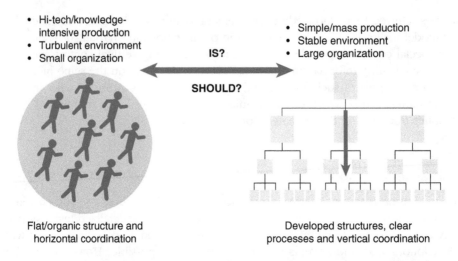

- Hi-tech/knowledge-
  intensive production
- Turbulent environment
- Small organization

IS?

SHOULD?

- Simple/mass production
- Stable environment
- Large organization

Flat/organic structure and
horizontal coordination

Developed structures, clear
processes and vertical coordination

Figure 2.3   A simple one-dimensional model for analyzing whether an activity is efficiently organized

If you *are* where you *should* be, the analysis explains why things are going well. You have efficient structures, given the level of uncertainty that characterizes the organization and its environment. If you *are not* where you *should* be, it indicates that there are problems that can be addressed through the reorganization of structures and processes.

For example, if we analyze the organizational structures and processes of the Stockholm School of Economics (SSE):[1] does SSE have optimal structures and processes, given the nature of its activities? In the last ten years or so, SSE has expanded its organizational structure and formalized previously informal processes. More hierarchical levels have been created and decision-making has been centralized, and the school is hence relatively bureaucratically organized. Overall, SSE *is* today further to the right on the scale in Figure 2.3 than it was 10–15 years ago.

If, instead, we look at how SSE *should* be organized, we can see that the school is very small compared to its competitors, and that there are no more teachers or researchers today than 10 years ago (although the administrative staff has increased considerably as a result of the expanded structure, formalization and bureaucratization). Moreover, the ambition is extremely high in terms of advanced knowledge content in the research and education being conducted. SSE is a distinguished elite school. All this means that it should not have an overly developed formal structure but instead work more with horizontal coordination.

A clearly formulated conclusion based on this analysis and on the one-dimensional structural model in Figure 2.3 is that SSE has changed for the worse, i.e. it has gone in the wrong direction. You should not move to the right on the scale. Today, the school is even smaller than before, relative to its large competitors, yet it has at least as high elite school ambitions as before (today, the school competes with major international prestigious schools more than ever before). This is an argument for more horizontal coordination, more work in teams and projects, and less hierarchy and formalism.

It can seem paradoxical that a top school with high-end master's and executive programs in management cannot organize its own activities according to this simple normative model. However, it should be added that it may not be as easy as the model makes it appear. We will therefore return to this example when we have further advanced the structural analysis. A strong argument suggesting that the above analysis bears some importance is that relatively recently, in the past few years, the newly appointed SSE management has abolished a number of formal positions and reduced the number of hierarchical levels. Maybe the current school management has better management skills than the previous one?

Although the above one-dimensional structural model is very simple, using it usually provides major new understanding. If the uncertainty of the organization and/or its environment increases, care should be exercised when investing in formal structures, formalized processes and greater division of labor. On the other hand, if an increasingly stable and predictable market is detectable, and there are opportunities to modularize and produce similar goods or services, then efficiency increases if you structure, systematize and formalize, or, in other words, 'set the processes'.

Uncertainty

The simple described model above talks about uncertainty. However, there are different types of uncertainty. We can distinguish between uncertainty in the production of goods and services and uncertainty in the environment, for example in different markets. You can also differentiate uncertainty in terms of employee skills and incentives, what kind of future goals and strategies are chosen, and so on.

In the following section, Mintzberg's structural configurations model is presented. This model distinguishes between different types of uncertainties and situational dependencies, which determine the ways activities should be structured.

Mintzberg's structural configurations

In order to facilitate the choice of efficient organizational form, that is, how to divide labor and coordinate, Mintzberg (1983) developed a typology consisting of five 'pure' structural configurations. With the help of Mintzberg's typology, more were developed and nuanced conclusions can be drawn on the type of structure and processes that are most effective in a given situation. The five configurations – machine bureaucracy, professional bureaucracy, simple structure, adhocracy and divisionalized form – are presented below. In the 'Dimensions and situational dependencies' section, Mintzberg's multi-dimensional model is then presented, which shows which configuration is most effective given different types of uncertainties (or dimensions of dependencies; see below).

However, we begin by reviewing the five basic parts from which the five configurations are built (see Figure 2.4).

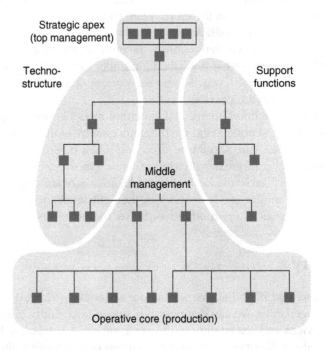

Figure 2.4   The basic parts of structural configurations

Source: Mintzberg (1983)

Each structural configuration consists of a *strategic apex* or *top*, which corresponds to the highest management group in real-life organizations. This is where the highest decision-making right resides in the organization, as well as the highest level of responsibility. You can also include the board and thus the owners in the strategic apex, but most often you treat these in the analysis as part of the organization's environment, at least when the owner and management team are not the same. Beneath the strategic apex are the line managers or *middle management*. In real organizations, the number of levels varies, but, in the model, they constitute one basic part. Under middle management is the *operational core*. This corresponds to the workshop floor, the restaurant and its kitchen, the cash office, the sales team and/or any of an organization's other core activities. Continuing our previous SSE example, SSE's operating core consists of teachers, students and classrooms, but the school's research activities are also part of the operating core.

In addition to these three basic parts, the model consists of *technostructure* and administrative *support functions*. These can sometimes be difficult to differentiate, but the main idea is that technostructure is designed to control the operating core, i.e. the division of labor and coordination of the operational core activities in a certain considered way. The clearest example is the conveyor belt, which defines tasks as well as when they are to be performed and by whom. A company's formalized project model is another example. Technostructure covers both the governing physical or formal structures and the people who design them. In other words, technostructure includes the staff function that, at the behest of the management, designs the new factory layout and its conveyor belts, for example, or the updated formal project model that everyone should use in their tasks. Support functions, in turn, lend their support to operational core activities rather than control them. A corporate staff restaurant, its payroll administration, free fruit and health care are relatively clear examples of support functions. However, it can be argued that all support systems have a controlling effect and that all technostructures provide support. The same structure can also be perceived differently by different people in an organization. However, such uncertainties and interpretations are best analyzed within the context of the symbolic framework (see Chapters 8 and 9). An analysis based on the structural perspective tries to keep these two basic parts separate.

By combining the five basic parts in different ways, Mintzberg (1983) designs five structural configurations: machine bureaucracy, professional bureaucracy, simple structure, adhocracy and divisionalized form. These five, their distinctive characteristics and their strengths and weaknesses are described below.

Machine bureaucracy

In a machine bureaucracy, labor division has been taken as far as possible, and coordination is conducted vertically through directives from the management at the top of the hierarchy or in the form of technical and formal structures designed by management and its staff. Machine bureaucracy is thus characterized by many formal and specialized roles and routines, by vertical coordination in the form of many hierarchical levels and a developed technostructure, as well as by many support functions (see Figure 2.5).

Of the five configurations, machine bureaucracy is that closest to Weber's classic formulation of formal-rational bureaucracy (see the section on historical roots earlier in this chapter), which Weber considered to be the most efficient organizational form. Machine bureaucracy can be said to be the core of the structural frame. If you can organize according to this configuration, you should do so. The strengths of typical machine bureaucracy are that it maximizes economies of scale, repetition and predictability in a stable environment and in an organization with production processes that are not overly complex. Because recruitment to different positions takes place on

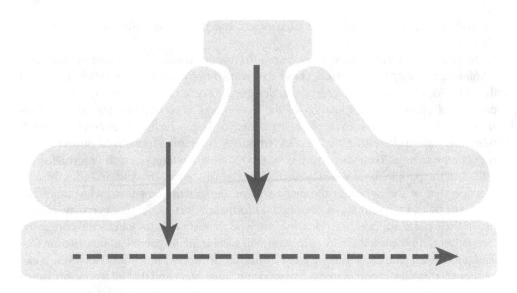

Figure 2.5 Machine bureaucracy

Note: The arrows symbolize vertical coordination, either through hierarchical management levels or through technostructure's design of processes and structures in the operating core (the dashed arrow).

the basis of formal qualifications and education, it counteracts arbitrariness, favoritism and irrational decisions. Two well-known examples of machine bureaucracies are the Ford Factory, which manufactured the Ford Model T, and McDonald's hamburger restaurants.

In a machine bureaucracy, labor division has been taken as far as possible, and coordination is conducted vertically through directives from the management at the top of the hierarchy or in the form of technical and formal structures designed by management and its staff. Machine bureaucracy is thus characterized by many formal and specialized roles and routines, as well as vertical coordination in the form of many hierarchical levels and a developed technostructure.

Machine bureaucracy is typically found in large organizations that mass-produce relatively simple and standardized goods and services in mature and stable markets. Even a product characterized by advanced technology, such as a personal computer, can be a simple product to manufacture and distribute. Most of the components of a personal computer are mass-produced standard products developed by companies other than the one putting it together and distributing it. Most personal computers are also sold through a system characterized by mass distribution through a small number of large retail chains and online stores.

One can even assert that knowledge-intensive service production, for example in major management consulting companies, is best done in the form of machine bureaucracy. This is because many of these companies' consultancy services make minor adjustments to highly structured models and are based on standardized and labor-divided processes. It is absolutely possible to argue that large parts of these company activities are too complex for a machine bureaucracy to be optimal. But developments over recent decades within the management consulting industry give machine bureaucracy support: the most successful consultancy agencies are large international companies with relatively formal structures.

Machine bureaucracy also has weaknesses, however. To begin with, it is unnecessary to develop extensive bureaucratic systems in order to coordinate activities in organizations with few employees. If there are five people whose work is to be coordinated, it is easier and cheaper for them to interact directly with each other, that is, to coordinate horizontally, than it is to create layers of hierarchical management levels, that is, to coordinate vertically. Neither is it rational to invest in large systems or build formal hierarchies if there are major uncertainties in the organization and its environment. If demand changes, or brand new production methods are developed, such systems can quickly become antiquated. Machine bureaucracy is thus slow-moving and difficult to change.

Another weakness is that there are often problems with work motivation in machine bureaucracies. This is due to decisions taken in the strategic apex usually being general and not adapted to the needs of the different departments further down the organization. However, this weakness can be analyzed in more depth, using models and theories that focus on human resources and relationships, namely the HR framework. We return to the conflict between efficient structures based on the structural framework and motivated staff based on the HR framework in Chapters 4 and 5.

In summary, machine bureaucracy has well-developed formalized processes and hierarchical structures with extensive specialization, large technostructure and vertical coordination. Its primary strength is efficiency and its biggest weakness is inertia.

Professional bureaucracy

Although activities in the operating core involve uncertainty in the form of complex production processes and technologies, the idea of formalized processes and bureaucratic structures should not be completely relinquished, according to the structural framework. If the operational environment is predictable and stable in terms of demand for the goods and/or services produced, complex activities should be organized in accordance with what Mintzberg calls professional bureaucracy.

Professional bureaucracy is a more decentralized organizational form than machine bureaucracy. Vertical coordination is not extensive, neither in terms of the number of hierarchical levels nor in the form of a developed technostructure (see Figure 2.6). It is not as easy to divide labor and formalize the production of goods and services that involve considerable uncertainty and complexity. Hence, complex production should

Figure 2.6   Professional bureaucracy

Note: The arrows from the SSE logo symbolize how business students are steered into homogeneous and predictable (professional) thinking during their education. This coordinates and stabilizes their work at future workplaces (the dashed arrows). Note how similar they are, and how they all run in the same direction!

be characterized by a lower degree of specialization and vertical coordination. Manufacturing amateur welding equipment, for example, requires a much simpler production process than developing software for next-generation spacecraft. Making and serving fast food is a relatively simpler service than a law firm's assignment in major business projects. Waste collection is a much easier service than emergency stroke surgery. In all these examples, the simple processes (welding equipment manufacture, fast food production and waste collection) are typically suitable for organizing as machine bureaucracies, while the more complex processes (software development, legal assistance in business projects, and brain surgery) are suitable for organizing as professional bureaucracies.

In professional bureaucracy, instead of by means of a developed technostructure and hierarchical levels, much of the organization is coordinated by the profession itself. Employees in a professional bureaucracy are characterized precisely by the fact that they belong to the same profession. This means that they have similar education and similar knowledge and skills that make their working tasks predictable and easy to coordinate. Coordination in a professional bureaucracy can be perceived to be largely horizontal, as there are no clear vertical coordination mechanisms as in a machine bureaucracy. However, by recruiting employees from one and the same field of education, for example from law school in the case of law firms, from medicine in the case of health and medical care, or from a business school in the case of management consultancy agencies, coordination can be said to be vertical to a certain extent. Management exerts some degree of control when recruiting from a specific profession.

Medical doctors have much more control over their working tasks than employees at fast food restaurant chains. A professional bureaucracy thus has a relatively undeveloped technostructure, but more support functions (see Figure 2.6). The work of a doctor, a lawyer or an equity analyst is simply too important for computers, projectors, stock exchange systems or assistants to go wrong: if a system breaks down in a hospital, patients can die; if a stock exchange system breaks down, large corporations can go under.

The strength of professional bureaucracy is that, at the decentralized level, in individual assignments and working tasks (the consultation assignment or the individual operation), it provides both efficiency and effectiveness. (Internal) efficiency is ensured by the profession having a stable and proven knowledge base that makes it possible to repeat difficult working tasks. Effectiveness (external efficiency) is guaranteed by the fact that employees are not controlled by rules but can adapt their theoretical professional knowledge to an endless variety of tasks.

A weakness in professional bureaucracy is that it is difficult to coordinate and control if you want to change it more fundamentally. For example, if management wants to change strategy for the entire organization, there is a great risk that the profession will dig its heels in. For example, an airline can relatively easily outsource its service and cabin crew but will find it significantly harder to outsource its pilots.

Simple structure

Mintzberg's third configuration, simple structure, can be said to be a miniature version of machine bureaucracy. It is characterized by clear vertical coordination, but, unlike machine bureaucracy, this is not in the form of many hierarchical levels or developed technostructure but in the form of a strong and dominant manager. The simple structure is common in small, young companies managed by their founder and owner. This person controls virtually everything, and the employees do as the manager (founder/owner) says (see Figure 2.7). A typical organization with simple structure is the small

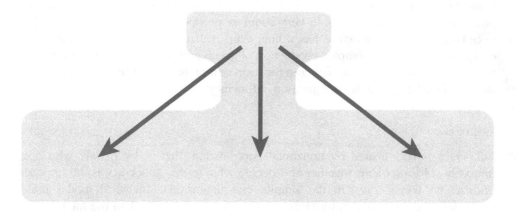

Figure 2.7   Simple structure

Note: The arrows symbolize how one or a few people have all the authority and micro-manage the work of all other employees.

architectural firm dominated by a more or less established architect. The employees work as the architect's assistants. Other examples include small industrial design companies, small consultancies and small subcontractors. These smaller companies, with up to around ten employees, are often organized into simple structures.

A strength of the simple structure is its flexibility. Because the manager decides and controls virtually everything, it's easy enough for that person to decide to do something slightly different and simply tell his staff to do it. The simple structure is more agile than machine bureaucracy because no formalized processes or hierarchical structures have been built up that need to be changed. Neither is there any large group of employees who are shaped and stabilized by a common profession and therefore dig their heels in when change is attempted.

But this concentrated authority has its limitations. If the manager does not understand or realize that changes are necessary, the simple structure becomes rigid and difficult to change. The risk of this increases if the organization grows and includes more and more employees. Then it becomes increasingly difficult for the manager to control everything. As managers are forced to devote more and more attention and energy to micromanagement, the risk of them missing the major strategic issues increases. For example, if changes occur in the customer market, if new competitors establish themselves or new technologies develop, there is a risk that the manager in the simple structure will not see it. If the organization grows even more, but maintains the simple structure, there is also a risk that the manager won't be able to cope with day-to-day micromanagement. Activities will then be unmanaged or under-managed, which can lead both to inadequate day-to-day coordination and a lack of longer-term strategic planning.

The simple structure therefore fits best in small organizations where its flexibility is its strength. It is also better suited to less advanced and less complex production processes, goods and services. In very complex production involving a high level of uncertainty, a simple structure has a limitation in that only one person determines everything. In the very complex production of goods and services, it is better if several people try to solve problems, either in the form of a professional bureaucracy or in the form of Mintzberg's fourth configuration, adhocracy.

Adhocracy

Adhocracy is coordinated by horizontal coordination, that is, by people who continuously solve problems together and decide what to do. Adhocracy is the opposite of machine bureaucracy. In the simple, one-dimensional analytical model previously described in this chapter (Figure 2.3), adhocracy is found to the far left (and machine bureaucracy to the far right). Adhocracy is characterized by its lack of vertical coordination. The pure adhocracy has neither technostructure, hierarchical levels nor authoritarian managers. It could be said to be managerless and self-organizing.

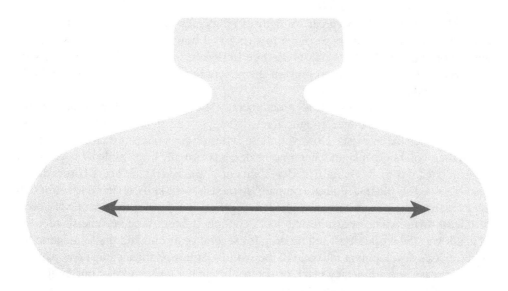

Figure 2.8 Adhocracy

Note: The arrow symbolizes horizontal coordination in the form of face-to-face interaction (or face-to-media-to-face). The bump in the middle symbolizes that there is always some form of limitation or vertical control, even in the most adhocratically organized organization.

Typical activities where adhocratic organization is suitable are research and development as well as temporary or time-limited activities such as projects, programs, assignments and investigations. In organizations where new products and technologies are developed, or which do extensive and complex customizations of existing components, adhocracy is often appropriate.

Just like simple structure, adhocracy best suits activities that involve relatively few people, such as the small research group or a small development team. However, with technological development and the advent of various social media, as well as the spread of *open-source*[2] development, the limits on how many people can be involved in an adhocratically organized activity may be questioned. As open source is a model that can be said to be both adhocratic and highly decentralized, the boundary of this configuration has to do with the ownership, control and distribution of created added value. In the context of profit-driven entrepreneurship, adhocracy can be said to be most suited to small groups. This is true since the horizontal coordination in the form of face-to-face interaction becomes too costly and clumsy if it comprises a large number of people. Here is a parallel to simple structure, which also has a limitation as regards size.

Adhocracy is an innovation-promoting and flexible organizational form. The lack of formalized processes, hierarchical levels and technostructure makes it agile. The horizontal coordination with people constantly interacting stimulates new thinking and problem-solving. If the great strength of adhocracy is innovation and flexibility, its weaknesses are mainly its resource intensity and how difficult it is to control. If a number of highly trained specialists are free to develop new technology, new goods and services, there is nothing to prevent them from developing products that nobody wants or is willing to pay for.

In a business context, therefore, an adhocracy should be framed by some governing constraint: a cost budget, rough targets, some sort of steering group or a representative of outside interests. However, these types of constraints are more difficult to design than you might imagine. For an outsider, it is virtually impossible to assess what a research team is really doing. The development of the gastric medicine Losec, developed by Swedish pharmaceutical company Astra, is a well-known example. Although Astra's management team formally decided to cancel the development work of Losec, on at least two separate occasions, the work continued. Losec then became so successful that it was the world's best-selling drug for several years and laid the foundation for AstraZeneca's development into one of the world's largest pharmaceutical companies.[3] In Losec's case, the adhocracy's lack of control became a great success, but things can just as easily go in the opposite direction.

When different types of control and constraints on an adhocracy are introduced, the pure theoretical form of this configuration, coordinated by horizontal control only, must be partially abandoned. In real organizations, it is difficult to imagine a completely 'free' and pure adhocracy. However, this applies to all the configurations presented here. Real organizations are more complex and usually include elements of several configurations. This leads us to the fifth and final configuration in Mintzberg's structural analytical model: divisionalized form.

Divisionalized form

The divisionalized form is a little bit of an odd configuration, and in various ways it does not fit the logic of the overall model. Its most important contribution is to problematize where an organization's boundaries are and to show that different configurations can be combined in all sorts of ways (see Figure 2.9). When analyzing real organizations using the described configurations, a number of choices must be made. One such choice is which unit or units to focus on. For example, in a large multinational firm, there are always a variety of activities that can be analyzed separately. At which level should you then focus your analysis? Throughout the multinational firm, in a subsidiary, department or particular business unit? The choice should be guided by, for example, the purpose, the issue at hand and the problems faced, but it is often appropriate to employ trial and error and analyze on several levels and at different widths and depths.

The divisionalized form is found in large organizations containing several different businesses (see Figure 2.9). Samsung manufactures everything from dishwashers

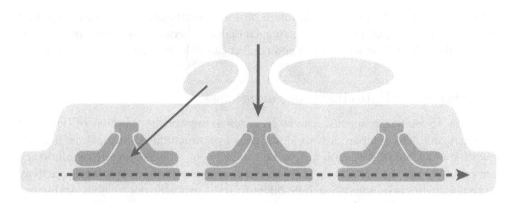

Figure 2.9   Divisionalized form

Note: The arrow from the technostructure symbolizes vertical coordination in the form of joint business systems and centralized resources in the form of, for example, marketing and contact with financial markets. The arrow from the strategic apex symbolizes financial return requirements but also complementary management dialogues.

to tablet computers and drones for military use. Should such different activities not be organized according to different configurations, perhaps? The answer is in the affirmative if these activities involve different levels of complexity and uncertainty. Is dishwasher manufacturing possibly more suited to being organized as a machine bureaucracy than, for example, the development of advanced military technology? An analysis involving such large groups with different products and customer markets, so-called 'conglomerates', should also include the divisionalized form configuration. Questions that should be asked are: Which configuration is similar for the entire group? Which configurations do we find in its different divisions? Are these forms of organization appropriate?

The strength of a divisionalized form is that different branches of activity can be adapted to their different conditions and that synergies between them can still be utilized. For example, the same administrative support functions and other resources can be shared, everything from product marketing to communication with financial markets.

The divisionalized form's weaknesses include the risk of conflicts between the divisions. Because the divisions share the same resources, they are dependent on each other, while they are organized according to different configurations and principles. How common resources are to be designed and distributed is a matter that can easily lead to conflict. There is also a risk of short-sightedness. Since the divisions are often evaluated and compared to each other in financial terms, there is a tendency to focus on aspects that are mostly easily and securely measured, i.e. the current and historical financial situation, rather than the future. The divisions will thus compete with each other, based on their financial performance in the current quarter, rather than on the basis of the expected five-year outcome. Short-term results are, in turn, easiest to achieve by cutting costs rather than investing in future business. Short-sightedness becomes a reality. Research shows that, by conducting regular dialogue between the group and division leaders, the risk of short-sightedness and conflict can at least in part be counteracted.

Dimensions and situational dependencies

One way to analyze a specific activity in order to answer the question of how best to organize it is to compare it with Mintzberg's five structural configurations. If it is a question of a large organization in a stable environment, simple structure or adhocracy are probably not the best configurations. If it is a question of a very complex activity in an uncertain environment, machine bureaucracy is probably not suitable. And so on. By comparing the studied activity with all five configurations, a reasonably normative response can be achieved.

An even more meticulous variant of analysis based on a structural perspective is to clearly distinguish between the description of the unit to be analyzed and the normative analysis that leads to an understanding of how the studied activity should be organized. By dividing the analysis into a clearly *descriptive* part and a clearly *prescriptive* or normative part, the analysis can be made clearer and more specific conclusions can be reached. Mintzberg's five structural configurations should then be used primarily in the descriptive analysis part. In the prescriptive or normative part, the uncertainty in and around the activity is instead analyzed by dividing up the uncertainty into six different dimensions. Each of these dimensions comprises a situational dependency, that is, depending on the situation, described in six dimensions, the activity should be structured in different ways. By analyzing all six dimensions and their respective situational dependencies, it is possible to draw fairly accurate conclusions about which of the five structural configurations the analyzed activity should resemble.

A thorough analysis based on a structural framework should thus comprise two separate parts. One part should answer the question: Which structural configuration/s resemble the organization in focus? The other part should answer the question: Which configuration/s *should* the organization in focus resemble? Mintzberg's structural configurations are used primarily to answer the question of which configuration/s the organization resembles, and the dimensions and situational dependencies listed in Table 2.1 can then be used to answer the question of which configuration/s it should resemble.

Of the six listed dimensions and dependencies in Table 2.1, the first three can be said to be the most central and well-researched from a structural perspective.

Size and age

The first dimension, *size and age*, is relatively easy to understand. It is quite obvious that a large organization, with perhaps tens of thousands of employees, requires more forms of coordination than, for example, a company with five employees. It is also

Table 2.1   Dimensions and situational dependencies

Dimension	Situational dependency
Size and age	The bigger and older the organization, the more formalized the processes and hierarchical structures
Central processes and core technology	The higher the complexity in central processes and core technology, the less formalization and hierarchy
Environment	The higher the uncertainty and turbulence in the environment, the less formalization and hierarchy
Strategy	The more 'high-end', that is, high quality and high tech, the less formalization and hierarchy
Information technology	The more developed the information technology, the more decentralized organization and the smaller number of middle managers, but also the more centralization and vertical control
Labor force	The more highly educated and skilled labor, the less formalization and hierarchy

Source: based on Mintzberg (1983)

quite obvious that the age of the organization has an influence – over time, you learn how activities can be conducted, and the opportunities to divide labor and formalize processes increase over time. As uncertainty decreases, you can set the processes. Often, size and age coincide; successful organizations often grow over time. The fact that McDonald's has a much more extensive, bureaucratic structure than a small fast-food stand is a clear example of how an activity can and should be structured according to this situational dependency.

Central processes and core technologies

The *central processes and core technology* and *environment* dimensions, respectively, can be seen as a breakdown of an activity's uncertainty into two dimensions: central processes and core technologies refer to uncertainty within the organization, and environment refers to uncertainty beyond the organization's boundaries. In the one-dimensional simple structure model described in the introduction to this chapter (see Figure 2.3), these two dimensions are clumped into one. However, when separated from each other, the analysis can be taken further and more precise conclusions on how to organize an activity (see Figure 2.10) can be drawn.

The central processes dimension consists of uncertainty in the production of goods and services, in regards to both the complexity of the product itself and the manufacturing process. Developing next-generation passenger aircraft is a technically complicated process. Flying and maintaining such an aircraft may not be as complex.

Selling tickets, receiving and filling planes with passengers, luggage, fuel and crew, and taking off and landing are even less complex, and can be both planned and structured using formalized processes. The mass production of nails is a much less complex activity than particle-physics experiments. The higher the complexity of the central processes, the more appropriate are less developed structures and less formalized processes.

Environment

An organization's *environment* can be turbulent in several different dimensions. The market for the organization's offerings may be more or less turbulent; the competitive situation likewise. Changes in laws and regulations can cause major and unpredictable challenges. The global economy, demographic development and other environmental factors may be more or less difficult to assess. However, with regard to the turbulence of the environment, it should be borne in mind that a temporary increase in uncertainty and turbulence does not necessarily mean that we should not formalize and build structures in the longer term. Reorganizations take time and constitute investments that cannot be realized directly. Therefore, we should try to assess the possible growth of an organization, the complexity of central processes and the relative turbulence of the environment in the slightly longer term. Even if you experience a radical and turbulent shift in technology, a crucial readjustment or another major change, the increased uncertainty may be of a more temporary nature. Perhaps you should therefore choose to organize as you expect the situation to look in the slightly longer term, rather than just what it is at the moment.

Strategy

The *strategy* dimension shows that, in principle, you do *not* need to consider the first three dimensions in Table 2.1. Instead, you can choose the size of the organization, the complexity of core technologies and in what environment you conduct your business. If you choose to conduct technically high-quality activities (*high-end*), instead of activities characterized by low technology content and low quality, then you should not formalize, divide labor and establish hierarchy. Alternatively, if you choose to invest in more standardized (*low-end*) activities, with low quality, low costs and low prices, then labor division, formalization and hierarchy should be introduced as far as possible. In this way, the dimension strategy is a variant of the above, but with the emphasis that organizations can choose. This means that uncertainties in the environment or in the production of goods and services are not seen as independent and as determining variables, but as something that can be influenced. Thus, one computer manufacturer who chooses a low-end strategy should organize its activities differently to a computer manufacturer who chooses a high-end strategy. The same applies to service production. A luxury restaurant should not be organized in the same way as a fast-food chain. The strategy dimension indicates a complexity, or even a logical contradiction, in the structural framework. On the one hand, the framework says that we should adapt our choice of organizational form to a number of objective facts (a so-called deterministic view). On the other hand, it says that an organization's management can choose different strategies and thus affect the conditions that need to be adapted to (a more so-called voluntarist view). In practice, this can be seen as a short- and long-term issue. In the short term, we should adapt to the uncertainties (analyzed in the form of a number of dimensions and situational dependencies) that characterize an organization and its environment, but, in the longer term, we can move and change our activities more fundamentally.

Information technology

The research on the *information technology* dimension is contradictory. There are many studies that show that the introduction of modern information technology reduces the need for middle managers and that you can 'flatten' the organizational structure, i.e. reduce the number of hierarchical levels. Decision-making can be decentralized, i.e. vertical coordination can be replaced by horizontal coordination. For example, in the armed forces, it has been possible to make battle units more independent and thus more flexible, by giving them access to comprehensive strategic information previously available only at the highest level. This is often how information technology is described in textbooks and in popular media. But there are also opposing tendencies. As information can be disseminated more quickly than ever, even the highest management can obtain information about conditions in the organization's core processes and its environment faster and cheaper than ever before. Information technology therefore also enables a higher degree of centralized decision-making and control, and more vertical coordination, than before. In addition, profits derived from the fewer hierarchical levels and the smaller number of middle managers can be 'eaten up' by growing IT departments or costs for external IT support. In other words, if the number of middle managers and levels decreases, the need for technostructure and support functions increases. The general idea is that IT rationalizes, but whether it does so by means of increased decentralization and horizontal coordination, or by means of increased centralization and increased vertical control, is not entirely clear. Perhaps it occurs by means of both increased vertical and increased horizontal control?

The information technology dimension, however, has a far more comprehensive and extensive impact on organizations and companies than those situational dependencies which only affect which formal structure is effective in a particular situation. Internet, social media, cloud data, artificial intelligence and block-chain technologies influence individuals, organizations and societies on all levels. We will return to this development in the chapters on the power (Chapters 6 and 7) and symbol

(Chapters 8 and 9) perspectives but also in a separate section in the next chapter, where we delve deeper into the structural framework.

Labor force

The *labor* dimension has some similarities with the information technology dimension. In both cases, the major changes that have occurred in these areas are seen as indicating that organizations should not organize their activities today in the same way they did a couple of decades ago. In addition to the fact that today there are completely different technological solutions, employees' knowledge and education levels, as well as the knowledge content of many organizations, have increased significantly. In short, this means that you cannot divide labor, formalize and coordinate vertically as much today as you could before. Countless times, it has been claimed that the 'death of bureaucracy' is upon us. But, at the same time, bureaucracy seems to be more tenacious than many believed. Despite the message from all consultants and popular management books, that we *must* now organize in terms of managerless, self-determining, autonomous teams, research shows that organizations with advanced bureaucracy continue to be successful, both those that have operated for a long time (for example, in the engineering and banking sectors) and those that have relatively recently been established (for example, in the telecom sector and the management consultancy industry).

Applying the dimensions in analysis

Regardless of these problematizations of the above situational dimensions and dependencies, it is extremely informative to analyze an organization based on all six. A good analysis of the structure and degree of formalized processes in an organization should be characterized by at least the first three established dimensions (size and age, central processes and core technology and environment). Even if unambiguous answers to individual dimensions cannot be reached, an analysis of the organization using them as a starting point will identify important considerations. In sum, they will point in a certain direction. A careful structural analysis will answer questions about whether and, to what extent, an organization is characterized by an appropriate structure and degree of formalization, or whether it should be restructured; and – given that there is room for improvement – the direction in which the organization should be steered. A very useful model for describing the structures a particular organization resembles (or *is*), and the structures an organization *should* resemble, is the four-square matrix shown in Figure 2.10.

The two-dimensional model in Figure 2.10 can be seen as a concentrated expression of a more accurate analysis based on a structural framework. It also constitutes an expanded or slightly more complicated version of the simple one-dimensional model described in the introduction to this chapter (see Figure 2.3). The four-square

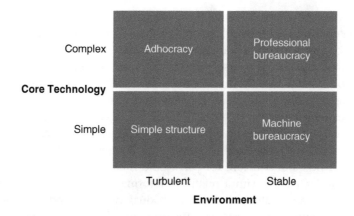

Figure 2.10   A two-dimensional structural analysis

Note: The two dimensions determine which of the four configurations is the most appropriate organizational form.

matrix can be used in several ways. You can illustrate which structural configurations an organization and its activities resemble, that is, answer the '*is*-question' by placing it in one of the squares. You can also show which configurations the same activities *should* resemble. If these two points coincide, the activities have an appropriate level of advanced bureaucracy. If they do not coincide, activities should be reorganized, according to the structural framework. You can also insert a time and change perspective regarding both *is* and *should*. Maybe these two positions coincided a number of years ago, but reorganizations may not have kept pace with technological development and/or changes in the environment. Or, restructuring has taken place, but in the wrong direction. Similar courses of events are then illustrated with two arrows. The one arrow describes what has been done (*is* and *where*) and the other one what *should* have been done.

If we look again at the case of SSE's increased bureaucratization, a much more far-reaching and nuanced analysis can be carried out than the one conducted using the one-dimensional model at the beginning of the chapter. With the greater accuracy of the two-dimensional model, we can see that there are different activities with partially different conditions within the SSE organization. Research, for example, is characterized by an extremely high degree of complexity but still has a relatively stable demand. Some form of professional bureaucracy might be appropriate. In individual research projects, where there is considerable uncertainty regarding process, results and demand, an adhocratic organization could also work well. Even with regard to educational programs, you might think that the development of programs and courses should take place in some kind of adhocratically organized team, albeit with more formalized processes than in research projects. Although the demand for graduate and master economists is relatively stable, there are constant changes in specific programs and their content. In cases where development work is not too complex, we can imagine that this occurs within the framework of simple structures, that is, a competent and experienced teacher or course director conducts a course development project relatively autocratically. In order to effectively provide these programs and courses, it should still be possible to structure activities with extensive support functions (professional bureaucracy elements), but also to divide labor, formalize and coordinate a lot of processes vertically (machine bureaucracy elements), especially with regard to the largest and most standardized programs, the Bachelor of Business and Economics programs. A possible structure for SSE would thus be to divide activities into two divisions: *one for research*, with a relatively informal professional bureaucracy as an umbrella structure and adhocracies for individual projects, and *one for education*, with adhocracies and simple structures for program and course development, and a professional bureaucracy with machine bureaucracy elements as an umbrella organization. In order to minimize the potential conflict within this divisional structure, and to avoid becoming a 'headless giant' (an organization with no clear direction and a top management with little control), it is also important to have ongoing dialogue and discussion between school management, division management, faculty and staff on strategy and goals. This rapid analysis of SSE's activities shows that, even in an analysis of a relatively small organization (SSE has just over 300 full-time employees, including researchers, faculty and administrative staff), all five structural configurations and several dimensions of situational dependencies can be helpful.

Matrix organization

The matrix organization was briefly mentioned in the introduction to this chapter in the section on how the labor involved in an activity can be divided. For example, if labor is divided based on both function and project, a two-dimensional structure, a so-called matrix, is created. Mintzberg (1983) mentions matrix organization only in passing and then as an example of a horizontal coordination mechanism. But, different variants of matrices are today very common in both large and small organizations. In addition, extensive research shows that a matrix organization is a much more complex phenomenon than just a horizontal coordination mechanism. There is therefore every reason to go a little deeper into the matrix organization and look at division of labor, coordination and control, and finally its strengths and weaknesses.

Division of labor in matrix organizations

Based on the different principles of labor division described earlier in this chapter (function, product, market, etc.), a matrix organization can be defined as an activity in which labor is divided on the basis of two or more of these principles. Large parts of an organization's resources, such as its employees, belong to two (or more) different structures. In a two-dimensional matrix organization, employees have two authority and responsibility structures to consider (see Figure 2.11). For example, you can have a manager for the function to which you belong (e.g. marketing or production manager) and a manager of the project, customer or product you are working with. The origin of the matrix organization can be traced back to US aircraft manufacturers in the 1950s and to the US space industry. Matrix organizations, at that time, consisted of a combination of functional structures that managed the manufacturing of, for example, aircraft, and cross-functional groups (or projects) that managed the development of new aircraft models (Allen 1984).

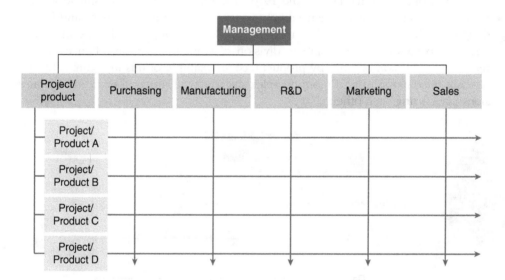

Figure 2.11   Dual authority and responsibility structures in a matrix organization

Source: Daft et al. (2014)

Note: Compare with the structure of a functional organization in Figure 2.2.

The development of matrix organizations was intimately associated with the development of project management (discussed in more detail in Chapter 3). One reason for the emergence of the matrix organization was the problems that were often encountered when functionally organized departments had to cooperate. As the basic assumptions of the structural framework imply, cross-functional cooperation was formalized and, together with the already formalized functional structure, formed a new kind of structural solution. The development of new products now took place in formally planned projects with formally appointed project managers. The project manager's task was to coordinate and control project resources in order to carry out product development, i.e. the project's goals. When a specific project's development work was completed, the group dissolved or received new assignments. For each assignment, however, the composition of the project groups could change, due to the organization's flexibility and resource utilization, and this increased the efficiency of the project's development work (Galbraith 1971).

The emergence of matrix organizations thus led to cross-functional projects forming entities in the formal organizational structure. In organizations with repeated and parallel projects, these formed a formal horizontal structure that cut across the various functions. This clarified an already emerging informal process in accordance with the structural perspective's view of how clear structures and formal processes lead to efficient organizations. During the 1970s, the matrix organization spread to other industries, companies and organizations. Today, it is found everywhere and is often designed to handle activities other than just product development. For example, multinational companies often combine division of labor by location, often country or region, with division of labor by product (see an example of this in Figure 2.12). It is also not uncommon to find more complex matrices with three, four or more dimensions intersecting each other.

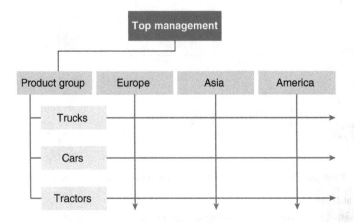

Figure 2.12   **A common matrix in multinational companies (exemplified by a vehicle manufacturer)**

Coordination and control in matrix organizations

If matrix organizations are relatively easy to understand in terms of labor division, they are more complex in terms of coordination. This is because the coordination between the different dimensions of the matrix is, among other things, about balancing different goals and interests. Dual coordination mechanisms can also create an ambiguity for the organization's employees. One could argue that restructuring a functional structure (see Figure 2.2 at the beginning of the chapter) into a matrix structure is to complement vertical control with horizontal coordination. This is in line with projects, teams and cross-functional groups listed as examples of horizontal coordination by, for example, Mintzberg (1983) and Bolman and Deal (2013). However, since the 'horizontal' dimension in matrix organizations is most often formalized in the form of its own management structure (such as project manager, project office manager, project coordinator), and moreover most often in the form of formal process descriptions (i.e. new technostructure; see, for example, project management models in Chapter 3), a matrix organization consists of two dimensions, both of which comprise vertical control. These two vertical control structures tend to collide. What benefits the effectiveness of research and development work does not necessarily benefit efficiency in more day-to-day production. What benefits an organization in a certain country is not necessarily what is best for a particular product group.

According to the structural framework, the solution to this problem is about trying to find a clear balance between the responsibilities and powers of the two dimensions. If successful, the matrix organization makes use of the benefits of several different principles for both labor division and coordination. Ideally, for example, a matrix organization may develop new goods and services faster than purely functional organizations, while being equally efficient in its more day-to-day activities. For example, a well-implemented matrix can enable an organization to quickly adapt to changing local market conditions, while, at the same time, producing products as efficiently as pure product organizations. However, failing to balance the dimensions of the matrix can cause confusion and conflict, and a time-consuming and inefficient bureaucratic superstructure can also develop.

Strengths and weaknesses of matrix organizations

Table 2.2 lists the strengths and weaknesses of the matrix organization. Based on a structural framework, the basic principle of creating a balanced matrix is to clarify, formalize and regulate the powers and responsibilities of the various managerial structures. However, as there is an almost infinite number of areas, issues and aspects that could be the source of confusion and conflict, such formalization risks resulting in an extensive, rigid and costly bureaucracy. Even if one tries to solve the balancing problem with more horizontal coordination, all calls and meetings are likely to take time and resources. Therefore, getting a matrix organization to work takes quite a long time, usually several years. The fact that an organization eventually succeeds in implementing a working matrix is also no guarantee that the organization will continue to work if you change the dimensions of the matrix or the balance between them. Although a well-functioning matrix organization is more flexible and better at development than a machine bureaucracy, it has similar problems in dealing with more extensive changes.

Table 2.2   **Strengths and weaknesses of the matrix organization**

Strengths	Weaknesses
Can create the coordination necessary to satisfy conflicting demands	May require a lot of time for coordination meetings and creates extensive bureaucracy
Has flexibility in its allocation of resources	Can create confusion and frustration
Is suitable in complex decision-making situations and turbulent environments	Assumes that managers and employees have high collaborative skills
Enables skill development in several dimensions	Assumes a 'collegial' rather than a 'competitive' culture
Fits organizations with many areas of expertise, products and markets	Requires great efforts to balance influence

Source: based on Duncan (1979)

To avoid political power struggles, time-consuming meetings and a sluggish and extensive bureaucratic superstructure, arenas for conflict resolution, functioning dialogues, trust and community spirit between managers and leaders in the different dimensions of the matrix need to be created. However, in order to really understand the problem of how this happens, it is necessary to go beyond the structural framework's focus on clarity and formalization. In other words, matrix organizations should also be analyzed using models and theories from the other fundamental frameworks of organizational theory.

Videos

Don't forget to watch the videos to discover more about the key concepts in this chapter: **https://study.sagepub.com/blomberg**

Notes

1   Stockholm School of Economics (SSE) is the only privately owned university-level school in Sweden. It was founded in 1908 by one of Sweden's wealthiest and most influential banking and industrialist families, and has since been regarded as an institution providing top-quality education in business administration and economics. Today, it has programs at bachelor, master's, PhD and executive levels and has students from all over the world. It also plays a comparatively large part in research. The school is small, having about 300 employees. It has gone through many changes but is, as it has been from the start, firmly positioned as the top Scandinavian business school.

2   What is open source? See, for instance, https://opensource.com/resources/what-open-source.

3   Read more on the history of Losec at, for instance, www.akademiliv.se/2013/12/15611.

3

An In-Depth Structural Framework – Lean, Team, Leadership and Projects

This chapter describes a number of models that complement and deepen the foundation, laid down in the previous chapter, of organizational analysis from a structural framework perspective. These complementary models will help you to understand the analyzed phenomenon even better, and they will enable you to develop even more precise conclusions on how to structure the analyzed organization at hand.

First, three established models are presented that can be used for an in-depth analysis of the first three of the six dimensions described in the previous chapter (see Table 2.1): the size and age of the organization, the complexity of its central processes and uncertainty in the surrounding environment. As already mentioned, these are crucial aspects governing how an organization should be structured.

We then describe a contemporary influential structural model, which often goes by the name of *lean production* or just *lean* for short. This is followed by a section that presents two very influential theories or approaches that can be used to analyze outsourcing and to understand how so-called virtual networks affect how business operations are structured, both within and between organizations and companies. Two sections are then devoted to understanding how leadership and work in teams and projects can be analyzed based on the structural framework. The chapter concludes with a section on the structural framework's generic questions, strengths and weaknesses.

Three models for an in-depth analysis of situational dependencies

It is possible to achieve more than you think in the form of informative conclusions using the one-dimensional structural model described in the introduction to the previous chapter. More substantially developed analysis is possible if one uses Mintzberg's more complex model comprising the five configurations and the six structural dimensions. But the analysis can be taken even further. In addition, parts of the model can be clarified and developed by supplementing them with more theory and less rigid, more nuanced concepts. It is possible to borrow some more theory when and where Mintzberg's model feels obtuse. Sometimes, for example, it can be difficult to determine whether an organization should be considered large or small. It can be difficult to analyze the degree of uncertainty and turbulence in the surrounding environment without using a more structured environmental description. And it is often difficult to determine whether a business's central processes should be considered complex or simple. Therefore, this chapter begins with a description of three well-established models that can be said to complement and deepen the three most central and well-established structural dimensions – size and age, process complexity and environment.

Size and age – evolution and revolution

Greiner (1972, 1998) has developed a very simple but useful model for analyzing what form of organization and what type of leadership are needed in the different growth phases of organizations. Greiner's model consists of five growth phases, each consisting of a period of stable growth, followed by a short 'crisis' (see Figure 3.1). Greiner (1972) claims that each phase of an organization's growth has its own unique characteristics and thus needs to be organized and managed in a unique way. According to Greiner, an organization's growth and development are mostly characterized by stable phases of evolution (typically 4–8 years long). The stable phases are a result of leadership that developed in response to previous problems and challenges, but which is not obviously adapting to the various changes taking place both inside and outside the organization. As such, these evolutionary phases are abruptly interrupted by short, intense crises – revolution – where the challenge for leadership is to find new structural solutions and ways to lead.

One argument that supports Greiner's theory is that organization, by definition, is about creating predictability and inertia and ensuring that the organization does not respond to everything in its environment (if this were the case, the organization would dissolve into a passively responsive organism without the ability to create added value). Since all organization and leadership must include some degree of stabilization

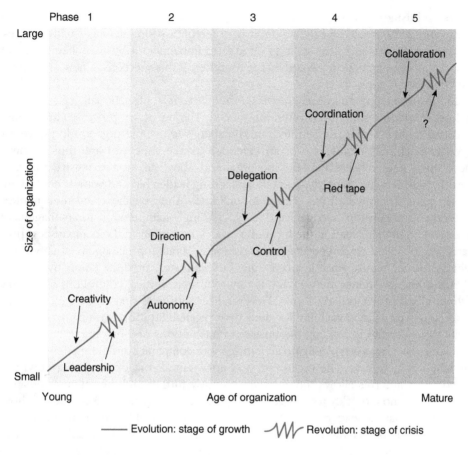

Figure 3.1   An organization's five growth phases

Source: Greiner (1972)

and inertia, businesses tend to become out of kilter with both the technology and the environmental factors affecting core processes. According to Greiner, this leads to a crisis, and radical reorganization eventually becomes inevitable.

Greiner's description of the first growth phase of organizations, *creativity* (see Figure 3.1), is very similar to the adhocratic configuration in Mintzberg's model. The founders are often technically or entrepreneurially oriented, and their attention is entirely focused on developing and selling a product or service. Interaction is informal, returns are low and the organization is responsive and flexible. As the number of employees grows and sales increase, the creative, adhocratically organized business becomes messy and inefficient. The founders are reluctant to structure and yearn for when the business was smaller and more manageable. A crisis in the form of a lack of *leadership* is the result, and the solution is to recruit a strong manager with business expertise and with sufficient skills to be able to implement a business-like approach and, at the same time, be accepted by the founders. If this succeeds, a new and calmer growth phase begins.

In the second growth phase, *growth through direction*, a functionally classified, formal organizational structure is often introduced. The necessary processes are formalized and middle managers recruited. In Mintzberg's terms, the organization develops towards machine bureaucracy (or an extended simple structure) and thus becomes increasingly internally efficient. But the larger and, above all, more extensive and complex the business becomes, the less efficient strong leadership and vertical control are. Lower managers and staff in core operations know their business and their markets better than strategic top managers and feel increasingly hampered by top management. A second crisis then arises in the form of a lack of *autonomy* in the company's various parts. Many skilled employees leave the company, while top management is typically reluctant to reorganize since it successfully built and structured the company.

According to Greiner, the solution is now not more vertical control but *decentralization*, albeit under orderly forms. Decentralized business units have much greater powers as well as responsibility for their own profitability. Top (group) management limits its leadership to reading the business units' reports and helping to solve major problems. The focus is typically on acquiring more companies and fitting them into the growing conglomerate. The organization is now reminiscent of Mintzberg's divisionalized structure. This allows the company to grow further and the different business units to react more quickly to changes in the market. The divisionalized structure, however, means that the leaders of the various business units will begin to pull in different directions. It is becoming increasingly difficult for top (group) management to make decisions on resource allocation and strategic direction, and the group falls into a crisis in the form of lack of *control*.

In Greiner's view, the solution for the company in terms of being able to grow further is increased *coordination*. This does not mean harder top-down control from a strategic apex but more and more sophisticated processes being formalized ('put in place'). Business units are grouped according to product or market. Group-wide training and promotion programs are introduced. The product groups are seen as investments and are managed using quantitative portfolio models. Profit-sharing models and bonuses are designed so that employees and managers consider the results of the group as a whole. According to Greiner, this will solve many of the conflicts that have arisen and distribute group-wide resources more efficiently. Gradually, however, all these formalized processes will lead to distance and a lack of trust between line managers and the staff that manage the technostructure. The group simply becomes too large to be manageable by formal programs and systems. A crisis in the form of an abundance of heavy and inefficient *red-tape bureaucracy* will be the result.

According to Greiner, the solution to this crisis is more *collaboration*. This is achieved through more spontaneous and action-oriented leadership and quick problem-solving with the help of teams. By simplifying formal systems and processes and introducing horizontal coordination in the form of teams, meetings, conferences and modern information systems, vertical control can be reduced and the organization's different parts made more responsive to each other. According to Greiner, however, there were signs that the next crisis would be about the mental health of employees and about burnout from all the intensive teamwork, hence the question mark in Figure 3.1. The solution in the form of a fifth revolution is then new programs that support employees and give them space to reflect and recover. Given that Greiner wrote this in the early 1970s and that burnout came to be a very prominent problem in the 1980s, resulting in an increasing number of organizations introducing different formal processes to manage the work–life balance of their employees, we have to admit that Greiner was on point in formulating this fifth crisis.[1]

We can also link back to the example of the Stockholm School of Economics (see Chapter 2), which, for many years, had been formalized and structured, despite the fact that, internally at the school, this posed major problems for ongoing operations. Over time, many talented teachers and researchers left the organization, and quality suffered. However, the management was opposed to a change in structure. It became something of a crisis and it required new management to take the school in a new direction.

Process complexity – three types of dependencies

It is not always easy to determine whether an organization's central processes should be seen as complex or simple. It may depend on what these processes are compared to, but also on a simple lack of knowledge about the organization in question. Thompson (1967), however, has developed a model that may be helpful. Thompson identifies three different types of dependencies, arguing that the types of dependencies that exist in an organization affect how it should be organized. If one can identify which dependencies characterize an organization's central processes, it becomes easier to draw conclusions about the degree of complexity and thus the appropriate degree of work division, formalization and hierarchy.

Pooled dependencies

Pooled, or parallel, dependencies are characterized by the fact that what is done in one unit has no direct influence on what is done in another, except that both units produce components that are part of the same overall product or service. For example, a telephone operator needs both a unit that takes care of payment and billing issues, and a unit that takes care of technical customer support, but one unit can produce its services without interacting with the other. At the same time, both units are needed for the telephone operator to be able to conduct their business. Pooled dependencies can be said to be very loose, indirect and almost invisible to employees in the different units. Therefore, coordination between them does not have to be flexible or agile. The most important thing is that they produce their components as predictably and in as standardized a way as possible in order to fit into the whole of the organization. Therefore, organizations characterized by pooled dependencies should be coordinated by a hierarchical structure and by formalized and standardized requirements for the results of the different units (or 'pools').

Sequential dependencies

Sequential dependencies are characterized by the fact that what one unit does cannot continue without the completion of what another unit produces. That is, the 'output' from one unit constitutes the 'input' in another. The most famous example of an operation characterized by sequential dependencies is the conveyor belt. The conveyor belt has been in use in various types of manufacturing for over 100 years, but it has been and still is perhaps most common in the production of cars. Although the conveyor belt is a kind of technostructure that in itself accounts for much of the continuous coordination, Thompson believes that it needs to be supplemented with additional coordination and control mechanisms. More detailed control in the form of scheduling and planning is required to avoid production halting or slowing down. In order to effectively coordinate operations characterized by sequential dependencies, a high degree of vertical coordination is thus required, either in the form of a developed technostructure or in the form of formalized plans. According to this model, sequential dependencies should be organized using vertical coordination mechanisms.

Mutual dependencies

Mutual dependencies are characterized by the fact that one unit's activity must be continuously adapted, based on what another unit does, and vice versa. Mutual dependencies are largely found in more complex operations. This means that, if mutual dependencies can be identified, it is an indication that the operation is more complex and should be coordinated more horizontally than vertically. A clear example of an activity with a high degree of mutual dependencies is brain surgery, not least if it is an emergency operation. If the surgeon makes a decision during the operation that causes it to take more time than estimated, the anaesthetist must also adjust their part of the intervention. For each step, the nurses and doctors must adapt their actions to each other. These mutual dependencies are a component of the great complexity and uncertainty that characterize this type of activity. Mutual dependencies can, however, be found, to a lower or higher degree, in many other, not quite so complex activities: in research, the development of advanced future technology, innovative consulting projects, and so on. We see here great similarities with Mintzberg's adhocratic configuration. In other words, if mutual dependencies can be identified, it is an expression of the fact that the activity is characterized by adhocratic elements and that horizontal coordination is thus more suitable than vertical coordination.

Uncertainty in the environment – PESTEL

Mintzberg's multidimensional analysis model (see Table 2.1) has many merits, but can be said to be rather obtuse in terms of how to analyze the environment dimension. An organization can be said to work in many different environments; alternatively, an organization's environment can be divided into several different dimensions or factors. Therefore, in order not to 'miss' important changes or the degree of turbulence and uncertainty when analyzing an organization's environment, it may be appropriate to use a more elaborate model. One well-established conceptual scheme is the so-called PESTEL model.[2] Each letter in the model's name symbolizes an environmental dimension:

- **p**olitical
- **e**conomic
- **s**ocial
- **t**echnological
- **e**nvironmental
- **l**egal.

By going through these dimensions separately, a more precise environmental analysis can be obtained.

Political

Is the political environment stable and predictable? Are major political changes expected to occur, with consequences that are difficult to predict? There is hardly any doubt that changes in the political environment affect many organizations. Straightforward legal changes can occur (see the section below), but it may also be the case that the agendas of different political representatives directly affect the organization's business dealings and markets. The political environment can be uncertain at local, national and international levels alike. The decisions of Stockholm politicians regarding whether the nearest local airport, Bromma, should be closed down or developed, is an example of rather local uncertainty. The fast-developing political landscape in many Western democracies, with an increasing support for anti-democratic parties, is an example of political uncertainty on a more international scale. The possible withdrawal application of various EU Member States, or ambitions for increased supranational cooperation, is another. However, the important thing in an analysis of this environmental dimension's uncertainty is whether it has consequences for the analyzed organization. If a company operates within the energy section, political decisions on, for example, the expansion of hydropower or the closure of nuclear power plants are of considerable relevance.

Economic

Economic factors that affect the environmental dimension are mainly macroeconomic. Examples of issues related to the economic environment are: What does growth look like in the country in which the organization is considering setting up? Will different interest rates and exchange rates change significantly? Is there any uncertainty about how inflation will develop? If there is considerable uncertainty about, for example, interest rates and thus the organization's capital costs, it should be prepared to rapidly change its capital structure, which is an argument for a more flexible, structured financial function.

Social

Social factors range from cultural and social attitudes and trends to population development and age structures. The social environment is perhaps one of the most important to take into account because it is in this environment that both labor markets and end-consumer demand can largely be said to be formed. Examples of trends are: attitudes to work, career and leisure; the desire to shop for food online; and the balance between security and private integrity and freedom. If a clear social trend can be identified, for example, that parents increasingly devote resources to protective equipment for their children (child seats, helmets, elbow, knee and shin pads, back protection, etc.), it may be appropriate to invest in processes and systems that can produce and distribute such things. However, it is usually difficult to accurately estimate the development of demand for a particular product or product area. The potential may be great, but the risk is often high.

Technological

We recognize technology from Mintzberg's organizational model with the structural dimension 'central processes and core technology' (see Table 2.1). But here it is about technology as an environmental dimension: if and to what extent there is rapid technology development, if there are several competing technologies, if these are at different maturity levels, which technology has the greatest potential and, if so, on what viewpoint, and so on. If it is difficult to answer such questions, there is considerable uncertainty in this area, and it is then less appropriate to organize the business according to more bureaucratic principles. Today, we can see different car manufacturers investing a lot in different types of engines: petrol, diesel, electricity, gas, hybrids, different types of battery technologies, hydropower, and so on. Another known example is insulin production. Before synthetic insulin became the industry standard, there was a great deal of uncertainty about whether it was organic insulin (from pigs) or synthetic insulin that had the greatest potential. Medicine and telecommunications are obvious areas where it is important to understand this type of environmental uncertainty, but it can also apply to less advanced goods and services. There are almost always technological choices to make: glue or rivet, plastic or aluminum, and so on. In all these cases, considerable technological uncertainty should be addressed with a less bureaucratic organization.

Environmental

Environmental factors are increasingly being highlighted. This dimension could be seen as being intertwined with some of the dimensions described above, but then we neglect the fact that changes are actually happening in the physical natural environment. These are so important that they should be described as a separate environmental dimension. Global warming means that green technologies are becoming increasingly important, that fresh water is becoming increasingly scarce and that gas and oil are becoming easier to exploit as the Arctic and Antarctic ice caps disappear (creating new opportunities for profitable exploitation that also makes global warming even worse). Extreme weather patterns affect and increase uncertainty in many areas, ranging from tourism, agricultural industries, financial markets and private individuals' choice of food to urban planning and public authority crisis preparation. The demand for organic goods, emissions-compensated travel and locally produced goods and services are all important aspects of this dimension. The environmental dimension is also associated with different degrees of uncertainty. Some trends may be more certain, while others are associated with great uncertainty. What happens in one area can have the opposite effect on another. It is therefore not obvious that investment and organization should be carried out on the basis of an overarching picture of increased environmental awareness. Instead, a proper analysis of what is happening and may happen should be carried out.

Legal

Legal factors can be seen as part of the political environment, but, when viewed as a separate environmental dimension, the focus is on laws and regulations. Legal changes – new regulation, deregulation or re-regulation – can create uncertainty in many areas. For example, in the banking and financial markets, international regulations have supplemented and/or replaced national regulations in the last two decades. These regulations have not only increased the requirements for highly formalized and regulated internal risk-control processes in banks and finance companies, but also created a completely new market for both large and small consulting agencies. The smaller ones mainly help small finance companies to meet the mandatory requirements for vertical coordination and risk-control processes. The large international management consultants have developed all kinds of models for how banks should develop 'healthy risk cultures'. In this banking example, regulation has involved absolute requirements for bureaucratization and opened up a market for new consulting services.

To sum up, the PESTEL model can be helpful when trying to understand the uncertainties in an organization's environment. Together with Greiner's organizational growth model (Greiner 1972, 1998) and Thompson's model of three types of uncertainties (Thompson 1967), we thus have three models that complement and develop Mintzberg's model, described in the previous chapter. Together, they can be used to analyze what kind of structure and formal processes a specific organization should have to be as efficient and innovative as possible.

Lean production

Over the years, organizational theory has become an increasingly comprehensive and multifaceted research area, with an increasing number of specialized sub-fields. One such field, which has also had a great practical impact, is *operations management*, specifically the perspective developed in this field that goes by the name of *lean production* or just *lean* for short. Although the seeds of this perspective can be said to have been sown by a few American scientists and writers, most of its roots were developed in Japanese car factories, in particular Toyota, in the 1970s and 1980s. Lean encompasses a variety of principles, concepts and models. Here, only a few basic principles and a central model will be described.

Continuous improvement – identifying bottlenecks and creating flow

A basic principle within lean is that an attempt is not made to optimize a business once and for all (or until further notice). Instead, continuous improvement is the aim. Lean can thus be said to be a more dynamic perspective than the traditional structural models (for example, Mintzberg's structural configurations, which are described in the previous chapter). In addition, the way to identify problems and implement changes is different. Based on a traditional structural framework, restructuring takes place by management analyzing the organization and thereby discovering any sub-optimal structures and processes. Based on the results of the analysis, a new structural solution is then implemented, using vertical, i.e. 'top-down', control. Both analysis and change initiatives are thus something that the organization's management (a strategic apex using the technostructure, in Mintzberg's terms) stands behind.

According to the lean perspective on continuous improvement, much of this improvement work instead takes place on site in the operational core. It is the employees at the assembly line in Toyota who are expected to constantly try to streamline operations. Instead of management deciding on an optimized flow, for example in the form of an optimal speed of an assembly line, the speed of the line is gradually increased in order to find out where and why problems arise. When problems arise, for example a bottleneck, the assembly line is stopped. Employees are trying to develop a solution to the problem on site, for example a redistribution of personnel along the assembly line that causes the bottleneck to disappear. This means that the personnel in the operational core have greater responsibility and power than in a typical machine bureaucracy, but also that they can never 'sit back' and be content with just doing their job.

Flow efficiency

One of the main points of the lean perspective is that organizations can become more efficient by constantly improving how well resources flow through them, rather than by optimizing them with regard to how well the available resources are utilized. Toyota's deceased, almost legendary, head, Taiichi Ohno (1912–90), put it as follows: 'All we are doing is looking at the timeline, from the moment the customer gives us an order to the point when we collect the cash. And we are reducing the timeline by reducing the non-value adding wastes' (Modig & Åhlström 2013: 76).

The above quote points to the fact that lean is not only about continuous improvement but also that the main focus of this improvement work is to try to shorten the time it takes to satisfy customer demand. This means that all forms of inventories, intermediate storage, inspections and buffers within and outside the organization's boundaries should be removed. This in turn leads to the fact that every small disturbance in production will be noticed (just as when the assembly line was stopped in the example above). 'Bad flows' will be discovered and opportunities to improve the flow will arise. This also has to do with 'zero-defects production' and *just-in-time*. If there is no separate inspection of the quality of what is produced, all responsibility for quality is shifted to the unit that is actually responsible for the production. As there are no buffer stocks (supplies of inputs held as a reserve to safeguard against unforeseen shortages or demands) and other reserves within the production process, a defective component in a product or service is likely to be detected immediately and, again, an opportunity for improved flow arises. The lack of buffer stocks means that each component must

$$\text{Flow efficiency} = \frac{\text{Value adding time}}{\text{Throughput time}}$$

Figure 3.2   Definition of flow efficiency

be manufactured at just the right time, in the right amount and with the right quality to fit into the production chain flow.

According to traditional structural models, a disturbance, for example an assembly line breakdown, is almost a disaster because it means that production is at a standstill. Therefore, it is good to have some 'slack' in the form of buffer stocks or other reserves. On the contrary, from the lean perspective, it is desirable to disrupt production to stop the assembly line, as it enables the discovery of bad flows and possible quality improvements. Thus, based on the principle of continuous improvement and flow efficiency, it is desirable to create a sensitive, lean and dynamic system, rather than a stable one.

The above quotation also points to another important component in the hunt for flow efficiency. All work stages should be about *creating or adding customer value*. Buffers and inventories of various kinds and transport to and from these add minimal value for the customer. The same applies to administration, planning and activities among middle managers, in the strategic apex, in overall technostructure and in support functions. Waiting for a referral to a specialist care unit after a visit to the healthcare center adds anxiety and dissatisfaction rather than value for a patient. From a flow efficiency perspective, not only should buffer stocks, transport and administration be minimized, but also waiting times in, for example, medical care. The definition of flow efficiency is given in Figure 3.2.

Flow efficiency thus closely resembles the concept of effectiveness/external efficiency (see the discussion on different types of efficiency at the beginning of Chapter 2), but with the emphasis on dynamics and time minimization rather than on cost minimization (i.e. cost efficiency or internal efficiency). Modig and Åhlström (2013) state that organizations must consider how much they should strive to be good at *resource efficiency* (internal efficiency) *and* flow efficiency (a dynamic variant of external efficiency). The ideal would be to be best at both forms of efficiency, but how such an organizational form would be structured is difficult to formulate in theory, as well as difficult to find in practice. If companies organize themselves according to lean principles, however, lean advocates say that the utilization of resources and time minimization between customer demand and delivery, can be combined better than if they are content with organizing themselves according to more traditional structural models. Modig and Åhlström (2013) have formulated an efficiency matrix with four typical 'operational states' that an organization can be in, given the balance between resource efficiency (internal efficiency) and flow efficiency (see Figure 3.3). They call these states of efficiency 'desert', 'efficient ocean', 'efficient islands' and 'the perfect state'.

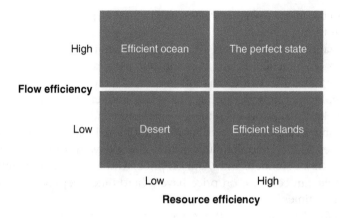

Figure 3.3   Four operational states

Source: Modig and Åhlström (2013)

The operational state *efficient islands* overlaps to a great extent with Mintzberg's (1983) machine bureaucracy configuration: the company is largely internally efficient and can produce goods and services at low prices. However, it is not self-evident that these are the products customers really want. But, if the company can get the customer to experience the value of the goods or services as acceptable, for example by means of a really low price, it can still be successful in this state. A clear example of a successful organization that has chosen an extreme version of this strategy is Ryanair. The airline has deliberately stripped off value-creating components and concentrated on maximum resource efficiency. Paradoxically, this has led to them being able to create added value for a large number of customers in the form of very cheap air travel. Really efficient machine bureaucracy can thus create stable and predictable demand and then it need not be flow-efficient in accordance with lean.

The operational state *efficient ocean* has similarities mainly with the simple structure and, to some extent, with the adhocracy in Mintzberg's structural model. In this state, the organization is good at flow efficiency and at quickly adapting the production of goods and services to a changing environment, at least in terms of variations of the organization's product offerings. A crucial difference, however, is that the effective ocean state, despite its flexibility, includes more systematically designed processes than the simple structure. Through continuous improvement, flows of information, materials and people, a large number of activities can be structured into one synchronized and increasingly optimized flow. Through lean, the advantages of the simple structure can thus be at least partially scaled up. For example, the computer manufacturer Dell can make certain configurations according to customer requirements, deliver quickly and still charge a relatively low price; but you cannot get your Dell computer configured however you want. For companies that specialize in building advanced computers according to customers' specific wishes, adhocracy is probably a more appropriate organizational form.

An organization that finds itself in *the perfect state* maximizes both resource and flow efficiency. In practice, this is difficult, but there are companies that have succeeded in doing this. The clothes manufacturer and store chain Zara has an extremely short timeline. From a new design idea to a new garment hanging in a store, it takes about two weeks. This covers everything from design and material purchases to manufacturing, pricing, transportation, and more. A traditional tailor can perhaps sew a new garment in a few hours, and definitely within a few days from the time the customer orders it, but cannot compete with Zara on price. And the clothing manufacturers and chain stores that can compete on price have a hard time keeping up with Zara's very short production times.

The *wasteland* or *desert* is the operational state to avoid at all costs, if the goal of a business is to produce goods and services efficiently. In this state, the organization is neither good at using its resources, nor at adapting its production to changing demands. Since the pursuit of some kind of efficiency is one of the fundamental assumptions of the structural perspective, there is nothing positive in the desert state.

Part of the principle of continuous improvement is to decentralize responsibility and authority from management to the employees in the operational core. Employees are given information about how the production flows, partly because there are no buffer stocks, and partly through support structures in the form of systems that give everyone in the operational core information on how well synchronized production is at the moment (everything from large, constantly updated information boards showing how each workstation is doing, to lamps located in the ceiling over each unit, visible to everyone, that flash red when there is a problem). Thus, the lean principles can be said to go against the basic structural perspective that maximum work division and vertical coordination represent the most effective organizational form. But, as the example of Ryanair shows, pure machine bureaucracy can certainly be a successful organizational form. In addition, one can question how decentralized organizations that apply lean actually are. Who or what has determined that employees in operational activities, in addition to managing day-to-day operations, shall also constantly strive to streamline them? Does not the removal of intermediate storage and buffers also mean that employees lack opportunities to take breaks and recover? The question can be reformulated using Mintzberg's model: Does lean simply mean that you scale up the adhocracy or the simple structure? From a structural perspective, this question is difficult to answer. Therefore, we will return to it in the chapters on the other three basic frameworks. Based on these, there are better models for analyzing centralization and decentralization, power and influence, and more 'invisible' and cultural control.

Virtual networks, outsourcing, markets and control

The previous chapter described six structural dimensions and situational dependencies that together determine the type of formal structure, or structural configuration, that maximizes an organization's efficiency. In the section on information technology, one of the structural dimensions (see Table 2.1), it was briefly mentioned that the development of IT, the Internet, social media and cloud data has influenced and still influences the conditions for organizing at individual, organizational and societal levels.

Here we discuss two models with strong roots in the basic assumptions of the structural framework and which can be used to both understand and practically organize and lead companies and other organizations. Together, they can provide a good guide on how to navigate the contemporary, network-based business world.

Williamson's transaction cost approach has its roots in the economic theory of organization, while the subsequently described network model is derived from industrial marketing and distribution economics. Both models can be said to treat markets and interorganizational networks as at least as important as organizations and their internal processes. For exactly this reason, they are useful instruments when analyzing organization and leadership in the rapidly emerging network-based society.

Williamson's transaction cost approach

In quantitative and economic organizational theory, organizations are treated in an even more 'reductionist' (simplified, pure, conceptual) way than in the more qualitative models that dominate other organizational theory. An example of a highly reductionist model is Williamson's transaction cost approach (Williamson 1973, 1975, 1981), which explains why some exchanges take place in *markets* (think of the perfect markets of economic theory) and why others occur within the framework of pure *hierarchies* (think of Weber's formally rational bureaucracy and Mintzberg's machine bureaucracy). According to Williamson, which of these two forms of organization is most effective depends on which of them has the lowest transaction costs. According to Williamson, transaction costs, i.e. costs that have to do with the exchange itself and not with the production of the good or service, arise because of human nature, the number of players who can offer the same or similar goods and services, and how the information on these players and their offerings is dispersed.

Williamson believes that human beings are opportunistic and try to maximize their material self-interest, but they also have limited cognitive and rational ability. Humans also have different preferences. For example, some strive for a high degree of freedom, while others strive for less. However, the decisive factor in whether human exchanges are organized most efficiently with market transactions or within the framework of hierarchical control are:

- how many market actors can offer the good or service to be exchanged
- how unevenly information about the product or service and about each other is distributed between the exchanging parties.

If the number of market actors is relatively large and the information about the goods and/or services to be exchanged is dispersed, then the transaction cost is lowest within the framework of a market transaction (see Figure 3.4).[3] Since there are a large number of actors offering similar goods (that is, there is homogeneity among the market offerings; and the offers represent each other's substitutes), it is easy to switch business partners in the event of being dissatisfied with the deal. This reduces the incentives for sellers to deceive. If the seller would deceive, it is easy for the deceived buyer to switch to another seller, when there are a large number of similar sellers offering similar products. The same applies if the information is dispersed. Since the seller does not have an informational advantage, there is no need for costly information gathering by the buyer, thus it is easy to switch to another seller.

If, on the other hand, there are relatively few actors that offer similar goods and services, the transaction cost is lower if the exchange takes place within a hierarchical organization. This is because we are more dependent on the other actor and are forced to continue exchanging goods and services with them, regardless of whether we are dissatisfied or not. If we also have an informational disadvantage, we need to put

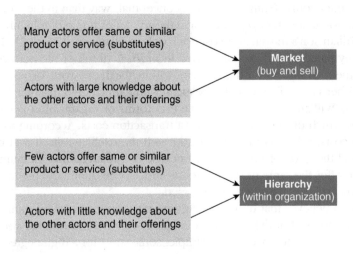

Figure 3.4   Conditions for when the market or hierarchy, respectively, is the most efficient form of organization

relatively large resources into information gathering for the transaction, to be able to switch to another seller. The total transaction cost will therefore be higher than when the market is characterized by many actors and dispersed information. It then becomes profitable to develop hierarchical control structures and to arrange production of the goods or services in them. By regulating and controlling exchanges in the form of formalized employment contracts, the scenario where parties deceive each other when exchanging their goods and services can be avoided.

Outsourcing – make or buy?

Williamson's model can be used to analyze what happens both within companies and organizations and in their external relationships. This makes the model suitable for use when deciding whether to do something within the organization or whether to buy this something from external actors, that is, when you want to answer the question 'make or buy?' (Walker & Weber 1984). Whether to run an operation to manufacture a product within one's own organization or to buy externally is a question that can be asked about virtually all less strategically important parts of a business – telephone exchange services, cleaning, and so on – but the trend over the last two decades is, increasingly, to outsource more strategically important parts of an organization's operations as well. Today, it is not uncommon for all IT support, all HR administration with several more complex services, to be purchased instead of being created within the organization. The production of components and development of new technology are also increasingly being outsourced. In addition, the hiring of management consultants as well as the utilization of so-called interim managers can be seen as a part of the development towards more and more organizational activities being purchased from external sources rather than being created internally.

Based on Williamson's model, everything that is characterized by relatively low uncertainty, that is offered by many external players and does not require extensive and costly information gathering, should be purchased. The trend towards increasing outsourcing can then be explained by the fact that information technology and virtual networks enable the identification of more sources that offer the same or similar goods and services, as well as the fact that the cost of gathering information about these sources is decreasing.

The industrial network approach

Williamson's model is very simple (and ingenious – in 2009 Williamson received the Swedish Central Bank's prize in economic sciences in memory of Alfred Nobel). However, it only covers two abstract types of relationships within which human exchanges can take place (markets and hierarchies). It also has a rather static view of transaction costs (see the previous section for an explanation of these concepts). One way to refine and make the analysis more realistic is to introduce a third type of relationship – networks – and a more dynamic view of transaction costs.

'Network' is a concept that, like 'structures' and 'processes', can refer to many different phenomena. Social networks refer to people's direct and indirect relationships with each other. IT networks can relate both to delimited, more internal networks and the more open and virtually global Internet. However, in the network model, or the industrial network approach, created primarily by Swedish distribution researchers (Hägg & Johanson 1982; Johanson & Mattsson 1987, 1988), it is industrial relationships between organizations, as well as relationships between units and resources within organizations, that are in focus. This network model complements and develops the more economic organizational theories and can be used to analyze and increase understanding of how virtual networks affect management, organization and leadership, not least with regard to the issue of outsourcing.

The network model differs from, for example, Williamson's model in that it is based on an assumption of heterogeneous resources rather than homogeneous ones. Resources can be everything from people, raw materials and products to services and organizations. The assumption means that, in principle, there are no substitute goods or services. One car manufacturer's car model can never be an exact substitute for another car manufacturer's comparable model. One supplier of engine parts can never supply exactly similar parts as another supplier. One person can never deliver exactly the same service as another. All resources are different from each other, albeit to varying degrees. People, products, services and organizations are different from each other, as are their goods and services. Sometimes these differences are considerable and important, and sometimes they play less of a role, but they are always there. This means that the conditions in Williamson's model, which imply that markets are more efficient than hierarchies, can never be fully met. There is always uncertainty, never very many similar market actors and always a need for more information. However, according to the network model, this does not mean that all exchange should take place within hierarchies. Instead, it takes place, and should take place, in the form of relatively permanent and dynamic exchange relationships between heterogeneous resources (people, knowledge, capital, machines, etc.). Whether it takes place within a formal organization or between organizations is not crucial. What matters is how the resources relate to each other within the network.

Since all resources (people, materials, products, services, organizations) are different from each other, it is not obvious how they fit together. Thus, there is a built-in coordination problem that creates what Williamson calls 'transaction costs'. But, according to the network model, resources cannot be coordinated solely by purely market exchanges or centralized control in hierarchies. Instead, coordination takes place by gradual adjustments between different resources. People and organizations invest time and money in other people and other organizations to learn about and adjust to each other. This learning and these adjustments create dependencies, or bonds (see Table 3.1),

Table 3.1   Different types of bonds between heterogeneous resources in networks

Type of bond	Possible adjustments
Technological	Adjustments to product and process technology can reduce production and transaction costs for the parties
Administrative	Adjustments to administrative systems can reduce costs for information exchange
Knowledge	Knowledge adjustments can increase the ability to communicate and facilitate process and product innovations
Social	Social adjustments can increase confidence and consensus, which in turn can enable further adjustments
Legal	Legal adjustments can increase transparency between the parties and reduce transaction costs even more

and the resources and their bonds together create the network. The network can be seen as a cross between or a combination of market and hierarchy, where heterogeneous resources have different kinds of real and potential bonds. In order for an organization to be able to acquire resources and sell goods and services, it must enter into relationships with others, just as resources within the organization must be coordinated with other resources, both internal and external.

An important practical implication with the network model is that the more resources are adjusted to each other, the lower the transaction costs will be. The more people and organizations interact, the more they learn about each other and the more they can adjust to make their resources and actions fit each other. Thus, over time, the transaction costs go down. The transaction costs are thus not given by the number of market actors or by whether the information is dispersed or not at a certain time (as in Williamson's model). It is thus not possible to calculate in advance whether an exchange should take place within the framework of a hierarchy or in a market. Instead, whether resources complement each other can be analyzed, for example a staffing agency's offering and a company's own operations, and a relationship initiated where one gradually tries to adjust to the other. If this proves successful, the initially high transaction costs will gradually fall and the efficiency of the network relationship will increase. As shown in Table 3.1, adjustments of the bonds in the network can also increase an organization's ability to learn from other organizations and enable areas for both product and process innovation to be detected.

The downside of the investments made in the form of adjusted bonds with external organizations is the lock-in effect that these entail. It is not easy to replace or break off a relationship once adjustments have started to take place. It is, in any case, associated with the fact that the profits from previous investments in the relationship cannot be realized. There can therefore be said to be at least three different ways of organizing in relation to heterogeneous/specialized resources:

- create market-like exchanges with external actors where investments in the relationship are kept to a minimum
- invest in long-term network relationships, both to reduce transaction and production costs and to create knowledge exchange that stimulates development and innovation
- create resources internally in the organization and thus have a greater opportunity to exercise control (which, however, does not necessarily provide the most efficient operations).

Which of these organizational principles is best can be analyzed using both Williamson's transaction cost approach and the more dynamic network model.

Vertical or horizontal relationships in the virtual networks?

As network-based information technology – virtual networks – makes it possible to spread information about and among various actors faster and at lower cost, it becomes even more advantageous for more activities to take place outside of one's own organization. Network-based information technology can reduce the costs that arise when organizations adjust to each other. Information about each other is more available, and media for information exchange and communication is already set in place, thanks to new network-based technologies. It should therefore be possible to accelerate adjustments and realize the efficiency gains more rapidly. Since the adjustments can take place at lower cost and go faster, the lock-in effects can also be less obvious. Even breaking off a long-term relationship with a subcontractor should therefore be possible at a lower cost. Organizing operations in the form of networks consisting of relatively small, cooperative organizations, rather than in the form of large hierarchical companies, should be more attractive than before, both according to an analysis based on the transaction cost approach and an analysis based on the network approach.

The choice between more market-like relationships, deeper cooperation in the form of network relationships and conducting activities within one's own organization, can be compared with the choice between vertical and horizontal coordination within one's own organization. According to Mintzberg's model (1983; see Chapter 2), adhocracy is preferable if the situation is characterized by high uncertainty, while machine bureaucracy is preferred where the situation is simpler and more predictable. However, according to Williamson's transaction cost approach, the market is better than the hierarchy at dealing with simple and predictable exchanges. According to the network model, more long-term cooperation is better than market exchanges precisely because all exchanges are seen as uncertain and thus require more mutual cooperation. Network relationships can thus be seen as an interorganizational counterpart to adhocracy, and markets can, paradoxically, be seen as an interorganizational counterpart to machine bureaucracy.

This also means that interorganizational relationships can be organized either with more vertical control, which (again paradoxically) corresponds to market exchanges, or with more horizontal control, which corresponds to mutual network relationships. By negotiating with and pressuring a subcontractor to deliver a standardized product at the lowest price, vertical control is exercised in relation to the subcontractor. By entering into long-term cooperative relationships, one can instead develop efficient processes, goods and services together. The network model can thus be said to recommend a horizontal and adhocratic relationship with the surrounding environment, while the transaction cost perspective recommends a vertical and hierarchical relationship with it. The different assumptions of the two models regarding homogeneity and heterogeneity respectively also imply that an adhocratic relationship with external actors is preferable when the organization's environment is characterized by great uncertainty, and that a hierarchical market relationship with external actors is preferable when there is relatively little uncertainty. The two models can thus be used both as independent analytical tools (and in combination with each other) and as an extension of the models described in Chapter 2. Even when the analysis of work division and coordination involves external actors and interorganizational networks (see Figure 3.5), benefit can be derived from reasoning about vertical and horizontal coordination, the one-dimensional structural model and Mintzberg's structural configurations.

However, one question remains: Does network-based information technology – virtual networks – constitute a kind of interorganizational support structure, that is, does it enable mainly increased horizontal coordination, or does it constitute a kind of

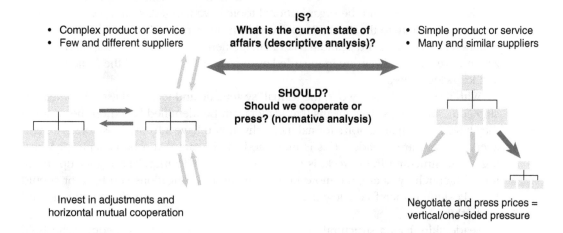

Figure 3.5   A simple structural model for the analysis of interorganizational relationships

Note: Compare with Figure 2.3. It is basically the same model, the previous focusing on organizing within organizations ('hierarchies' in Williamson's terminology), and this later model focusing on organization between organizations ('networks' in Johanson and Mattsson's terminology).

interorganizational technostructure, that is, a kind of vertical control mechanism? The answer is, as so often, not clear-cut. Some network-based information technology is horizontal, while some is vertical. In addition, the same technology can be used both for mutual horizontal cooperation and for exercising vertical influence and control. In addition, there is a more theoretically complex analysis of whether virtual networks lead to more vertical control or to more freedom and cooperation. However, such analyses are best suited to being performed from those perspectives based on basic assumptions rather than the structural perspective. We therefore return to this question in the description of more complex power theories in Chapter 7.

Structural leadership

The models presented so far have a clear foundation in organizational theory (except PESTEL, which is derived from the topic of marketing and strategy, and the two models described above, which have their roots in economics and distribution research, respectively). Leadership research and its applications have long been regarded as a separate topic to organization theory in the Anglo-Saxon world, with its own history and models. However, it has increasingly come closer to the organizational and management disciplines. Today, for example, the talk is of organizational leadership, of leadership not taking place without followers, of leadership being a social relationship and of leadership taking place in different ways in different situations. Previously, leadership research focused heavily on the characteristics and styles of individuals – now it is more about relationships, situations and organization (Northouse 2019). The leadership topic and the organizational topic have merged, so to speak. However, this applies mainly to the Anglo-Saxon world. In other parts of the world, not least in continental European and Scandinavian management research, leadership and organization have almost always been regarded as two aspects of one and the same research and knowledge area.

With a structural framework, the formal, systematic and technical aspects of leadership come into focus. This means that leaders can be identified based on the position they have in an organization's formal hierarchy. If you have a formal position as a manager, then you are a leader. This is motivated by the fact that a bureaucracy, according to the structural framework, is or should be a *meritocracy*. The higher up in the formal hierarchy you are, the more knowledge and qualifications you have or should have. Position is therefore a legitimate and sufficient basis for exercising authority and leadership.

Leadership from a structural perspective thus focuses on those people who hold formal managerial positions. Ideally, such managers/leaders should possess great knowledge of both their own organization and the surrounding environment. This is because it is the manager's task to analyze whether the organization has an optimal structure and degree of formalization. By systematically gathering facts about the

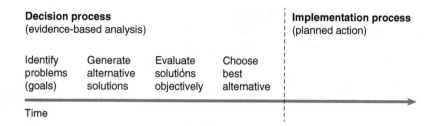

Figure 3.6 **The rational decision model**

environment (for example, using the PESTEL model) and about their own organization (information via the formal organizational structure), the structural leader can
analyze and optimize operations. The higher up in the organization you are, the more
time is devoted to major strategic issues: What does our market look like in the short,
medium and long terms? What does our financing situation look like? What are our
competitors doing? What about technology development? And so on. The closer to the
operational activities you are, the more micromanagement of daily operations comes
into focus.

Based on these analyses, the structural leader makes rational decisions about how
the organization should develop and act (see Figure 3.6). Both facts and conclusions
include and are based on objective, formal, material and physical facts. Measurability
and evidence are important to avoid subjective and emotional decisions. Recruitment
and promotion are based on objective assessments of qualifications and skills, as are
remuneration and pay. Establishment in new markets is determined by their actual
measurable economic potential. The choice of organizational form takes place on the
basis of thorough analyses based on established models (for example, Mintzberg's
(1983) structural configurations and situational dependencies). Implementation of new
organizational structures, new technologies or new processes takes place according to
carefully defined plans, based on evidence-based studies and analyses. The structural
leader is thus a kind of architect or 'social engineer', who measures, analyzes, makes
rational decisions and formulates careful action plans.

Traits of successful leaders

There are surprisingly few analytical models for leadership that are based on an
explicit structural framework. This is partly due to the fact that the structural perspective focuses precisely on structures and formalized processes, rather than on individual initiatives and social, informal processes. In a formalized and well-organized
system, the need for leadership can be less than in a less well-organized organization.
However, the motto 'the right person in the right place' can be said to indicate that

the most individual-oriented leadership research fits well into the framework of the structural perspective. This is also reinforced by the history of leadership research; once upon a time, the totally dominant purpose of leadership research was to satisfy the military's need for officers (which escalated sharply during the First World War) and other individuals 'of the right stuff'. During the early years of industrialism, both leaders and structural solutions and perspectives were imported from military organizations.

Trying to determine which individual traits characterized successful leaders heavily dominated leadership research until at least the 1950s. This research tradition was almost entirely condemned by later leadership research, but has been given fresh impetus and almost a complete reboot as a result of the much younger, specialized entrepreneurship research.

Trait-based research also fits into the structural framework, in that measurable facts are in focus. Psychological traits can be perceived as being difficult to measure, but that is still the aim. Table 3.2 shows two established leadership researchers' summaries of what characterizes successful leaders.

The problem with these types of lists is that they have little explanatory value, both when trying to understand what distinguishes leaders from non-leaders and when trying to explain what distinguishes good leadership from less good leadership. For example, in some situations social skills are crucial, while in others they are completely meaningless. In addition, similar traits have been identified in completely different people than leaders. Most of the listed traits also characterize talented mathematicians, athletes, craftsmen and nannies. They seem to explain top-performing people in general rather than successful leaders specifically. Fortunately, there are more useful leadership models in the other three theoretical frameworks presented in this book. In these, the structural framework is also strongly criticized, which is why we have reason to return later to the view of leaders and leadership processes from a structural framework perspective.

Table 3.2 Traits of successful leaders

Stogdill (1974)	Yukl (2002)
High energy level	High energy level
Great need for social status	Think the world can be controlled/changed
Intelligent	Emotionally competent
Verbal	Great self-confidence
Dominant	Great integrity
Self-controlled	Great need for power
Great self-confidence	Moderate need to belong
Persistent	
Socially competent	

Source: Stogdill (1974), Yukl (2002)

The fact that leadership based on a structural framework focuses on the traits of individual leaders may seem somewhat paradoxical – should the structural frame not focus on structures rather than individuals? But there is some logic to this. Since the general focus of the structural framework is on formal and material structures, it is a question of trying to find individuals that fit into the positions defined by the structures. The higher up in the hierarchy, the higher the demands on the individual in terms of traits, knowledge and rationality. However, the structural perspective can also be used to analyze operations and processes that are often described as less hierarchical and formally structured, such as work in teams and projects. The following section provides a brief review of how teams can be analyzed, based on a structural framework. It also describes the more extensive research that, on the basis of a structural perspective, explains and prescribes how to work in and control projects.

High-performance teams and efficient project management

Both research on high-performance groups (teams) and research on project management can be said to be about how to get a small group of people to work together in the best way to effectively achieve more or less specific goals or solve more or less defined tasks. Based on the established models described in both this and the previous chapter, such work should be organized in accordance with how much uncertainty surrounds the forthcoming work. If it is a routine assignment, with a well-defined goal that can be achieved with well-established and relatively simple processes, then the team should strive to structure and plan its work to the greatest possible extent. This means that the work of the group should be divided up according to the members' qualifications and skills, that the task should be broken down into parts and specialized sub-tasks and that a team or project manager with formal authority should be appointed. If there is a standardized process model developed in previous and similar projects, it should of course be followed – if not, one should be created. A simple structure with elements of machine bureaucracy may be suitable. If the task is instead shrouded in major uncertainty, if there is only a vague goal or vision that is difficult to break down into sub-goals and parts and if there is major uncertainty about how to approach these vaguely formulated goals, then the work should be organized more according to adhocratic principles.

The established structural models may be considered more than sufficient for organizing teams and project work effectively, but there is more analytical power to be derived from the more specialized research on structured teams and projects.

Structured teamwork

Just as with leadership, research on teams is conducted based all four basic frameworks. The team models of a more structural nature are either more or less replicas of the established structural models or simple checklists for what to consider when organizing and working in groups. In Chapters 4 and 5, on the HR framework, a number of team models will be presented. Here we focus on two of the most fundamental dimensions of organizing teams according to the structural framework: work division and coordination.

Division of work in teams

Many groups are quick to divide their work, and according to a structural analysis, this is good, provided that it is done to a sufficiently high degree and depending on how well defined the work is and what degree of uncertainty it is characterized by. But groups are often careless about the grounds on which the work is divided. According to the structural framework, the division must be based on knowledge and skills. Who is most suited to gathering information and facts? Who is best at performing an analysis based on a particular model or theory? Who is best at writing reports? And, perhaps most importantly, who is most suitable as a team leader? Work can also be divided to varying degrees. What should be done individually? What should be done in pairs? What is it appropriate to do together as a group? Here the complexity, the uncertainty and type of dependency should be taken into account in accordance with the established structural models.

Coordination of work in teams

Where many groups fail, however, is not in how they divide their work but how they coordinate it. Often, they don't bother appointing a leader, and no coordination mechanisms are formalized, neither horizontal nor vertical. Since many assignments performed in teams are time-limited – something must be achieved by a certain time – coordination over time is crucial to ensuring the quality of the team's work. That is, there are sequential dependencies between different stages of the work. This means that knowledge must often be transferred between those who perform tasks in the early stages and those who work on the later stages of the project. For example, if some team members collect data, others perform analyses and a third group writes a report, how can it be guaranteed that the report takes into account the most relevant data and covers the analyses that have the highest relevance? Some sort of timetable should therefore be designed to formalize and structure the subsequent work. The plan can also be seen as a collection of rules in the form of deadlines that everyone must keep to. Individual elements such as meetings should also be structured. What do we have to deal with first? How long should we discuss different solutions before we make a decision on how to proceed? The formal leader has the responsibility and authority to control both the overall structure of the work and the various sub-elements, for example ensuring that meetings take place in a structured and efficient manner.

Structured projects

Although structural models for how work in teams should be organized are relatively scarce, there is more research, theory and models on project work from a structural perspective. In a way, project management and organization and leadership in teams are about the same thing. However, team models are often based on basic theoretical assumptions that belong in the HR perspective; the research on teams is, to a large extent, the domain of the behavioral scientist. On the contrary, project management is an area traditionally populated by engineers. The area has its roots in engineering schools, the military and the engineering industry, where a structural perspective can be said to dominate. Here we discuss two models for structuring projects: the waterfall model and the stage model, before looking at two well-established tools within the project management arena, based on the basic assumptions of the structural framework: the Gantt chart and the PERT chart. These and similar project tools can be said to constitute the technostructure of a project.

The waterfall model

Projects from a structural perspective are defined as a goal-oriented rational activity characterized by limited resources and a limited time period. The definition of project is thus very similar to the definition of an organization, with the addition that it is a time-limited activity. The traditional and most comprehensive project model known as the 'waterfall model' can almost be equated with a structural perspective on projects. The main idea of this model is that everything included in the project must be analyzed, planned and decided first, before being implemented.

The waterfall model's description of projects is thus very much in line with the rational decision model, which, in its simplest form, is illustrated by Figure 3.6 in the section on structural leadership. One problem with both the waterfall model and the rational decision model is that they are more or less impossible to apply in practical project work. There are always uncertainties that cannot be 'planned away'. Regardless of the quantity of facts collected, and no matter how many advanced analyses and risk assessments are carried out, there will always be lessons to be learned, new conditions and changed goals during the course of the project. Thus, decisions are made that are never implemented, as are actions that are neither planned nor preceded by explicit decision-making processes (Blomberg 2003, 2013).

The stage model

A well-established and more specific variant of the more comprehensive waterfall model is the so-called *stage*, *phase* or *toll-gate* model. Compared to the waterfall model, the stage model is a more realistic and practical variant of the theoretically refined

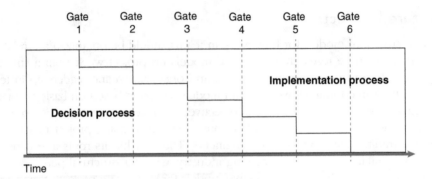

Figure 3.7   The stage model for project management

Note: This is a variant of the rational decision model (see Figure 3.6).

generic rational decision model. Instead of thinking, planning and deciding everything before moving on to making, implementing and executing, the project is divided into a number of clear formal stages or phases. At the end of each stage, which is also the beginning of the next, there is a *gate*, *toll-gate* or *stage-gate*. If the planned sub-goal has been successfully achieved, the gate will be passed, and work begins to try to reach the planned goal of the next stage. In this way, the transition from the planning and decision-making process to the execution and implementation process takes place gradually over time (see Figure 3.7).

As the goals for each project stage apply to *time* taken, *cost* budget and qualitative *content* alike, any deviations will in some way affect the project's goals in some of these dimensions. Although the goals for qualitative content are retained intact, all unplanned adjustments and additions will use up either time or cost – or both. In cases where the project's limited resources do not allow such unplanned work, costs will nevertheless arise in some way. For example, a project member can work on the project when they are formally paid to work on something else. Or the costs will be borne on a more personal level by the project members who work overtime, but without extra payment. A fundamental feature of the structural view of project management is that the entire project should be planned so carefully that the project work is done optimally and according to plan. If the plan is well supported by a proper factual basis and rational analysis, it will take care of all possible disruptions and changes.

Gantt chart

The Gantt chart is a graphical planning model that is used to divide up work and follow a project's progress. The Gantt chart is a horizontal bar chart where each bar symbolizes a specific activity (see Figure 3.8). When the bars are laid along the project

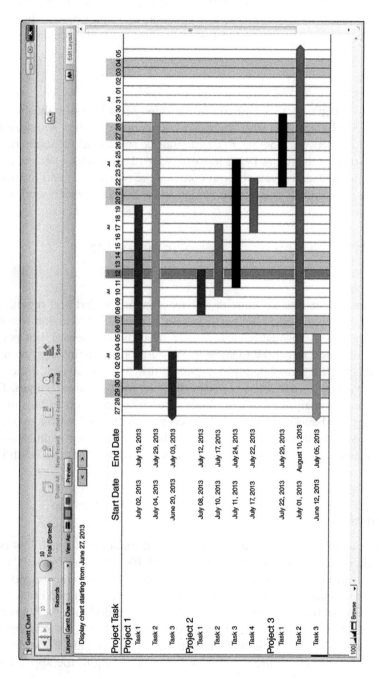

Figure 3.8   A typical Gantt chart

Note: This is as it looks in one of many computer programs developed for project management.

timeline, a clear picture of the project plan and the ongoing work is obtained. The length of the bars shows the activity's planned duration. In some variants, the surface area of the bar depends on the amount of resources assigned to the activity.

PERT chart

The PERT chart (see Figure 3.9) is a variant of the Gantt chart.[4] It not only shows the different work-divided stages but also the logical sequence that they should follow. The result is a kind of network diagram. PERT can thus be said to include more information, but it can also be perceived as being less easy to read. By drawing vertical arrows between the bars in the Gantt chart, you can combine the two models and include the time management, cost budget and interdependencies of the task-divided work stages.

The structural framework's generic questions, strengths and weaknesses

The reason behind an analysis of how an activity is managed, led and organized is usually to solve a problem. Something isn't working as it should and action is needed to fix it. Often, there is a reasonably clear idea of what the problem is, but perhaps not what is causing it and thus how to solve it. But all problem definitions, no matter how vague or precise, are formulated from a perspective. This means that if the activity in question is viewed from a different perspective, the problem also changes. There may also be reason to analyze an activity even when it is perceived to be functioning smoothly. Perceived success often makes even the smartest of managers, change agents and professionals blind to signs of trouble. Therefore, it is important to analyze activities and organizations even when they are perceived as being successful and problem-free.

Generic questions

One way to initiate an analysis based on the structural framework, regardless of the problem, is to ask a number of generic questions (see Table 3.3). Their 'generic' nature means that they can be adapted and asked in all situations and with regard to all activities and phenomena. The 'IS' question in Table 3.3 is about to find out how the analyzed organizational unit *IS* organized. The 'SHOULD' question in Table 3.3 is about how the unit should be organized. It is always best to keep these questions and their following analyses apart, since this will make it easier to conclude if the analyzed organizational unit *is* organized the way it *should* be, according to the applied structural theories.

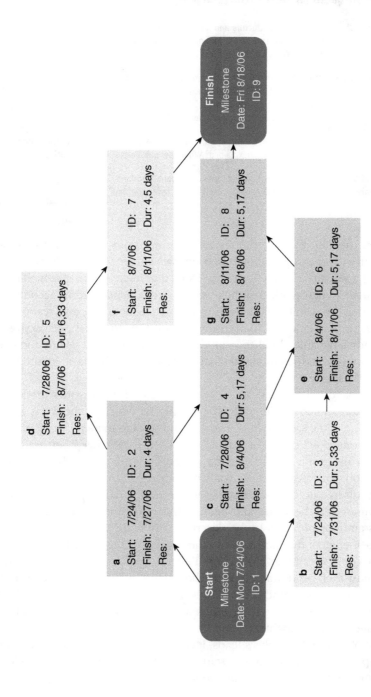

Figure 3.9   A simple PERT chart

Table 3.3   Generic questions from a structural perspective

IS? (descriptive analysis)	What structure and formal processes does the organization have? Which structural configuration/s is it similar to? What are the pros and cons?
SHOULD? (prescriptive/normative analysis)	What structure and formal processes should the organization have? What are the ideal structural configurations – which configuration should it be similar to – and why? Start analyzing from the situational dependencies
→ (conclusions)	To what extent does the structural analysis explain the phenomenon? What is unexplained? What new questions will be relevant?
Greiner? (example of a complementary analysis)	Which growth phase is the organization in? So how should it therefore be led/organized?

In addition to using these questions as a starting point, the analysis can also be complemented with more questions based on the different models. In what way and to what extent are lean principles applied? Does that make sense? Are well-structured processes in place when working in teams? Are projects planned in accordance with the phase model? Are Gantt charts used to facilitate scheduling and resource allocation? Is leadership implemented in accordance with the structural perspective, that is, are leaders knowledgeable about the nature of the business and its environment, and are things structured and restructured in accordance with the basic assumptions and models of the perspective?

Which of these questions and which of the structural framework's models receive the most attention should be determined primarily by which of them has the highest explanatory value in the specific case. They should be able to identify any fundamental problems, tensions, conflicts, inconsistencies or even paradoxes. They are extra valuable if they can also result in such specific and concrete responses that they constitute a basis for action. Analyses do not always provide a full explanation for why a phenomenon has arisen, but, even in these cases, the analysis usually points in a direction that allows progress to be made and enables the organization to be analyzed using other models and perspectives. In the description of lean, it was found, for example, that it is not self-evident that personnel in the operational core wish to take the initiative to continuously streamline production. Perhaps a structural analysis based on the lean model must then be re-framed using the models of motivation found in the HR framework (see Chapters 4 and 5)? Or are lean's successes built on a certain type of corporate culture? We may have to re-frame and instead analyze using models in the symbolic framework (see Chapters 8 and 9).

Regardless of where the analysis leads, it is important to test the different analytical models. An appropriate approach is to start the analysis by applying the models in the structural framework, and by asking the generic questions.

Strengths of the structural framework

One of the major strengths of the structural framework is its potential to create a clear description of a business or an organization in terms of structures and formal processes. Based on such a foundation, the same phenomenon, problem, activity or organization can then be problematized, discussed and analyzed with models from the other frameworks, but armed with greater insight than before the initial structural analyses were carried out.

Another strength of the structural framework is its normative power. If a proper structural analysis is carried out, it will be possible to draw conclusions regarding how, from a structural perspective, a business *should* be structured. This is partly due to the structural models' clear causal relationship and partly due to the fact that they focus on formal and material aspects. The clear cause–effect relationships mean that if we can 'only' determine whether something is present, for example if the environment is uncertain or not, then the model prescribes how we should structure it. According to most models in the structural framework, there is a best way to organize, given a number of situation-specific conditions.

Weaknesses of the structural framework

The strengths of the structural framework also constitute its weaknesses. By focusing on the formal, the material, the rational and the planned, the framework fails to deal with the informal, the idealistic, the emotional employees being reduced to a formal position and their work reduced to planned formal work descriptions. People are reduced to a material utility maximizer, and their social relations are reduced to employment contracts or market transactions. Leaders are reduced to rational, calculating analytical tools.

The normative power of the framework also makes it possible to 'hide' behind a structural analysis. The responsibility for one's actions can, so to speak, be passed on to the analysis and the analytical tool. Since the analysis has been done thoroughly and correctly, and action has been taken in accordance with its conclusion, it can be argued that no personal responsibility is taken for the consequences of the actions implemented. Once again, it can be said that the perspective reduces the human factor to a rational, formal and technical process.

Max Weber, who laid much of the foundation for the structural framework, described how the rationalization of human social life makes it possible to produce goods and services more efficiently than ever before. But Weber also argued that the very same development can result in us becoming caught in an 'iron cage of rationality ... which transforms us into specialists without spirit, sensualists without heart; this nullity imagines that it has attained a level of civilization never before achieved' (Weber 1905/2003: 124).

The fact that the weakness of machine bureaucracy is a lack of flexibility and adaptability to changing conditions, and that employees have difficulty in finding motivation within it, can thus be seen as something far greater than just a problem with one of Mintzberg's five structural configurations. The structural framework as a whole can be criticized on the same grounds. The more we analyze, structure and formalize, and the more we strive for career and material wealth, the poorer life becomes.

Videos

Don't forget to watch the videos to discover more about the key concepts in this chapter: **https://study.sagepub.com/blomberg**

Notes

1 In a supplement written over 25 years after the original article came out, Greiner (1998) states that a sixth phase is visible in the form of new leadership that focuses on cooperation with other companies and organizations in the form of strategic alliances and industrial network structures. Organizing business efficiently then becomes something that lies between 'market' and 'hierarchy'. According to Swedish research on industrial markets and distribution networks, the success of large Swedish export companies can be explained by just such a focus (Johanson & Mattsson 1988). See also the section on Williamson's transaction cost approach a little later in this chapter.

2 The origin of the PESTEL model is not fully understood, but can be traced back to the marketing and strategy topics of the 1960s. Since they originate at least as much from a consulting and education context as from academic research, the lack of sources is evident. During the 1960s and 1970s, different variants and abbreviations existed, of which PEST and STEP were the most frequent. The last two letters, E and L, are more recent additions that can be traced back to the late 1980s.

3 Williamson uses concepts that are common in economics theory. Thus, he writes 'information' when talking about what is commonly referred to as 'knowledge' in business and management theory and practice. 'Dispersed' information means that the level of knowledge of, for example, goods and services is substantial among both sellers and buyers.

4 PERT stands for Program Evaluation Review Technique and was originally developed in the 1950s by the US Navy (see Sapolsky 1972).

4

Human Resources, Relations and Competence – The Basics of the HR Framework

Charlie Chaplin's masterpiece movie, *Modern Times,* premiered in 1936, and can be viewed as an important part of the early development of the HR framework. One of the most famous scenes in the movie is when Charlie works in a large factory at an assembly line. The factory is organized and managed as a machine bureaucracy with an extreme level of division of labor, extensive technostructure and top-down control (see Mintzberg's model in the structural framework in Chapter 2). The scene starts with Chaplin and another employee working hard at the conveyor belt. Chaplin and his coworkers are controlled by the speed of the belt, the local boss, and the top manager who supervises everything via TV monitors. Chaplin has no time to take a break and becomes quite manic in trying to keep up with the gradually increasing speed of the conveyor belt. He is finally swallowed up by the factory's large machines, where he literally becomes a 'cog in the machine'.

Chaplin's film is more important than you might initially think for the development of management and organizational analysis and for the strong criticism of bureaucratic and top-down controlled organizations. The film was premiered (in 1936) at about the same time as the publication of the first influential scientific articles within what came to be a new research area of organizational research: *human relations* (HR). The concept of HR and the later developed concepts of *human resources, human resource management* (HRM), *organizational behavior* (OB), *organizational development* (OD) *and agile HR*, all relate to the HR framework, the first framework to seriously challenge the then dominant structural framework.

In this chapter, we begin with the historical roots of the HR framework, before moving on to its basic assumptions. We then focus on three important areas of this framework – *human needs, human relations and communication* and *organization of work.*

The historical roots of the HR framework

A common view of scientific knowledge acquisition is that it develops in a linear or accumulative fashion. New knowledge is added to and on top of old knowledge. This view corresponds to how the HR framework was developed on the basis of the structural framework, but only to some extent. There are other important circumstances to take into account in order to understand the advent of the HR framework.

Technological development

Just like the structural framework, the emergence of the HR framework can be explained by developments in the industrialized world. Technological development during the interwar period meant that manufacturing machinery became increasingly sophisticated, more expensive and more difficult to operate. This meant that those who operated these machines needed ever-greater competence, which in turn made them more difficult to replace. Business owners and managers were quite simply forced to take better care of their staff, regardless of any new scientific achievements within management research.

Industrial structures and political circumstances

Although there was a large surplus of labor after agriculture was first rationalized and people flocked to young, growing industrial cities, the entry of women into the labor market during the First World War, and the return of soldiers after the end of the war, further diluted the excess supply of labor. At the same time, the unions were growing bigger and better organized, not least in the United States (until the Second World War), and, despite the excess supply of labor, it became increasingly difficult for companies to exploit human resources without facing fierce opposition.

Economic and social unease

The Wall Street crash in 1929 and the subsequent economic and social depression were also powerful catalysts for the development of the HR framework. During the 1920s, the growing middle class was able to buy shares and become increasingly wealthy. The American economic miracle, with stock markets and corporate business as its engine, was admired all around the world. 'The great crash' of 1929 changed all this and led to a public distrust of business, capitalism and the financial market. Widespread social unease, along with new ideas among intellectuals (expressed, for example, in Chaplin's *Modern Times*), provided an ideal breeding ground for the emergence of new perspectives.

Scientific (and practical) legitimacy

Just as the structural framework developed and gained its legitimacy from new research by people like Taylor, Fayol and Weber, the HR framework gained its legitimacy from new research findings. One of the most influential pioneers in the field, the American researcher Mary Parker Follett (1868–1933), is sometimes referred to as the mother of organizational theory. Her extensive research on horizontal and mutual interactions in organizations challenged the then established bureaucratic theory's focus on specialization and vertical interactions (Follett 1924, 1927). Follett argued that neither society nor business corporations benefited from increased specialization, standardization and vertical control. Instead, she urged that working life be based on a positive group dynamic that could fulfill human needs (Follett 1924). She also stated that the leader–follower relationship should be characterized by mutuality, questioning the prevailing ideal of vertical control. Publishing these arguments in the 1920s, she preceded the birth of the human relations school of thought by at least a decade. She was a pioneer in organization theory and in being an influential management authority.

Another American researcher, Elton Mayo (1880–1949), was one of many involved in the extensive research carried out in the 1920s and early 1930s at AT&T's and Western Electric's huge factory, The Hawthorne Works outside Chicago. The researchers experimented with working conditions in all sorts of ways, ranging from the cleaning of desks and adjusting of lighting, to the length of work shifts and breaks. The studies were conducted in experimental form where employees were divided into two groups: a test group, where changes were made, and a control group, where they were not. To the surprise of the research group, the test group's work performance increased regardless of what changes were made. For example, when the lighting was gradually dimmed (to lower costs by saving electricity), performance increased until it was so dark that it was almost impossible to see anything. Initially, the researchers were at a loss to understand this. The experiments were therefore supplemented with extensive interviews with the employees, and after excluding all other, more structural and material explanations, only one remained: it was the attention from the researchers that had increased employee efficiency! The employees had a psychological and social need for positive attention. Giving such attention was more important than any structural design. This revolutionary discovery was called *the Hawthorne effect* after the name of the factory. Now there was suddenly scientific evidence that large, formal, hierarchical systems might not be the superior organizational principle. Rather, the most important thing was that the needs of the employees in the core business were satisfied, due in part to social attention.

While Mayo (1924, 1933, 1945) and his colleagues, Roethlisberger and Dickson (1939), were publishing the results of their studies at the Hawthorne factory, Chester Barnard was publishing his book, *The functions of the executive* (1938), in which he summarized the experience he had gained over a long managerial career. According to Barnard, the success of organizations was a consequence of how well people cooperated within them. In Barnard's opinion, the primary task of the leader was to stimulate and maintain good communication within the organization so that common goals could be translated into working tasks and actions. If Follett and Mayo et al. gave the HR framework scientific legitimacy, Barnard can be said to have given it practical legitimacy. Now, in the late 1930s, there was the basis for studying, developing and practically applying models that focused on people's psychological and social needs, and, as a result, this model came to be in fierce opposition to the then established structural and bureaucratic models.

Today, the HR framework constitutes a multifaceted field with many sub-areas and specializations. One of these areas consists of models that have emerged from the extensive research on leadership based on an HR framework. However, we will save the area of leadership for the next chapter. This chapter describes three other, just as important, areas – *human needs*, *human relations and communication*, and *organization of work* – and central models that can be used to analyze them. In the next chapter, we will look at these areas in more depth and supplement them with models for how to analyze and possibly create successful leadership, effective development projects and high-performance teams.

First, however, the basic assumptions of the HR framework are presented.

The basic assumptions of the HR framework

The HR framework can be said to be based on a number of basic assumptions about how people and organizations work. Although the framework has gone through many phases in the form of new knowledge and the development of new models and concepts, the basic assumptions have held true for the 80-plus years that the framework can be said to have existed.

Organizations should satisfy human needs

The fact that organizations should satisfy human needs sounds like the rather trite phrase 'the human is the organization's most important resource'. At the most basic level, according to the HR framework, it is more about 'the organization being the human's most important resource'. The human needs that are to be satisfied are not only the needs of the customers, but also, and primarily, the needs of those who work in the organization. And, even if the organization's primary function is seen as producing products and services as efficiently as possible, the organization should still be adapted to meet the needs of its employees. This is due to the next assumption.

The needs of organizations and people must coincide

According to the HR framework, the structural framework's models for efficient organization are incorrect. Extensive work division, hierarchical coordination and control structures create inhumane work environments that cause employees to underperform. If workplaces and working tasks are instead designed according to human needs, employees will take responsibility, develop high work motivation and maximize their performance. If you want your employees to do a good job, you have to give them a good job to do. If you design workplaces and work tasks that satisfy the needs of employees, both employees and the organization will be rewarded – if you do not, both will suffer.

The human is a complex biological (and social) psychological being

If the path to successful, efficient organizations goes via the satisfaction of human needs, the question arises as to what these needs are. In the HR framework, that question is answered by results based mainly on individual and social psychological motivational research. In particular, early HR research was based on individual psychological models for human needs satisfaction. However, this does not mean that the human was or is seen as an atomistic individual. Individual psychology also acknowledges that the human has a need for fellow human beings. This assumption means that a much more complex picture of the individual and their needs emerges compared to that of the structural framework, where the human is reduced to a rational, selfish utility maximizer. It follows from this that hierarchical control and salary are not sufficient means to get employees to perform well. The human need for other people's friendship and appreciation, together with the desire to learn new things and develop, means that there are many more ways to motivate both managers and employees.

Human needs

The research on human needs is extensive and long. The most well-known and disseminated model, Maslow's hierarchy of needs, is known to many far beyond organizational research and business management circles. It also forms the basis for many other and more specific HR models.

Maslow's hierarchy of needs

According to American psychologist Abraham Maslow (1908–70), how people prioritize between different needs can be described by dividing them into five hierarchical levels (see Figure 4.1). According to Maslow, people must satisfy their lower needs before attempting to satisfy their higher needs. In the obvious cases where it can be observed that an individual ignores his lower needs, Maslow believed that this is only possible if this individual, at an earlier stage of his life, had been able to largely satisfy the lower needs that are now being ignored. For example, the fact that an individual resigns from a safe workplace and moves to a highly uncertain war zone is only possible if the individual has experienced a high degree of security in their early life.

Applied to management and organization, Maslow's model means that attempts to increase employees' work motivation by satisfying their higher needs are fruitless if their lower needs are not satisfied first. It does not matter how much appreciation

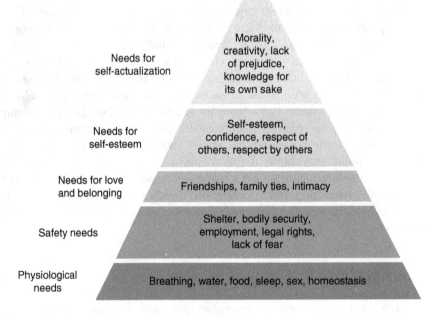

Needs for self-actualization — Morality, creativity, lack of prejudice, knowledge for its own sake

Needs for self-esteem — Self-esteem, confidence, respect of others, respect by others

Needs for love and belonging — Friendships, family ties, intimacy

Safety needs — Shelter, bodily security, employment, legal rights, lack of fear

Physiological needs — Breathing, water, food, sleep, sex, homeostasis

Figure 4.1   Maslow's (1943) hierarchy of needs

a manager shows an employee if the salary is so low that the employee cannot live on it, or if the working hours are so long that the employee does not have time to sleep and eat. In Maslow's opinion, the model is universal, that is, it applies to all people in all societies and environments. But, since people can be at different levels in the model, it can still explain why they strive in different directions and are motivated by different things. A very well-paid partner in a management consultancy may therefore be less motivated by a pay rise than temporary and low-paid staff at a fast-food chain.

Herzberg's two-factor theory of motivation

Herzberg's two-factor theory has great similarities with Maslow's hierarchy of needs, but is specifically developed to analyze how best to motivate employees in the workplace. Herzberg (1964) divides people's needs into two main groups: *hygiene factors* are needs that largely overlap the two lowest levels in Maslow's needs hierarchy; while *motivators* correspond to the needs of Maslow's three higher levels.

The two-factor theory (see Figure 4.2) is based on the same idea as the hierarchy of needs: that people first strive to satisfy the lower needs (the hygiene factors), and then strive for satisfaction of the higher needs (the motivators). Herzberg's model, however, adds that the hygiene factors are primarily about eliminating dissatisfaction. If the hygiene factors are not met, employees will be dissatisfied and also show it in different ways. If the hygiene factors are met, employees may be satisfied, but they will still not be particularly motivated to put that little extra into their work. In order to really get employees to commit to their work, the motivators must also be satisfied.

Herzberg also shows that the hygiene factors all constitute 'external' aspects of work, that is, they are about things outside the employee's person. Thus, it is an authoritarian style of leadership, low wages, limiting or cumbersome rules and the

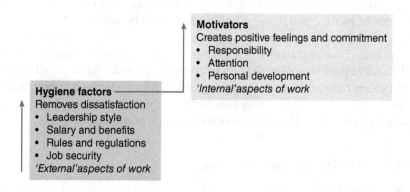

Figure 4.2   Herzberg's (1964) two-factor theory

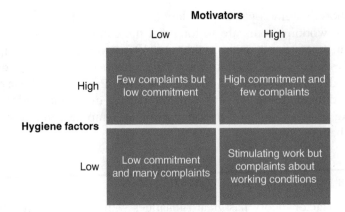

Figure 4.3   Herzberg's model (1964) as a four-field matrix

lack of job security that lead to dissatisfaction, while a leadership style that involves delegating, an acceptable or high salary, sensible rules and job security eliminate dissatisfaction. None of these factors is about the employee's 'inner' state.

The opposite applies to the motivators. They are about the employee's feelings and psychological state. If employees feel responsible, view themselves as noticed and appreciated and have opportunities for self-realization at their workplace, they will perform at a high level, according to Herzberg. Dissatisfaction (hygiene factors) and commitment (motivators) thus become two different dimensions which act and can be analyzed independently of each other. According to this model, different combinations of how well an organization satisfies its employees have different consequences (see Figure 4.3).

The four-field matrix can be used as an analytical tool to increase the understanding of why employees are more or less satisfied and motivated, but also as a normative tool that can be used to improve the ability of organizations to get their employees to commit. If employees complain a lot, it can be an expression of a dissatisfaction with mainly hygiene factors, and this is when these should be addressed. Can the external working environment be improved? Are wages too low? Can unnecessary, formal processes and rules be eliminated? If complaints are conspicuous in their absence, but it is still difficult to get employees to want to commit and really make an effort, then it is not worth either raising wages or improving benefits and other conditions. Instead, the scope for restructuring the business should be examined so that tasks become more interesting in themselves. Has work division perhaps gone too far?

Internal and external commitment

According to the HR framework, it is more important to satisfy human needs than to divide work and coordinate activities vertically in order for a business to be

Table 4.1   **Internal and external commitment**

Internal commitment	External commitment
Individuals define their tasks	Tasks are defined by others
Behaviors necessary to execute the task are defined by individuals	Behaviors necessary to execute the task are defined by others
Leadership and individuals together define challenging goals for the individual	Goals are defined by the management
The weight and importance of goals are defined by individuals	The weight and importance of goals are defined by others

Source: Argyris (1998)

high-performing. Translated into theories on motivation, this means that 'internal' and 'psychological' commitment is more important than 'external' and 'economic' commitment (see Table 4.1).

Despite the HR framework's criticism of the structural framework, and its explanation of efficient organization, hierarchically structured organizations and extensively work-divided processes seem to survive, as do performance-based salaries, bonuses and benefits. Argyris (1998) argues that this does not prove that the structural framework is right and the HR framework is wrong. Instead, he gives a more complex explanation for the lack of application of 'empowerment' and the lack of attempts to create internal commitment. Argyris believes that the following factors explain why organizations still do not focus more on internal commitment:

- Leaders and managers like decentralization in theory, but exercise authoritarian and vertical control in practice (see also the section below about single- and double-loop learning, as well as on espoused theories and theories in use, respectively).
- Employees want to participate in decision-making to varying degrees, for example regarding the design of their working tasks. It is not realistic to believe that everyone would like to be involved in everything.
- All centrally initiated decentralization projects increase the organization's internal conflicts. In practice, all organizations have both vertical control and decentralized decision-making. Managers tend to both consciously and unconsciously hide the vertical control when they describe and talk about change projects and the importance of employee commitment. This inhibits open and honest communication.
- Internal commitment is not necessary for employees to be able to perform simpler and more repetitive working tasks.

Human relations and communication

According to the HR framework, humans have a need for social appreciation and honest, loving social relationships. Applied to organizations, this means that employees and leaders should make both major and minor decisions together. Well-functioning, decentralized, horizontal coordination requires that all parties involved can cooperate and talk. Therefore, the HR framework encompasses theory and models for how honest and open – or, if you like, effective – communication takes place. These communication models are also an important component of the HR framework's many normative models for how groups should work.

Espoused theories versus theories-in-use, single- and double-loop learning

According to Argyris and Schön (1978, 1996), people's actions are a consequence of their personal theories of action. People are not fully aware of their own theories of action, nor of the extent to which they affect their behavior. As a result, an individual's *espoused theory* (theory that we say we believe in and say that we act upon) does not completely coincide with their *theory-in-use (theory we actually act upon but not necessarily say we act upon)*. For example, what a leader says is rarely the same as what a leader does. Leaders can see themselves as rational, caring and open to new knowledge and employees' different perspectives, but, at the same time, exert more authoritarian leadership and seek supportive information. This need not be an expression of such leaders consciously trying to hide or embellish their actions, but rather is a consequence of them not being fully aware of their theories-in-use and actions.

Such blindness to their own theories-in-use and actions also impedes leaders' ability in more extensive re-framing, critical thinking and learning (see Chapter 1). In a social context, this leads to a group's or organization's communication and learning being characterized more by argumentation and competition between individual positions than by a joint examination of perspectives and new knowledge. Argyris and Schön (1978, 1996) call more self-protective and self-reinforcing learning *single-loop learning* and more challenging and perspective-breaking learning *double-loop learning*.

The idea of espoused theories and theories-in-use and the two types of learning can also be formulated as two basic types of communication, Model 1 and Model 2. If communication can be achieved according to Model 2 below, the conditions are good for double-loop learning.

Model 1 and 2 communication

The basic idea of all communication models in the HR framework is that communication is about understanding each other openly and honestly, utilizing each other's

Table 4.2   Communication according to Models 1 and 2

Model 1	Model 2
If the other person does not understand the problem then they are the problem	Emphasize common goals and mutual understanding
Do your own analysis	Open communication: question your own (and the other person's) assumptions and interpretations, together
Use facts, logic, criticism or anything else to get the other person to understand the problem/change their view	Combine claims with questions
If the other does not agree, take it as proof that they do not understand the problem (and thus are the problem)	If the other does not agree, continue to investigate the problem using open communication
Advocate	Inquire

knowledge and together achieving common goals, decisions and practical solutions. To highlight the differences between poor and good communication, Argyris and colleagues have developed a model describing two typical ways (Models 1 and 2) of communicating (Argyris et al. 1985, Argyris & Schön 1996). Model 1 describes ineffective communication, which Argyris says characterizes how many people, not least leaders, communicate. Model 1 communication overlaps with vertical control because, in many ways, it is about persuasion or giving orders, rather than a more equal exploratory conversation and collaboration. The latter, however, is the basis of horizontal coordination, and this type of communication – the ideal – is what Argyris calls Model 2 communication (see Table 4.2).

Since many leaders and managers communicate more according to Model 1 than Model 2, Argyris thinks that organizing in accordance with the HR framework is difficult to introduce, although, according to him, it is the best way to organize. According to Argyris (1998), there are more reasons why organizations continue to be characterized by far-reaching work division, vertical control and the lack of motivators, despite the fact that decentralization, horizontal control and motivators are absolutely necessary for long-term successful enterprise. According to Argyris, managers are afraid that the costs will sky-rocket. In the short term, order-giving and structural thinking can work, while decentralization and investment in employees do not obviously pay off in the short term. Leaders may also be afraid of losing their authority. If employees start to have more autonomy and make decisions on their own, it can be difficult to see where such a development ends.

In addition, Argyris adds, it is not certain that all employees always want to participate and decide. This conflicts with the basic human needs models of the HR framework. According to these, all people strive to satisfy increasingly higher needs (see, for example, Maslow's hierarchy of needs or Herzberg's two-factor theory above). Argyris suggests that this only applies occasionally. This opens up the possibility for a more complex HR model. Just as the structural framework has evolved from seeing maximum work division and vertical control as the form of organization to always strive for, it is now seen as only the best solution given a number of circumstances (see Mintzberg's model in Chapter 2). In the same way, the HR framework has also been developed, and, in the next chapter, a couple of more complex models will therefore be presented. However, here we focus on the original HR framework and its view that horizontal cooperation is always preferable to vertical control, despite many organizations continuing to be characterized by extensive vertical control. This view depends on what assumptions leaders and managers make about the needs of their employees, assumptions that tend to be self-fulfilling. This phenomenon can be analyzed using McGregor's model (below), which describes two sets of assumptions that leaders make about what motivates their subordinates.

Leadership theory X and Y

All people make different assumptions about each other, but McGregor's model (1960) (Figure 4.4) focuses on leaders and managers, and their relationship with subordinates. Managers' assumptions about subordinates govern how leaders act in and interpret their surroundings. Leaders' actions are, in turn, interpreted by their subordinates, who act on the basis of their interpretations, and leaders interpret this and act, and so on. Leaders' different assumptions therefore create different patterns of behavior in both the leaders themselves and their employees.

Theory X assumes that employees are basically lazy and must be controlled and rewarded for doing their job, i.e. assumptions about people in accordance with the structural framework. When employees are exposed to control, they tend to resist, which leads the leader to think that even more control is needed. The leader's assumption becomes self-fulfilling. McGregor also divides Theory X into 'hard' and 'soft' versions. The hard version focuses on strict control and punishment, while the soft

Theory X

People are lazy, but with carrot (money) and whip (control) one can make them work.

Theory Y

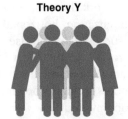

Work is as natural as play is for children. If one supports them to self-actualize at work, they will perform.

Figure 4.4   Theories X and Y

Source: McGregor (1960)

version focuses on rewards. However, soft Theory X is also problematic, according to McGregor, as it leads to constantly increasing demand for rewards and constantly decreasing commitment. This development, in turn, often results in leaders concluding that rewards are not enough, and must be supplemented with stricter control, i.e. hard Theory X. Even the soft version is thus self-fulfilling.

Theory Y aligns with the HR framework, that is, if employees are given influence and responsibility, they will grow and gradually be able to shoulder this responsibility. If employees are given space and the opportunity to satisfy their higher needs in the workplace, their own goals and those of the organization will merge. Even Theory Y can thus become a self-fulfilling prophecy.

McGregor's model suggests that far-reaching work division and extensive vertical control characterize certain organizations not because it is the most effective form of organization, but because of leaders' self-fulfilling enactment of Theory X. In addition, we can explain the survival of bureaucratic organizations by stating that their leaders communicate in accordance with Argyris' Model 1, and fear both sky-rocketing costs and the loss of their authority. According to the HR framework, on the other hand, if leaders change their assumptions to those in Theory Y, change their communication to Model 2 and overcome their fear of short-term costs and loss of authority, then horizontal coordination and satisfaction of both low and high human needs will lead to successful organization.

An analysis of a particular business or organization from an HR framework perspective should thus include both analysis of whether the organization satisfies the needs of its employees, and analysis of how its leaders and employees communicate, as well as of what view of employees leaders express in their statements and actions. A great deal can be achieved in the latter analyses by comparing the leadership actually exercised with the quite simple Model 1 and 2 communication and Theory X and Y assumptions.

Intelligence – IQ versus EQ

All the above models include a one-dimensional or dualistic structure. Just as the HR framework can be contrasted with the structural, intrinsic motivation is contrasted with extrinsic, Model 1 is contrasted with Model 2, and Theory Y with Theory X. An additional variant of these simple dualistic or one-dimensional models for needs, communication and leaders' assumptions is to set intelligence (IQ) against emotional intelligence (EQ or EI).

It was the German psychologist William Stern who launched both the concept of IQ (*Intelligenz-Quotient*) and the IQ measurement method in the 1910s, that is, the same period as Taylor, Fayol and Weber published the texts that form the basis of the structural framework. The IQ test was far from the only intelligence test that was developed during this period. Although different tests were based on different perceptions of psychological skills, they all attempted to measure the qualities and skills of individuals in an as objective and scientific manner as possible. It was considered possible to categorize people as static objects and then place them in the right place in the emerging bureaucracies that increasingly dominated both society and companies. The history of the IQ test is thus intimately intertwined both with the advent of the structural framework and with so-called leadership traits research that focuses on the qualities of individual leaders (see 'Traits of successful leaders' in Chapter 3 and Table 3.2). It is therefore no coincidence that IQ tests usually focus on people's cognitive, analytical and more rational/logical side. IQ can be said to be an expression of the structural framework's rational *homo economicus* and of the well-structured organization with the right person in the right place.

Emotional intelligence (EQ or EI) can be said to both complement and criticize the focus of the IQ test on analytical ability (Salovey & Mayer 1990). Since the mid-1990s, high EQ has been viewed (and popularized) as the most important psychological skill of successful leaders (Goleman 1995). Emotional intelligence can be said to fit well with the HR framework's more complex and playful *homo ludens* and, above all, its perception of what constitutes successful leadership. Emotional intelligence is, according to Goleman (1995, 1998), an innate, basic emotional talent, but there are also five types of emotional skills that one can develop with the help of training and experience:

- *Self-awareness* – understanding your own feelings, strengths, weaknesses, driving forces, values and goals, and understanding how these affect others when making decisions based on your common sense.
- *Self-regulation* – being able to control and change your feelings and impulses and adapt to changing circumstances.
- *Social skills* – being able to control your relationships to influence people in the desired direction.
- *Empathy* – being able to recognize and consider other people's feelings in decision-making.
- *Motivation* – wanting to perform for performance's sake.

The difference between IQ and EQ is obvious. The former includes technical, analytical and rational thinking, based on a comprehensive objective and a measurable factual basis. EQ is more about a 'feeling for feelings'. It can be said that EQ is also a rational and logical idea of what should characterize working interpersonal relations and successful leadership, but this rationality is based on the HR framework's assumption that human beings need more than just to maximize material and economic benefit. By comparing real leaders' and employees' interpersonal relations with the five skills of emotional intelligence, the reasons why these relationships work well or not can be explained.

We will return to this kind of analysis in the next chapter, focusing on leadership. First, however, we will present a very central and useful model in the third major area of the basic HR framework: workplace design or organization of work.

Organization of work

Given that people have more complex needs than the structural framework assumes, and given that Maslow's, Herzberg's and other theories about needs are fairly reasonable, how then should work in companies and organizations be structured? Based on an HR framework, the answer to this does not lie with the method prescribed by the models of the structural framework. Theory X leadership, far-reaching work division and extensive vertical control reduce employees' ability to satisfy their higher needs and lead to dissatisfaction, low performance, resistance and high staff turnover.

However, there are HR models that prescribe how organizations should be designed to maximize the opportunity for employee self-fulfillment at work and thus allow them to contribute to an effective organization. In this section, two such influential models will be described. The first of these – the *job characteristics model* – is a well-established model that was developed as a result of the very extensive HR research in the 1960s and 1970s. The second model – Hansson's model for different *competence strategies* – may not be as rooted in extensive psychological and social psychological research, but is a more contemporary attempt to link the HR framework with both business strategies and the assumptions of the structural framework. Like Mintzberg's structural configuration (Chapter 2), adhocracy can be seen as the structural framework's variant of an HR model, and Hansson's model for different competence strategies can be said to cover a lot of the structural framework's mindset.

Job characteristics model

The most famous of the HR framework's models for how the ideal workplace should be designed is undoubtedly Hackman's and Oldham's *job characteristics model* (1976, 1980). According to this model, working tasks and workplaces should be designed so that each employee can (1) feel that the work is meaningful, (2) feel responsible for it, and (3) see how it contributes to the results of the business. To achieve this, the business must be designed in accordance with five basic features:

1. Skill variety: the business should be characterized by employees being able to use different skills at different steps, that is, they do not have to repeat the same steps over and over again (compare with the extremely specialized work in a machine bureaucracy).

2. Task identity: work tasks should be designed so that employees feel that they can identify with them. For example, if different teams are responsible for the maintenance of bus stops on different streets, instead of one person emptying the trash cans at all bus stops, one changing timetables at all stops, another replacing broken glass panes at all stops, and so on, the teams will be able to identify with the bus stops on 'our street' and feel pride if they give a complete, clean and pleasant impression.

3. Task significance: the importance of the work in a larger context should be clearly conveyed – for example, that pleasant bus stops lead to more people choosing to go by bus instead of car, or that well-managed bus stops reduce vandalism.

4. Autonomy: the work should not be defined and specified in detail by anyone other than the employees who perform the work. In other words, employees should themselves, individually or in groups, be allowed to specify the details of how, where and when they solve their tasks. Autonomous or self-determining teams feel more responsibility than if someone or something else has decided exactly what to do and how. The more autonomy, the greater the sense of responsibility.

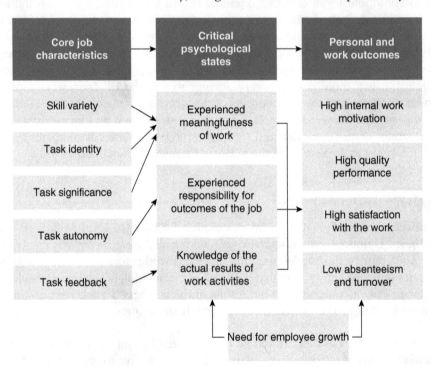

Figure 4.5   Job characteristics model

Source: Hackman & Oldham (1976)

5. Feedback: the more feedback employees receive about how the work of the individual or group affects the performance of the business or organization (productivity, profitability, innovation or other measures), the more knowledgeable they will be about how they can contribute to this result. For example, if the teams that provide the maintenance of bus stops know the costs of more extensive repairs, the incentive to keep the stops in such a fine condition increases in order to keep repairs to a minimum.

If a workplace is organized so that it is characterized by the above five features, the work will feel meaningful, and employees will take responsibility for it. The result, according to the job *characteristics* model, is that employees feel high internal motivation, that the goods and services produced are characterized by high quality, and that both sick leave and staff turnover are minimized (see Figure 4.5).

There are many interpretations and variants of Hackman and Oldham's model. What is perhaps missing most in Figure 4.6 is an additional arrow that shows how the increased motivation leads to a higher-performing business. High quality is included in the model, but not higher efficiency or productivity. This can be explained by the fact that it is self-evident, from a HR framework perspective, that increased needs satisfaction among employees leads to both increased motivation and increased commitment, but also better results in terms of efficiency and profitability. One way to clarify the outlook of the HR framework on how to create efficient, successful organizations is to compare it with the structural framework. Both frameworks can be said to strive for and prescribe efficient organizations, but in fundamentally different ways (see Figure 4.6).

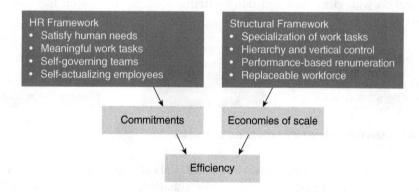

Figure 4.6   Two frameworks and their explanations of efficient organization

Competence strategies

Hansson's theories on how personnel strategy and business ideas can be seen as a development of Hackman and Oldham's job characteristics model. Unlike Hackman and Oldham, however, Hansson (2005) does not prescribe a best way, but believes that different competence strategies are appropriate in different situations. Thus, Hansson's model is reminiscent of, for example, Mintzberg's model with different structural configurations (see Chapter 2). It is also reminiscent of the models that describe high-performing teams and situational leadership and which are presented in the next chapter.

The basic idea in Hansson's model is that an organization's human resource and competence strategies must be in line with its business idea and competitive strategy. This can be seen as a development of the basic HR assumption that the needs of organizations and employees must coincide, but also be in closer alignment to the structural framework. This means that not everything is about maximizing employees' work motivation but rather about having to adapt how employees are managed according to the type of business being conducted.

The model has two dimensions. One is the organization's *attitude to business development*. Depending on its attitude to this, an organization can and should design different competence strategies. Different attitudes to business development are manifested in Hansson's model as three different competition strategies. The *customer-driven* and the *competence-driven* competition strategy can be seen as each other's opposites – they constitute the poles of the dimension – and the third, the *relationship-driven* strategy, is an intermediate form (see Figure 4.7). These three competitive strategies can be said to correspond to how companies can formulate their strategy according to research on business strategy, that is, based on an external analysis, in collaboration with customers and other external stakeholders, or on the basis of an analysis of their core competencies.

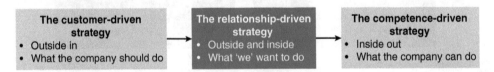

Figure 4.7 Starting points for competence strategies

The second dimension in Hansson's model is about company management's *attitude to employees* (compare with McGregor's Theory X and Theory Y). According to Hansson, leaders can view their employees either as *actors*, who interact with each other and management to create development and business, or as *recipients* of working tasks determined by management (see Figure 4.8). When leaders view employees as actors, the tasks are often more openly formulated and described as assignments

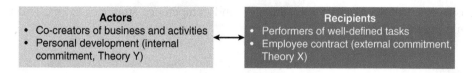

Figure 4.8   How management views its employees

Source: Hansson (2005)

or projects. The work becomes part of employees' personal development, and they are largely driven by internal motivation (compare with Argyris' concepts of internal and external commitment). When managers look at their employees as recipients, they become more executors of what the management has decided and is defined in the employment contract. For recipients, external motivation becomes more important than for actors.

Hansson believes that both competitive strategies and how management views its employees influence the choice of competence strategies. The model lists four typical or pure strategies: molding, matching, challenging and buying (see Figure 4.9). In reality, competence strategies are always a mixture of these, but the pure types can nevertheless be used as an analytical model. Given a certain business situation and competitive strategy, as well as a certain attitude to employees, different competence strategies are more or less effective. Just as with a structural analysis using Mintzberg's structural configurations and situational dependencies (see Chapter 2), one can choose to analyze entire companies or different parts within them. There can thus be different

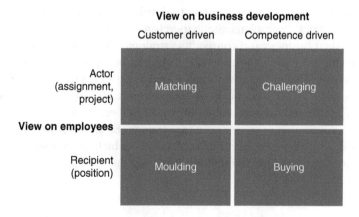

Figure 4.9   Four pure competence strategies

Source: Hansson (2005)

business situations, competition strategies and competence strategies in one and the same organization.

Molding

The molding strategy involves employees being adapted to a marketing plan or market strategy. The work and competence development of employees are governed by what is perceived to be customer requirements. Learning and competence development are guided towards what appears to be needed based on market requirements, often formulated in a company or business unit's marketing plan. Learning takes place in the form of clear working tasks and training initiatives.

The strategy is, according to Hansson, common and appropriate in companies whose business and competition strategy is aimed at 'cost leadership', that is, having lower costs than the company's competitors. The strategy is common in service, retail and industrial production companies. In order to reduce costs, the emphasis is often on economies of scale, standardization and continuous improvement. In addition to recruiting the right staff, i.e. sufficiently competent, 'cheap' and, at the same time, 'malleable' staff, the molding strategy includes a systematic introduction to and training for the job in question. Since these initiatives are also relatively standardized and large-scale, they lead to a homogeneous staff group. The employees are selected, aligned and often form a 'strong culture'. This coordinates employees but also makes them less open to new thinking and changed behaviors. Despite the idea of easily exchangeable employees, the molding strategy can therefore lead to an inertia that makes it difficult for companies to adapt if the market changes rapidly. Thus, a risk is that in a rapidly changing environment, companies with a low-cost and molding strategy may find it difficult to offer what customers really want. It is usually faster to analyze customers' needs and formulate marketing plans than to develop (mold) the right competencies to be able to implement these plans. Skills therefore lag behind and prevent companies from realizing their business and competitive strategies. The molding strategy therefore has clear limitations in more dynamic and turbulent business situations.

Molding as a competence strategy can be said to assume a high level of competition for customers and that success comes from developing offerings that customers appreciate more than the offerings of competitors. Therefore, market analysis and market strategy take precedence over competence strategy. Employees are to be molded to suit the business strategy, not the other way round – which bears a striking similarity to the basic idea of the structural framework of putting the right person in the right place.

Matching

The matching strategy involves taking into account employees' ambitions and competencies as well as customer requirements and needs. Space is created for mutual influence on the business process, that is, employees, management and customers alike are actively and jointly influencing the business and its development. Performance reviews, management by objectives, decentralized decision-making and horizontal coordination provide scope for competence development in daily operations.

The strategy involves trying to create a close relationship between management, employees and customers. The purpose is to create both employee loyalty and customer loyalty. Employee loyalty is created by investing in employees, motivating them to remain in the company for a long time, take responsibility for customers and develop their competence. By matching employees' needs and expectations with those of the company, and thereby creating benefits for both, competence development becomes a common concern for managers and employees. Leadership and followership partly merge as a result of a mutual responsibility for management work being created. If the molding strategy has many similarities with the basic assumptions of the structural framework, the matching strategy can be said to be true of the pure HR framework.

The matching strategy is, according to Hansson, a common and appropriate strategy in various forms of knowledge-intensive service and industrial activities, such as more advanced consulting and the manufacturing of high-tech products. In some ways, the strategy includes a similar array of problems as the molding strategy in terms of the emergence of a strong culture, even though the mechanisms behind it differ. As employees stay in the company for a long time and interact with each other and with managers, there is a great chance that a homogeneous thinking will be formed. This can also be reinforced by the fact that a certain specialist competence is often recruited, perhaps in the form of employees with similar higher education, which has already shaped their perspective and mindset. This facilitates coordination but also creates inertia, similar to the molding strategy. Companies with a matching strategy, however, can more easily adapt to changes in the market because employees are close to their customers, but more revolutionary changes can still be difficult to manage. Similarities can be seen between Hansson's matching strategy and Mintzberg's structural configuration of professional bureaucracy (Chapter 2).

Challenging

In the challenging strategy, the commitment and competence of employees are the very foundation of the company's business development. Skills development is seen as a strategic activity that requires significant and partly risky investment. The basis is not the market's or customers' direct requirements and needs, instead several development projects are run in parallel. Investment in competence can then be seen as an investment portfolio containing more and less risky projects. The business is flexible and stimulates learning. Employees are given the opportunity to work with increasingly large projects and be involved in their results. Flexible forms of organization provide the opportunity to gain new competencies.

Compared to both the molding and matching strategies, the challenging strategy is a much more proactive competence strategy. Instead of allowing the business strategy and marketing plan to determine competence requirements, as in the molding strategy, or allowing customers together with employees to govern competence development, as in the matching strategy, the challenging strategy involves allowing competence to take precedence over business strategies, marketing plans and existing customer needs. Instead of somehow listening to what customers want, goods and services are developed that, once they exist, can hopefully create new markets and customer needs. Everyone can be said to be actors and part of the company's business development. Employees are given considerable scope for self-development and thus for company development. One starting point is that employee competence cannot be forced or planned; rather, it must come from employees' own initiatives and activities. The function of managers is more to create conditions for learning and commitment than to govern and control the business. The focus of the management team is to set up competence objectives and decide whether the desire for competence development is strong enough, if the creative ability is sufficient and whether the company is innovating quickly enough.

The challenging strategy is often presented as the very image of 'good work'. It can be seen as a way to create extremely decentralized organizations with self-governing teams and self-fulfilling individuals. The strategy is also suitable in a rapidly changing world where it is inefficient to plan and manage the business vertically.

But the challenging strategy also involves risks. First, there are obvious business risks in developing competence and offerings without having any sort of systematized information (such as a marketing plan, or through close cooperation with customers) about what the market might want. It is also expensive to develop a diverse collection of competencies and offerings when it is likely that only a few will lead to profitable business. Second, there are tangible risks for employees, that is, those that can be said to be at the heart of the HR framework. The challenging strategy attracts and perhaps even creates employees with a great need for personal development, which risks leading to stress and increasingly burnt-out employees. The lack of vertical control means that there can be a horizontal control or pressure to perform that has no ceiling.

Another risk, or perhaps rather criticism of this competence strategy, is that in practice it is often about getting employees to perceive themselves as free, self-fulfilling individuals, when in fact they are manipulated to work more and more intensively than any hierarchical system could force them to do. This criticism can be said to apply to the entire HR framework and is something we will return to in subsequent frameworks. Based on the basic assumptions of the HR framework and its original theories and models, the challenging strategy is ideal. However, this competence strategy can also be linked to the structural framework, since it has major parallels with Mintzberg's structural configuration adhocracy.

Buying

The buying strategy, the fourth and final competence strategy in Hansson's model, involves management recruiting specific employees to meet specific competence requirements. They can be recruited or hired more or less temporarily. Management has a clear picture of what competence the company needs and how to obtain it. In addition to this knowledge of the company's competence requirements and where this competence can be acquired, activities that enable the competence to be transferred from specifically recruited/hired personnel to other employees are required. The competence requirements are thus defined by management and its knowledge and perceptions of what is needed to create attractive customer offerings. The buying strategy can at best bring increased flexibility and the ability to change a company's competence profile, compared to, for example, the molding strategy.

A clear trend over at least the last 20 years or so is large traditional companies and organizations becoming smaller in terms of number of employees. This is partly due to the automation of not only manufacturing but also service production (where machines and computers do what was previously done by people), and partly to operations previously done within an organization now being outsourced to external organizations. (This trend was described in the previous chapter, in the section on Williamson's transaction cost theory.)

The advantage of this type of more streamlined company is that its staffing can more easily be changed when required. It can be said that employment contracts and bureaucracy have increasingly been replaced by markets and buy–sell transactions. But since the latter can consist of highly detailed and extensive contracts – often more extensive than any employment contract – it is not obvious that they provide the flexibility intended. It may even be the case that more flexibility and fast changes can be created by using traditional permanent employees and decentralized and horizontal coordination, than via outsourcing and complicated contracts. Particularly when employing the challenging strategy, it is possible to achieve more flexibility with one's own employees. According to Hansson's model, creating a successful organization is primarily about different basic attitudes to business and employees, and developing a harmonizing or appropriate competence strategy.

Both a structural and a human model?

Hansson's four competence strategies can be seen as an HR version of Mintzberg's structural configurations of the structural framework. With these less rigid models, the contradiction between the structural framework and the HR framework is not as stark. However, it is not completely erased. The ideal structural configuration of the structural framework is machine bureaucracy. Based on a structural framework, the aim should always be to specialize, standardize and control, even if it is not always possible, in any case in the short term. The HR framework's ideal competence strategy is the challenging strategy, which is the opposite to an organization characterized by specialization, standardization and vertical control. If possible, according to the HR framework, the competence strategy should be allowed to take precedence over the business strategy. If possible, investment in employees should be maximized and they should be allowed to coordinate horizontally. In other words, although the structural framework's structural configurations overlap the HR framework's competence strategies, they are based on contradictory fundamental assumptions, providing two completely different normative answers to how an organization should be organized.

Videos

Don't forget to watch the videos to discover more about the key concepts in this chapter: **https://study.sagepub.com/blomberg**

5

An In-Depth HR Framework – Motivation, Learning, Teams and Leadership

In this chapter, the basic HR framework is developed further. This will increase your understanding of how human motivation works, and how you can create more or less committed organizational members. The more advanced HR framework will also increase your understanding of what knowledge is and how it can be managed in organizations, teams and projects. It will also enhance your ability to develop a more nuanced view of, as well as work with, human competence in the workplace.

First, we look at a model that both problematizes and deepens the motivation theories described in the previous chapter. Ryan and Deci's SDT model (2000) is based on extensive psychological research on the relationship between intrinsic and extrinsic motivation. It shows, among other things, that extrinsic rewards can be provided without necessarily leading to reduced intrinsic motivation, and that employees can be motivated even if their working tasks are boring.

Following this in-depth study of motivational theory, a well-established model follows in the field of 'knowledge management' that can be used to analyze whether and how learning takes place in organizations. Nonaka and Takeuchi's model (1995) for effective knowledge dissemination is based on the basic assumptions of the HR framework: by supporting and investing in employees and their learning and competence, organizations can improve their performance. It is also based on the idea that knowledge should be spread horizontally and shared, rather than divided up and controlled vertically.

We then describe HR-based models that can be used to characterize high-performing groups. In Chapter 3, we noted that there is not much research on group dynamics and teams based on a structural framework. However, for team research based on the basic assumptions of the HR framework, it is exactly the opposite: there is an abundance of it. This chapter describes some of the most influential models for the analysis of what makes groups high or low performing.

This is followed by a presentation of the 'agile project (and organization) model', which has major similarities with the HR framework's basic assumptions and principles. It can also be seen to criticize the structural frameworks' description of effective project management and the 'waterfall model' (see Chapter 3).

This is followed by a description of a few very central leadership models. In addition to being able to use these for an analysis of leadership based on an HR framework, they also function as a gradation of the HR framework in general. They can be said to correspond to Mintzberg's various structural configurations in the structural framework (Chapter 2), and to Hansson's competence strategy model in the basic HR framework (Chapter 4). In this case, these leadership models recommend leading and organizing in different ways in different situations, also according to the HR framework. The chapter concludes with a formulation of the HR framework's generic questions as well as a summary of the framework's strengths and weaknesses.

The SDT model - a more nuanced picture of motivation

Many of the models that form the basis of the HR framework are based on a dualism, that is, a one-dimensional theme where one pole consists of some kind of ideal comprising real, inner, genuine, free, higher human behaviors, and the other pole consists of more rational, external, controlled, lower behaviors. These behaviours can be in the form of different leadership styles, different ways of communicating or, as in the case of motivation, a difference between intrinsic and extrinsic motivation (Argyris 1998; see Table 4.1). More recent individual and organizational psychological research on motivation has, however, resulted in the earlier divisions of motivation into higher and lower needs (Maslow 1943; see Figure 4.2), hygiene factors and motivators (Herzberg 1964; see Figure 4.3) and intrinsic and extrinsic motivation, being partly abandoned.

The SDT (self-determination theory) model is built on contemporary individual psychological motivational research and is based on a developmental psychological view of the individual. Humans are considered to have an inherent basic need to be active, curious and playful, regardless of any external rewards (Ryan & Deci 2000). Internal motivation is therefore seen as the primary and most basic motivation.

According to *cognitive evaluation theory* (CET), the innate need for intrinsic motivation factors can be reformulated into three subsets, or three different basic needs: the needs for competence, autonomy and relatedness (Ryan & Deci 2000, Gagné & Deci 2005). The individual, and especially the young child, wants to learn to manage to do things without external help. However, this intrinsic motivation can be disturbed by various external conditions. According to CET, some types of extrinsic rewards reduce intrinsic motivation, others do not affect it, while others increase it (Gagné & Deci 2005). For example, material rewards in the form of bonuses and other, performance-based pay reduce intrinsic motivation, while monthly salary and other material rewards not directly linked to performance neither increase nor decrease it. External factors such as moderately challenging tasks and praise, on the other hand, can increase intrinsic motivation. There are thus good and bad combinations of intrinsic and extrinsic motivation. Thus, intrinsic and extrinsic motivation are not two mutually exclusive motivational forms, just as extrinsic motivation does not always adversely affect intrinsic motivation. In the latter stages of life particularly, combinations of the two motivational forms can lead to both psychological well-being and high performance.

A slightly different interpretation of the same research findings is to see the two types of motivation as dimensions more or less always present in the driving forces of individuals. This is what is done in the SDT model, which can be seen as a development, or an extension, of the CET model. In this model, intrinsic and extrinsic motivation have been replaced with a scale consisting of different degrees/types of *perceived autonomy* and *external regulation* (Ryan & Deci 2000). According to SDT, pure intrinsic motivation is something very unusual and extreme. Neither is its opposite extrinsic motivation but instead a lack of any motivation at all, which, in the STD model, is referred to as amotivation (see Figure 5.1).

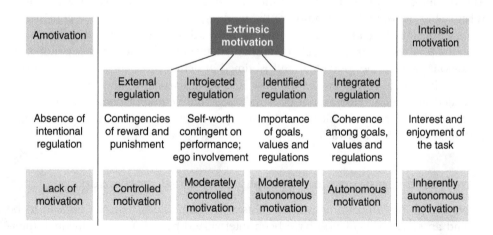

Figure 5.1   The SDT model and its continuum

Source: Ryan & Deci (2000)

Note: This consists of different types of external regulation and degrees/types of perceived autonomy, as well as two extreme points in the form of amotivation and intrinsic motivation.

In amotivation, no active action occurs at all, or it happens without the individual knowing why or being motivated by it in any way. The individual does not know why they performed a specific behavior or not. According to this model, intrinsic motivation is when the actual working task itself is interesting and gives joy to the person who performs it, regardless of what the other consequences of the action are. For example, consider a nurse who thinks it is interesting to talk to colleagues and patients, no matter how useful these conversations are for the treatment of patients; or an equity analyst who thinks that analyzing a company's value is the most enjoyable work there is, regardless of whether the analyst or anyone else benefits from it. However, this is the exception, according to the SDT model. Purely intrinsic motivation in this model is indeed the highest sense of autonomy, but it is very unusual for this to be the basis for people's actions. However, it is not just pure intrinsic motivation that makes individuals experience autonomy; according to SDT, externally regulated actions are also characterized by feelings of autonomy. Different types of external regulation affect motivation in different ways. Here we look at extrinsic regulation, introjected regulation, regulation through identification and integrated regulation in relation to controlled and autonomous motivation.

Extrinsic regulation and controlled motivation

Working tasks and specific behaviors that are uninteresting for the individual require some kind of extrinsic motivation or regulation for the individual to perform them. This extrinsic motivation means that the individual needs to be able to see a causal relationship between the execution of the working task and a demanded consistency, for example avoiding a penalty or obtaining a reward. This type of situation is referred to in the SDT model as 'externally controlled' motivation. The action is dependent on conditions outside the individual and is aimed at achieving a certain condition outside the individual. 'I work when the boss is looking' expresses this type of externally regulated motivation. However, it does include some degree of perceived autonomy. One can choose not to work when the manager is looking, but they then risk being punished or missing a reward.

Introjected regulation and partially controlled motivation

Another type of extrinsic motivation exists when the values that can be said to be behind an external regulation have been internalized by the acting individual. Internalization means that people take in the underlying values, attitudes and regulatory structures of a behavior and transform them into intrinsic perceptions. If this happens, no clear external control is required. 'I work even if the boss is not looking' expresses an internalized external control. However, behaviors and their underlying values can be internalized to varying degrees. The higher the degree of internalized behavior and regulation, the higher the sense of autonomy. Working even when the boss is not looking does not mean that you work entirely voluntarily. There is an awareness of a manager and an external regulation that has an effect, albeit in a more indirect way.

Regulation through identification and partly autonomous motivation

A higher degree of internalized external regulation is referred to in the SDT model as 'regulation through identification'. This means that the values and motives behind the external regulation have been identified. It is therefore not a question of being exposed to direct or indirect control, but of having an understanding of why there is external regulation at all. Even if the underlying values of the regulation or their underlying motives are not fully shared, they can be perceived as important. This understanding means that less concrete control is required and that the execution of working tasks is perceived as being more voluntary. The nurse might not like to wash patients, but does so because the nurse knows that patients need to be washed and that there is no one else who will do it. The nurse might not think it should be a part of her or his job, but, since nobody else is doing it, the nurse does it.

Integrated regulation and autonomous motivation

'Integrated regulation' causes the greatest sense of autonomy in the acting individual. The external regulation has then been completely internalized. An analyst can, for example, make a recommendation to buy, sell or retain for the investor collective, not because the actual making of the recommendation is interesting or fun in itself, but because it is part of what the analyst sees as an important function of their role in the financial system. A nurse may want to wash a patient, not because it is an interesting or fun job, but because it is in line with the nurse's values in terms of taking care of patients. It is about the consequences of the action, not the action itself. In this case, the external regulation and the person's own values have been integrated. The goal of acting in accordance with one's own values can be seen as a kind of internal mechanism, but this is not to be equated with the task being satisfying in itself or not being regulated externally. On the contrary, nurses are expected to wash patients and equity analysts are expected to make recommendations to buy, sell or retain.

Competence, autonomy and relatedness – implications for leadership

The SDT model can be said to nuance the individual psychological image of humans as independent individuals, driven by innate basic needs. Innate 'internal' driving forces are partly replaced by an internalization process that involves different degrees of external influence and different degrees of perceived free choice. This image of the human largely overlaps with both the power framework's view of exercising power through manipulation (see Chapters 6 and 7) and the symbolic framework's view of how strong cultures are created and developed through socialization (see Chapters 8 and 9). But the SDT model for motivation nevertheless adheres to the HR framework's foundations. The individual and organizational psychological research on which the model is based shows that internalization is facilitated by three factors, all of which can be seen as variants of some of the basic assumptions of the HR framework. According to the SDT model, both the creation of intrinsic motivation and internalization are natural processes fed by three basic human needs. In addition to the developmental psychological needs for *competence* and *autonomy*, individuals, according to the SDT model, need to feel *relatedness*. If they do not, internalization cannot occur efficiently.

From an organizational and leadership perspective, leadership that expresses confidence in employees' ability and independent action is therefore preferable to leadership that expresses control and a need to reward each individual achievement. Using performance-based rewards does not have to be wrong at all, given that it does not happen regularly and is only for specialized and defined achievements. Trying to micro-manage using performance pay can create a feeling among employees that they cannot choose and think for themselves. External rules and structures need not reduce motivation, given that they can be justified in a way that employees can relate to.

The third basic need that the SDT model assumes – relatedness – also has clear practical implications. Performance-based pay can be given, for example, at group level, which then stimulates a team atmosphere that in turn increases the ability of individuals to internalize external regulation. However, more individual *performance management* (PM) individual perspectives on competence, training and reward systems (today often grouped under the epithet *talent management*, TM), individual grades, individual '360-degree' manager evaluations, regular individual prices and appointments, and so on, are not effective ways to motivate people. This applies to both students in elementary schools and colleges, and to employees in companies and other organizations.

An even more general implication of the SDT model is that people can certainly be motivated to perform at a high level, even if the actual task itself is not perceived as interesting or fun. By stimulating the internalization of external values ('Equity analysts should make recommendations') and the internalization of external regulations ('If we exceed the expected result, our team will get an extra bonus'), you can get managers and employees to perform to a high level even if the work itself is really boring.

Nonaka and Takeuchi's model for the creation of organizational knowledge

If Ryan and Deci's SDT model can be described as highly individual, although with a clear social dimension, the model presented in this section is largely organizational, albeit with a clear individual dimension.

Nonaka and Takeuchi's model (1995) is one of the most central within 'knowledge management', an area that can be said to be a mixture of research and practice with a focus on the knowledge and learning of people and organizations. Nonaka and Takeuchi's model for how knowledge is created and disseminated in organizations is largely based on the basic assumptions of the HR framework, but it also has clear elements from a structural framework perspective. Nonaka and Takeuchi's model (1995) admits that there are both advantages and disadvantages to formalized processes. Basically, however, the model expresses that an organization, by supporting and investing in employees' learning and competence, can improve the organization's performance. The model is also based on the idea that an organization in which individuals learn through new experiences, and where individual learning is spread to other employees within the company, is a more successful organization than if the knowledge is divided into different formal groups or concentrated at the top of the organization's hierarchy.

Nonaka and Takeuchi's model consists of a general description of how individuals develop new knowledge and how this is then spread from individual to group and then to ever-higher organizational levels. The explanatory and normative power of the model comes from the fact that it can be applied in an analysis of why knowledge is or is not created and disseminated in a particular context. It is thus possible, with the help of Nonaka and Takeuchi's model, to identify obstacles and limitations to the effective creation and dissemination of knowledge and thereby also identify how these obstacles and limitations can be overcome.

Particularly in companies that perform and sell advanced services, where the competitiveness lies in employees' knowledge and competence rather than in machines and material production systems, employees' competence is a key factor for the organization's well-being and survival. Typical organizations where this is considered relevant are consulting companies that sell more knowledge-intensive and complex services. Examples of such organizations include different types of technical, legal and financial consultants as well as management consultants. At the same time, it can be argued that employees' competence becomes an increasingly important resource in all types of organizations – since the simpler, more standardized parts of the production of goods and services are so rationalized, standardized and nowadays increasingly automated that they are also easy to copy. In order to create sustainable competitive advantage, therefore, in addition to efficient production, it is necessary to offer services in which the building blocks are greater knowledge and competence, which are more difficult to copy.

The problem is that such difficult-to-copy knowledge and competence are also difficult to transfer between employees within one's own company. How then can employees' individual competencies and knowledge be made scalable? For example, how can an entire management consulting firm benefit from an experienced consultant's or consulting group's unique lessons and knowledge? Perhaps an enormous amount of learning takes place within a consulting project at a customer operating in, for example, the biotech industry in Sweden. How can the consulting firm effectively disseminate this experience and new knowledge to other consultants and other projects, perhaps spread all over the world?

Nonaka and Takeuchi's model (1995) consists of two dimensions: an ontological dimension (roughly meaning 'reality') and an epistemological dimension (roughly meaning 'knowledge of reality'). The ontological dimension extends from the individual level to the level of the team, group, organization, and so on. The epistemological dimension consists of a division of knowledge into two types – *tacit* and *explicit*. Explicit knowledge can be formulated in words, written down and transferred relatively easily from one person to another, for example in the form of a written instruction. Tacit knowledge, on the other hand, is difficult to conceptualize and is created when an individual gains practical experience without necessarily knowing exactly what they are learning. Most of us can walk without a written instruction telling us how to do it. Most of us can also walk on a crowded pavement without crashing into others, without following explicit rules on how to navigate.

Four stages of knowledge transfer

The model describes how individual knowledge is transferred to an ever-higher ontological level in the form of a spiral that moves through four states of knowledge transfer: socialization (from tacit to tacit knowledge), externalization (from tacit to explicit), combining (from explicit to explicit) and internalization (from explicit to tacit) (see Figure 5.2).

Through *socialization*, employees can make and share experiences with each other. Typically, this happens during the actual work, assignment or project. Consultants solve problems more or less together with clients and others. Most of this work is never formalized, and learning is done informally and implicitly. The knowledge is highly practical and linked to the specific situation in which it originated. The employees do not have to be aware of their lessons. If they find themselves in similar situations, they will be able to use their new knowledge, but it remains implicit, tacit knowledge within those employees who helped to create it. However, by mixing experienced with less experienced employees, for example in a consulting team or in the

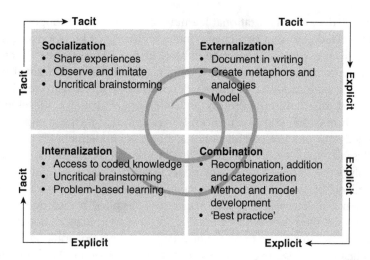

Figure 5.2   Nonaka and Takeuchi's model (1995) for the creation of organizational knowledge

form of a teacher and an apprentice, less experienced employees can take advantage of experienced employees' knowledge. By working together, they can gain common experience, but less experienced employees can also observe experienced employees 'in action' and try to imitate them. The close and information-rich relationship between experienced and less experienced employees means that tacit knowledge can be transferred from individual to individual. However, it takes time and does not work over great distances in time or space.

Therefore, many knowledge-intensive companies are investing in extensive *externalization*. By translating the experiences of individuals and teams into more general and abstract lessons, more unique and situational knowledge can be disseminated. More general knowledge can consist of all kinds of texts, manuals in the form of bulleted lists, short descriptions or some sort of model. Most consulting firms and many other companies have some kind of system for this, usually in the form of an IT system where experiences from each completed project are described. However, the design of these systems can vary, from responding to a number of standardized questions to an extensive, more structured system where different information is imputed in different parts of a more standardized project or process model. Knowledge can then be divided into sector knowledge, process knowledge, 'who can what' knowledge, and so on. Tacit knowledge can thus be externalized to become explicit knowledge available to a large number of employees who have neither been involved in the project where the lessons are learned nor socialized with those who have been. Individual knowledge has been transformed into 'structural capital' (support functions or technostructure, to use Mintzberg's terminology).

New knowledge, or organizational learning, can also arise through the *combining* of explicit knowledge from a particular context with explicit knowledge from another. Experiences from a project team externalized in the form of texts describing their project can be combined with similar experiences from another team. By means of an analysis of a large number of project descriptions, patterns can be identified and lessons learned regarding contributory and inhibiting factors for successful projects. Based on such material, *best practice* can be created, that is, the company's accumulated knowledge of how successful projects should be implemented.

Regardless of the extent to which explicit knowledge is combined, externalization always involves the standardization and generalization of tacit, individual and contextual knowledge. This means that knowledge is always 'lost' about how to act in specific contexts when tacit knowledge is externalized into explicit knowledge. Regardless of how extensive are the systems for externalization and combination, not all tacit knowledge can be transformed into explicit knowledge. In addition, someone is required to use the explicit knowledge in a practical context in order for it to have any significance at all for how a particular activity is conducted. A library full of books has no practical function if no one visits the library and reads the books.

In order for the formalized explicit knowledge to be of significance for organizing and business, it must be used, which in turn requires that the explicit knowledge through *internalization* once again takes the form of tacit knowledge. Upon internalization, explicit knowledge is converted into tacit knowledge. A clear example of internalization is when the junior consultant in his first project tries to apply the formal models and formalized processes that were part of his initial training. Another is when a small working group of students tries for the first time to use the models and theories that they have just read about in the course literature in the analysis of a 'real' case. In both situations, an attempt should be made to translate the more theoretical, abstract and pronounced knowledge into a practical, unique and very complex situation. When written instructions and formal processes are put into action in a specific situation, the explicit instructions are never complete. It is required of the individual (the consultant or the student) that they interpret both the instructions and the situation. This 'filling in' means that the instructions and the explicit knowledge are supplemented with new tacit knowledge.

We have completed a circuit of the model, and now the next circuit starts, but this time with a higher degree of common tacit knowledge and with a higher degree of written explicit knowledge. In this way, an organization can create learning that spreads individuals' experience and implicit knowledge over time and space and ever-greater distances. But, if there is no opportunity for the experienced and inexperienced to work and socialize together, if there is no system to allow externalization and combination to happen, and if the written explicit knowledge is not available to an organization's employees, then organizational learning will fail, according to Nonaka and Takeuchi's model. In other words, using this model, we can analyze whether and how organizations have structured themselves in terms of employee interaction and formalized processes and whether these support or hinder learning and the creation of organizational knowledge.

High-performance teams

There is extensive research on high-performance teams/working groups that is based on the basic assumptions of the HR framework.[1] In this section, we present some basic questions that can be asked at the onset of a group project, before detailing the development phases of high-performance teams. We then take a look at effective communication in high- and low-performing teams.

Four basic questions

Before any of the established models are described, it can be useful to have a simple list of questions that individuals can ask themselves and each other at the beginning of a forthcoming joint assignment to be performed in a group. These questions are based precisely on research on communication in and the development of smaller working groups. By posing the questions as soon as possible, the time it takes to get a number of individuals to work together and work as a high-performance team can be reduced.

Am I willing to listen and can I adapt to others?

According to the HR framework, collaboration is the basis of successful organization, not formal processes, authoritarian leadership and control. This means that a person should have both the ability to listen to others and be willing to work towards joint goals rather than their own individual goals. For many motivated and ambitious people, this can be a big challenge. Are they able to take a step back and allow others, with their knowledge and perspective, to step forward?

Do I dare to talk and take a more prominent role than I usually do?

In newly formed groups, there are usually members who observe and listen, rather than communicate and contribute, regardless of their ambition and drive. The reasons for this can be many, ranging from timidity and insecurity to a reluctance to create conflict. Just as those who often take up a lot of space should take a step back, it is important for the more passive listeners to dare to take a step forward.

What competence does each group member have?

This question should not be asked primarily for the purpose of finding an optimal work division in the group (such as based on a structural framework), but is more about taking an inventory of the competences and perspectives that exist within the group. Such an inventory can speed up the group's dynamic development over time and facilitate collaboration, understanding and knowledge transfer within the group.

What are our common goals?

Regardless of whether the goals of a particular work effort are defined in advance, there are differences between group members both in terms of how these set goals are perceived and interpreted and in terms of the scope of the work effort and the working method (doing everything together and/or dividing certain parts of work). Therefore, an inventory should also be taken of these differences and an attempt made to create a common set of goals. This can be anything from how much work group members are expected to do, to what is actually the main objective of the work effort (e.g. achieve the set quality goals within the framework of a specific budget, satisfied customers, interesting and educational work, an investment for future assignments, high grades, and other possible goals) and how to go about achieving these goals. According to the HR framework, if such objectives can be agreed, the likelihood of being able to function as a high-performance team increases.

Development phases of high-performance teams

Wheelan (2015) has summarized the research on group dynamics and the development of groups from the time a group starts working together for the first time until it constitutes a high-performance team. Wheelan's model describes four phases: the dependency phase, the conflict phase, the confidence phase and the productivity phase (see Figure 5.3). The model is based on extensive research on group dynamics that has resulted in similar phase models. Perhaps the most famous of all these models is Tuckman's (1965) 'Forming, storming, norming and performing' theory. In the following formulation, we start from Tuckman's model but make additions based on Wheelan's summary of subsequent related research. In addition to describing what characterizes each phase, parts of this research also describe what constitutes a suitable leadership style in each phase. However, we will save the leadership part of this research until the description of another very influential model, Hersey and Blanchard's 'Situational leadership model', which is one of the leadership models described at the end of this chapter.

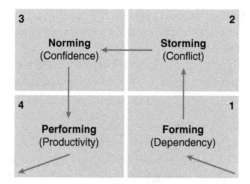

Figure 5.3   Tuckman's model (1965) for team development with Wheelan's concepts (2015) in brackets

Forming

In the initial phase of group development, *forming*, the group's behavior, according to Tuckman, is characterized by its lack of guidance and direction. There is not much agreement on the group's goals or work processes, and there are many unanswered questions about purpose and goals.

According to Wheelan, this 'dependency phase' is characterized by a cautious courtesy where the various group members try to predict each other's behaviors. Members feel a need for recognition, while having a low degree of identification with the group. Group members avoid conflict and risk-taking behaviors. The conversation in the group is characterized by many suggestions but few decisions and implementations, as well as by much discussion about topics that have little to do with the group's assignments or actual tasks. The group lacks leadership.

Storming

Gradually, the group passes into the *storming* phase. In this phase, decision-making is cumbersome and time-consuming. Group members try to establish relationships with each other and look for a possible leader, who is often challenged by other members. The group's tasks and its purpose become somewhat clearer, but extensive uncertainty remains. Alliances are formed and there is a high risk of power struggles. The group or the incipient team needs to focus on its goals to avoid being distracted by relationship-building and emotional reactions. Compromise can be necessary to enable progress and further development of the group.

Wheelan adds that, in this 'conflict phase', group members are often put under stress by issues that do not have to do with the actual task. There is open competition among members who make various excuses for not contributing to the team, nor its task. Members strive to persuade each other (compare with model 1: communication; see Chapter 4) rather than to cooperate. Group members try to convince each other to share their own motives and values. Members now take higher risks, and there is a great deal of variation between the activities of individual members.

Norming

If the group manages to manage the conflict, positioning and competition in the *storming* phase, the group can gradually progress to *norming*. Members become closer to each other and the degree of consensus increases. The group focuses increasingly on making decisions together, and the motivation to implement them increases. The group engages in fun and social activities, as well as in discussing and developing its working methods. Any leaders are respected, but much is determined and implemented jointly without any clear, individual leadership.

Wheelan believes that more recent research has contributed to our understanding of this 'confidence phase'. This research shows that, while team members strive for consensus and are open and spontaneous in their approach to each other, the group as a whole is quite ineffective. It spends more time on social activities and conversations on how to work than on the actual task or assignment and its implementation. In addition, there is a clear risk for 'groupthink' (see Chapter 8), which involves not reflecting on the pros and cons of the ongoing work and unconsciously taking greater risks than would have been the case if the work had been more critically examined. Members identify so much with the team that they laud their own team's efforts and belittle the efforts of other teams.

Performing

In the *performing* phase, the ideal phase, the team is performing at a high level. Members are so confident that they do not have to strive for consensus or spend time discussing how the work should be organized. They still devote time to social activities, but not to the same extent as before. Instead, the focus is on the task, the assignment or the work. The group now has a more strategic focus – it knows what it is doing and why. The team has a common vision, but members also dare to stand up for different views because conflicts can now be resolved positively, that is, differences drive forward development and create better results rather than leading to power struggles and discord. The team can work towards achieving its goals (and often strives to 'over-deliver') and, at the same time, develop its work processes if it finds reason to do so. The team does not need leadership or control, but works independently and makes joint decisions, and members take care of each other.

In the description of this ideal 'productivity phase', that is, in the description of how groups should work to become high-performance teams, Wheelan believes that later research does not have much to add. Rather, Wheelan reiterates Tuckman's description of how these teams have clear goals, allow conflict management to drive forward development, and how a warm and caring attitude allows team members to handle relationship issues effectively without losing focus on the work and its goals. An important addition, however, is the empirical support that these phase models have received in all kinds of studies. Among other things, Wheelan shows that high-performance teams (in the *performance*/productivity phase) on average focus 75 percent of their time on the task, in contrast to average-performance teams (in the *norming*/confidence phase) which, on average, focus only 38 percent of their time on the task.

Analysis of group efficiency using the phase model

An analysis of the efficiency of a small working group using the above phase model involves trying to identify which phase the group is in, and why. Has the group got stuck somewhere in its development, that is, in a phase before the productivity phase, and, if so, why? The 'why' question can in turn be answered with the help of analyses based on other HR models. What does communication look like in the group? How are conflicts dealt with? Has work division been taken too far? Do any or some members practice Theory X and authoritarian leadership? As regards leadership, Hersey and Blanchard's highly influential and useful model will be described below, but first we briefly describe a slightly more developed communication model.

Effective communication in high- and low-performance management teams

As regards communication, research on high-performance teams has developed and supplemented Argyris' communication theory 'Models 1 and 2' (see Chapter 4). Losada and Heapy (2004) compared the communication in 60 more or less well-functioning *business teams*. In the study, three dimensions emerged, which correlated strongly with group performance. These three dimensions were: (1) degree of connectivity, (2) self versus other focus, and (3) advocative or investigative communication style (see Figure 5.4). The groups could also be divided into three performance levels: high-, medium- and low-performance teams. It emerged that high-performance management teams demonstrated completely different communication patterns to those of medium- and low-performance teams. Of the three dimensions, whether group members focused their own thinking and actions (*self-focus*) was the most basic dimension. In teams where members self-focused, communication became predominantly

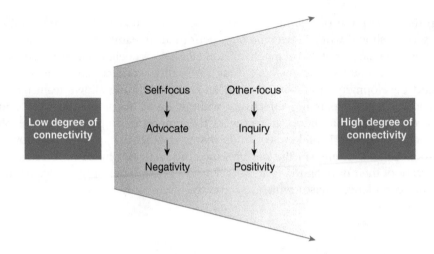

Figure 5.4 **The effect of three dimensions on team interaction and performance**

advocative (compare with *advocate* in Model 1). In teams where members focused on each other (*other focus*), communication was much more investigative (compare with *inquire* in Model 2). These differences, in turn, meant that high-performance teams communicated more and more positively with each other than medium- and low-performance teams.

Creating a high-performance team is thus about achieving positive and comprehensive communication with considerable focus on the task, which in turn is about how individual members of the group behave. If members want to contribute to a group's performance, they should start by analyzing their own contribution. Do I focus (too) much on myself, my own opinions, perspectives and actions, or am I more interested in the other members of my team?

In high-performance teams, members devoted 50 percent of their total communication time to examining what their own and others' perspectives, knowledge and proposed solutions were and why (*inquire*). The other 50 percent devoted themselves to advocating their own perspective, knowledge base and proposed solutions (*advocate*). This means that they balanced an investigative and curious communication style with an advocative, argumentative one. In addition, members of high-performance management teams devoted 50 percent of their total communication time to talking about themselves based on their own perspective, and 50 percent to talking about other members of the group based on other members' perspectives (see Figure 5.5). Low-performance management groups advocated their own solutions with arguments taken from their own knowledge and perspective. In addition, low- and medium-performance teams devoted much less time to the task and more time to social activities.

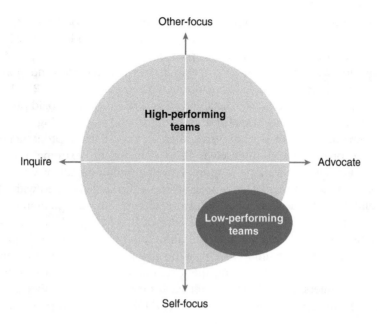

Figure 5.5   Communication patterns in high- and low-performance teams

In an analysis of groups and teams, their varying achievements can therefore be explained by what the group's communication patterns look like. Further, according to this model, communication patterns are a consequence of individual group members' perspectives and approaches to themselves and other group members.

Agile projects

Research on project management based on a structural framework is as extensive as research based on the same framework on group dynamics and teams is scant. Regarding research on teams and projects within a HR framework, the opposite is true. The most typical project model based on a structural framework is called the waterfall model within project research and practice, meaning that projects are planned from start to finish in the form of a linear, formalized and rational process (see Chapter 3).

Over the last 15–20 years, however, an alternative model for project management and project organization has been developed, which is both a criticism of linear project models (or waterfall models) and firmly anchored in the HR framework's basic assumptions. The 'agile' project model originates from software programming in Silicon Valley, that is, in northern California in the United States. During the 1990s, more and more large IT companies tried to lower their programming costs by employing cheaper labor, often migrants from countries like India, or by outsourcing operations to low-wage countries. In this way, established, experienced and relatively highly paid North American programmers could be replaced.

In connection with this, programming was also formalized more and more towards resembling a 'machine bureaucracy' organizational form (see Chapter 2). The criticism of these changes came mainly from established and relatively well-paid programmers. They thought that this more formalized and controlled programming became stiffer, more cumbersome and more expensive than if experienced programmers could manage their programming themselves. The concept of 'extreme programming' was coined, as well as a variety of more 'extreme' methods, all of which involved programming being best managed by programmers, who collaborated with each other and with end-users of the developed software; all with minimal planning in advance and minimal documentation and vertical control.[2] Continuously documenting the programming work and the emerging program code in the form of logbooks took unnecessary and expensive time away from the actual programming, and, in addition, the logbooks never matched, making them unusable when troubleshooting, it was claimed. Programmers could instead meet each other and prospective users face to face in small teams and continuously assemble different program parts into working software.

From the discussion on pros and cons of 'extreme programming' and more 'traditional' or more planned and formalized programming, the *agile manifesto* was born. In 2001, 17 programmers formulated a list with 12 basic principles on how to work in programming projects. These principles came to lay the foundation for what are today called agile projects and which have spread far beyond just software programming (Beck et al. 2001):

1. Our highest priority is to satisfy the customer through the early and continuous delivery of valuable software.
2. Welcome changing requirements, even late in development. Agile processes harness change for the customer's competitive advantage.
3. Deliver working software frequently, from a couple of weeks to a couple of months, with a preference for the shorter timescale.
4. Business people and developers must work together daily throughout the project.
5. Build projects around motivated individuals. Give them the environment and support they need, and trust them to get the job done.
6. The most efficient and effective method for conveying information to and within a development team is face-to-face conversation.
7. Working software is the primary measure of progress.
8. Agile processes promote sustainable development. Sponsors, developers and users should be able to maintain a constant pace indefinitely.
9. Continuous attention paid to technical excellence and good design enhances agility.

10. Simplicity – the art of maximizing the amount of work not done – is essential.
11. The best architecture, requirements and designs emerge from self-organizing teams.
12. At regular intervals, the team reflects on how to become more effective, then tunes and adjusts its behavior accordingly.

The similarity with the basic assumptions and principles of the HR framework is striking. The emergence and development of agile project methodology can almost be seen as a repetition of the advent and development of the HR framework, albeit with a time-lag of half a century or so. The similarity becomes even more apparent if we look at the latest developments in project management. Over the last 5–10 years, 'bio-modal' project methods have been launched by all sorts of project experts. The basic idea in these is that, depending on the nature of the project, the traditional, linear waterfall methodology should be combined in different ways with agile methodology. The traditional, linear project model (that is, the more bureaucratic model; see Chapter 3) is best suited for IT projects aimed at developing stable and large systems that have nothing to do with the company's innovative or developmental capability, for example email systems or financial monitoring systems. Agile project models are best suited to the development of new, constantly improved systems that are crucial to companies' competitiveness, for example the development of the technical systems and algorithms that make trading decisions in high-frequency security trading (Gartner 2015).

It is basically the same fundamental idea as the one behind Mintzberg's structural configurations – sometimes more adhocratic (agile) organizing is best suited, sometimes machine bureaucracy (linear) is best, and sometimes a combination of the two is the best option (simple structure or professional bureaucratic/biomodal). However, whether we lean towards the project model of the structural framework or the HR framework, one basic assumption is unchanged: that it is possible to optimize the project work given the project's objectives and prevailing circumstances.

Working 'agilely' is no longer limited to project work. The term 'agile' has spread and is used today in all possible contexts. Talk is of agile organization, agile HR and even agile lean. These concepts are all about working with less formalized processes and vertical control and are more in line with the HR framework's basic assumptions and Mintzberg's adhocratic configuration.

Leadership based on a HR framework

There is extensive leadership research as well as many leadership concepts, models and theories based on the basic assumptions of the HR framework. The perspective of the HR framework on what constitutes effective leadership is in sharp contrast to the corresponding ideal of the structural framework. Many of the slightly older leadership models within the HR framework can be seen as a direct criticism of the structural framework's leadership ideal. But later, less rigid models have been developed which can be seen as both a criticism of and a complement to the structural framework's description of effective leadership. In this section, a couple of very simple concepts and models will first be described which can be said to criticize the rational, system- and task-oriented structural leader. We then present a more complex model – Hersey and Blanchard's situational leadership model – which prescribes different leadership styles in different situations.

Management versus leadership

A very popular distinction in both leadership research and practice is that between managers/management and leaders/leadership (Zaleznik 1977, Kotter 1987, 1990a). A person who holds a formal managerial position is not to be equated with a person who is a leader, just as management is not always the same as leadership. There are just as many definitions and descriptions of the differences between the two concepts as there are leadership researchers and leadership consultants. One common expression is that managers control employees, while leaders are followed by employees. Another is that managers administrate systems and formal processes, while leaders achieve change. A third way of describing the difference is that management is what leaders do, based on a structural framework (see Chapters 2 and 3), while leadership is what leaders do, based on a HR framework. These distinctions can be seen as variants of the theme in 'Theory Y and Theory X' (see Chapter 4). Another influential variant of this theme is the distinction between 'transactional' and 'transformational' leadership (Bass 1985, Burns 1978). Transactional leadership corresponds to Theory X and the structural framework, transformational to Theory Y and the HR framework (and, to some extent, to the symbolic framework; see Chapter 8).

The list shown in Table 5.1 is a reasonably compact summary of how the differences between leadership and management are described in the extensive leadership literature.

When analyzing leadership, the distinctions in Table 5.1 can be used to clarify whether leadership or management is exercised in a particular situation. If, for example, it is a development project in a turbulent environment and with many difficult technology choices, perhaps an outright manager is less suitable than a leader. Another way of looking at the distinction is that all leaders should be able to exercise both leadership and management, a perspective that is relevant in recruitment, promotion and training contexts. Seeing leadership as an ability to more or less successfully combine more task-oriented and controlling management with more employee-oriented and motivating leadership is also the theme of the extremely well-known managerial grid model, described in the next section.

Table 5.1   **Leadership versus management**

Category	Leadership	Management
Thinking	Focuses on people Looks inward	Focuses on things Looks outward
Objectives	Formulates visions Creates the future Sees the wood	Implements plans Improves the existing Sees the trees
Relation to employees	Motivates Colleagues Shows trust and develops	Controls Subordinates Instructs and coordinates
Behaviors	Does the right things Creates change Supports subordinates	Does things right Manages change Supports superiors
Leadership style	Uses influence Uses conflict Acts clearly	Uses authority Avoids conflict Acts responsibly

Source: Based on Lunenburg (2011)

The managerial grid

Another variant of the distinction between leaders and managers is Blake and Mouton's managerial grid model (1964). This model assesses the extent to which leaders care about their employees (*concern for people*) and the extent to which they care about production targets (*concern for production*). By combining three positions (low, medium and high) on these two scales, five different leadership styles can be formulated (see Figure 5.6).

Leaders with an *indifferent* leadership style (1.1) are those leaders who do not really care about their employees or about the production targets. Leaders with this style care most about keeping their job and protecting themselves from getting into hot water. The main focus of an indifferent leader is to not be held responsible for mistakes and bad results.

Managers who exhibit the *accommodating* leadership style (1.9) care to a high degree about their employees' working environment and working conditions in the hope that it will lead to improved performance. This, according to Blake and Mouton, results in a pleasant work environment, but not necessarily in efficient production.

Leaders with a *dictatorial* leadership style (9.1) control and dominate. With a great deal of concern for production but little concern for employees, this leadership style implies a Theory X-like behavior (see Chapter 4). Leaders with a dictatorial style are, according to Blake and Mouton, common in companies that are doing, or are perceived to be doing, really badly and are in crisis.

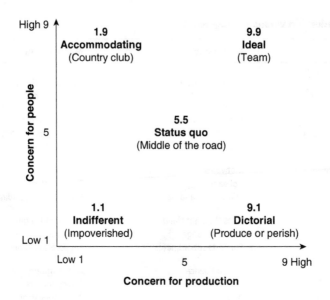

Figure 5.6   The managerial grid

Source: Blake & Mouton (1964)

Leaders who exhibit a *status quo* leadership style (5.5) balance and compromise between employee needs and production goals. In this way, the hope is to have reasonably satisfied employees and, at the same time, satisfy production rates and quality goals. However, according to Blake and Mouton, the risk of failure in both is considerable.

The *ideal* leadership style (9.9) entails great concern for both employees and production. Leaders with this style create the motivation to produce efficiently. The sound leadership style is about getting each employee to be themselves and, at the same time, become a productive force in the organization. It is worth noting that the sound leadership style in Blake and Mouton's original version was called *team leadership style*, and that contemporary research on high-performance teams can be interpreted as being strong empirical support for this leadership style being preferable. High-performance teams balance communication with a focus on their own and others' competencies and solutions, as well as balancing an investigative and advocative communication pattern (see Figure 5.4). This can be seen as a development of, but still basically the same idea as, Blake and Mouton's sound leadership style, which balances concern for employees with concern for production goals.

But the managerial grid model can also be criticized. Are there really leaders out there who are good at everything, or at least good at both taking care of employees and focusing on production goals? And is it always necessary? According to the next leadership model, the last one described in this chapter, the answer is at least partially no.

On the contrary, it describes and prescribes that different situations require different leadership styles, that is, there is no obvious style of leadership that is best in all situations.

Situational leadership

Hersey and Blanchard's situational leadership model is perhaps the most established and well-known of all models that describe and prescribe 'situational' leadership (Hersey & Blanchard 1969a, 1969b). According to this model, different leadership styles are functional in different situations; although it differs from Blake and Mouton's managerial grid model in that it does not prescribe the same leadership style in all situations. The model suggests that leadership should not only be adapted to the prevailing short-term situation (the four boxes in Figure 5.7) but that it should also transform the situation over time to create both highly motivated and competent employees (the direction of the red arrows in the figure).

Telling/directing. If employees in a particular operational unit are characterized by low competence, that is, they do not know how to solve a certain task, but are motivated to do the job, then an authoritative leadership style is appropriate. The leader simply gives clear and detailed instructions on what the employees should do and how.

Selling/coaching. In this situation, employees have begun to learn how to perform the task, but their initial motivation has decreased, partly because of the authoritarian

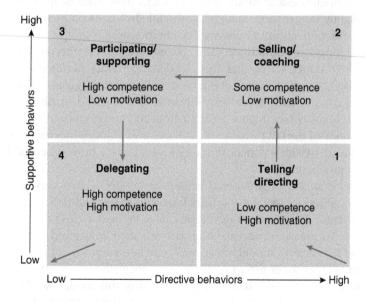

Figure 5.7   Situational leadership

Source: Based on Hersey & Blanchard (1969b); Blanchard et al. (1985)

leadership style. At this point, it is appropriate to combine a supportive and an authoritarian leadership style. The leader should encourage and support, but also guide employees in how they work.

Participating/supporting. If competence is high but motivation is lacking, the leadership style should aim to increase intrinsic motivation. That is, in accordance with the HR framework's models, the tasks should be designed to be varied and enriching, and vertical coordination should be avoided. Instead, participatory, more horizontal leadership should be employed.

Delegating. In the ideal situation, employees are both competent and motivated to a high degree. Leadership (in terms of a leader influencing followers) can then be minimized and delegated to employees. Employees are then 'self-governing' or can be said to work in 'autonomous teams' (compare with Mintzberg's structural configuration 'adhocracy' in Chapter 2, and with the 'challenging strategy' in Hansson's model for competence strategies in Chapter 4).

Hersey and Blanchard's model for situational leadership thus prescribes different leadership styles for different situations, but, at the same time, it prescribes that one of these leadership styles is the most desirable one, as well as the situation in which it fits. Thus, Hersey and Blanchard's model is both relative (different leadership styles are appropriate in different situations) and more absolute (there is, after all, a leadership style and a situation that are most desirable). A leader should thus analyze their employees' competence and motivation and adapt their leadership style accordingly. But, in the slightly longer term, leadership should also focus on increasing employees' competence and motivation to contribute to the business.

This more long-term dimension, and the more absolute interpretation of Hersey and Blanchard's model, show that their leadership model fits nicely into the basic HR framework. Delegated responsibility and self-governing groups driven by intrinsic motivation *are* the path to successful business. Compared to Blake and Mouton's managerial grid model (see Figure 5.6), it can even be said to be more faithful to the basic assumptions of the HR framework, as Blake and Mouton prescribe a combination of a pure HR leader (with a concern for employees) and a pure structural leader (with a concern for production).

Hersey and Blanchard's situational leadership model is also very consistent with Tuckman's phase model for high-performance teams (see Figure 5.3), as well as with the many variants of this model developed later (Wheelan 2015). The fact that the four phases in Tuckman's model for high-performance teams and the four situations in Hersey and Blanchard's model are so well matched means that they are suitable for combining in an analysis of group performance. Since situational leadership is considered important in other contexts as well as in teams, this model can be said to have a broader scope of use, though it may be the case that Tuckman's phase model for high-performance teams can also be applied to operations not performed by smaller groups and teams.

The HR framework's generic questions, strengths and weaknesses

Just as with the structural framework's concepts and models, those that belong to the HR framework can be used for analysis of the management and organizing of all kinds of activities. Sometimes organizations and businesses have obvious problems, which makes it easy to formulate a set of problems that can control the more theoretically driven analysis. Sometimes, however, the problems are vague and difficult to formulate. In addition, the problem definition can be completely different, depending on which framework we base our view of reality. There is also reason to analyze activities that, at first glance, appear to be completely problem-free. An activity that is perceived as problem-free can actually appear to be extremely problematic when looked at from one or more precisely specified theoretical perspectives. In addition, analyzing success is just as educational as analyzing setbacks.

Generic questions

One way to get started with the analysis work is to ask more general or 'generic' questions based on each framework. The generic questions based on a HR framework (see Table 5.2) can be asked in more or less all situations and just about all activities. They can thus provide a direction and help us to get started with a theory-driven analysis of management and organizing based on a HR framework. The 'IS' question

Table 5.2   Generic questions based on a HR framework

IS? (Descriptive analysis)	What needs do employees have?
	Can vary between different staff groups
	What needs are met by the organization?
	Can differ between different parts of the business
SHOULD? (Prescriptive analysis)	Is there a reason for restructuring?
	Should the organization change other HR practices?
	Recruitment, investment and competence strategy
IS? (Descriptive analysis)	Does the management practice Theory X or Theory Y?
	Not obviously the same as they say they do – read critically!
	Is communication good (Model 2)?
SHOULD? (Prescriptive analysis)	Is there any reason for changing leadership?
	To fit the situation and/or to change the situation in the long run?
→ (Conclusions)	To what extent does the HR analysis explain the phenomenon?
	What is unexplained? What new questions will be relevant?

in Table 5.2 is about to find out how the analyzed organizational unit *IS* organized (here in terms of human needs and motivation). The 'SHOULD' question in Table 5.2 is about how the unit *SHOULD* be organized. It is always best to keep these questions and their following analyses apart, since this will make it easier to conclude if the analyzed organizational unit *is* organized the way it *should* be, according to the applied HR theories.

The questions align the analysis to a number of more basic models, but these should of course be supplemented with more analytical instruments to provide additional knowledge, explanatory value and guidance.

Strengths of the HR framework

One of the strengths of the HR framework is that it complements the structural framework at precisely the points where this is weak. Thus, the HR framework encompasses many analytical models that focus on a more complex and psychological person, compared to the economic and rational human implied by the structural framework. Although the HR framework can be seen as a criticism of the structural framework, if we choose the less rigid models, which include more situational analyses, we find major overlaps between the frameworks. These enable the creation of syntheses and analyses that include models based on both frameworks. If the structural framework focuses on the structural and formal, the HR framework focuses on the human and informal. Both frameworks also have the same strength in the form of normative power and 'functionalism'. A rigorous analysis using the HR framework results, just like an analysis based on the structural framework, in conclusions in the form of normative/ prescriptive recommendations. This also means that it is relatively easy to develop proposals for concrete actions based on these frameworks.

The differences between the two frameworks can be seen as a strength at an even deeper level. Although several models from the two frameworks can be said to overlap, they have different normative 'directions'. If it is possible to structure and formalize more, then this should be done, based on the structural framework. If it is possible to enrich, delegate and enable more autonomous and self-governing employees, then this should be done, according to the HR framework. This conflict is a strength because it helps create multi-frame analysis. If we focus on similarities and complements, we miss the opportunity to create the alternative and conflicting conclusions that really force us to understand an organization, a business or a situation in depth. The main strength of the HR framework as an analytical instrument is thus that it both *complements* and *contradicts* the somewhat cold, rational and formal world of the structural framework. As a complement, it makes the overall impression of real business a little more complex but also warmer and more 'human'. As a criticism, it produces conclusions that help us to re-frame reality more in depth.

Weaknesses of the HR framework

As in all basic frameworks, the HR framework sheds light on some aspects of reality, while, at the same time, it more or less completely shields it from others. The normative power of both the structural and the HR frameworks means that they prescribe relatively clearly what is right and what is wrong. This power often facilitates analysis and the development of concrete, alternative courses of action, but it also means that reality is taken more for granted than with frameworks that do not have the same normative power. Analyses of the HR and structural frameworks are more *for* practice than analyses *of and about* practice. Therefore, the structural and HR frameworks can be said to be somewhat naive, in that they take more for granted than the power framework and the symbolic framework. The structural framework can be said to include a naïve belief in rationalism and fact-driven (or 'evidence-based', to use a popular concept) analysis. The HR framework can be said to include a naïve belief in the willingness of good people to contribute to organizations and to the benefit of others.

More specifically, this criticism of the HR framework can be said to be that (1) it is based on a 'middle class' or 'petty bourgeois' ideology that is taken for granted, (2) the almost romantic description of reality misses all the conflicts, influence processes and power struggles that frequently occur in most organizations, and (3) the many models simply cannot cope with an empirical examination. As far as ideological criticism is concerned, the HR framework can be said to take for granted that all people want to advance towards ever-higher ideals, and that we want to do so in our working time and through our work. It is far from self-evident that everyone wants to achieve higher goals and feel intrinsically motivated within their work. It might equally be the case that people want to relax, small-talk and work just to be able to bring home a salary that enables them to enjoy their spare time – the whole idea that self-actualization through work is the meaning of life is perhaps only valid for some.

With regard to the lack of analytical instruments that include analyses of influence, conflict and power, the HR framework can even be criticized for actively concealing such processes, and not merely toning them down. Perhaps it is no coincidence that most analytical models for leadership in companies and organizations can be found within the HR framework. Senior managers usually have a lot of power, a high salary and a privileged position in society. Describing the power and influence processes that enable this is perhaps not so convenient for those at the top – it is better to describe enterprise as a matter of common goals than as skillful management of conflicts and politics. Better to describe organizing as 'management' rather than 'manipulation', given that the aim is to maintain the power structures that are reproduced in our companies and organizations. The lack of power in the HR framework's description of reality can thus be seen as an expression of precisely the power and influence processes that the HR framework helps to conceal.

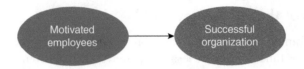

Figure 5.8   An assumed empirical relationship

The models of the HR framework often appear logically and intuitively reasonable. If employees feel happy, they should do a better job. If employees are allowed to participate and decide, their workplaces and tasks should be designed so that they feel happy. High motivation should affect the business for the better. This also has empirical support. Studies show that high moral standards and motivation co-vary with high performance, efficiency and successful organizations (see Figure 5.8).

But covariation is not the same as a cause–effect relationship. There are also studies that suggest that the cause–effect relationship is exactly the opposite, that is, successful organizations create motivated employees. Longitudinal studies show that corporate successes and failures often precede changes in employee motivation. It is more fun to play in a successful team, no matter what causes the success, than to play in a losing team. Why a particular business or organization is successful is not always easy to determine. Perhaps they have an efficiently formalized hierarchical structure? Perhaps they are simply lucky with regards to external circumstances? Whatever the reason, successful organizations will exhibit more motivated employees than less successful organizations, perhaps completely independent of how competence strategies, rewards and actual working conditions and tasks are designed (see Figure 5.9).

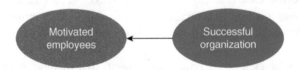

Figure 5.9   A possible reverse cause–effect relationship

If the above is reasonable, then the description of reality that the HR framework offers appears to be even more naive and political than the other frameworks' realities. Therefore, it is even more important to have the ability to re-frame reality using the framework presented in the next two chapters, that is, applying the power framework in a multi-frame analysis.

HR practice versus the HR framework – a final comment

HR as in *human resources*, HRM as in *human resource management*, PM as in *performance management*, TM as in *talent management*, and many similar concepts, are widely used in business practice. These concepts and their closely related processes are part of what is seen as HR practice in companies and organizations. However, this does not mean that they are based on the theoretical human relations/resource framework, which in this book is called the HR framework. On the contrary, much of current HR practice can be said to be based on the basic assumptions of the structural framework. Measuring talent as accurately as possible as an individual trait, or steering and controlling people's performance with the help of quantitative evaluation and reward systems, are very common HR practices. However, they are much closer to how things should be organized, according to the structural framework. The abbreviation HR is therefore somewhat confusing – are we talking about HR *practice* or HR *theory*? This highlights the importance of distinguishing between the two. Sometimes the distinction is made between hard and soft HR. Hard HR practice can then be said to be closer to the structural framework, while soft HR practice can be said to be closer to the HR framework.

The problem surrounding the difference between HR practice and HR theory also identifies a more general dividing line: different theoretical frameworks can be used to analyze the same phenomenon, one and the same practice. Thus, a HR practice of, for instance, a performance management system, can be analyzed with models from all four theoretical frameworks, that is, from the structural, HR, power and symbolic framework perspectives.

Videos

Don't forget to watch the videos to discover more about the key concepts in this chapter: **https://study.sagepub.com/blomberg**

Notes

1 There is some confusion about the concepts of group, working group and team. Some equate 'high-performance group' with 'team', which means that you can write neither low-performance group nor high-performance team. Here, this concept use is not adhered to. 'Group' can be anything from all people who, for example, are over 180 cm tall or a number of people waiting for a bus at a bus stop, to a closely collaborating and high-performance project group. A 'team' is a narrower concept that can be equated with a 'working group', i.e. a group of people who together try to solve a problem or carry out an assignment, a task or a project. Such a working group, or team, can be high-performance, low-performance or something in between. In the following, 'group', 'working group' and 'team' are used interchangeably.

2 The best known of these methods is probably SCRUM. Scrum is a concept taken from rugby where it is the name of the moment at which the ball is set in motion, beginning a play. See www.mountaingoatsoftware.com/agile/scrum or www.scribd.com/document/35686704/Scrum-Guide.

6

Stakeholders, Power, Politics and Conflict – The Basics of the Power Framework

There are many definitions of what constitutes an organization. Most of these emphasize some kind of structure, in the form of common goals, a common culture or a common value system. All these definitions agree that organization always includes some sort of stable and continuous whole. If the system, group, culture or common values were constantly changing, and the organization reacted to everything in its environment, it would no longer be an organization. Instead, it would be some sort of dissolved, reactive organism. The definitions also have in common that they are explicitly or implicitly based on individuals in the organization subordinating themselves to the system, the collective, the culture or the values. If everyone did exactly what they felt like doing, spontaneously, creatively or reactively, the organization would not work. A functioning organization requires that it does not respond to everything in its environment, that is, it has a certain inertia, and that it controls and restricts its members' individual desires and actions. This is important to emphasize at a time when all popular texts – in best-selling management books, on blogs and in other media, in education programs and in a lot of research – without further thought present the image of present-day and future businesses being all about speed, flexibility, innovation and creativity. Management is now said to be about change, not about creating inertia and continuity. If one draws the reasoning to its extreme, no organizations could exist.

A stakeholder and power framework constructs a powerful argument against the above reasoning. How can we talk about common goals or a common culture, or an optimally efficient structure, when our organizations and our society consist of such a multitude of individuals with different backgrounds, education, interests and positions? Shouldn't these at least have some different interests and goals? And how can we speak in terms of efficiency without first saying something about efficiency for what, for whom and based on what goals? The concept of efficiency becomes quite meaningless if we don't tie it to something around 'efficiency for what?' What goals, or who's goals, should the efficient organization fulfill as efficiently as possible? If we do not include the formulation of goals, and the process used for choice of goals over others, in the analysis, the conclusions reached might be quite flawed. And even more importantly, our actions and organizations might work in directions that do not benefit anything or anyone. For example, is the fact that our companies and organizations are better than ever at exploiting the Earth's resources an example of desirable efficiency? Do we really want a working life that makes us sit still in front of screens most of the time we are awake? Do we become happy and satisfied by displaying our toughly disciplined exterior and ideal image of our lives on social media? Are we becoming happier by consuming clothes, food, electronics, home furnishings, cars and other products at a higher rate than ever, instead of being outdoors, walking to the grocery store, repairing and reusing our clothes and, above all, socializing face to face, being neighborly, showing trust and talking about how we want the world to develop and about how to achieve that? Who or what is it that has decided that it should be the way it is? Why do so many seem to equate the meaning of life with career and consumption – even though this may end up being the main cause of the destruction of life as we know it?

Answering these questions requires an analysis of stakeholders, that is, actors with different agendas, and of power processes, that is, how we place ourselves above or below others, in our inner circles, in organizations, and in society in general, a society that is nowadays increasingly global.

We begin the chapter by looking at the historical roots of the power framework and how the political environment shaped its development. We then outline the basic assumptions of the framework before discussing why power, and thus the power framework, is often perceived to be insensitive, irrational, unprofessional and illegitimate. We then present two key power models: Lukes' (1974) three dimensions of power, the first two being focused on this chapter, and Pfeffer's (1983) model of conflict and power struggle. We look in detail at the importance of mapping the political landscape to identify actors, their interests and their power bases, and then use this as a starting point for designing an effective power strategy. This is followed by a discussion of two established negation models, before the chapter concludes with a brief discussion of the limitations of these models that primarily focus on the first and second of Lukes' dimensions of power.

The historical roots of the power framework

Like most theories and perspectives in contemporary management research, the power framework has 'always' existed, albeit beyond what we now define as management or organizational theory. In philosophy, sociology and, not least, political science, models and theories about stakeholders, power, influence processes and conflicts have been around for a long time. Historically, the framework has, if anything, dominated studies of politics, political leadership, military organization and military strategy. A classic book still present in both the exercising of power and military organization is *The Art of War*, which is often attributed to the Chinese strategist Sun Zi (500BC/2015). The origin of the book is much debated but dates back at least to around 500 BC. This classic text has inspired many, from Napoleon and Mao to the fictional financier Gordon Gecko in the movie *Wall Street* from 1987. Another classic dealing with political leadership and the exercising of power is Machiavelli's *The Prince*, first published in 1532.

However, within the current management and organizational research field, the power framework did not develop as a distinct perspective until the late 1960s and early 1970s. At the time, this new perspective was part of the prevailing spirit of the age, which was expressed in, for example, the civil rights movement in the USA during the second half of the 1950s and into the 1960s, 'the Summer of Love' in San Francisco in 1967 and the student revolts around the world, culminating in the May Revolution in Paris in the spring of 1968. Common to these events was a reaction to the establishment and a political force that concerned, among other things, a redistribution of resources and a struggle for freedom and solidarity against racism and class oppression. In Europe, this can also be linked to the ending of dictatorship in both Spain and Portugal in the 1970s. Acting politically and discussing power, conflict and revolution became an integral part of both younger and older people's everyday lives in the late 1960s and 1970s.

The development of the power framework can also be seen as a direct consequence of a number of empirical studies, the most influential of which was Andrew M. Pettigrew's (1973) acclaimed study of decision-making in a British clothing and furniture chain. After an extensive anthropological study (long-term participatory observations within the company), Pettigrew showed that a decision made on which new administrative data system to purchase was not primarily a result of some sort of rational or functional process in which the company's needs and the offerings of various suppliers were evaluated. Neither was the decision-making process characterized by communication aimed at different actors in the company coming to a consensus on which system would be the most appropriate. Pettigrew's study resulted in organizing and decision-making being described as a political process in which different stakeholders with different goals and agendas use different power strategies and methods to seek support for the alternative that is best for them in a constantly ongoing political power game. The study can be said to have shattered the then prevailing image of management as a rational process, as the design of functional systems, or as the creation of common goals and committed employees. Once Pettigrew had broken down the door, a tsunami of studies followed, which showed that companies and organizations are primarily arenas for political processes and power struggles, and that large companies and organizations are power-exercising entities with considerable power held over society and its citizens.

The fundamental assumptions of the power framework

The power framework includes theories and models with quite different starting points. Some are about how to practically act within the framework of organization and leadership, while others express more critical analyses of how companies, organizations and society develop over time. Formulating basic assumptions upon which these rather different models and theories are based is thus problematic. The four basic assumptions formulated below are more consistent with the action-oriented and more practical models described in this chapter than with the more complex, critical and explanatory models in the next chapter, where the power framework is elaborated on in more depth. However, they constitute a good starting point for providing an initial understanding of the framework:

1. There are always interests, agendas and goals that contradict each other. Individuals, groups, organizations and various social bodies are therefore always in conflict with each other.
2. Conflicts cannot be resolved by making rational decisions about solutions that are best for everyone, or by agreeing on common goals. One cannot therefore design effective organizations. What is an effective way of achieving one stakeholder's goal is not necessarily effective for other stakeholders.
3. Organizational structures, formal and informal processes are always an expression of stakeholders' exercise of power and influence.
4. Conflicts cannot always be resolved, but they are managed more or less rationally. Studying power and influence processes can increase the likelihood of getting through a certain agenda and achieving specific goals.

Conflict should not, however, be equated with open political power games. Conflict can prevail (or, rather, always prevails, according to the power framework) silently, completely unnoticed. According to some power theories, it is precisely when power cannot be seen – it might even look like everyone is united and wants the same things – that power is most skillfully exercised and most effective. Neither is conflict obviously negative. According to the power framework, there is always conflict, so it is rather a question of managing conflicts in a sensible way. A hidden or unnoticed conflict becoming visible and taking the form of an open power struggle can even be a solution, rather than a problem. In particular, when looking at organizational changes in old, large and rigid organizations, or at innovation and creativity, making underlying conflicts visible can be the beginning of a solution. On this point, the

[handwritten margin note: 4 Basic Assumptions Of Power Framework]

power framework can be said to be in stark contrast to the HR framework, which, on the contrary, states that conflicts by definition are dysfunctional and that they should and can be resolved with the help of the right kind of communication. The HR framework's ideal regarding honest, open communication, common goals and consensus is, from a power framework perspective, an impossibility. If a situation is characterized by interacting stakeholders perceiving there to be consensus, then we can assume that one or more stakeholders are playing a skillful power game.

A hushed-up and critical perspective

In more public conversations between employees in companies and organizations, between managers and, not least, between senior managers, power is rarely talked about using the terminology of the power framework. Management, organizing and leadership are said to be about 'setting the processes' (structural framework) and finding, developing and investing in talents (HR framework). In addition, the concept of core values is usually mentioned (this can be seen as an expression of the symbolic framework; see Chapter 8). Even in popular management literature and in business press, business and organizing are usually described as a rational process, where both the goals and the means are clear and desirable for most. Leadership is described as 'coaching' and motivating, rather than as 'controlling' and manipulating. Goals are often described as some kind of universal given that benefits everything and everyone: organizations must be innovative and efficient, companies must increase their competitiveness and profitability.

There is a notable absence of the power framework in the public debate and texts on management and leadership. As part of the Stockholm School of Economics' executive education program, course participants, in the form of experienced practitioners, managers and leaders, are sometimes given short, introductory examinations. Their responses to the questions 'What is an organization?' and 'How do you manage them?' have been categorized based on which of the four basic frameworks they can be said to express (see Figure 6.1). The structural and HR frameworks strongly dominate in participants' responses. The symbolic framework (discussed in Chapters 8 and 9) is in a clear third place, and the power framework is definitely last. Experienced practitioners, managers and leaders do not seem to consider that organizing and leadership have so much to do with power and influence.

In public descriptions of management, organizing and leadership, the power framework is thus conspicuous in its absence. But it doesn't take much for the exact same people who don't talk about power publicly to begin talking about it. In the elevator, at the coffee machine, behind closed doors and in other informal contexts, people talk all the more about power and politics in organizations. However, these conversations are often perceived as insensitive and unprofessional – power is seen as something

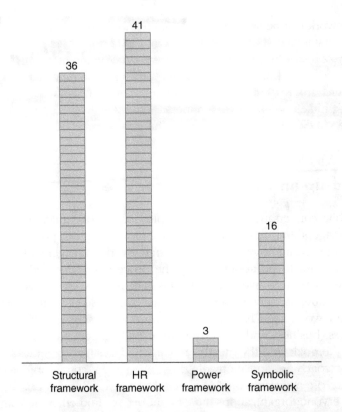

Figure 6.1   Responses by participants on an executive education program to the question 'What is an organization?' categorized into four basic frameworks

that cannot and should not be analyzed or structured in a more formalized way. One business leader expressed this as follows: 'The fact that everything is about power is common knowledge, but there is nothing anyone can do about it.' From a power framework perspective, a great deal can be done – however, perhaps not *about* it, but *because of* it.

There are several reasons why the power framework is not expressed in more public contexts:

- It is not perceived as being something scientific or rational that can be managed using structured knowledge and analysis.
- It is perceived as being illegitimate and immoral and therefore better suited as material for gossip than as a management method.
- It is perceived as being insensitive to unsuccessful or vulnerable people and groups who may be disturbed by their situation being described.

- It is perceived as being insensitive to those who possess a lot of power and/or are in superior positions – power-makers do not benefit from the power processes that have led to them occupying superior positions being revealed.

The reasons listed above are related. The fact that 'power and politics' in organizations is not perceived as a rationally or scientifically based way of organizing, also leads to it being perceived as less legitimate. The fact that it is perceived as irrational, unscientific and immoral also means that those who hold a lot of power and a superior position would be perceived as being less entitled to these if it emerged that their position had more to do with the exercising of power than with knowledge, competence and hard work. From a power framework perspective, for example, senior managers are better off emphasizing the structural and HR frameworks rather than the power framework. It follows from this that the power framework can be seen to be highly critical of other frameworks, for at least two reasons:

1. The power framework is critical of the structural and HR frameworks' description of organizing and leadership as rationally and scientifically based activities aimed at benefiting all actors involved. According to the power framework, organizational structures and processes are not some kind of optimized tool for producing goods and services as efficiently as possible. Organizations are not characterized by people working together to achieve common goals.
2. The power framework is a more ideological criticism of how other frameworks, as well as more popular descriptions of management, organization and leadership, hush up the exercising of power and political processes that favor certain groups at the expense of others. This more ideological criticism becomes even more relevant when we analyze power, influence, social groups and minorities. When analyzing, for example, the scarcity of women and ethnic minorities in high management positions, the models of the power framework have a high explanatory value.

Despite, or perhaps thanks to, the critical aspect of the power framework, its analytical concepts, models and theories can be used to understand and form the basis for decisions and actions in organizations. They can be used by managers, leaders and others alike. However, they cannot prescribe strategies and solutions that are best for everyone in a more specific situation – just what is good for some stakeholders and thus less good for others. What is good for the marketing department may not be so good for the production department. What is good for senior management may not be so good for middle managers. What is good for one consulting team is perhaps less good for another. From a broader societal perspective, however, the power framework, precisely because of its more 'revealing' and critical direction, can certainly be said to contribute to fairer and more rational organizations. What can be seen as a loss in the short term, based on the position of a particular actor, can, in the longer term and with a broader perspective, be seen as something that is good for everyone. If the goal is to create a just and reason-based society, where all individuals and groups have the same opportunities and conditions to survive, acquire jobs, educate themselves, make a career and live meaningful lives, then the power framework is highly relevant.

Lukes' three dimensions of power

There are many different, complementary and partly contradictory definitions of power. An influential categorization is Lukes' formulation (1974) of the three faces or dimensions of power: decision-making power, power over the agenda and power over thought. These three dimensions can be seen as an analytical division of power exercised simultaneously in one and the same situation. To understand power in depth, the analysis must include all three dimensions. Lukes' categorization can also be seen as a description of the evolution of power theories over time, from relatively easily identifiable and analyzable processes based on a narrow dimension of power, to becoming wider and including more and more vague dimensions of how power is practiced. This chapter, looks at the analytical models that focus on the first two, more concrete dimensions of power. In the next chapter, these are supplemented with analytical models that largely focus on the third dimension of power.

Decision-making power

The first dimension, the power of decision-making, constitutes an application of Dahl's well-established definition of power (1957: 202–3):

> A has power over B to the extent that A can make B do anything that B would not otherwise have done.

The first dimension of power focuses on how one or more actors influence one or more other actors to perform or refrain from performing a particular act or making a certain decision. Applied to a decision-making situation, an analysis of this power definition becomes relatively simple to implement. For example, the analytical work of describing what two or more actors want to achieve in a particular situation will study how the different actors work to push their agenda. The results of these processes can then be compared to see which one or more actors have succeeded best in influencing the others and thus fulfilling their own goal/s better than other actors. Such an analysis provides a lot of information about how a political power process happens. According to Lukes, an analysis of the first dimension of power still only provides limited knowledge of how power is exercised. The analysis needs to be supplemented with analyses of the second and third dimensions of power.

Power over the agenda

Regardless of which interest or alternative decision 'wins' in competition with other interests and alternative decisions, we can ask why these particular alternative decisions, and the subject matter they are about, ended up on the agenda in the first place. Power is not only about what alternative decision is taken, given a particular matter, but also about why some issues end up on the agenda, while others don't. In other words, if you can control the context within which decisions are made, you can control much more than the outcome of a single decision-making process. A power analysis therefore needs to include why some issues ends up on the agenda while others do not.

The importance of such an analysis is well illustrated by the anecdote about the whiteboard. Discussions at workplaces, even among managers and leaders and at formal meetings, can be taken up by questions such as where to place a whiteboard or which coffee machine to buy. Senior managers and competent employees devote precious hours to such trivial issues, instead of dealing with more important and perhaps more conflict-ridden questions. An analysis of the second dimension of power – power over the agenda – focuses precisely on why these more important issues do not come up on the agenda. Who are the actors who have power over the agenda, and what do they do to obtain this power?

This dimension can also be said to be relatively simple to analyze, albeit somewhat trickier than the first dimension of power. Instead of studying a specific issue on the agenda, and the decision-making process concerning that specific issue, you need to identify issues that are not on the agenda that could have been there. You can start with what is on the agenda and then add more issues that are not. Which actors and interests exist in the studied organization? Which actors have the power to get their interests represented as issues on the agenda? Which actors do not have that power? The most interesting issues for study might not be on any formal agenda, but still be possible to identify by studying actors, interests and issues in the context of, but not included in, the agenda. When these actors, interests and issues have been identified, the processes that lead to some issues ending up on the agenda but most not, can be studied.

Although power over the agenda is included in the analysis, Lukes believes that perhaps the most important dimension of power still might be missed, namely the very formation of interests, goals and definitions of problems and solutions – in other words, how it happens that some actors want something specific in a given situation, while other actors do not seem to want anything in other situations. How is it that certain things are perceived to be problematic, while others are perceived as self-evident or natural – or are seen as non-issues?

Manipulation – power over thought

The third dimension of power, according to Lukes, is the most basic and most insidious. It is invisible and therefore difficult to study and analyze. Manipulation is a form of influence on how others think, perceive and define themselves and their surroundings. Manipulation can be more visible in the form of an actor consciously and systematically exposing other actors to different stimuli that together shape thoughts and perceptions. By describing reality in a certain way, it is possible to control how others perceive it. For example, a situation can be defined as a crisis to create support for more extensive change work. Conversely, problems can be understated if it suits the purpose. In these cases, you do not primarily control which solution is chosen in a specific problem situation, or which of a number of specific issues are put on the agenda. The impact is more indirect and happens by influencing actors' thoughts and experiences, and whether what is perceived is a problem or a solution at all.

This third dimension can thus be even more elusive than the first two. An analysis of it can lead to the identification of taken-for-granted frameworks and implicit common-sense thinking among actors that benefit and disadvantage various actors.

Specific sources cannot always be identified for why actors have specific perspectives and think in certain ways. Who or what has the power then? We can then talk about cultural control or a norm-controlled activity where no actor is actually aware of how it is controlled and by whom. Thus, actors can sometimes be identified who deliberately exercise manipulation, while, in other cases, we have to settle for seeing power over thought as originating from more cultural and/or structural processes without any individual actor's conscious influence. Analyzing this type of diffuse power process may be best suited to the help of models belonging to the symbolic framework (see Chapters 8 and 9). It follows from this that the power and symbolic frameworks largely overlap and complement each other in terms of analyses of cultural control.

Both a meta-model and a precise analytical tool

Lukes' three faces or dimensions of power can be seen as a meta-model, according to which other, more specific models can be sorted. Some analytical models are best suited to analyzing the first and second dimensions of power, while others are best suited to analyzing the third. Lukes' model can, however, also be adapted to more specific analyses of organizing and leadership. Can, for example, the exercise of power by actors be explained by what dimensions these have or do not have power over? Another model that can also be seen as more bridging and general, and which, at the same time, invites more precise analysis of specific conditions, is Pfeffer's model for analyzing the strength of conflicts and causes of political power struggle.

Pfeffer's model of conflict and power struggle

According to the power framework, there is always conflict. However, conflict can vary in strength: from being unnoticed by and unproblematic for the actors involved,

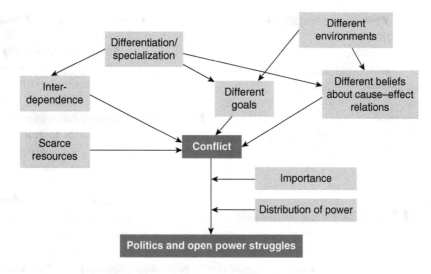

Figure 6.2   **Pfeffer's (1983) model of causes of conflict and power struggle**

to constituting the basis of open power struggle. Pfeffer's model (see Figure 6.2) can explain why there is always conflict, why it can vary in strength and why the conflict sometimes flares up into open political power struggle. It can also form the basis for developing different strategies for managing conflict.

Causes of conflict and open power struggle

The variables in the upper half of Figure 6.2 are what Pfeffer (1983) thinks are reasons why there is always conflict in organizations. Different parts of an organization – people, functions, departments and levels – are in different environments or surroundings. Top management works with other managers and management teams, they meet owner representatives and analysts from the financial sector and they represent their companies in the media. A sales department interacts with customers and their buyers. Product developers move in technical circuits where new technology and construction are in focus. Organization members are influenced by the different environments in which they operate, and, since these are different, organization members also differ in their mindset, perspective and goals. Although they might agree on common goals, for example that the organization should achieve a certain profitability, it is highly likely that staff have different views on how to achieve these goals. A salesperson may feasibly think that an increased sales budget would increase sales and thus profitability. A product developer may instead want to invest in the development of better products.

Another root cause of conflict in organizations is division of work or specialization (differentiation in the figure). Due to work division, different people do different things, they develop different competencies and thus also different perspectives and objectives. Work division therefore precludes the inequality created by different parts of the organization operating in different environments. This means that the more extensive the work division is (which is the basis for efficiency, according to the structural framework), the more conflicts there are. Work division also creates dependencies between the work-divided parts. A sales department has no products to sell without a manufacturing department that manufactures them or a purchasing department that purchases them. More work division leads to increasing dependencies, which leads to even more conflict.

One final basic reason why there is always conflict in organizations is limited resources. Resources are always limited, but to varying degrees and of different types. Money is a resource to which there is rarely unlimited access. But limited access to personnel, management positions, premises, time constraints and more can also constitute grounds for conflict. If a company is doing well in terms of sales and profitability, conflicts will be mitigated by the abundant supply of resources. If things are going badly and resources become increasingly limited, conflicts increase. There will simply be more fighting over how a small, shrinking pot of resources should be distributed, compared to a large and growing one.

But, in order for a conflict to really flare up to an open power struggle, with parties who are actively trying to fight each other and each other's agendas, Pfeffer's model requires two conditions (the lower part of Figure 6.2). The first is that there is something that is important enough for the parties involved to care about and spend time and energy arguing about. It might be about the implementation of new systems or new strategies that could greatly change the prevailing power relations. It might be about redundancies or about significantly redistributed resources. But, even if there are actors with conflicting interests in an issue that is perceived as important, it is not certain that there will be an open power struggle. For that to happen, power must be reasonably dispersed. If an actor is superior with regard to their possession of power bases, that is, that power is very concentrated, other actors will find it hard to challenge them. However, if power is more widespread, there are opportunities to fight back.

Strategies for managing conflict

Pfeffer's model can be said to be primarily analytical. It gives an answer to the question of why there is more or less conflict in organizations, and why there are sometimes open power struggles. However, it can also be reformulated into a number of highly normative recommendations for how to deal with conflict and power struggle. Each explanatory variable points to a concrete strategy for how this might be done.

Create homogeneity and consensus on goals and means

According to the power framework, people can never completely agree, but they can disagree more or less. As disparity, according to Pfeffer's model, is one of the root causes of conflict, one can thus reduce the degree of conflict by reducing this disparity. By focusing on more comprehensive and abstract goal formulations, space is created for actors to interpret and formulate their own agendas into these goals. For example, setting a goal of a 17 percent margin does not stipulate which specific actions should be performed in order to achieve this. Another way is to reduce work division and the degree of heterogeneity in staff and unit environments. You can rotate staff between different units, or you can work in teams instead of with individual working tasks. Although this may be ineffective (at least according to the structural framework), as it increases homogeneity and thereby reduces conflict, it can still be an effective power strategy. The fact that an inefficient structure can be an effective power strategy shows how different frameworks are in opposition to each other. But, even with a power framework, a relatively homogeneous workforce is associated with risks. Heterogeneity and different experiences and interests can, if properly managed, be a prerequisite for organizational change, innovation and creativity. If disparities are reduced and/or avoided and hidden by skilled rhetoric, then organizations risk becoming stiff and sluggish. In such situations, conflicts and even open power struggles can be part of a solution, rather than a problem.

Create a surplus of resources

As scarce resources are a reason why conflicts are intensified, a logical conclusion is that conflicts can be reduced by creating more resources. That is why there is less conflict in profitable companies than in crisis-ridden companies. The problem is how the surplus should be created. Acquiring capital via the financial market (through bank loans, bonds/private investments, preferred stock, new issuing of shares, etc.), that is, other than by selling goods and services to your customers, is one way to go. If there is a shortage of, for example, managerial positions (perhaps due to a merger), these can be increased via various structural solutions. Extra-large management groups are sometimes formed in order to avoid power struggles about who will become what. The same can apply to other positions in an organization. It may not be effective from other perspectives, but it may be according to a power framework. Conversely, if there is a shortage of staff, they can be employed or hired temporarily or consultants and others can be brought in. However, all these ways have a common disadvantage: they are usually quite costly. The financial market wants to get paid for its money, managers and other employees want a salary, and so on. Often, this type of measure is therefore time-limited, in order to avoid conflicts developing into open power struggles in a particular situation, rather than a long-term strategy.

Reduce and downplay the significance of a decision

The third and final strategy, based on Pfeffer's model, is to downplay the importance of a certain decision. One concrete way to do this is to divide it into several small decisions. Instead of deciding on a large initiative in the Chinese market, for example, it may be decided to implement a less costly pilot project, but one designed so that it can be easily scaled up. Another way is to put a time limit on initiatives. For example, it is much easier to agree on granting a temporary building permit than a permanent one. However, there are always opportunities to extend temporary building permits or make them permanent. A third way is not to change anything from a purely formal point of view, but rather to downplay the importance of a decision by how it is described to the involved actors. If it can be assumed that there are strong opponents to it (something which should be analyzed with the aid of theory; see below), it is perhaps better to describe a decision as less important than to describe it as absolutely crucial for the company's survival. How this type of description can affect actors, their interests and actions is an issue that is addressed in more detail in Chapter 8 in the sections on symbolic leadership and action rationality. With regard to this more manipulative and symbolic exercising of power (the third dimension of power), the power and symbolic frameworks overlap each other considerably.

Mapping the political landscape

Pfeffer's model, described above, is a suitable starting point for an analysis of power and influence in organizations. However, it requires 'support' in the form of complementary models to provide a really informative picture of what the political landscape looks like in an organization. If supplemented, the analysis can result in even more action-based knowledge, that is, it can inform actors about which options are more suitable to act on.

In order to answer the question of whether power is concentrated or dispersed, that is, one of the two variables that, according to Pfeffer's model, sometimes cause conflicts to develop into open power struggles, most of the relevant actors and their interests need to be identified and how much power each one has must be analyzed. Independent of Pfeffer's model, it is also appropriate to map the political landscape before attempting to implement a certain action. The chances of being able to manage any resistance to this action will increase considerably if you map out which stakeholders are for and against it, and what power bases they possess. It is smart to identify where any mines are located before choosing which path to take over the field.

An initial listing of actors and their interests

The identification of stakeholders is facilitated by listing all possible actors with a direct or indirect interest in a particular issue – the more the merrier. It is often enough as a careful thought exercise, that is, you simply think through which actors might have some sort of stake in the current problem. You can also let it become a topic for creative discussion with people who share your own interest. However, it is important to think broadly – there are always more stakeholders than those who seem obvious, so it is about trying to identify the less obvious actors in the current political landscape.

Once this list is in place, you can identify the interests, objectives or agendas of each actor with regard to the issue in question. Sometimes it is enough to try to determine whether each actor is for or against a particular issue, for example a planned reorganization. In practice, it is likely that a number of actors are more or less in favor of or against certain parts of a planned reorganization. But, even if all the nuances of different actors' interests are not identified, the analysis can provide a lot of information on what the political landscape looks like. It is worth noting that there can often be individuals (often managers but also others) who very clearly state their support for or against a particular issue, such as a reorganization, but it does not necessarily mean that these individuals have the support of their group, department, division, and so on. You then have to mix up the list of individuals and groupings.

In the example given in Table 6.1, there appears to be disagreement in the production department. One should then break up the various actors there and handle them separately. Could it also be the same in the group executive and in other departments? It may also be relevant to identify actors outside the focused organization. What about suppliers, customers, owners and other actors who might have an interest in the organization and in the planned reorganization?

Table 6.1 A simple list of actors and their interests, given a reorganization

Actor	For or against
Group executive	Declared support FOR the reorganization
R&D department	Strongly FOR the reorganization
Marketing department	Clearly AGAINST the reorganization
Production department	No consensus – individual manager FOR, employees AGAINST
Purchasing department	AGAINST
Administration	Indifferent, slightly FOR
Supplier A	FOR
Suppliers B and C	AGAINST
B2B customers	FOR
Private consumers	Probably AGAINST

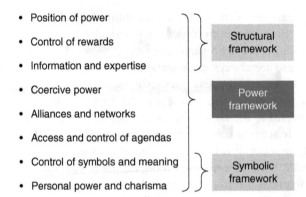

Figure 6.3   A categorization of different power bases and their relation to the four basic frameworks

Source: Based on Bolman & Deal (2013)

Power bases

After identifying the relevant actors and interests, an attempt is made to determine how much power each actor has with regard to the current issue. Who is not just against the reorganization, but may even have the clout to counteract it? Who does not only support the reorganization, but may also be an important power factor in overcoming opposition to it, that is, a candidate to create an alliance with? To answer these questions, the above list can be filled in by noting the sources of power, that is, the power bases, each actor possesses. By starting from a categorization of different power bases, you can both describe an actor's total power and obtain information about what type of power bases it consists of. There are many categorizations of power (the three dimensions of power can be seen as one of them). Figure 6.3 summarizes the many categorizations of power bases and the organizational framework they fall under.

As shown in Figure 6.3, the power framework comprises a more comprehensive and complex picture of what constitutes sources of power compared to the structural and symbolic frameworks (symbolized in Figure 6.3 by the top and bottom groupings). The structural framework reduces power to formal hierarchical position, rewards (in the form of salary and promotion) and knowledge (information and expertise). These power bases can be seen as the rational, formal and structural functional power bases.

The power framework adds a handful of power bases, however. No matter what position you have, what ability to influence rewards or what knowledge base you possess, you can sometimes force others to perform or refrain from performing a certain action. Compulsion may be forced by an explicit threat of violence, by slander or harassment, or by subtler expressions, such as sanctions (ridicule, questioning) or rewards other than salary and promotion (such as friendship, an invitation to attend an informal circle). By building relationships and networks with other powerful actors, you can increase your power despite a low formal hierarchical position. Through the active and proactive exercising of power, you can take initiative and gain control of the agenda. Through symbolic and charismatic leadership, you can create commitment and meaning and define situations and options so that others perceive them as being beneficial to their own agenda.

With the latter two power bases, the power framework significantly overlaps the symbolic framework (as Lukes' third power dimension, 'manipulation', indicates; see above) and will be discussed in more depth in Chapters 7 and 8.

In Figure 6.3, the HR framework is conspicuous in its absence. This is because, from this perspective, power and influence processes, conflicts and open power struggles are seen as dysfunctional and as something that cannot exist in well-functioning organizations. Knowledge could indeed constitute a power base – also according to the HR framework – but since the ideal from this perspective is to spread knowledge and minimize work division, that is, to make individual knowledge collective and common, knowledge does not constitute a clear power base either. According to the power framework, such a perspective is naïve and risks concealing rather than identifying, analyzing and managing power and influence. The power and HR frameworks thus lie in stark contrast to each other.

A generic stakeholder matrix

To obtain an overview of the political landscape, all relevant actors, their respective interests and their power bases can be summarized in a matrix (see Figure 6.4). The different power bases can be weighed together and summed up into a total power position for each actor. Such a matrix also shows which actors have similar interests, which power bases the actors have and thus which actors complement and/or compete for a certain type of power. The matrix and its contents can then form the basis for the design of effective power strategies. This is not effective in any superior, objective or universal sense, but effective given the interests of a particular actor or actors.

When the actors' power bases are summarized, an overview is also obtained of whether and to what extent power is concentrated or dispersed. This can then constitute the input value in the overall analysis of power, according to Pfeffer's model (see above). If power is dispersed, the risk/chance of conflicts developing into open power struggles increases; if it is concentrated, the risk/chance of this is less, all other factors being equal. But the Figure 6.4 matrix and its contents are also the first step for an actor who wants to design an effective power strategy. The first step in designing an effective power strategy is to map and analyze the political landscape.

Goals and power sources \ Actor	A	B	C	D	E	F
Goal						
Position						
Knowledge						
Control of rewards						
Coercive power						
Alliances and networks						
Control over agendas						
Control over symbols						
Charisma						
Total power						

Figure 6.4   A generic stakeholder matrix (describes the political landscape)

The generic stakeholder matrix in Figure 6.4 includes a lot of information and many estimates. Sometimes it is therefore appropriate to further simplify the description of the political landscape. When an analysis is conducted, the aim is to find out as much as possible, but when the conclusions of the analysis are to be presented, a simplified picture can form the basis for more effective communication. One way to simplify the generic stakeholder matrix is to reduce the goals and interests of all actors to two alternatives, for example for and against a particular proposal, such as a reorganization. All power bases can also be added together into total amounts of power for each player. The political landscape can then be described as in Figure 6.5. It is important to emphasize that there is large scope for interpretation when trying to determine how much power a particular player has. However, it is better to try to make an estimate than not to do it at all. Regardless of what material the assessment is based on and how carefully the parts in this are considered, the result will never be more than an approximation.

There are many informative variations of the above image of the political landscape. For example, you can select a number of actor groups and try to assess how these groups perceive the political landscape. How does management perceive the political landscape? How is it perceived in the marketing department? Based on such analysis, a power strategy can be set up (see below): Which actor should you try to influence in terms of how the situation is perceived? Which are suitable to approach and build an alliance with? Which should be co-opted? You can also illustrate how the landscape changes over time, or how it would need to change over time, given a

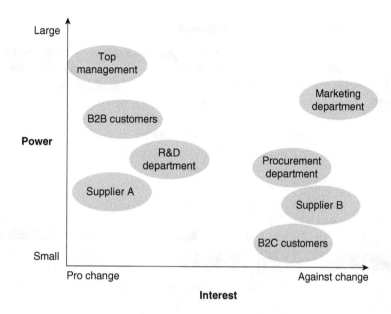

Figure 6.5 An even more simplified picture of the political landscape

Source: Based on Bolman & Deal (2013)

certain actor's agenda (for example, your own). A very simplified picture of the complex power and influence processes, which, according to the power framework, are always going on, can thus inform actors and be the basis for more knowledge-based and effective decisions and actions.

An effective power strategy

It is thus advantageous to begin designing an effective power strategy by mapping the political landscape, preferably with the aid of the above analytical models, that is, by listing actors, their interests and power bases. According to Bolman and Deal (2013), however, the design of an effective power strategy includes further steps and can thus be summarized in the following five points:

1. map the political landscape
2. design and customize the agenda
3. build networks and alliances
4. bargain and negotiate
5. co-opt and manipulate.

Design and customize the agenda

Designing and adapting the agenda, that is, designing a concrete proposal, solution or option that can actually be implemented, means that the agenda should, to some extent, be a consequence of what the political landscape looks like and how it can be managed. Although an analysis based on a structural or HR framework may result in a clear and optimal strategy, this may be completely unrealistic given the interests and agendas of other powerful actors. From a power framework perspective, the agenda should then be adapted to what is reasonable to carry out on the basis of a power analysis.

If, for example, a structural analysis of a company results in a conclusion that the company should be restructured from a professional hierarchy into more of a machine bureaucracy, but powerful actors representing the profession oppose this, according to the power framework, the restructuring should be adapted to suit these powerful actors slightly better. One should definitely adapt how the proposal is formulated and how it is implemented, but one is often also forced to adapt the more substantive content of the proposal. In this imaginary example, instead of centralizing with the aid of an expanded technostructure, it is perhaps enough to expand the support structures (see Mintzberg's structural configurations in Chapter 2 for a review of these concepts). At a later stage, these support structures can then be made increasingly powerful, that is, transformed into a technostructure, and thus achieve a centralization, an expanded technostructure and a more machine-bureaucratically organized company.

Build networks and alliances

Although it may not be possible to push through the exact strategy that is considered the best in a given situation, it is not always necessary to completely adapt it to the interests of other powerful actors. Instead, power bases can be increased by building networks and alliances. However, in order to implement as much of your agenda as possible, you should not build networks and alliances with just anyone. By studying the political landscape, you can instead identify those actors whose agendas most closely resemble your own and those who have as many power bases as possible. Building an alliance with an actor who has similar goals means that you do not have to compromise so much within the alliance, and building an alliance with actors who have many power bases makes the alliance powerful. It is thus a matter of balancing the alliance's power with the amount of compromise required within the alliance. Effective networking and alliance building can lead to seemingly weak actors, that is, actors with few power bases, being able to jointly implement options that have large and strong opponents.

Bargain and negotiate

It is always possible to bargain and negotiate about different options, and there is more to such negotiations than just the content of each option. Negotiation technique is an extensive subject in itself. Two influential and practically useful models for how to negotiate effectively are described in a separate section below. However, the main point, according to these models, is that bargaining, negotiation and persuasion are about much more than compromising on the actual content of a proposal or business deal. By separating the more personal from the more task and formal side of a negotiation, or by using seemingly objective or at least socially approved proofs for your arguments, you can be much more successful in a negotiation.

Co-opt and manipulate

A final step in an effective power strategy is what can be seen as an expanded or more long-term negotiation strategy, namely, co-optation and manipulation. It can also be seen as a more insidious way of forming alliances and networks. Co-opting means that instead of circumventing, winning over, bargaining or cooperating with your opponents, you invite them in. By getting opponents to work close to you, over time you can influence how they look at different issues and their own role in relation to these issues. By co-opting opponents, you can make them change their perceptions and interests so that they are closer to your own. A clear example of this is the Swedish law on trade union representation on company boards. Since the unions are on the board and actively participate in the work of the board together with the board's (many more) owner representatives, it is quite likely that the union's representatives perceive the company's operations, its opportunities and problems, more from an ownership and management perspective than if they were not included on the board (as union representatives are in a clear minority, their position on the board can also be analyzed using Kanter's minority theory, which is described in the next chapter). By getting your opponent to take a role similar to your own, you can thus influence the opponent's thoughts, perspectives and goals.

Two established negotiation models

Based on behavioral theories (individual and social psychology), studies on persuasion and negotiation have resulted in practically useful models and theories. The two most established of these are Ury, Fisher and Patton's model for 'principled negotiation' (1992) and Cialdini's six principles for persuasion (Cialdini 2009, Cialdini et al. 2002). Negotiations can be both evaluated retrospectively and designed in advance (and continuously) using the principles of these two models. The models can be said to deepen the 'bargaining and negotiating' stage in the above description of an effective power strategy.

Principled negotiation – 'getting to yes'

An important component of a successful power strategy is to negotiate in an effective manner (that is, to avoid compromising on more than is absolutely necessary). An influential model describing what an effective negotiation consists of is the four principles of *principled negotiation* (Ury et al. 1992). According to this negotiation model, a negotiation should be characterized by trying to avoid both hard negotiations on positions and soft negotiations where relations are more important than factual issues. According to this model, a principled negotiation must be characterized by the fact that it can:

- separate the people from the problem
- focus on (the counterpart's) interests
- generate more options
- refer to 'objective' evaluation criteria.

Separate the people from the problem

Instead of being a 'soft' negotiator, who mainly strives to create a good and long-term relationship with their negotiating party, and instead of being a 'hard' negotiator, who does anything to enforce their agenda, including jeopardizing all possibilities for continued business and collaboration, you should combine the soft and hard negotiating styles. The combination means that you are soft on people and hard on problems. This, however, requires you to separate people and problems. Avoiding personal attacks and criticism, and instead devoting energy to listening, confirming and showing consideration and affection to the other person, increases the chance of getting more of your agenda through. It is a question of creating a relationship where the parties perceive each other as partners in problem-solving, rather than opponents in a conflict.

Focus on (the counterpart's) interests

The second fundamental principle of a successful negotiation is that it should be characterized by focusing on interests rather than on positions. If two actors have conflicting positions with regard to which path to follow, it is difficult to agree on any kind of option that does not mean that one of the actors loses. If you instead look at the interests behind different options, an option that benefits (or is perceived to benefit) both actors can be more easily formulated. Although the interests of the actors differ, it is always possible to find some common ground. The further from concrete solutions and options you argue, the easier it is to identify common interests. For example, most actors feel the need for fundamental security and an economic situation that is reasonably sustainable. If you first identify and talk about the other person's interests, the smaller the chance that this other person sees themselves as an opponent. It is also a question of identifying common interests early on and showing how the more concrete options you are advocating can be seen as an expression of these. If you can show that both you and your counterpart love skiing (and that melting glaciers is a major problem), and that you both think that short-term profits are usually over-emphasized compared to sustainable businesses, you will have an easier task in getting both to agree to a long-term investment in high-risk green research and development.

Generate more options

The principle of generating more options is related to the last principle, focusing on interests rather than on concrete actions. If, after all, it is the case that two (or more) parties come to the negotiation, each with their own concrete and contradictory option, one way forward is to try to generate more options. It is a question of avoiding a win–lose situation where fixed positions are in opposition to each other. Instead of centralizing or decentralizing, perhaps you can develop more efficient communication processes. For example, a new IT system may be perceived as (horizontal) communication support, but, despite this, it also implies greater (vertical) governance and control.

Refer to 'objective' evaluation criteria

If, after all, it is not possible to agree on an option, instead of continuing to negotiate which is the best one, you should try to agree on a joint evaluation process. The first step in such an attempt is to try to identify criteria that the parties involved can agree to use in the evaluation of options. More objective criteria are then preferable, that is, criteria that are perceived as objective and exist beyond the parties involved in the conflict. This may be industry standards, research findings or 'best practice'. If other successful organizations have acted in a certain way in a similar situation, then it should be able to work here as well. If IBM became very successful by developing its consulting and solution business, as did HP some years later, why shouldn't we do the same? Once a number of more objective criteria have been identified and accepted, the possibility of agreeing on an option that can be implemented increases.

Whether this is really a 'common' option can be questioned. The choice of criteria is not always obvious, no matter how objective they are perceived to be; and, also, how the criteria are subsequently used provides great scope for different actors to get their particular agenda through. The idea is, however, that it is easier to agree on an evaluation process than on a certain solution. If two children argue about who should get the biggest slice of cake, they might agree on a process that solves this problem: one child gets to divide the cake into two pieces, while the other child gets to choose their piece.

Six principles of persuasion

Another established model for setting up a negotiation has been developed by Cialdini (Cialdini 2009, Cialdini et al. 2002). It has many similarities and overlaps with the 'principled negotiation' model described above (Ury et al. 1992). For example, 'perceived objective evaluation criteria' (the fourth principle in the above model) overlaps partly with the authority principle and the principle of social proof in Cialdini's model (the last principle below). However, they focus on slightly different modulations, even where they overlap each other and can therefore be seen as good complements to each other. Cialdini et al. (2002) formulate six basic principles for how to influence and persuade another person. These principles are so fundamental that they may be said to apply in a wider context than just obvious negotiation situations where two or more parties meet to try to reach agreement or persuade each other on a particular issue. They can also be adapted to situations such as an informal conversation at the photocopier or the seemingly conflict-free conversation at a formal meeting. However, the principles are particularly relevant for exercising influence in the short term in relation to a given issue or situation. In the longer term, indirectly and in the wider context, 'symbolic leadership' and 'manipulation' can take place in several ways (see Chapters 7 and 8).

The liking principle

Research shows that people are more affected by people they like than by people they dislike. Research also shows that there are many different reasons why we like other people more or less: physical attraction, similar perceptions, previous collaborations, and so on. The factor that has proved to be the most important in various studies, however, is how similar you perceive the other person to be to yourself. Experiments show, for example, that questionnaires are filled in more often if they are accompanied by a covering letter that is signed by a name similar to the recipient's. For example, if the recipient is called Anna Johansson, her inclination to fill in the questionnaire will be higher if the sender is an Alva Jonsson rather than, say, a Sergei Lechner. This and other, seemingly trivial similarities have proven to play a major role in how we let ourselves be influenced by others. In a negotiating situation, you should therefore try to identify similarities between the parties. By identifying similarities with respect to previous assignments, similar situations in each organization, similar private lives and, of course, even similarities with regard to interests concerning the current issue, it will be easier to persuade the other party. Of course, talking about differences should also be avoided. It is important to remember that both parties have the same interest in building a business relationship, and should avoid talking about what the construction of such a relationship might cost.

The authority principle

People become more influenced and more easily persuaded by others who they perceive to have legitimate authority. Authority is often perceived as legitimate if it is based on knowledge, skills and experience. Position and title are also often associated with legitimate authority, given that the latter can be linked to competence. However, there is a tendency for people to take their own knowledge and position for granted, and therefore they do not establish it in negotiation situations. An experiment (see Cialdini, 2009) has shown, for example, that if occupational therapists hang up their education diplomas and certificates on the wall in their reception, their patients, who might not usually continue to follow a practitioner's instructions after they are discharged from hospital, will follow their instructions to a much greater extent. It is also good to establish your authority early on and preferably before you meet to negotiate. You can, for example, mention your experience and expertise in a preliminary informal conversation before the actual negotiation. In written documentation or a meeting request, for example, you might briefly and factually describe your knowledge bases and positions, which can increase your legitimate authority. In order to be perceived as truly credible, it is also appropriate to mention some minor knowledge gaps or weaknesses. This reduces the risk of the described knowledge base and strengths being perceived as bragging or boasting.

The scarcity principle

The scarcer a resource is, the more attractive it becomes. There is not just an economic connection between supply and demand in markets, but also a psychological phenomenon at play in negotiations. In 2001, when General Motors released the news that it would stop production of the Oldsmobile (which many analysts, even General Motors themselves, thought was simply an outdated product), the Oldsmobile set a new sales record. As a negotiator, you should therefore always make an effort to describe the solution, the option you are advocating as unique and as the only, final opportunity to achieve an important goal. It is also important to describe the option you want to use as being a way to avoid a big loss, rather than as making a big profit.

A large number of studies (see Cialdini, 2009) show that people value losing something much higher than not winning something, even if this is exactly the same thing, formally speaking. In a negotiating situation, you should thus highlight as many potential large losses as possible, rather than as many large profits as possible.

The consistency principle

People strive to think, speak and act in a consistent way (which, however, can never be the case all the time). That is, if you say that you are going to do something, the chance increases that you will subsequently do it. If you can thus get your counterpart to imagine acting or say they will act in a way that is in line with what they want to achieve, then the chance increases that you will be able to get the other party to translate this into action. For example, a restaurant has problems with a large number of guests who do not show up even though they have booked a table. When they call and book tables, the restaurant employee ends the call by saying: 'Please call us and cancel if you can't come.' When the restaurant turns this statement into a question: 'Would you be so kind and call us if you can't come?' the guest replies that they will do this, and the proportion of 'no-shows' decreases from 30 to 10 percent. Because the guest was asked to express an intention to perform a certain action, the guest's inclination to perform the action markedly increases. When it comes to negotiating situations, this means that if you make an initial decision on a comprehensive issue, the chance of you standing by such a decision increases if you write it down or repeat it orally, preferably in a public context. Writing *letters of intent* also increases the chance of later reaching a comprehensive agreement.

The reciprocity principle

People tend to give back what you give to them. If you smile when you meet people, chances are they will smile back. In other words, the principle of reciprocity does not only apply to material or financial resources, it also applies to attention, information, recognition and respect. The principle of reciprocity can be seen as a variant of distinguishing between problems and people, that is, the first principle, according to the model of 'principled negotiation' (see above). Treating the other party in a pleasant, informative and appreciative way increases the chance of the other party feeling obliged to repay you in some way.

The principle of social proof

The last principle in this description of how to increase your influence and persuade other parties is the realization that what people often choose to do in a particular situation is what they perceive other, similar people would do in similar situations. If many people like me do something in a certain way, it should be right for me to do so as well. The tendency to do as others do is extremely strong in situations that are perceived to be highly uncertain. When you lack experience of similar situations yourself, it becomes difficult to anchor your actions in yourself – instead, you go outside yourself and are influenced by how others do things. By pointing out how others (people, companies and organizations) have acted in similar situations, you may thus increase the chance of the other party agreeing to act in a similar way.

The problematic first and second dimensions of power

The models and concepts described in this chapter include everything from theory that explains why there is more or less conflict in organizations, to concrete tips on how to set up a negotiation and persuade other people to support a certain option. Although these models and frameworks include manipulation in the sense of trying to influence how other actors perceive reality, they can still be said to primarily address the first and second dimensions of power – decision-making power and power over the agenda – rather than the third dimension: manipulation. This is because they all assume that people and groups have more or less fixed goals that they try to achieve by exercising power over others. The idea that individuals and groups can *have* more or less power also implies that power and power bases exist, as it were, as concrete units or objects, and that, as an actor, you can gather these power units together and bring them with you into various contexts. According to Lukes (1974) and other, more recent power theorists, this is an almost naïve approach to power that is easy to problematize and criticize. Power is something that *is exercised* in specific situations where people's relationships rather than power bases determine who influences who. Power can also be seen as something that exists, or is exercised beyond such 'micro' situations in the form of overall structures and cultural norm systems, that individuals are neither aware of nor can do anything to change.

The models outlined in this chapter are most suitable for use in practical contexts, for designing more informed agendas, decisions and actions. In the next chapter, however, we will study more complex and critical theories of power in more depth. These models often have high explanatory value, and, in spite of their increased complexity and critical stance, they have clear implications for how we might operate in companies and other organizational contexts.

Videos

Don't forget to watch the videos to discover more about the key concepts in this chapter:
https://study.sagepub.com/blomberg

7

The Power Framework In-Depth – Structures, Norms and Fair Organizations

Efficient processes, optimal structures, *lean* production systems, the right skills, talented employees and a willingness and courage to think creatively and develop innovative new products and services – this is usually how we describe a successful business. The first and second dimensions of the power framework – decision-making power and power over the agenda – as described in the previous chapter, are in part a criticism of this popular description of business and organization. This argues that it is not possible to optimize structures and formalize processes so that they are effective and efficient 'for all'. A process can never be 'neutral' – it can, however, be an effective way to achieve one actor's agenda at the expense of other actors. But such a perspective on power assumes that there are actors who know what they want, who have solid, stable goals and know how to impose their will. This assumes that actors are competent and rational individuals who can pick and choose between alternative courses of action and power strategies to achieve their goals. The first and second dimensions of power also view power itself as being an object. As an individual, you can collect such power objects, or power bases, which can then be used in the struggle to gain influence and achieve your own goals.

Both of these views – that of the power-maker who makes more or less rational choices and that of power as an object – are, however, heavily criticized, even within the power framework. In this chapter, therefore, a more complex picture of power is described. The concepts and models that this picture encompasses can enhance our understanding of how power is created and creates, but they can also be used practically – as a basis for more informed decisions and actions.

The first and second dimensions of power comprise a perspective that is both 'instrumental' (power seen as an instrument) and 'actor-oriented' (people seen as individuals with stable goals and the ability to choose appropriate methods to achieve them). This chapter describes a more 'structural' and a more 'cultural' perspective of power and influence. This means that we move from a 'micro level', focusing on individuals and small groups, to 'meso' and 'macro level', focusing on organization and society.

The following descriptions of complex and extensive theoretical constructions are simplified to the highest degree. In addition, they are simplified for a specific purpose: to highlight useful analytical tools. This means that many theories and models are simply not included. There are also aspects of those models included that may be fundamental in other contexts but are not included in the descriptions below. If you want to have a broader, deeper and more accurate picture of the theoretical work of social scientists, such as Robert Michels, Rosabeth Moss Kanter, Michel Foucault and others discussed in this chapter, then go to the sources or to a more comprehensive introductory text. In this chapter, however, some selectively chosen and highly relevant power theories are presented, which can be used, without extensive theoretical knowledge, to analyze organization, management and leadership. We then look at the practical benefits of more complex power theories and the consequences of these models and analyses for leadership and organization in practice. This is followed by a brief discussion of how we use language to exercise power, along with how leaders are viewed from a power framework perspective. The chapter concludes with a presentation of the power framework's generic questions, strengths and weaknesses.

Kanter's structural explanation of power and influence

One of the most influential theories about how more concrete structural conditions change how people unconsciously perceive, judge and act towards each other, is Kanter's (1977) theory of minorities and *tokens*. Tokens and 'tokenism' are concepts that were given meaning and significance during the civil rights movement for equal treatment and human rights in the United States in the 1950s and 1960s. In the early 1960s, Malcolm X (1963) commented on the alleged progress of the black population with:

> What gains? All you gotten is tokenism – one or two Negroes in a job, or at a lunch counter, so the rest of us will be quiet.

Kanter (1977), however, was not studying the black population's situation in American society but executive levels in a major US industrial company. In management teams at different levels and in different departments, she found that women were either conspicuous by their absence, completely alone or in the minority. When the women were

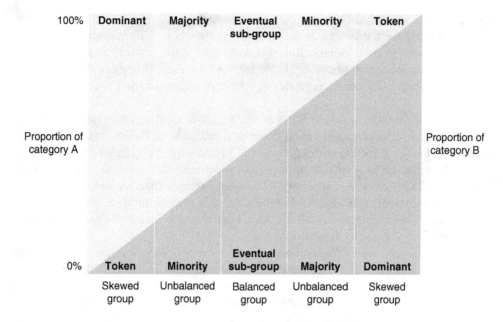

100% | Dominant | Majority | Eventual sub-group | Minority | Token

Proportion of category A

Proportion of category B

0% | Token | Minority | Eventual sub-group | Majority | Dominant

Skewed group | Unbalanced group | Balanced group | Unbalanced group | Skewed group

Figure 7.1 **Kanter's (1977) model of majorities, minorities and tokens**

very much in the minority or alone (tokens), it had several consequences for how both the majority and the minority acted. The actual proportion of men to women influenced the way the management teams functioned. It was not primarily one or more actors' conscious power and influence strategies that governed, but it was primarily a question of a structural effect of the majority/minority relationship (see Figure 7.1).

Kanter identifies three concrete effects of a group having a clear majority, minority or token position, that is, three effects of the group being 'skewed' or largely 'unbalanced':

- a minority or token receives a lot of attention
- there is a greater contrast between the majority and the minority/token
- the token/minority adapts to the majority by assimilation and distancing.

Attention

If you are a token or belong to a small minority, you stick out and get more attention than those belonging to the majority. This could be something positive, for example from a career perspective. You are more visible and would feasibly therefore receive more feedback and learn faster. You could get recognition for the good things you achieve, and so on. However, Kanter says that it is, first and foremost, visible and external aspects, such as clothing and appearance, which receive attention, rather than qualifications, skills and achievements. Neither is this necessarily a negative, bad thing from a career perspective, given that we want to and can dress up and show off external factors that are valued highly. However, it is more problematic if the goal is an efficient meritocracy, that is, where people hold their positions because of their skills.

Even more problematic is the fact that studies show that the single largest explanatory variable for people liking each other is similarity (see 'Liking principle' in the section on the six principles of negotiation in Chapter 6). If you belong to a minority that is characterized by a specific appearance, you are, by definition, different from the majority, and thus there is a tendency to be disliked more than individuals belonging to the similar majority. This means that there is a tendency to judge actions performed by individuals belonging to a small minority more critically than if the action had been performed by someone in the majority.

But it does not stop at tokens and minority members receiving attention for their external appearance and being judged more critically than the majority. According to Kanter, the major attention is not focused on a token or minority member as an individual at all, but on the person as a representative of one, or 'his/her', category. This means that if a woman in a male-dominated group says or does something that is perceived as negative, it will not be seen as the individual woman's mistake. Instead, it is seen as typical of the category she is considered to represent in the group, that is, typical of women. If Maria, who is the only woman in a management team, makes a mistake, it will thus be seen as a mistake that is typical for women to make. If Andrew in the same management team makes the same mistake, it will not be seen as a typical mistake for men, but as Andrew's individual mistake. Had there been a larger number of individuals belonging to the minority group, they would be considered more as individuals than as categories. The greater attention of the minority or token thus both focuses on the external, leading to a more critical attitude and an assessment of an entire category, rather than of an individual person.

Contrast

A skewed or heavily unbalanced group has a different dynamic to one that is balanced. This is particularly noticeable as the composition of the group changes. You can imagine a group without a token or minority who gets a new token member, that is, a member who, on the outside, markedly differs from the others and therefore is classified in a different category to the majority, for example a woman who becomes a member in a management group that until now consisted only of men. In such a group, the presence of a token will cause how the group thinks and acts to be strengthened. This contradicts the idea that new group members bring new mindsets and behaviors with them, and make a group more dynamic and less averse to change. Kanter argues that the entry of someone who is perceived differently poses a threat to the mindset and behaviors of the group. The threat means that group members unwittingly stand up for and therefore strengthen their mindset and behaviors. For example, if a group of men sometimes expressed a certain macho culture, then there is a tendency for the majority (in this example men) to amplify this when a token (in this case a woman) enters and becomes a member of the group. The majority reinforces, maybe even creates, a contrast and disparity between the majority and the minority in the group. One can thus assert that a newly arrived minority or token, merely by its presence, reinforces or can even be the co-creator of an exclusive and prejudiced group culture.

Assimilation and distancing

The critical and categorical attention and exclusive group culture put considerable pressure on a token or minority member to adapt to the majority. This can be done by accepting and laughing at what is not necessarily an easily digested joke. One can try not to be crushed by the superficial and extremely critical review, but, at the same time, not imitate the majority's behaviors, but rather try to fit in more discreetly. Performing without taking credit can be such a strategy. Kanter does not advise that tokens adopt these strategies. In fact, the account is rather a critical description of survival strategies that tokens are forced to employ, often without a conscious awareness of it. An indirect consequence of this assimilation and survival strategy is that tokens and minority members also distance themselves from other members of the same category who are outside the working group. For example, new women in a male-dominated group therefore distance themselves from other women in order to show their loyalty to the majority in their new group. It's not necessarily something a token wants to do but rather a condition for being accepted by the majority. This means that a token or minority tends to remain a token or minority, and thus an unbalanced group tends to remain so.

Applying Kanter's model

Kanter's model provides an explanation for and reasons why some people become more vulnerable and subordinate to other people in a kind of structural majority–minority relationship in groups and organizations. Although interpretations and actions of individuals are included in the model, the main explanation is placed at a level above the individual. In this way, Kanter's model is a structural explanation on the organizational or meso level, rather than on a micro level. The explanation can also be said to be 'materialistic'. Although the effects of skewed groups include people's experiences and perceptions, the explanation is based on the breakdown between physical human beings and their visible external differences. Kanter's model thus represents a partial materialistic explanation on a structural meso level.

However, this does not make the model unusable for individuals who want to influence how organization takes place and how individual issues and problems are addressed. For example, if you want to influence the effects of unbalanced groups in terms of examining some people more critically than others, you can make the group's composition less skewed. In the case of management teams dominated by men, recruitment of several women, according to Kanter's model, would lead to a fairer, more equitable, more rational and more efficient evaluation of the management team members – all else being equal. On the contrary, if you want to protect the interests of the majority, in this case the male majority, then it is appropriate to recruit one or a few women to the group who, because of the assimilation effect, will 'protect' the group from more women coming in to it.

Kanter's model is the result of studies of unequal management teams. But it is formulated in more general terms – the relationship between minorities and majorities. Therefore, it could be applied to completely different groups. In many large, Western-based companies, many ethnic groups are in the minority, whose situation could be analyzed using Kanter's model. Within companies, it is sometimes possible to see quite clear differences between employees in different parts and at different levels. A young male MBA graduate from an elite business school can be easily identified in his first managerial job in an administrative unit where most employees are middle-aged women. Even a young female graduate from the same business school would stick out both in the way she dresses and in the words and expressions she uses, and could thus be suitable material for an analysis à la Kanter. Another example is the older male manager with a background in the venture capital industry, who takes over as the new president of a clothing brand focusing on well-off women with an avid interest in yoga and well-being. Kanter's model can simply be used to analyze all kinds of groups in which members might see and divide themselves into two groups reasonably well.

More recent research, which has tested Kanter's model, shows, however, that the effects can be quite different, depending on who makes up the majority and minority respectively. In groups dominated by women, but with a male token or a small male minority, the structural imbalance has completely different effects than in the original study with a converse 'gender order'. In such cases, it seems as though the few men are taken care of a bit more, valued uncritically and even praised, and are also expected to reach the top quickly (Ott 1989, Williams 1993, Simpson 2004). If Kanter's study of male-dominated management teams can explain the so-called glass ceiling, that is, women have worse conditions for career progression, the converse relationship seems instead to give the minority of men a glass elevator, as it seems easier for them to progress quickly (Warming & Ussing 2005).

Why this is so can be explained by, among other things, how different norms, values and stereotypes interact and counteract each other, which leads us into even more complex power theories and models. Such models are even more remote from the first and second dimensions of power, that is, the individual-focused micro-level models. Instead, these more complex models focus on how power works at both the organizational and society macro level, as well as on how material and formal aspects interact with cultural and value-based ones. The cultural and value aspects of organization and leadership are the main focus of the symbolic framework and will be discussed in Chapters 8 and 9. Some additional power-theory models that are described below overlap with the symbolic framework, but also focus on power and control to a greater extent than many of the models found within the symbolic framework. However, the following models are as much part of the power framework as they are part of the symbolic. Here, these two perspectives overlap each other almost completely.

Weber's three types of legitimate authority

Weber is not only one of the founders of modern organizational theory, and the person who first and most clearly formulated a theory on why bureaucracy is the most effective way of organizing all kinds of business activities (see Chapter 2), he is also one of the great power theorists. In his extensive historical description and analysis of how industrialism, democracy, technology development and increasingly advanced artistic expression emerged from more traditional and religious societies, he also shows how the exercising of power and control has changed over time (Weber 1924/1983). Weber shows that violence was replaced by other grounds for power and influence. In order for these later forms of authority to function, they must be perceived as legitimate by those people who allow themselves to be subsumed by and who subordinate themselves to them.

Weber thus defines *authority* as *power which is accepted as legitimate by those who are exposed to it*. For example, holding a high position in a bureaucracy is not enough, according to Weber, to be able to exercise power based on this position alone. It is also necessary that the bureaucracy itself is perceived as legitimate and that the person holding the position is perceived as a legitimate holder of that position. For example, if a senior manager is not considered competent enough to hold his high position, it is far from certain that they will be able to govern and control their subordinates.

Weber distinguishes between three pure types of authority: charismatic, traditional and formal-rational (Weber 1924/1983). Weber also argues that these three types constitute a hierarchical development system. Historically, societies have evolved from being governed by charismatic and traditional authority to being ruled by formal-rational authority. Applied to organizations, the same pattern can be observed. Young companies, so-called start-ups, are often managed by charismatic and traditional authority, but, as they age and grow, are increasingly managed by formal-rational authority.

Weber's power theory and the structural models found in the structural framework (not least Greiner's model) have great similarities. For example, it can be argued that in a simple structure, charismatic authority rules; in a professional bureaucracy, traditional authority is most important; and in machine bureaucracy, it is formal-rational authority that governs (see Chapter 2 for a description of Mintzberg's different structural configurations).

Charismatic authority

According to Weber, charismatic authority is based on personal qualities and individual strengths. Subordinates let themselves be governed, not because of traditions or rules but because they believe in the individual leader as a person. What other power bases or competences the charismatic leader has is of less importance, since it is the individual charm and charisma that form the basis of the leader's power. Entrepreneurs and known medial, 'heroic', 'larger-than-life' leaders can be said to exercise power by means of charismatic authority. However, charismatic authority is vulnerable. If a leader loses his or her charisma, dies or disappears, the organizations and societies governed by them tend to be transformed and increasingly governed by traditional or formal-rational authority.

Traditional authority

Traditional authority derives from traditions, customs and history. Authority is attributed to powerful individuals and groups due to traditions and beliefs accepted by the subordinates. Religion and royalty have historically been the most important source of traditional authority, with clergy and royals as proprietors and practitioners of this form of power. Even the mill owner, the head of the family, the veteran political party leader and the company founder can exert power and influence through traditional authority. According to Weber, inequality and injustice are created and cemented using traditional authority. This is because tradition and customs hinder the most competent or merited person from gaining the position they would have in a formal-rational bureaucracy or meritocracy (see next section). Unless traditional authority is challenged, dominant leaders and groups will continue to be superior and prevent the creation of fair, rational and effective organizations and societies.

Formal-rational authority

According to Weber, formal-rational authority is the most developed and civilized form of power. It is based on neither custom nor personality but on position. The position is defined by the rationally designed hierarchical structure to which it belongs. A person's power is thus defined by the position that person holds. If the position is high, the power is considerable; if it is low, the power is minimal. If a person leaves their position, for example after their formally regulated (rationally designed) working day, the person's authority also disappears until the person returns to his position and office. A person who deputizes in a certain position temporarily has the same authority as the absentee (and which the latter will regain when they return to their job and position).

The positions and the systems or structures that these people are part of are governed by rules formulated as rational solutions to problems that the organization and society want to solve. A company's task may be to produce goods and services as efficiently as possible. A democratic political system can be rationally designed to formulate social development goals and organize the implementation of these goals as efficiently as possible. In its purely ideal form, bureaucratic systems are based on knowledge, that is, bureaucracies are also meritocracies. Those who hold different positions are then most suitable for the tasks that these posts involve. Recruitment and promotion are based on knowledge and skills – not on friendship, personal chemistry or personal judgment – and the authority is thus perceived to be legitimate, effective and fair.

According to Weber, formal-rational authority and the formal-rational bureaucracy are both the fairest and the most efficient ways of producing goods and services, as well as of organizing entire societies. But Weber also saw that the ongoing rationalization and 'disenchantment' of the world over a long historical period was draining human life of deeper meaning. Faith, hope and love were increasingly being replaced by rational decisions, bureaucratic structures and formalized processes. Weber thus had a split – both positive and negative – view of social development.

Michels' theory of the iron law of oligarchy

Another theorist whose early ideas were close to Weber's view of the bureaucracy's ability to create justice and efficiency was the German sociologist Michels. However, after a study of the then young but increasingly organized labor parties in Europe, Michels (1915/1968) formulated a very harsh criticism of bureaucracy. In his view, bureaucracy, instead of creating a rational and fair world, by definition involved top-down management and an undemocratic social order.

Michels' criticism leads to, among other things, a model describing bureaucracy as a tool for a new ruling class – an *oligarchy* – consisting of the most senior management levels of increasingly numerous and powerful organizations. As organization and management require extensive administrative knowledge, a knowledge gap arises between organizations' most senior management and those who populate the lower organizational levels. Administrative knowledge unites and rectifies senior leaders and civil servants in major organizations and leads to senior executives and civil servants obtaining a kind of knowledge monopoly. Instead of directing and representing their various organizations, in competition or in collaboration with each other, senior management teams collaborate with each other to superordinate themselves to the working classes and other citizens.

Michels' (1915/1968) image of major hierarchical organizations differs significantly from the established image of markets and hierarchies found in both the economics media and economically inspired structural organizational theory (see, for example, Williamson's transaction cost theory in Chapter 3). Instead of describing large organizations as competitors, which continually streamline their production and develop their products, the economic elite cooperates across organizational boundaries to reproduce its own superiority and the subordination of others. Within this new leadership elite, or oligarchy, there are strong bonds, common interests and a regimented knowledge base – contrary to the rest of the population, which is characterized by diversity, heterogeneous knowledge and weak bonds. According to Michels, Weber's meritocratic ideal is not found in real-life large organizations. The lower classes, ethnic minorities, women, small savers and other categories of people have no chance of gaining access to the ruling elite, regardless of knowledge and skills. Applied to, for example, stock market actors, Michels' model can be illustrated as in Figure 7.2 which describes an elite group

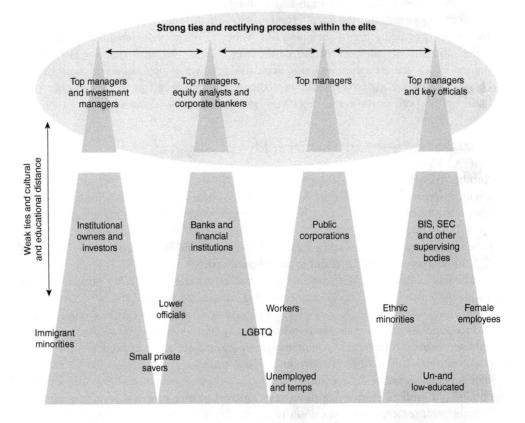

Figure 7.2   The iron law of oligarchy applied to some of the financial sector's key players

Source: Based on Blomberg (2005)

of higher managers and investors in various types of powerful organizations active in the financial sector. No matter if these organizations are competitive corporation and investment firms, surveillance bodies or financial institutions, the powerful people in these organizations have a lot in common and strong bonds between them. They have similar education and management knowledge. They move between these organizations and in the same social circles. They form an oligarchic elite that is very hard to become a part of if you are a mid-manager, a regular employee, a member of a minority group or do not have a degree from a top university.

Although bureaucracy constitutes a tool for creating a fair, rational and efficient world in theory, and thus combats injustice, favoritism and inefficiency, Michels believed that in practice it was creating almost the opposite conditions. Bureaucratic organizations became the center of a power concentration in which owners and management teams in both different and similar companies, authorities and other organizations form an oligarchic elite. Michels' theory of the iron law of oligarchy – that organization, by definition, is undemocratic, and that senior executives and officials are characterized by consensus and rectification (cf. 'groupthink' in Chapter 8) – is today highly topical when scandals among senior executives in industrial companies, banks and other organizations alike are rife, despite an ever-increasing focus on 'risk-control systems' and more formal processes regulated by laws and directives. Michels' model might also be relevant when trying to understand the richest and increasingly powerful owners of the world's largest social media technology corporations.

Acker's theory of bureaucratic control and society's gender systems

A similar picture emerges from Acker's more contemporary research and theory about the emergence of bureaucracy in symbiosis with society's so-called gender order or gender systems (Acker & Van Houten 1974, Acker 1990, 2006). Regardless of Weber's optimistic theory of formal-rational bureaucracy, Acker argues that the rationalization of enterprise and industrial production has prompted an increase in the unfair and irrational division of labor between men and women.

According to Acker, the development of formal-rational bureaucracies also requires the development of a special kind of person that holds the positions of these bureaucracies. Like Weber, in his more pessimistic view of the consequences of bureaucracy for meaningful human life, Acker believes that, in the bureaucratic system, there is no room for people's feelings, beliefs or relationships. Bureaucracy has also changed within the framework of late-modern capitalism. Today, in addition to abstract rational officials and workers, large companies and bureaucracies also demand that these officials and workers display unlimited loyalty to their positions, work and employers. A successful career is more important than ever for the professional worker of today. Careerism and careerists are not any more seen as something odd or bad. In order to become a successful careerist, you are required to have support functions outside work, which can take care of the more interpersonal, emotional and practical aspects of life. These aspects, such as feeding and raising children, cooking food and washing clothes, have therefore been passed on to people who are not expected to work and make a career in the major capitalist bureaucracies. According to Acker, the cold rational and now unrestrainedly demanding capitalist bureaucracy – large companies – is male in its basic structure and can only exist if the men who make careers in it have a female support structure that manages their personal lives outside the companies' business operations (Acker 1990). This, says Acker, makes it easier for men to devote themselves to their work and career, while preventing women from doing the same.

Acker's model can be used as an explanation for women's poorer working conditions, such as lower pay for the same work and the expectation of taking greater responsibility than men for children and household work. But, it can also be seen as an explanation for the fact that many people, both men and women, strive for successful careers. This careerism means a willingness to work hard over extremely long days. But, as careerists equate success and happiness with material rewards and career advancement, their hard work will not focus on creating a more humanistic, industrial or entrepreneurial society. Acker's model can thus be regarded as a highly critical theory, with implications beyond both gender equality and the clever exercising of power in organizations.

Burawoy's labor process theory – manufacturing consent

Another model with a similar and highly critical approach to how we organize both companies and society is Burawoy's labor process theory. Unlike Acker's model, Burawoy's model does not focus on the lack of equal treatment of men and women in organizations. On the contrary, Burawoy complements both Acker and Michels in regards to explaining the individualism and careerism that they believe has spread and continues to spread throughout society.

Michels' model focuses on hierarchical tops – the management elite – that is, the leaders of large companies, authorities and institutions, while Burawoy (1979) focuses on the lower levels of hierarchies, that is, those who perform the actual production of goods and services. The model examines how the design of the labor process in contemporary organizations affects the power relationship between employees, managers and owners. Burawoy's theory is based on Marx and other neo-Marxist theorists, but rephrases Marx's classic question as to why workers work at all in capitalist organizations, and instead asks why they work so hard – or, in Burawoy's words, why they *consent* to working so hard – when they receive such a small portion of the added value that this work creates. Burawoy's model also distinguishes itself because it does not, like most Marx-inspired organizational models, assume that organizations are the tools capitalists use to de-individualize workers' knowledge and skills. On the contrary, Burawoy believes that organizations and their senior executives encourage their employees and coworkers to develop their own individual skills. As knowledge is one of several power bases (see Chapter 6), this encouragement could lead to the spreading and decentralization of power in companies and other organizations.

This is exactly how the 'knowledge society', 'network organization', 'flat organizations', 'self-management work groups', 'leaderless organizations' or 'the death of bureaucracy' is portrayed in the media and popular management literature: due to employees' extensive knowledge, companies and organizations can no longer be organized in accordance with the principles of the structural framework. As a recently qualified MBA graduate from a top business school, one cannot be exploited or become 'de-skilled' by management and owner representatives. On the contrary, a free choice can be made between everything from a glittering career in the big banks and consultancies to realizing oneself as an entrepreneur or a 'digital nomad', it is said. But, according to Burawoy, instead of capitalists exploiting the labor collective by depriving them of their knowledge, organizations can today make employees work harder than ever, because employees today have accepted the basic (capitalist) order that controls them. Instead of alienating their employees, business executives in today's organizations manage to co-opt them. By means of more indirect and structural control, business executives manage to split and individualize potential employee collectives, and thus lower their potential influence. According to Burawoy's model, this is done in three ways:

- performance-based individual compensation
- an internal, flexible labor market
- collective bargaining.

Performance-based individual compensation

By means of individual performance-based remuneration, vertical control and conflict (due to the potential resistance of an employee collective) are transformed into a vertical contest between individual employees. Coworkers not only receive a higher salary if they work harder than their colleagues, but they also obtain status and admiration from them. Marginal individual wage increases therefore mask the fact that it is senior managers and owners who earn the most from the hard work of their coworkers due to the competition among them. An alliance or a collective of employees is divided into a number of tough, individually competing careerists. Burawoy's description of today's individually competitive employees fits well with many of the present and future workplaces of newly-graduated MBA students. In banking, consulting and the new technology-based businesses, individual performance-based renumeration is commonplace. In addition, grades and individual development plans throughout the school have laid the foundations for this individual competition.

An internal, flexible labor market

Increased career opportunities, but also changing working tasks and positions within organizations, create an illusion that employees have high degrees of freedom. It also means that employees who work together are separated and thus cannot build alliances and create more influential and stronger negotiating positions. What is presented as a flexible and creative work organization with a great deal of co-determination, based on Burawoy's model, can be seen as an intricate system that prevents employees from forming stable groupings and alliances. Additionally, if we add phenomena such as outsourcing, time-limited project employment and distance work, the logic of Burawoy's model becomes even more convincing: what is perceived as a modern way of organizing and managing operations is a system that both creates an illusion of individual freedom and prevents employees from collaborating to obtain greater influence.

Collective bargaining

When individually competing employees are also members of trade unions that negotiate wage levels and terms for the workforce (a collective) with business executives, this creates an illusion of participation and opportunities for influence. Even this can be perceived as counter-intuitive – trade unions consist of individuals who join together to become a stronger negotiating party. However, with a direct reference to Michels' description of the oligarchical elite, this elite also encompasses the hierarchical top of the trade unions. Trade unions therefore create an illusion of, rather than real, increased influence.

Burawoy's model and more

The three mechanisms mean that the vertical conflict between management and employees is transformed into a horizontal competition among employees and creates a false sense of freedom and influence. The term 'There is nothing as easily manipulated as a careerist' has, with Burawoy's model, received theoretical backing. In addition, Burawoy's model can be combined with Michels' oligarchical elite model: management and owners, as well as the top echelons of authorities and trade unions, have joined together and formed a powerful political ownership and leadership elite across organizational and societal boundaries, while employees are split by individualized wage-setting and a false sense of individual freedom.

Burawoy's model is a result of his empirical studies of work at a manufacturing company. The model can thus be said to handle power at the micro level (individual level) and meso level (organizational level). But it also constitutes criticism of both Marxist theory and the capitalist development of society on a macro level. There are many more and similar contributions that emphasize even more strongly how individualization is both a consequence of and a reason for how we organize and lead companies and organizations. At the macro level (society level), for example, Chomsky's (1988) 'propaganda model' is highly critical of what Chomsky describes as a leading owner and management elite that, through its control of news media, consolidates its role in society. With Michels' model as a base and with Chomsky as an addition, one could plot the big media companies in Figure 7.2, shown earlier in this chapter. Habermas' (1984) theory of 'communicative action' and comprehensive analysis of how the 'world of systems' is increasingly taking over the 'lifeworld' can be seen as a continuation of Weber's pessimistic analysis of how we imprison ourselves, in the name of rationality, in an increasingly meaningless and cold iron cage. Even Foucault's historical 'genealogy' and theory of 'self-discipline' and 'truth regimes' can be seen as power theory developments of Weber's rationalization theory (Foucault 1969/2002, 1977, 1980). Therefore, Foucault's model of how we increasingly discipline ourselves in structural and mental prisons created by ourselves is described in the next section.

Kanter, Michels, Acker and Burawoy alike base their criticism of bureaucracy on studies of real organizations. Acker and Burawoy also collect, at least in part, theoretical power for their criticism of Marxist theories. Foucault's theory of structuring and self-discipline, which is the last overarching power theory in this chapter, however, retrieves its theoretical power from post-structuralism, rather than Marxism. The theory can be said to be even more complex and hard to grasp than the previous ones, but, despite this complexity, it produces a relatively clear interpretation of how power works through individuals (micro), organizations (meso) and comprehensive social structures (macro) at the same time.

Foucault's theory of structuring and self-discipline

Foucault, like Weber, Michels and Acker (and many other social scientists), describes how society has become increasingly structured over a long period of time. The division of labor continues to increase, and coordination and control become increasingly complex and technically sophisticated. Just like the aforementioned theorists, Foucault believes that this development imposes demands on the human being as well. Unlike Michels, Acker and Burawoy, Foucault doesn't believe that most power in organizations and society is exercised by certain groups and interests systematically placing themselves above other groups and interests (the highest echelons of bureaucracy place themselves above workers and citizens in Michels' model, while male wage earners and careerists place themselves above unemployed and underpaid women in Acker's model). Foucault, instead, posits that it is every single individual who disciplines themselves (Foucault 1969/2002, 1980). This is similar to Burawoy's model, but Foucault believes that even owners, senior executives and others are 'victims' of this historical and all-embracing process. Foucault describes society's increased structuring not as a Weberian rationalization process, but as a disciplinary process. The individual's self-discipline and society's structuring are two sides of the same coin. One presupposes the other. Power exists in the subject (in the individual person), in our language use and in more material structures.

Bentham's panopticon

Foucault (1977) uses the 17th century philosopher Jeremy Bentham's prison design as a metaphor for how he thinks we, as human beings, constantly self-discipline ourselves and do so to an increasingly higher extent. In Bentham's prison, a watch tower was placed in the middle, with prison cells in the shape of pieces of cake set all around (see Figure 7.3). From the tower, the prison guard could see all prisoners, but not all

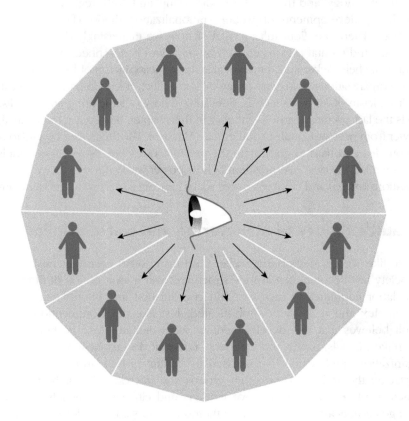

Figure 7.3   Bentham's panopticon

at the same time. The prisoners, however, could not see the guard and therefore did not know when they were being watched and when they were not. It was enough to keep them calm, however, to know that they *could* be under surveillance. Although the prisoners could not know if they were actually being monitored, they nevertheless felt they were. The prisoners guarded, or disciplined, themselves. Bentham's panopticon was effective, partly because only one guard was needed to monitor a large number of prisoners, and partly, and above all, because the prisoners disciplined themselves. The watch tower did not even have to be manned all the time, as it was the feeling of being constantly watched that disciplined the prisoners, rather than them actually being watched at all times.

Increasingly widespread self-discipline

Foucault (1969/2002, 1977, 1980) believes that the increased structuring of society is leading to the introduction of more and more panopticon-like institutions and systems. We measure everything more thoroughly, we increasingly separate, divide up, evaluate and rank. We have individual performance reviews at all school levels, as well as in working life. We have increasingly finely gauged grading systems and increasingly sophisticated *performance management* and *talent management* systems. We are increasingly connected via IT and social media. Our lives are increasingly monitored and recorded in the form of 'big data'. Just like in Bentham's panopticon, our phone, tablet, computer, watch, loudspeaker, car, kitchen or even our own bodies (via our devices' 'health apps') can call upon us at any time. We are always expected to answer, and we discipline ourselves to structure all emails and information flows into different boxes and apps. Not least, we make ourselves constantly available to everyone and everything.

All these measurements, evaluations and connections make us constantly discipline ourselves. We act in accordance with what we think is important for our next evaluation; we manage, sort and respond to emails; and post on our chat threads. We post pictures of our feigned and toughly disciplined lives. We distinguish and control ourselves using all the structures that we both create and reproduce with our toughly disciplined bodies, actions and thoughts. It is even the case that we increasingly go beyond accepting to be controlled or exposed to all of this – we actually demand to be evaluated. We 'want' to be graded on increasingly detailed levels. We need to know what a specific achievement is 'worth' on a grading scale, in terms of bonus or career opportunity. We demand to be evaluated according to our organization's promotion and remuneration criteria. We are so self-disciplined that a world without these kinds of panopticonic prisons, be they in the form of course grades, performance appraisals, Facebook communication or Instagram posts, is almost unthinkable. This very special world, which includes both our self-identities and our relationships, becomes the only possible one. We become victims of our own 'regime of truth'.

Who then exercises power over whom? And how can Foucault's and similar power theorists' insights be used more practically? When the executor and sender of power are the same as the subject and recipient, it might be argued that all individuals are in conflict with themselves.

The practical benefit of more complex power theories

Michels and Acker believe, like Kanter, that the bureaucratic organizations of reality are far from Weber's theoretically idealized, formal-rational bureaucracy. Based on a reinterpretation of Marx, Burawoy believes that today's 'flattened' and partially 'dissolved' bureaucracy reinforces rather than weakens the prioritized situation of elites at the expense of others. Foucault adds that our extremely structured, disciplined society affects us all, regardless of which community, group, class, profession or organization we belong to, and, in addition, we are all co-creators of this structural and mental self-disciplining prison.

But what are the consequences of these models and analyses for leadership and organization in practice? How can we use these models practically? First of all, like any other model and perspective, they can help us to see beyond our common sense and break with the norms and values that we perceive as self-evident and given. When we think we recruit on the basis of individual skills, perhaps we mix what we consider a comfortable, non-threatening person and social relationship with knowledge best suited to a particular job. Instead of being a victim of seemingly obvious truths, group thinking and homogeneous cultures (see Chapter 8), we can see that what we perceived as self-evident is actually one of many other perspectives.

The more complex and critical power theories in this chapter can also help us to nuance our images of various measures, actions and strategies. For example, if we want to improve an organization's gender equality and diversity, we should ask whether it is primarily a question of formalizing and making processes more transparent, or whether it is primarily about the education and criticism of prevailing norms and values. For example, an analysis based on Kanter may lead to the fact that quotas can be an effective way to avoid the negative effects of 'tokenism'. If we can see that a real organization can never be the same as the ideal image of meritocracy, quotas can instead be a method of coming closer to meritocracy than departing from it. According to Weber, greater formalization, policies and regulations should lead to fairer and more efficient processes, but, based on Acker's theory, greater formalization and regulation can instead have the opposite effect. It is then a question of thinking through, but also being responsive to, the real effects of well-meaning policies and reforms, and then adjusting and developing the rules accordingly.

For example, if the intention is to reduce segregation in the recruitment of new employees, great importance can be attached to recruitment based on anonymously written CVs. Since these are anonymous in terms of gender and personal names (that can indicate ethnic minorities), actual skills can be valued higher than gender and ethnicity. But the design of an impressive CV, as well as the ability to write one, can differ widely between different cultures and social backgrounds. To attach great importance to anonymously written CVs may therefore reduce rather than enhance the capacity to include job-seekers who are highly skilled but have different backgrounds. The result will be departing further from rather than coming closer to a meritocratic, fair and rational organization. The anonymized process should therefore be complemented by a process where people can meet and describe themselves verbally and through their actions. The written CVs could perhaps be complemented by some kind of open house or aptitude test in which the applicants can demonstrate their skills.

Foucault's model for simultaneous structural and cultural self-discipline can also be used in both the analysis and the design of concrete organizational processes. Since both our self-images and our truths are created by ourselves, via self-disciplinary structures, we can make changes by just changing ourselves and the 'panopticonic' structures we have created. Maybe we should have an email-free morning? Perhaps we should stay offline when we eat food and instead talk to those sitting next to us? Perhaps we should abolish some of our individual and quantitative evaluation instruments and instead try to develop both individually and, above all, together? Even though a process can be formalized and apparently solve a specific problem, perhaps we should still refrain from building another panopticonic prison cell which, together with other, similar structures, makes life even more abstract, controlled and cold.

A number of power strategies were described in the previous chapter. It is hard to design a list of effective strategies based on the kind of power theories developed by Foucault, Acker, Michels and other, similar researchers, but, at the same time, it is exactly these theories that make us see the world in a different way. They can help us to re-frame, to change our perspective more radically, and thus gain insights that will potentially free us from ignorance and structural cages to a much greater extent than the simpler and more practical models of the previous chapter. The models in the previous chapter are mainly useful when we want to get a particular alternative course of action, a certain agenda adopted in a more precisely defined situation. The theories in this chapter are better suited to an analysis of where we are heading in a larger and more obscure context. Together, they give us the opportunity both to operate on a small scale and to influence the bigger picture.

Thoughts, texts and conversations – linguistic and symbolic models of power

The power theories described above cover both hard material and formal structures as well as physical and formalized processes. The positions of bureaucracy, all evaluations and measurements, and the constant presence of media technology in our lives constitute a kind of control. These theories also deal with how people think about, interpret and describe the world. But there are power theories that focus even more on how we think and describe our world, and that play down even more material structures and formal processes. However, these 'semiotic' and more radical 'post-structural' theories overlap the models and theories that make up the core of the symbolic framework, discussed in the following two chapters, to such a degree that it is sufficient here merely to highlight their existence.

What they have in common is that organization, power and social phenomena can be scrutinized by analyzing norms, texts and language that are taken for granted. Conversations and texts – descriptions of all kinds of phenomena – are never neutral in terms of who and what benefits or is at a disadvantage. By analyzing conversations and texts, power and influence can be identified.

Gustafsson (1994) describes this hidden power as a *wall of self-evidence*, that is, customs, behaviors, problem definitions, solutions and alternative courses of action that are so obvious and natural that they are not even perceived as customs, problems or solutions. These walls of self-evidence can be found in language and, above all, in the concepts that, in this particular case, are perceived as most self-evident, axiomatic, natural, real and good. Candidates for such obviously positively charged concepts in our Western contemporary culture are 'happiness', 'fairness', 'efficiency', 'development', 'rational decisions', 'success', 'perseverance', and perhaps even 'entrepreneurship' and 'creativity'.

The wall of self-evidence does not need to be seen as something inevitably negative. We have to take things for granted, and, without any kind of scale that can be used to evaluate all kinds of phenomena, including ourselves, as good or bad, we would have difficulty thinking and doing anything at all. But, if we connect Gustafsson's wall with the pessimistic Weber's iron cage, as well as with Foucault's self-disciplining regimes of truth, then the wall of self-evidence becomes something which, by seeing and describing, we can also free ourselves from. We can thus see the obviously positive charge of the words 'fairness' and 'success' as an expression of our subordination to our language use. What do we really mean by an 'effective innovation system', and what effects does the use of such a term have? Is 'happiness' always something desirable, and can it be used synonymously with 'development' and 'success'? Can 'success' perhaps be equated to 'career' and/or 'entrepreneurship'? The intention here is not to try to answer these questions, but merely to show that, according to the power framework, even the most innocent use of spoken and written language includes the exercising of power.

Leadership from a power framework perspective

Just as in the structural and HR frameworks, leadership based on the power framework can be seen as a process in which one or more people apply all the concepts, models and theories of the frameworks in practice. In other words, as a leader, let analyses based on the frameworks' models form the basis of how to exercise leadership. But it is also possible to focus leadership more directly and with a greater focus on individuals, their thoughts, skills and behaviors. We then focus once again on the first and second dimensions of power (see Chapter 6). Metaphorically, a leader viewed from the power framework perspective can be seen both as a manipulative deceiver and as a lawyer who manages differing interests and conflicts as rationally as possible. However, if the power framework's leader is seen as a lawyer, it is important to remember that even lawyers have a client with a specific agenda, and, just like everyone else, lawyers also have their own agendas. But, since the power framework can be viewed as a criticism of both the structural and HR frameworks, it can also be used to criticize these frameworks' view of leadership. Thus, for the power framework the idea of a leader who designs rational structures and effective instruments for achieving goals that benefit all, is naïve. The HR framework's idea of communicative and honest leaders who help people understand each other and who support them to reach common goals, is even more naïve.

Another variant of this more individually focused type of criticism is formulated by Maccoby (2004). Based on the psychodynamic theories of Freud and Fromm, Maccoby claims that great and often heralded leaders frequently have clearly dysfunctional personality traits. Maccoby believes that the glorification of major 'heroic' leaders is dangerous, as these leaders can pose major problems for both organizations and their various stakeholders. We now describe Maccoby's categorization of different types of leaders as the final model within the power framework.

Maccoby's Freud-based leader types

Maccoby's criticism is directed neither at all managers/leaders nor all senior executives. His purpose is more to warn us about our praise and admiration of a certain kind of leader. Maccoby (2004) thinks that 'heroic' and 'larger-than-life' leaders, who often receive great attention in media, literature and research, often pose a threat to the company or organization in which they operate. This is because these leaders often have a clear narcissistic personality disorder. Maccoby formulates three typical leaders based on Freud's categorization of the basic personality types: erotic, obsessive and narcissistic. Maccoby also believes that the prevalence of leaders with these personality traits differs in different professions and industries. However, it is the narcissistic leader who is the main focus and who receives the most attention here (see below).

According to Maccoby, *erotic* leaders have personality traits that make them extrovert and communicative; they are perceived as warm and like to show emotional affection for others as well as to receive emotional approval from others. Although erotic leaders are sensitive, in terms of them wanting to approve others and receive approval emotionally, they are not sensitive in terms of being delicate or having uncontrolled emotions. They could be said to have high emotional intelligence and correspond to what the HR framework stipulates to be the perfect leader, one who supports their followers and allows them to grow. The erotic leader creates strong emotional ties, which can create both loyalty and a willingness to cooperate, but also a reluctance to change. According to Maccoby, this type of leader is common in schools and educational organizations, as well as in healthcare. If we look at current popular texts and descriptions of leaders, the erotic leader is often a celebrated ideal in most types of organizations, especially in fast-growing entrepreneurial businesses.

Obsessive leaders are, in Maccoby's opinion, introvert, analytical and structured. They create and maintain good order. If the erotic leader corresponds to the leadership ideal of the HR framework, the *productive* obsessive leader can be said to correspond to the structural framework's ideal leader. Obsessive leaders do not need social approval, nor do they seek to approve others; they instead prefer to immerse themselves in huge amounts of facts and to conduct extensive analyses. An obsessive leader can communicate clearly but lacks vision. As an entrepreneur, the obsessive leader is not a risk-taker, but systematic and persistent. The obsessive leader can be seen as an asocial nerd, a know-all and a bureaucrat, but they are also highly self-critical and careful when going beyond their area of expertise. The obsessive leader can therefore become unproductive when their expertise and analytical ability are insufficient. According to Maccoby, obsessive leaders are common in more structured and analytical activities, such as investigative work, accounting and business planning.

The narcissistic leader

It is, as already mentioned, the narcissistic leader who is Maccoby's main focus. According to Maccoby, narcissistic leaders are self-reliant in the sense that they do not need either solid social relations or large amounts of data and comprehensive analyses to exercise strong leadership. Narcissistic leaders are hard to impress. They are innovators and driven by a will for power and influence. They love to possess expert knowledge in a particular area or industry, but they do not hesitate to go beyond their area of expertise or take great risks. Narcissistic leaders can ask critical and uncomfortable questions, and, unlike erotic leaders, they do not strive to be popular among friends – they want to be admired heroes. Unlike obsessive leaders, they are not hampered by a self-critical superego but aggressively work towards their goals without hesitation. Because of their independence and aggression, they are constantly on guard against opponents and enemies, which can lead to isolation, even though they are successful. In connection with extreme stress, their suspicion and aggression can develop into paranoia.

Strengths of the narcissistic leader

According to Maccoby, erotic leaders' great need for support and friendship makes them quite bad leaders. In Maccoby's view, obsessive leaders are better because they can structure and make rational decisions, but without major risk-taking. But it is narcissistic leaders who best live up to the widely accepted image of the great leader. This is because, first of all, they have great, appealing vision, and, second, because they have the ability to attract followers. Instead of analyzing trends, narcissistic leaders try to create them. They do not follow but change the rules of the game. Their ability to pave the way forward and dare to act is very positive in situations characterized by extreme uncertainty and crisis. In situations where environmental analyses and rational choices between carefully studied alternatives are almost impossible to implement, when organizations are characterized by confusion and paralysis, it is here that a narcissistic leader is in their element. The narcissistic leader creates energy in situations in which other leaders are paralyzed.

Weaknesses of the narcissistic leader

Despite the commitment that the charisma of the narcissistic leader evokes, they have poor contact with and control over their own feelings. They only listen to positive information. They have difficulty learning from the experience of others, and, instead of informing and educating, they indoctrinate and manipulate with great rhetorical ability. This often leads to tension and competition between managers and employees, rather than cooperation and rational communication. The narcissistic leader's weaknesses also tend to be amplified the more successful the leader is.

Narcissistic leaders are bad listeners, are sensitive to criticism, lack empathy and are extremely competitive. This makes them bad team players, even though they claim to like working in teams. Emotionally, they are isolated and keep followers at a distance. Their poor contact with their own feelings makes them uncomfortable when others express theirs, especially if they are negative. Their inability to handle their own and others' feelings makes them extremely sensitive to criticism. If they feel questioned or attacked (which does not require much), they can respond brutally. They can then humiliate, dismiss and punish employees without hesitation. This leads to them often being surrounded by sycophants. It also means that, despite being admired and often holding 'star status', they are often disliked. Narcissistic leaders usually receive a bad evaluation regarding their person-oriented leadership style, and efforts made to improve this are commonly ineffective. Narcissistic leaders do not feel the need to listen to others because they think they know best themselves, especially if they are successful. Young narcissistic leaders often appear to be sociable and comfortable in their relationships with others, but they still dislike intimate relationships with coworkers and colleagues. This makes mentorship and coaching difficult.

Managing the downsides of narcissistic leadership

According to Maccoby, there is a scarcity of research on narcissistic leaders as well as good advice on how to deal with the dangers of their leadership. The majority of leadership research deals with *obsessive* leaders and with how they can improve their communicative ability and team leadership (see the HR perspective's models in Chapters 4 and 5). The reasons for this, according to Maccoby, are that narcissistic leaders are admired and reluctant to change and that it is hard to get close to them. However, two strategies have proven to be effective:

- complement the narcissistic leader with a trustworthy 'side-kick'
- increase their self-reflective ability through therapy.

As for a so-called side-kick, this person not only has to understand the narcissistic leader, but also has to be sufficiently trustworthy for the narcissistic leader to want to establish a close relationship. Usually, this side-kick is a successful obsessive leader. The obsessive leader's orientation towards facts, clarity, stable processes and self-criticism can complement the narcissistic leader's more spontaneous and irrational leadership. As for therapy, there are examples of leaders who, despite their reluctance to change, have realized that their own emotional outbreaks and aggressive responses are not functional and have subsequently learned to express their feelings more productively.

Maccoby exemplifies his Freud-inspired construction of narcissistic leadership with famous leaders such as Bill Gates, Jack Welch and Jan Carlzon. A more current example might be Donald Trump. Leaders in reality, however, always have varying elements of the different types and usually have elements of several of them. According to Maccoby, Jack Welch (the legendary head of General Electric), for example, is a productive narcissistic leader with a clear element of *obsessive* personality traits. Therefore, in an analysis of an individual leader, all three types should be used. Which type or types are most prominent? What are the strengths and weaknesses of this leader, given the prominent personality types? What does this explain? Can leadership be improved based on this analysis?

Fromm's marketing personality

It is also worth noting that Freud's disciple and contemporary psychoanalyst, Erich Fromm supplemented Freud's personality types with a fourth type: *the marketing personality*. Maccoby (2004) believes that this type of personality has become increasingly common due to the growth and development of the services sector. A similar and perhaps even more interesting link is to the more complex sociological power theories described in this chapter. The marketing personality type is characterized by being motivated by constant anxiety about not fitting in. Marketing personalities are completely preoccupied with always being second to none, and are therefore both adept at and occupied with constantly selling themselves to others. They are experts in presenting themselves as attractive people. Unproductive marketing personalities lack direction and an ability to focus, while productive ones are good process leaders, team players, and focus on customer benefit or benefits to colleagues. They are major consumers of self-help literature and are bad leaders in a crisis.

What makes Fromm's addition interesting is that it enables us to include a historical time axis and a social perspective in Maccoby's otherwise micro- and individual-focused typology. In our increasingly rationalized and self-disciplinary society (see Weber's and Foucault's theories above), we are becoming increasingly concerned and adaptable, similar to both Foucault's post-structural power theory and Fromm's marketing personality type. Similarly, it can be argued that Freud's *obsessive* personality type is a development of the previously dominant erotic personality type, seen from Weber's theory of social rationalization. Maccoby's superficially static and individually focused leadership model thus has clear links with overarching social theories and descriptions of long historical processes. In order to truly gain an in-depth understanding of management, organization and leadership, we should analyze such phenomena on the micro, meso and macro levels.

The power framework's generic questions, strengths and weaknesses

Just as with the concepts and models belonging to the other frameworks, those that belong to the power framework can be used for the analysis of all kinds of activities, organizational processes, management and leadership practices. Even when there is no obvious problem or specific phenomenon to analyze, there might still be a lot to be learned from a theory-driven analysis. Trying to answer the power framework's generic questions can then be a good way to get started.

Generic questions

As the power framework offers no objectively optimal solutions to organizational problems, the generic questions are not about what an organization *should* look like in order to be good or efficient. Such issues are replaced with more descriptive questions, which are then supplemented by how a particular actor, stakeholder or party has acted or can/should act (see the generic questions in Table 7.1). In addition, there are questions to pose based on the more complex and overarching power theories. Both the more descriptive questions and the more complex analyses can, however, serve as a basis for how to act as leaders and members of an organization both in the short term in specific situations and in the longer term in general. Just as with the generic questions based on the structural and HR frameworks, these questions can always be asked when analyzing any organizational phenomenon. Their function is to get the analysis started. In addition to using these questions as a starting point, the analysis should also

Table 7.1   Generic questions from a power framework perspective

IS? (descriptive analysis)	What are the conflicts? Is there an open power game? Why/why not? Analysis based on Pfeffer's model
	What does the political landscape look like? Actors, goals and power bases
IS/SHOULD? (descriptive/ prescriptive analysis)	How have/might/should conflicts and power struggles been/be managed by different actors? Political landscape, agenda adaptation, networking, negotiations, co-opting and manipulation
IS? (descriptive analysis)	The third dimension of power? The influence of majorities and minorities (Kanter)? The exercising of power by elite groups (Michels)? Organizations' power relations to macro structures (Acker)? The individual's power relationship to meso and macro structures (Acker)?
SHOULD? (prescriptive/normative analysis)	Is there any reason to change the leadership or organizational processes? Re-balancing between minorities and majorities? Too much (or too little) segregation (gender, class, ethnicity, etc.)? Too many or too few panopticons?
→ (conclusion)	To what extent does the power analysis explain the phenomenon? What is unexplained? What new questions will be relevant?

be complemented by more questions based on the different models. Which specific models to use depends on the problem at hand and on the purpose of the analysis. Regardless of this, the generic questions are a good starting point.

Strengths of the power framework

A major strength of the power framework is that it re-frames and presents a critique of both the structural and HR frameworks. It is critical of the rational optimization–logical structural framework, and it is critical of the innocent, conflict-free HR framework. It also goes against the way in which management, organization and leadership most often are presented in public descriptions and conversations in the media, in education and in all manner of more public contexts. Since the power framework does not entertain the quite naïve, modernist and rationalistic assumptions that form the basis of both the structural and HR frameworks, it has much greater explosive force in terms of re-framing both everyday theorizing and politically correct descriptions of business and organization.

At the same time, however, the framework includes models and concepts that, relatively easily, can be used to create a highly actionable knowledge base. The strengths of the power framework therefore do not only consist of an intellectual critique and deconstruction of rational myths, but also of models that, properly applied, produce down-to-earth, concrete advice. The framework also offers analytical power for those who want to go further into social science management and organizational research, as well as for those who don't just demand tools to streamline their own actions. For those who want to work for fairer and reason-based organizations, the power framework also offers more complex analytical tools. A strength of the power framework is that it has a wide span, from practical and relatively easy-to-apply models, to more analytical, complex and critical models. There is, so to speak, something for everyone and for different kinds of problems.

Weaknesses of the power framework

Like all perspectives, the power framework includes models and theory that do not automatically merge with each other. On the one hand, exercising power is described as something that is about trying to influence others to act for one's own benefit (see Chapter 6), and, on the other hand, the exercising of power is described as something that is primarily about a less conscious self-discipline in which there are no obvious goals. Sometimes, a person is described as a relatively rational individual who more or less cleverly exercises power, and sometimes she is described as a victim of structures and norms in society for which no single individual can be responsible. The span of the power framework thus implies a problem with regards to logical consistency. But, to some extent, this applies to all frameworks and theories.

Perhaps a more serious shortcoming is that the framework's descriptions of reality are so interesting and 'revealing' in their nature that we become so convinced by its analyses that we are unable to re-frame *from* the power framework. We see power in everything and everyone. This can lead to us underestimating the possibility that people can actually agree and create reasonably common goals, and that they can come up with fairly rational solutions that benefit several different actors.

The structural framework can be said to be naïve in regards to objectively evaluating facts and specializing in and coordinating tasks using formalized processes and structures. Similarly, the HR perspective can be said to be idealistic in its view of how people want to work, collaborate and develop at their workplace. But the same kind of criticism can be directed towards the power framework, which – at least in terms of the first and second dimensions of power – has more of a cynical image of our constant lust for power and our unwillingness to collaborate towards common goals.

The solution to the weaknesses of these three frameworks regarding naïve, idealistic or cynical images of people, management, organization and leadership is partly to utilize several frameworks – multi-frame analysis – when analyzing any empirical phenomena. Another solution might be a framework with a more nuanced view. The fourth and last framework of this book – the symbolic framework – represents just such a view. It makes less essential assumptions about what a human being is, and therefore facilitates even more basic analyses and even more challenging conclusions as to how management, organization and leadership might be exercised.

Videos

Don't forget to watch the videos to discover more about the key concepts in this chapter:
https://study.sagepub.com/blomberg

8

Organizational Culture, Values, Interpretations and Norms – The Basics of the Symbolic Framework

Why do all the old banks have thick stone walls, while newly built banks have glass walls?

Why do most management consultants wear expensive suits, while IT consultants often wear jeans and T-shirts?

Why can't you find any organizational charts that describe companies' formal organization on their websites, while it is easy to find their (often very similar) core values?

The above questions can be answered from many and different perspectives. From a structural framework perspective, one would seek the answer in the material, formal and functional, as well in the idea that it is possible to optimize wall materials, consultants' clothing and information on corporate websites based on clear goals for achieving profitability and the efficient production of goods and services. Today, technical development enables completely different materials other than thick stone blocks in the construction of large buildings. The tasks of IT consultants sometimes include manual work which make durable jeans much more functional for them than a suit. Today, work is increasingly being done in teams and in flat, flexible organizations, unlike in the past, when large companies were organized in the form of top-down hierarchical structures. Describing companies as large bureaucracies would give a false picture of their value-based activities.

But, even if the above answers explain a lot, they don't explain everything. Glass is unnecessarily expensive to use as the main surface material in office buildings. In addition, glass walls present problems with regard to the internal working environment, such as light and temperature conditions. It is only a small minority of IT consultants who lie on the floor laying network cables, and this does not explain why strategy consultants in most cases dress in the most expensive suits. In addition, today, large global companies have more complex formal processes, more developed structures, policies and rules than ever before. An organizational chart would make it much easier for both employees and other stakeholders to understand how these companies work. It becomes even stranger when you look back a decade or two – when virtually all companies and organizations had organizational charts in their company presentations on their web pages, in their annual reports and in other contexts.

It becomes even more difficult to explain how companies and organizations can be successful, even when they are neither particularly efficient nor especially profitable. Shouldn't less efficient companies be driven out by more efficient ones? Why can entire industries continue to exist, year after year, even though they hardly show any profitability at all, while other industries have dramatic profitability levels? Shouldn't owners withdraw from less profitable industries and invest their capital in more profitable ones?

For example, how can a business school like the Stockholm School of Economics exist? The cost per educated pupil is sky-high compared to other business and economics programs in Sweden. With premises in the inner city of Stockholm, where the square meter rent is ridiculously high, with more professors per pupil than any other university, with extremely well-paid senior executives and board members from Sweden's largest company who regularly participate in the school's undergraduate education, with overhead costs (subscriptions to international databases with research publications, alumni activities, student services, etc.) that are spread among a very small number of students compared to other universities … how is this possible?

Based on a structural or HR framework, these high costs can only be justified by the fact that the Stockholm School of Economics does not just produce slightly better bachelor and master's students, but far and away better ones. However, while newly graduated students from the Stockholm School of Economics are extremely attractive to the labor market, there is no actual measurement that shows that they can really do more or perform better than newly graduated economics students from other universities. Very high costs to produce possibly slightly better goods and services cannot equal an efficient organization, and yet the small elite school exists and, in many people's eyes, is also very successful.

To understand why it is so common for bank offices to have glass façades, why certain professional groups dress in specific ways, why some things are hidden and other things are highlighted on corporate websites, and how obviously inefficient organizations can be successful, we must look beyond objective, material, measurable and functional explanations. We must interpret and understand, rather than measure and explain. We must go beyond what is visible and into the meanings, values, interpretations, ideas, perspectives and taken-for-granted assumptions that lie behind and are expressed in the glass walls, the suits, the company descriptions, and in the creation, existence, success and failure of companies.

The symbolic framework offers powerful analytical tools to do just that. Based on a symbolic framework, we can see glass walls, clothing styles, buildings, organizational structures, formalized processes, company descriptions and entire organizations not as measurable, given facts, but as symbols and artifacts. By looking at these phenomena that are constructed from certain specific ideas and taken-for-granted perspectives, we can put them into a cultural and understandable context. We can understand and explain phenomena that appear to be completely irrational and illogical – not to say impossible – when analyzed using models belonging to the other frameworks. And, importantly, the explanations that these powerful analytical tools can produce, assuming that they are properly used, open up a vast array of opportunities for action in terms of smart, sensible and effective exercising of management, organization and leadership. The symbolic framework can make us both much wiser and more effective as leaders and organizational members.

Once upon a time, long ago, money consisted of physical coins and banknotes. In order to dare to leave these in a bank, it was important that we could trust that the bank was safe. The thick stone walls and the heavy vaults gave an air of safety and confidence – they should be able to keep our money safe. We want to be able to rely on banks today, but we no longer see traditional bank robberies as the biggest threat to the security of our assets. Instead, it is banks themselves that we believe trick us into paying all kinds of fees for their sometimes quite incomprehensible services. What do they actually do in there with our hard-earned assets? We require transparency in order to trust them. Glass walls are more transparent than both stone and steel walls and symbolize a bank's (possibly high level of) honesty and openness. The glass façades may be unnecessarily expensive and not very functional for the work carried out behind them, but they symbolize openness and honesty, which creates confidence in banks and is a basic requirement for them having something to do at all, efficiently or not.

Perhaps the increasingly costly and comprehensive risk-control functions, which banks invest heavily in, can be understood in the same way as their choice of expensive façade materials. Whether their costly internal control functions are effective or not is perhaps not the most important thing. Perhaps the most important thing is that the large investments in these systems mean that we trust banks, despite all the scandals and crises. Might it even be the case that we give companies and organizations a better assessment the higher their costs are (and thus the more inefficient they are) because the value of their goods and services is so difficult to measure? This would explain both banks' expensive office buildings and their extensive risk-control systems, strategy consultants' expensive clothes, and the School of Economics in Stockholm's long-standing and continued success.

After this lengthy introduction, the historical roots of the symbolic framework are described below, as well as its basic assumptions. There then follows a detailed presentation of Schein's model which describes the three levels of organizational culture. This model is then complemented by a description of Hofstede's dimensions for describing and comparing cultures, and by Janis' 'groupthink' theory. After a section on symbolic leadership, the chapter ends with a presentation of Brunsson's somewhat provocative model of organized hypocrisy..

The historical roots of the symbolic framework

Like a great deal of other management and organizational research, research based on a symbolic framework can be said to have 'always' existed. Plato's idealism, medieval theology, hermeneutics, philosophy of mind, pragmatic psychology, psychoanalytical theory, phenomenology, social anthropology, interpretive and historical sociology, cognitive psychology, continental social psychology, semiotic linguistics and post-structuralism, along with other heavy, comprehensive and complex philosophical, social theoretical and behavioral fields, constitute both the basis and parts of the symbolic framework. This means that it is, relatively speaking, more difficult to reduce this framework to a number of handy analytical tools, compared to the other frameworks. The framework can also appear to be more fragmented, complex and difficult to understand. Its focus on what is difficult to observe, what is non-measurable and cultural, also means that, from an everyday understanding of science, it can be perceived as both unscientific and irrational.

From an academic perspective, it is rather the opposite: the symbolic framework is based on explicit and elaborate philosophy of science perspectives rather than on a naive and taken- for-granted scientific view. This makes the symbolic framework more scientific and robust than many other frameworks. It also has the ability to analyze exactly what is perceived as irrational and inexplicable from other frameworks and therefore has a high academic and scientific value.

However, as a part of current management and organizational theory, the symbolic framework can both be delimited in scope and seen as a relatively young research area. As its own research field, the symbolic framework can be said to have emerged in the late 1970s and early 1980s. At that time, within more popular management literature, a number of best-selling books were published that focused on the role of corporate culture as an effective coordination mechanism alongside the formal structures and rules found in the structural framework (Deal & Kennedy 1982, Peters & Waterman 1982). Within more academic organizational research, the increased interest in symbols and cultural expressions can be seen in light of the fact that the already existing management research based on a power framework increasingly erased the boundary between what was organizational theory and what was more general social theory. By importing theory from closely related fields, such as social anthropology, sociology and social psychology, academic organizational research developed at a rapid pace. But developments in philosophy, linguistics and sociology – with post-modern and post-structural criticism as both a rejection of so-called positivist research (which both the structural and HR frameworks are expressions of) and an alternative to a Marxist-based critical analysis (which constitutes the foundation of some of the more critical models in the power framework) – were also an important source of inspiration. Today, so-called interpretive or constructionist approaches are almost mainstream if we look at academic organizational research, outside the United States in particular, where mainstream can still be said to be rooted in the structural framework and 'positivism'.

The basic assumptions of the symbolic framework

The structural framework is based, among other things, on an assumption that the essence of mankind is a *homo economicus*. We are seen as autonomous individuals with stable preferences, with the ability to make rational decisions and with a desire to maximize our material utility function. The HR framework considers us to be more complex psychological beings who only want to maximize our material benefit to a limited extent, and in addition want to learn, realize ourselves and feel social affinity and love. The power framework can, in its simplest form, be said to assume that we are driven by the desire for power. How we use this power is subordinate to the desire for power itself.

The symbolic framework has a more open, flexible or relativistic view of human beings. It is based on less essential and universal assumptions about how we work. We can be utility-maximizing, calculating egoists, but, in another context, in another culture, we can be loving altruists. In yet another context, we can be something completely different. This, in turn, is based on a model in which the foundation of what is human is not in our genetic material, brain structures or consciousness, but in interpersonal interaction. In order for a newborn child to develop into a thinking, reflective subject, rather than being driven by her innate instincts, she must interact with other people. This interaction can look very different in different social and cultural contexts, and thus humans develop differently in different social environments.

This applies both in a historically large geographical context and in the small local context. How a highly educated Londoner experiences the world, thinks and acts in 2020 can have much more in common with how a highly educated resident of Osaka thinks and acts in 2020, than with a highly educated Londoner in the 18th century. An upper-class man in Paris in 1720 perceived the world, thought and acted much more like an upper-class woman in the same city, than like a French male farmer that same year. But this also applies at the micro level. Two people sitting in the same room cannot perceive or experience the world in exactly the same way, because of their different past experiences. Two managers in the same company, two students in the same school, two leadership researchers, two readers of this text, can never perceive the text and its meaning in exactly the same way. Furthermore, none of them can perceive the text in the same way as its author. This also means that it is impossible to describe the world completely objectively. We can neither perceive the world 'as it is' nor perceive it exactly the same as someone else. Therefore, we can never be completely sure – about anything.

This, in turn, means that all our information, all our decision-making bases, all our thoughts and analyses include a fundamental uncertainty that cannot be eliminated, no matter how many facts we use and how robust our measurement and calculation methods are. We can never be absolutely sure of what we see, whether banks are trying to help or fool us, which products are good, which people we should cooperate with, who we ourselves are and what we really want with our lives or how we should organize our companies and organizations.

In order to deal with this fundamental uncertainty, we create common cultures, norms and value systems. Thus, despite our unique, individual experiences and interpretations, we are not imprisoned in our isolated heads and bodies. Through social interaction and communication, we, as humans, according to the symbolic framework, create sufficiently common cultures and norms in order to avoid devoting all our energy to worrying about who we are and whether we understand each other. Through language, our bodies, and by creating artifacts and symbols, we can make ourselves sufficiently understood by each other. These cultures, norms and taken-for-granted perspectives can be seen as templates that we can use as a basis and can then fill in with more specific experiences and impressions. These cultures mean that we can never see everything, but they also allow us to at least see something and thereby make decisions, act, organize and lead ourselves and each other.

The basic assumptions of the symbolic framework can thus be formulated as follows:

- *All people are unique*. No single individual has exactly the same experiences as someone else. A person's experiences, thoughts and actions are shaped by their interaction mainly with other people but also with technology, artifacts and other objects. Thus, two people can never perceive the world exactly the same, nor exactly 'as it is'.
- *Norms and cultures reduce uncertainty*. Everything we know, experience, feel, think and do involves a basic uncertainty. We may have misunderstood, we never know for sure and we can be misinterpreted. We manage this uncertainty by creating communities, cultures, norms, values and perspectives. These act as templates and require much less cognitive and emotional energy to fill in than trying to see everything 'as it is'. Without these cultures, norms or values, we would not be able to act as individuals, in groups or in companies and organizations.

- *Norms and cultures are created and reproduced through everything we do*. In our thoughts, actions, conversations and texts as well as in our artifacts, we express and interpret our culture. This culture helps us think and act, while our actions re-create it. Artifacts such as clothing, buildings, technology, organizational charts, strategies and texts on, for example, core values have no meaning 'in themselves', but they convey meaning, perspective and values that help us interpret, act, organize and lead each other.
- *The meaning and interpretation of things and events are more important than 'the things themselves'*. Since we can never obtain accurate, objective or perspective-free knowledge of the world or know exactly what is happening, why it happens and what the consequences are, it is the interpretations of the world and of what happens that are important for what we do and what we think we should do.
- *Management, organization and leadership are about creating meaning and interpretations*. Through 'symbolic leadership' or 'management of meaning', we can get employees and colleagues to interpret the world, the organization, each other and themselves in specific ways. Employees' (including managers') actions can therefore be influenced indirectly and unnoticed, which in turn can reduce the need for formalized rules and processes, micromanagement and joint decisions.

The symbolic framework, as a basic perspective for analyzing management, organization and leadership, can also be divided into sub-groups. Such a division is made between models and theories that see culture as something that organizations *have*, and models and theories that see culture as something organizations *are*. If we see culture as something organizations have, like an object, this object can be used to organize and lead the organization's activities. Culture becomes a tool alongside others. As a leader, you can then choose which tool you want to use – formulate rules and formalize processes, micromanage in the form of personal presence and influence, or use symbols and stories to influence culture (more on this below). Instead, if we see culture as something organizations are, it becomes problematic to use culture as a means of control. If everything in an organization is culture, then the choice of control method is also a consequence of norms and cultural templates. Managers and leaders are themselves symbols and artifacts of a culture that they cannot perceive objectively or control and govern as they please.

This chapter mainly describes theories, models and concepts that see culture as something that organizations have, that is, they view culture as a control instrument. In Chapter 9, it becomes more complex than this.

Schein's three levels of culture

A well-established model and a tool for analyzing corporate and organizational cultures is Schein's model of the three levels of culture (1996, 2004). The model can

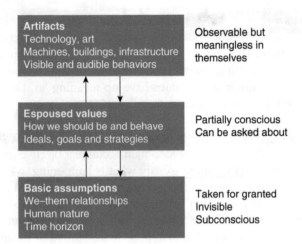

Figure 8.1   Schein's three levels of organizational culture

Source: Based on Schein (2004: 26)

function both as a specific analytical instrument and as a more comprehensive model that other models might use as a supplement. Schein's cultural model is therefore a good starting point for a symbolic analysis of a company or an organization. Schein (2004: 17) defines organizational culture as:

> a pattern of shared basic assumptions that the group learned as it solved its problems of external adaptation and internal integration, that has worked well enough to be considered valid and, therefore, to be taught to new members as the correct way to perceive, think, and feel in relation to those problems.

Schein (2004) adds that the group's shared basic assumptions are about how the world is and should be, and these assumptions determine their perceptions, thoughts, feelings and overt behavior. Schein believes that organizational culture can never be described in its entirety or exactly as it is, no matter how much data there is or which methods are used. Only the parts or elements of a culture can be described. Studying and analyzing organizational culture should therefore be done through observation, but also through communication and interaction with the analyzed organization and its members. Schein divides the elements of a culture into three levels – artifacts, espoused values and basic assumptions – which arise in chronological order when organizational culture is created (see Figure 8.1). The three levels are also, to varying degrees, concrete and material, and their identification varies in simplicity.

Artifacts

Artifacts are all kinds of objects that people have created and which our minds (usually) can perceive. Artifacts are everything from buildings and their design, machines in offices and on factory premises, wall materials and decorations, to how people move, dress and talk. Artifacts are logotypes, images in company presentations, but also the actual text and figures in both organizations' descriptions of themselves and in internal work material. Even how a company's car park is organized is an artifact. Do managers have their own space, or can anyone park anywhere, regardless of their function or hierarchical position? Do managers fly first class or business class, while employees fly economy class? Do they eat together or in different places? Artifacts are also sounds; in addition to what people say and how, there may be music or the sound of heels walking quickly over a marble floor. An artifact might be both a laser printer and the profanities expressed when it does not work, but also the hissing sound, as well as the smell, of an espresso machine. At a technical consulting agency's head office, it can be quite silent, and the conversations that are conducted can be quite low-key and mostly concern technical constructions, finance and administration. At another consulting firm, there may be considerably higher noise levels, loud calls and laughter, and conversations about the company's upcoming volleyball tournament. Formal work descriptions, contracts and formal organizational structures are also examples of artifacts. In other words, a machine-bureaucratic organizational structure (see Chapter 2) is an artifact and as such can be an expression of a specific organizational culture. Maybe the structural framework is taken for granted as being the right path to a successful organization; maybe not.

Artifacts are relatively easy to observe. But, even though they are simple for our minds to perceive, they can be difficult to interpret as symbols of a specific culture. We recognize that a car park looks a certain way because we are part of the same culture as the one that the artifact is created by. If we didn't know what a car was or had never seen a car park, the physical matter that constitutes the car park would not tell us anything. The same applies to all artifacts. For example, if we placed a person from the deepest rainforest into the middle of a big city, all artifacts would appear incomprehensible and the indigenous person would be very confused. For a resident of the same city, the same artifacts appear as a natural part of everyday life and its meaning, and their significance is seen as self-evident. We know that it is advisable not to cross the street just anywhere, but only when the signal for walking is showing at a pedestrian crossing. The indigenous person may not even know what a street is for, let alone a traffic light. The same phenomenon applies if we were to place a city-dweller in the deepest rainforest. The city-dweller would find it extremely difficult to see, interpret and understand all the behaviors and artifacts of those who live there.

But the very fact that most of our companies' and organizations' artifacts are obvious to us also makes them difficult to 'discover' and see as symbols of an underlying culture. Things that are really familiar and obvious do not stand out; they constitute neither something enigmatic nor something problematic. To be able to see and analyze the meaning and significance of artifacts in a particular culture, we must therefore try to estrange ourselves. Perhaps not to the extent of the totally confused stranger – because then we would not understand anything at all – but a certain amount of alienation is necessary to be able to see and analyze artifacts and their meanings. This is also a leadership issue. If we cannot distance ourselves from our taken-for-granted perspectives and interpretations, we cannot consciously control and create desirable cultures. Instead, we become 'victims' of our perspectives and the culture that defines our 'truths'.

Espoused values

Espoused values are all manner of explicit value statements – the message in a business corporation's mission statement, or the values expressed in their publicly stated core values, or an employee's opinion on what characterizes good leadership. The vast majority of people have opinions and make judgments about things and people more or less consciously. Some like to have things in good order, while some like spontaneous and creative people, but dislike those who are provocative and seek conflict. We like a certain type of art and we dislike some sports. Some believe that the primary task of a company is to generate profits for its owners, while others see companies as social institutions that have more important tasks than being simple 'money machines'. Some think that a certain type of decoration makes a workplace beautiful and stimulating, while others think the opposite. And so on.

The point is that these types of values cannot simply be observed, they always have to also be interpreted and they are often not expressed if not asked for. The boundary between what is to be considered a visible or audible statement, that is, an artifact, and a value is not self-evident. Audible artifacts can be seen as things that you talk about in the organization without asking about them, while values are espoused and audible if you ask questions that are usually not asked in day-to-day work. You can also see espoused values as interpreting observable and audible artifacts, that is, the talk and the texts that already exist, by asking them questions, instead of interpreting them 'verbatim'. What values, assessments and cause–effect relationships, for example, imply a company's formulated strategy or mission? How are opportunities and threats valued in the environment? Questions can thus be asked both of organization members and about already observed conversations and texts.

An additional way to distinguish the two levels is to see an artifact as that which exists, that which is, while a value is about what should be and how it should be. Espoused values can explain things that can be observed at the artifact level. But there is no one-to-one relationship between the two levels. Espoused values can be just stated values, that is, something that you say you think should happen, but it is far from certain that the same person who says they think something will also act in accordance with this view. Many of us do not like how animals are treated in industrial food production. We want chickens, cows and pigs to be bred under reasonably 'humane' conditions, but this does not prevent us from taking the food store up on its offer of cut-price chicken fillets. To understand what drives us as individuals, in companies and organizations, we need to analyze artifacts, espoused values and our basic assumptions alike.

Regardless of where the line is drawn between the artifact level and espoused values, we might say that by interpreting statements and asking specifically about values, artifacts give us more clues and information that lie slightly below the concrete material surface. We approach the deeper essence of culture by asking questions about how it should be, what things mean, and what is perceived as good, bad, right and wrong.

Basic assumptions

According to Schein, all three levels in the model are elements of an organization's culture, but it is the basic assumptions that make up the essence of the organizational culture. By putting these basic assumptions into words, our understanding of the entire organization, its processes, strategies and employees and their actions increases. An organization's basic assumptions should not be confused with the culture, or the core values that representatives of the organization say the organization has. Core values in the form of a bulleted list on a website, or a manager's description of their organization's values and culture, can instead be interpreted as being artifacts and espoused values. However, these core values do not always align with the same organization's culture and basic assumptions, and this difference can be analyzed with the aid of Schein's model. The difference between the explicitly expressed culture and the basic assumptions, according to the model, can be large or small, but it is always there. In an organization that claims to have core values based on meritocracy, diversity and competence, there may well be an assumption about who 'we' are and who 'they' are that is not at all based on merit and competence. In an organization that claims to have a creative and open culture, there can very well be hard, top-down pressure for conformity, recruitment and promotion of yes-people and a management group characterized by group thinking (see the section 'Groupthink' a little later in this chapter).

Putting basic assumptions into words is difficult, as their wording is never an unambiguous consequence of the identified artifacts and espoused values. Describing basic assumptions requires weighing different possible interpretations against each other, judging and evaluating. There are always competing interpretations, and you can never prove that a certain interpretation is obviously better than another. In addition to being able to substantiate the description of basic assumptions with information on artifacts and values, you should strive for a description of your basic assumptions that is short, clear and yet explains as much as possible.

Another way to articulate basic assumptions that explains as much as possible is to formulate assumptions that break as much as possible with more superficial and already existing descriptions of the organization and its culture. A clearly different or alternative interpretation can be said to provide added value compared to an interpretation that is in line with already existing descriptions. The added understanding is then a result of the theoretical interpretation – and re-framing – that is as different as possible from the common-sense interpretation of the culture (see the section on critical thinking and re-framing in Chapter 1). At the same time, this re-framed interpretation of an organizational culture must still have a robust link to the observed artifacts and espoused values. But this interpretative work is difficult and it does involve a trade-off – maximum fit with the identified artifacts and espoused values, or a completely different and alternative description? In practice, it is often possible to achieve a good fit with the artifacts and values and to contradict and say something new. This is because it is often quite obvious that neither the artifacts nor the espoused values tally particularly well with different kinds of empirical impressions. Artifacts are opposed to artifacts, which in turn are opposed to values that are opposed to other values.

The often complex and exciting, perhaps even paradoxical, picture of reality that emerges when artifacts and espoused values are considered without a deeper analysis often gives the best clue to formulating basic assumptions that are both in line with empirical material and 'contradict' it, that is, provide a new understanding of the analyzed organization and its culture. A typical example of this kind of paradoxical empirical impressions is that an organization that describes itself as flat and decentralized can also be described as an extensively work-divided and top-down organization based on a structural analysis, even though the organization itself does not provide any such organizational charts; or that a company constantly describes itself as being entrepreneurial, creative and innovative, even though its profitability comes from advertising revenues from one and the same business that has looked the same for many years and despite the fact that most attempts at new, profitable products have failed.

Another way of identifying tensions that can form the basis of an analysis using Schein's model is to see what conclusions the other three frameworks have resulted in. Is there a conflict between the structural and the HR analyses? Is the power analysis in line with the structural and HR analysis or not, and can any tensions between these analyses be seen in new light based on an analysis of the organizational culture?

Schein (2004) provides five dimensions which he believes are suitable to describe the basic assumptions:

1. us and them
2. human nature
3. time and space
4. work and leisure
5. feminine and masculine.

According to Schein, by formulating basic assumptions in terms of these five dimensions, a description of the essence of culture can then be formulated. Here, Schein's model can be supplemented by many other models, theories and perspectives. For example, assumptions about human nature can be understood based on McGregor's Theory X and Y (see Chapter 4), and Kanter and Acker's power theories are relevant for the analysis of assumptions about what is typically masculine and feminine (see Chapter 7). We can also benefit from the basic assumptions of the four frameworks. According to the structural framework, work and leisure time should be kept strictly apart. At work, rationality, knowledge, facts and competence should govern, while leisure time may also include emotionally controlled actions, subjective assessments, personal tastes and pleasures. According to the HR framework, working life is and should be driven as much by emotions and values as are family life, friendship relations and leisure time. If the structural and HR frameworks often contradict each other, the power framework, when applied in organizational analyses, sometimes contradicts itself. According to the power framework, all people seek to increase their power, but why then are some people not that interested in such power games? Maybe the assumption of the power-seeking individual is only valid in specific cultural contexts? All these assumptions made by the other frameworks can be used to understand the underlying basic assumptions that characterize organizational cultures. Which framework(s) seem(s) to characterize the culture of the analyzed organization?

Assumptions about *us and them* and assumptions about *time and space* often have a high explanatory value, that is, by formulating basic assumptions about these aspects, we often get a deep understanding of why organizations work the way they do. Who is defined as 'us', and who is excluded by this definition? By studying how to recruit, promote and talk about 'us' and 'them', we often identify assumptions that are not obvious at first glance. A company that describes itself as an inclusive meritocracy may in reality have a very narrow definition of who fits in and gets to be part of 'us'. A company that describes itself as the ultimate expert organization, which solely employs the absolute best in its field, can in fact hire anyone who is willing to work hard and conform to the company's many formalized processes and control structures. As far as 'time and space' is concerned, an organization may say that it promotes social responsibility and environmental sustainability, but the same organization may produce its products in distant, low-wage countries with working conditions that are worse than those of its competitors and with a strongly negative environmental impact with regard to both the local environment in the producer country and globally due to long haulage. An analysis of assumptions about us–them and about time and space often makes it possible to go beyond explicitly formulated strategies, objectives and values.

A dynamic model that includes learning, socialization, success and crisis

The above review of the three levels may give the impression that Schein's cultural model is static and results in a static description of organizational culture at a given time. However, Schein's definition of culture already shows that the model should be seen as, and can be used for, a more dynamic description of culture. The definition includes concepts such as 'learning' and 'work well' and 'new members', which implies change over time and means that the model includes a theory of how culture is created, strengthened and weakened. Figure 8.1 illustrates this dynamic by the vertical arrows.

According to Schein, groups are formed by one or a few initiators, such as a company's founders or managers, gathering people around them to solve a task, reach a goal or perform a certain activity. There is not necessarily a common view on how this should happen, but typically the initiator, founder or manager exercises leadership, that is, exerts power, to bring others round to a certain way of acting. If this works – that is, leads to a positive result, or at least is perceived as a successful activity – the likelihood that the same group of people will act in a similar way in a future similar situation increases. Each time this similar action is repeated and perceived as successful, this way of acting will increasingly be perceived as obviously the best way to act. At the beginning, members might disagree, and there might be strong arguments for solving the task in other ways, but, with time and success, the group will become increasingly united, and arguments for other options will be forgotten. The visible and audible behavior at the artifact level will increasingly be based on the group's shared espoused values and on taken-for-granted basic assumptions about how the world works (the arrows pointing downwards in Figure 8.1). When new members come to the group, they are socialized into the group's obvious way of thinking and acting.

Organizational culture and common basic assumptions are (1) thus created by repeating similar actions, and (2) that these are (initially) perceived as successful (in order to be perceived as obvious). Thus, with time and success, an organization's visible activities (on the artifact level) become more and more based on taken-for-granted assumptions (the arrows pointing upwards in Figure 8.1).

Successful organizations base their strategies, processes, structures and business on implicit unproblematized and taken-for-granted basic assumptions to a greater extent than less successful or 'crisis-ridden' organizations.

The two sides of strong culture

Success is a contributory factor to the creation of a 'strong' organizational culture. 'Strong culture' means a high degree of homogeneity in the basic assumptions that an organization's members make, that is, a similarity in how they think, interpret and thus act. In an organization with a strong culture, members are largely homogeneous in terms of thought and action, while members of organizations with a weak culture (or several subcultures; see below) think and act differently. Once established, a strong culture can coordinate the activities of people and organizations and thereby contribute to efficiency and success. A strong culture can thus supplement and even replace rules and formalized processes as an effective coordination mechanism. A strong culture can therefore be both a consequence of an organization's success and a contributory cause of the same organization's success.

In addition, basic assumptions are more inert and more difficult to change than both espoused values and artifacts. This means that organizations with strong cultures are also difficult to change. The strong culture coordinates and leads to efficiency, while, at the same time, inhibiting innovation and adaptability. The inertia of the basic assumptions means that they 'lag behind' the more superficial levels of culture. Even if you restructure, perhaps in accordance with the structural configurations of the structural framework, it is not certain that this will have the planned effect that you expected. Based on a symbolic framework, you have only changed on the artifact level, perhaps justified the change at a values level, while the basic assumptions create resistance.

A few examples may clarify how this can happen: a large, old and relatively successful company is characterized by an organizational culture whose basic assumptions include an idea that hierarchy and vertical control are the best way to coordinate large companies. A newly appointed CEO and partly new management decide to introduce a new support system, which aims to make it easier for employees at lower hierarchical levels to make their own decisions. The system is thus part of a decentralization. However, most employees and middle managers perceive the system as an expanded control structure and increased centralization and therefore oppose its implementation. As a result, the system will never be used. In another company, a large international strategy and management consultancy, there is an elitist organizational culture, which, among other things, puts a premium on employees with diplomas from highly rated business schools. Explicitly, it describes itself as a meritocracy, that is, it employs and promotes on the basis of knowledge, qualifications and competence. Despite this, a couple of highly motivated, hard-working and highly competent 'junior partners' do not receive the promotion that the young consultants should receive on the basis of their competence and business results, because they did not go to the same schools as their colleagues and managers. Educational background is confused with qualifications as a result of an elitist basic assumption.

A strong organizational culture can thus create both effective coordination and rigid organizations. In addition, the actual content of the basic assumptions can create problems when trying to organize in ways that are not in line with these. Basic assumptions are not only rigid, they also reformulate the reality in an unconscious and thus partly uncontrolled manner. This is why it is important to analyze organizational culture, for example using Schein's model – it creates a deeper understanding of how and why an organization functions as it does. Such an analysis should begin by attempting to answer two main questions:

- How 'strong' is the culture that the organization is characterized by?
- What characterizes the 'content' of this culture's basic assumptions?

How strong or homogeneous an organizational culture is also has to do with phenomena such as 'sub-cultures' and 'group thinking', which we will return to shortly. First, however, an additional model will be described which can be used to supplement Schein's model when trying to put the content of a culture into words. The content of the basic assumptions can be described with the aid of Schein's five dimensions (see above), but also with the help of the dimensions that Hofstede believes are the most decisive in comparisons of cultures.

Hofstede's model for comparing and describing culture

Describing the essence of culture – or, if we start from Schein's model, the basic assumptions – is difficult. However, there are more models that can help and complement the dimensions that Schein proposes (us–them, human nature, and so on; see above). Hofstede (1980) compared cultural conditions in different countries by studying IBM offices worldwide. The study resulted in a model describing the content of culture in four dimensions. Subsequent research has resulted in two more dimensions being added so that the model now comprises six dimensions which characterize and distinguish the culture of groups (Hofstede et al. 2010). Hofstede's own research focuses on differences between national cultures, but the descriptive model can also be used to analyze organizational cultures.

Power distance

The first dimension, power distance, describes how subordinates and people with relatively little power relate to powerful individuals. According to this model, power distance is not about the actual distribution of power, but is a description of how people perceive power and powerful individuals. In cultures with high power distance, people accept that those in power exercise that power to a greater extent than those in in cultures with low power distance. However, how people perceive power distances also affects real power and influence processes. In cultures characterized by high power distance, organizing often takes place with more authoritarian structures, while organizing in cultures with low power distance often takes place more democratically. According to Hofstede's research, Nordic countries are characterized by lower power distances than, for example, southern and eastern European countries. The fact that Sweden is known for its non-authoritarian leadership is thus supported by Hofstede's research.

Individualism versus collectivism

Cultures can be described as individualistic or collective. In cultures that are highly individualistic, people identify with 'I' rather than with 'we'. A high degree of individualism means that individuals prefer and are expected to live in loosely knit and changing social networks, and that they primarily take care of themselves. A high degree of collectivism means that people identify with 'we' rather than 'I'. Individuals in these cultures are very loyal to other individuals in the same cultural group and they take care of each other. According to Hofstede's studies, Latin American countries are the most collectivist, while English-speaking and western European countries are the most individualistic. If we loop back to the concept of 'strong culture', such a model can also be characterized by a high degree of individualism – all share the assumption that individuals primarily take care of themselves. Is then a strong individualistic culture equally effective in terms of coordination as a strong collectivist culture? Is it just as bad at creativity and innovation? Can a strong and, at the same time, individualistic culture be a way of bridging the contradiction between (static) efficiency and development over time? Or does a weak collectivist culture work better?

Femininity versus masculinity

Hofstede uses the terms femininity and masculinity in a way that can be perceived to be largely stereotyped and prejudiced with regard to women's and men's characteristics, behaviors and values. It is therefore very important to point out that the two concepts describe 'traditional' or 'stereotypical' values about what is feminine and what is masculine. The terms here should not be confused with how people behave, think or are characterized in real life. In so-called feminine cultures, relationships, cooperation, care for the weak and quality of life are highly valued. The so-called feminine culture is collaborative and consensus-oriented. In so-called masculine cultures, courage, toughness, initiative, success and material rewards are highly valued. The so-called masculine culture is competitive. Sweden is the world's most feminine country, according to Hofstede's studies, while Japan and Slovakia are ranked as the most masculine.

Uncertainty avoidance

Uncertainty avoidance is what Hofstede calls the extent to which the members of a culture feel uncomfortable with uncertainty and ambiguity. To what extent do the members feel a need to try to predict and control the future? To what extent do they let the future 'just happen'? Cultures characterized by high uncertainty avoidance put a lot of energy into homogenizing and standardizing members' values and behaviors. They develop different kinds of standards, rules and codes to be followed. Cultures with low uncertainty avoidance have a more relaxed and distanced view of which values and behaviors are acceptable. Principles are valued relatively lower, and there is a relatively higher tolerance for deviating values and behaviors.

Long-term versus short-term orientation

All cultures have a specific way of associating the present with the past and the future. Cultures with a long-term orientation, according to this dimension, have a pragmatic approach to the future. The future and its possible long-term changes affect how to deal with the present, for example through education initiatives and planning in response to long-term trends and future needs. Cultures with a short-term orientation, according to this dimension, have a more normative, conservative and historical perspective. They focus on traditions and customs as well as on contemporary related issues within the framework of these traditions and customs. This short-term and historical time perspective can be seen as an important part of what, according to Schein, creates strong cultures, and it can also lead to 'groupthink' (see below).

Indulgence versus restraint

An indulgence-oriented culture provides space for fun and allows for the gratification and expression of human emotions and needs. Organizing and successful enterprise are seen as means for being able to live an enjoyable (including working) life. On the contrary, a restraint-oriented culture is strongly disciplined and regulated in terms of rewards. Success and results are rather goals than means, and created values are reinvested in the business.

Hofstede's six dimensions (Hofstede et al. 2010) can be used to formulate the basic assumptions that characterize an organizational culture, according to Schein's (1996, 2004) cultural model. When used in conjunction with Schein's own dimensions, and with the four basic organizational frameworks, a description of the essence of culture can be created. By first listing artifacts that somehow express culture, then supplementing them with espoused values and finally looking at the different dimensions of Schein and Hofstede, a culture's more invisible and taken-for-granted perspectives can be described. In such a description, not all dimensions and perspectives usually need to be included – some provide much more information than others. In the actual analytical work, however, we should initially try to include as many dimensions as possible, and then gradually reduce them to the most informative.

Sub-cultures

Most definitions of culture contain something about culture being a social, collective and common phenomenon. Culture is something shared by several individuals. Organizational and corporate culture is thus something that is shared by the members of the organization or company. But there are, of course, collectives, groups and communities other than the organization and the company. An analysis of organizational culture should therefore also include any other cultural contexts that affect the organization in question. This may be different kinds of sub-cultures, such as management cultures, local workplace cultures and professional cultures. Some sub-cultures can also be seen as cross-organizational, such as professional cultures, industry-specific cultures and national cultures. For example, an organization with units in several countries will likely include several national cultures. An analysis of organizational culture should therefore be open to communities and cultures that can be said to both split organizations and unite them with others. In management, organizational and leadership analysis, however, different types of sub-cultures have received the most attention.

Schein and many others believe that a company or an organization can have strong sub-cultures. It can, for example, be about two departments in the same company that have completely different sets of basic assumptions, even though they have many common artifacts and also a lot of common espoused values. The classic example is when two companies are merged. Although the formalized processes and structures of the two companies are integrated, and even if the merger is expressly supported and great advantages are seen with it, problems often arise in the real integration process. One common explanation for such problems is that the two companies have different cultures that collide. That is to say, the integrated structures and the common formal processes are interpreted completely differently.

Another example of a company with strong sub-cultures is the large, successful truck manufacturer. In its manufacturing organization, efficiency is in line with the structural framework, with assumptions about formalized processes, continuity and continuous improvement work in line with lean (see Chapter 3). However, in the same truck manufacturer's growing and increasingly strategically important IT department, flexible and informal – 'agile' (see Chapter 5) – project organization is the obvious way to organize the business. Since agile projects are about developing and producing specific systems in small project groups together with users, and not about fine-tuning formalized processes and flows in the manufacturing organization, the IT department and the manufacturing organization have major difficulties working together. Although both express their belief in systems and cooperation, and although both understand that IT and traditional production need to be increasingly integrated, both misunderstandings and power struggles arise due to different interpretations of the same activities based on different basic assumptions.

In addition to sub-cultures in different departments or working groups, there may be different national cultures in a company's different national offices. There may also be different cultures at different hierarchical levels, for example a culture on the shop floor and another culture in higher management. Partially overlapping these possible sub-cultures are different professional cultures. A company's legal department can be characterized by a professional lawyer culture, while an engineers' culture characterizes production and product development, and a market and customer-oriented perspective characterizes the same company's sales department. A conflict-ridden relationship between technology and marketing departments is often explained by referring to just such different sub-cultures.

When analyzing the cultures of organizations and companies, we should therefore be open to the fact that there is likely to be different kinds of sub-culture in one and the same organization. Some of these sub-cultures, as previously mentioned, can also constitute cross-organizational cultures (for example, management cultures, industry cultures or professional cultures). Culture can thus exist at different aggregated levels. In addition, cultures are always changing, even though change often occurs slowly and with difficulty. Part of this changeability consists of different cultural categories having different degrees of significance in different situations. That is, although a certain organizational culture is very stable, and although a certain professional culture is at least as stable and other cultural categories are highly stable, the importance of these different categories varies in different situations. For example, in Sweden, I do not greet all Swedes, but if I encounter a Swede on a small island in the Indian Ocean, my Swedishness suddenly becomes an important category to act on. Here, organizational culture approaches the nearby area of identity (individual, social and organizational identity), which we will study in more depth in the next chapter. Regardless of the influence of different kinds of identities, an analysis of organizational culture should include analyses of the different levels of culture, of the strength of culture and of possible sub-cultures, of the dynamics of culture and possible loosely knit connections between its different levels and/or sub-cultures, as well as changes in terms of shifts in cultural content.

Regardless of whether a strong homogeneous organizational culture or any type or types of subcultures are identifiable or not, it is important to understand how these have been created and how they are constantly recreated and changed. Schein's model offers both a description and an explanation of this, but it can be supplemented with other, strong explanatory models, including the Janis formulation of the causes and consequences of *groupthink*.

Groupthink

A detailed explanation of why 'strong culture' can arise quickly and perhaps unexpectedly, and can also have very negative consequences, can be found in the research on so-called groupthink. Janis (1971) borrowed the concept of groupthink from Whyte

(1952) when he analyzed the decision-making processes behind the 'Bay of Pigs Fiasco', that is, the United States' failed invasion of Cuba in 1961, and the US Navy's decision-making in connection with the Japanese attack on Pearl Harbor in 1941. Janis' analyses result in a model explaining why groups, often composed of highly skilled members, sometimes make more or less insane decisions. According to Janis (1971: 185), the main principle of groupthink is:

> The more amiability and esprit de corps there is among the members of a policy-making in-group, the greater the danger that independent critical thinking will be replaced by groupthink, which is likely to result in irrational and dehumanizing actions directed against outgroups.

Janis' model represents an important contrast both to descriptions of organizational culture as something unambiguously good and to a lot of research within the HR framework (not least on high-performance teams), which gives a picture of groups making better decisions than individuals. Today's major focus on the common core values of organizations and companies can also be problematized using the groupthink model. According to Janis, groupthink has a number of symptoms that can be divided into three main groups:

1. *Overestimation of the group*. Groupthink means that the group creates an illusion of invulnerability and excessive optimism, which in turn leads to increased risk-taking. It also leads to an unquestionable belief in the inherent morality of the group. This belief leads group members to ignore the consequences of their decisions and actions for others.
2. *Closed-mindedness*. Group thinking means that the group members rationalize and explain away signals and warning signs that the group is wrong. It also means creating stereotypes for those who are against or who criticize the group. These people are perceived as weak, evil, insecure, partial and generally unintelligent.
3. *Illusion of unanimity*. Groupthink puts pressure on the members to appear uniform and equal. This involves group members exercising self-censorship of ideas that deviate from those of the groups. This silence with regard to deviant perceptions, in turn, leads to an illusion of unity in the group. Groupthink also means that more direct criticism is directed at members who question the group, who are often labelled 'disloyal'.

The above symptoms do not characterize the decision-making of all groups. According to Janis, groupthink is more likely to arise in groups where the following three conditions are fulfilled:

- high group cohesion
- structural shortcomings
- pressing external conditions.

Groupthink can arise even if all three conditions are not met. Janis believes that high group cohesion is necessary but not sufficient. If either of the two other conditions are fulfilled, the risk of groupthink increases markedly.

High group cohesion

If group members see it as more important to belong to the group than to express their individual freedom, the risk of groupthink increases. High group cohesion can in turn be a consequence of having been involved in a lot together, or coped with difficult situations together, or where the group is difficult to become a member of and has a high status. Companies that are difficult to be recruited by, management teams and corporate boards are examples of groups that can tally with several of these conditions in order for high group cohesion to prevail. Perhaps the regularly revealed corporate scandals, as well as 'business deals' in the top echelons of political parties and trade unions, can be explained by this aspect of groupthink.

Structural shortcomings

According to Janis, there are four structural shortcomings that lead to an increased risk of groupthink. The first is where the group is 'isolated' – for example, a management group that is rarely present on the shop floor, or a finance research group that relies on statistics and has very little direct contact with the practical issues being studied.

The second structural shortcoming is a lack of impartial leadership. Such leadership could be exercised by an external leader or an external steering group, to which the group reports. If such a function is missing, the risk of groupthink increases.

The third structural shortcoming is the lack of norms regarding the importance of formalized regulations and processes. Here Janis can be said to support a structural framework and the idea that rational organizing is best done through formalized processes, structures and regulations. In any case, this aspect implies that norms and culture as a control mechanism are not as predictable as formalized regulations (compare this with Weber's three forms of authority, described in Chapter 7).

The fourth and final structural shortcoming is when the social and ideological backgrounds of group members are homogeneous. If, for example, you only recruit newly graduated students from the Stockholm School of Economics, the risk of groupthink is greater than if you employ from several different universities. If you only recruit students from the Stockholm School of Economics who have completed the same program, the risk of groupthink increases even more. Furthermore, if you employ mainly Swedish citizens, mainly men, and primarily Swedish men with a certain social background, the risk of groupthink is even higher.

The structural shortcomings listed here have clear links to ongoing discussions on elitism and diversity, as well as to several models in the power framework, not least Kanter and Michs' models (see Chapter 7).

Pressing external conditions

External circumstances may require a rapid decision from a group, and if the decision is made under stress, or in a threatening situation, the risk of groupthink increases. Janis' own analyses were based on decisions in politically and militarily threatening situations, but, even in less dramatic contexts, we are often pressured by deadlines and by potentially serious consequences if we do not decide to act. Another factor here are trends towards an increasingly short-term way of running companies and towards ever more frequent changes of jobs and employers. Companies must achieve profit levels and improvements every quarter, and therefore senior executives, middle managers and other employees, many of whom have temporary, time-limited and part-time jobs, are all eager to show results quickly. This increases the risk of decisions being rushed, even though there is no obvious or externally demanded crisis situation. Based on this condition in Janis' model, it could be argued that increased shortsightedness and the stress it creates also produce a negative spiral of increasingly poor decision-making.

Remedies to avoid groupthink

According to Janis, groupthink can be avoided in most decision-making groups by taking a number of steps. First of all, a group leader should assign each group member the role of critical evaluator as well as trying to encourage the group to air openly any objections and doubt. An organization could also set up outside evaluation groups to work on the same issues as the internal decision-making group. The group might also invite outside experts to their meeting with an explicit role to challenge the group's view, or at least, one of the group members could be assigned the role of 'devil's advocate'. The group could also be momentarily split into two groups that work in parallel to open up the possibility of coming to different conclusions. The last action proposed by Janis to avoid groupthink is that when a group reaches consensus and agrees on an important decision, it should always be followed by a 'second chance' meeting at which every group member should really try to come up with doubts and objections. As simple as these steps sound, they all comprise costs, time and risks of leading to conflict and power struggle. But perhaps the most important objection to the remedies suggested by Janis is the fact that many important actions are never preceded by any formal decision-making process at all. This objection points straight to the core of Brunsson's model, which is described at the end of this chapter.

Janis' model gives a picture of homogeneous, collectivist and delimited groups often making poor decisions, that is, they are unable to analyze situations and strategic choices together in accordance with more rational assumptions about how people work. It is therefore a criticism of the basic assumptions of the structural framework, but also of the normative and rational sides of the HR framework. At the same time, it is based on an assumption that rational decisions would be good if only they were possible. It can thus be said to also support the basic assumptions that it, at first glance, is a criticism of. Janis seems to think that we are not rational, especially not in certain types of groups, but that with properly designed structures and processes, we can improve and become more rational in our decision-making.

Another model for decision theory, which is even more skeptical of the type of rational decision that is implicated in normative decision theory, is Brunsson's model, which is described at the end of this chapter. First, however, a couple of models that deal with charismatic and symbolic leadership will be described. The logic behind presenting these leadership models before Brunsson's organizational model is that 'symbolic leadership' in many ways works similarly to what Brunsson labels 'organized hypocrisy'. The main difference is that the leadership models' focus is individual people, while Brunsson's focus is on more systematic organizational processes. Thus, the leadership models are a little bit easier to grasp, and work as an introduction to Brunsson's somewhat more complex model.

Charismatic, transformative and symbolic leadership

Charismatic leadership can mean many different things, depending on theory, model and context. Charisma is found in the power framework as a power base (see Figure 6.3) and as one of Weber's three types of legitimate authority (see Chapter 7). Below, we describe *one* model for charismatic leadership which is in line with the basic assumptions of the symbolic framework and is developed from relatively contemporary research. Then, we take a brief look at transformative leadership, and a closely related concept to charismatic leadership, before discussing symbolic leadership. The presentation of symbolic leadership includes concepts such as manipulation and power over thought, which are also found in models within the power framework (see Chapter 6). Here, the symbolic and power frameworks clearly overlap.

Charismatic leadership

Seeing charisma as a power base or – as it is often seen in everyday contexts – as the unusual personality trait of 'personal charm', contradicts both the basic assumptions of the symbolic framework and contemporary theories of how charisma arises. According to the perspective of the symbolic framework of human beings being shaped by their social experiences and relations (and continuously being reshaped), neither charisma nor other 'qualities' are something given or static in an individual. On the contrary, it is something social that arises in interaction between people, given certain preconditions.

Since we can never be absolutely sure of what we want (we have no 'given preference function', to borrow a concept from economic theory) or who we are, we put a lot of cognitive and emotional energy into creating and maintaining our identities. One way to create and maintain a reasonably stable identity is to identify with different groups. We thus perceive ourselves as members of 'we-groups' and contrast ourselves and our groups with 'they-groups'.

Our relationship with ourselves and our relationship with other members of a we-group are both dynamic. If we are exposed to great uncertainty, we have a tendency to reduce this through our social relationships in our we-groups. If, for some reason, we perceive someone as more influential and perhaps more charismatic than the other group members, the probability is high that we will seek support and guidance from this group member. This is regardless of whether this member really has more influence than other team members. Other group members will be aware of how one member is drawn to another, which increases the likelihood that they will also begin to perceive this member as influential and perhaps charismatic. The member who is 'exposed' to these subtle expectations will in turn have a tendency to start acting to fit into them. That is, the group member who more or less arbitrarily and unknowingly was 'appointed' to the charismatic leader role will increasingly adapt to the growing group pressure. This leader will increasingly exercise leadership and influence, which validates the interpretations and expectations of other group members (see Fielding & Hogg 1997, Chemers 2001).

A social development spiral is thus created, and charismatic leadership gradually emerges. The process can be viewed as a kind of social diffusion that is stimulated by (1) high uncertainty or crisis, (2) people's need to reduce uncertainty through social relations, and (3) the fact that there is always a certain heterogeneity in groups and that someone therefore best fits the norms and values of a charismatic leadership personality (Hogg 2001).

Transformative leadership

Closely related to charismatic leadership is so-called transformative leadership (Bass 1998). This refers to leadership that causes followers to want to achieve goals that are beyond their own self-realization (cf. Maslow's needs pyramid and its highest levels; see Figure 4.2). Transformative leadership is about transforming the members of a group or an organization. It is therefore focused on more comprehensive and bold changes than 'transactional' leadership, which is more about satisfying the existing needs of an organization's members in return for the members working towards the goals of the organization or leader. Transformative leadership is thus 'visionary' or 'ideological' in terms of both method (it conveys visions) and objectives (it goes beyond the prevailing and realizes ideas).

But how can charismatic leadership be transformed into a social identification process using ideas about transformative leadership in practice? How can leadership be exercised in practice from a symbolic framework perspective?

Symbolic leadership

The basic principle of symbolic leadership is that it is about influencing how others interpret and experience their surroundings and themselves. Instead of directly influencing what organizational members do, the symbolic leader affects how they think. As a leader, they help others find meaning, interpret and understand the world – in a specific way. This is often described as ethically completely unproblematic – often, it is even praised to the skies as something 'fine' (visionary leadership is often described as being much more advanced than structural leadership, Theory X leadership or transactional leadership) – but it may be noted that it is basically the same as what Lukes and other power theorists call manipulation (see Chapter 6). Symbolic leadership also overlaps with much of what Maccoby describes as dysfunctional (often dangerous) and narcissistic leadership (see Chapter 7). According to Bolman and Deal (2013), symbolic leadership is characterized by the leader:

- using symbols to get attention
- framing and formulating perspectives for the experience of others (Bolman and Deal use the word *framing*, which has just this double meaning: to frame but also to formulate)
- formulating and communicating visions
- telling compelling stories.

These are explained below, using a number of examples.

Using symbols to get attention

The founder, CEO and head designer of a highly successful industrial design company lamented that he could not wear his usual suit when he met customers: 'I cannot dress as an economist or engineer, because then they do not think we have any creative design skills.' Thus, he and the company's other project managers/designers dressed in T-shirts and fleeces when they had meetings with what were often very large customers. It made them easy to identify as experts in creative design – that is, they received attention for their competence thanks to their clothing.

We have already touched on this idea of clothes, and their symbolic value, at the beginning of this chapter. The most exclusive business lawyers and strategy consultants (those with the highest hourly rates) often wear the most expensive suits, while IT consultants (even those who cost the most) often wear jeans and T-shirts. You can thus dress in such a way that signals creative design skills or legal expertise, but this does not mean that you know a lot about either design or law. The prerequisite for successful symbolic leadership is *not* that the leader has some form of technical competence as a base, but that they have the skills to carry themselves and use symbols that create meaning. A skilled symbolic leader looks at their work as a performance where every expression, in clothes, actions and speech, will be interpreted by an audience consisting of employees, customers and other stakeholders. By analyzing their audience (for example, using Schein's cultural model), these symbolic expressions can be designed to create specific interpretations among the audience.

However, symbols can be much more than clothing and personal expression. All kinds of artifacts can be used as tools for symbolic leadership. Free fruit, coffee, lunch buffets, candy and more at the offices of a well-known, large, global IT company, along with its colorful interior design, can be interpreted as an expression of a flat, non-hierarchical and creative business. The fact that the absolute majority of all employees are involved in standardized traditional sales of advertising space on the company's search engine is no obstacle to such an image. The work performed is seen in a different way because of the symbolic leadership and management's almost unlimited control over the symbols used.

Framing and formulating perspectives for the experience of others

If the students at the Stockholm School of Economics are told that they are the leaders of the future, in companies, in politics and in other organizations, and that they thus have a great responsibility for how both working life and society will develop in the future, they will probably be affected by this and, to a high degree, see themselves as prospective prominent leaders. To a large extent, they will take their studies seriously and also spend a lot of time outside their studies on building their CV, creating contacts and laying the foundations for their important future role in society. If they instead were told that they are a group of individuals who, to a greater extent than the rest of the working population, will suffer from stress, panic attacks, cardiovascular disease and even sudden adult death, due to their upcoming work assignments and related lifestyles, they would probably not be as positive about their chosen career. Their studies at the School of Economics are framed by a perspective formulated by the faculty, industry representatives and others. Even the students themselves are very active in developing their perspective on the future, as well as taking it increasingly for granted. Still, they would have found it much more difficult to develop and take the perspective for granted had it not been framed by teachers and members of the business community.

Formulating and communicating visions

Instead of focusing on facts, how things are and have been, the symbolic leader focuses on what could be. Everyday life in many companies and organizations can be quite boring, at least not quite as exciting as it could be. That is exactly why more transformative and symbolic leadership is visionary and ideological. Building the world's largest spherical building is more engaging than building another cultural and sports arena in Stockholm (a vision that lay behind the construction of the Globe Arena in Stockholm in the late 1980s). The fact that *time-based management* became such a big reorganization success at ABB (a Swiss-Swedish multinational technology corporation) during the 1990s was largely due to it being decided that all the hundreds of subsidiaries with quite different operations would halve the time taken from new product idea to finished product on the market. The project was christened 'T50', and the fact that there were quite different conditions and that a 50-percent time reduction was more or less unrealistic for the many different subsidiaries were nothing to be concerned about. The name T50 was as powerful as it was unrealistic – but it worked.

Formulating a vision is thus neither about sticking to facts nor about planning real-istic processes to reach a high but realistic goal. Visions are about daring to formulate a more unexpected and incredible future state. Not only does a vision not have to be close to the truth, it does not have to be based on logical reasoning either. Instead of a systematic logic, it should be based on a narrative or narrative logic (Bruner 1987, Czarniawska-Joerges 1997). Instead of constructing a consistent message based on clear facts and logical arguments, the narrative logic means that the message should have some kind of drama, a beginning, a plot, heroes, villains, and an end. It becomes more forceful if it is vague and has gaps that the receiver's imagination can fill in. This narrative logic can draw inspiration from everything from Greek myths, detective novels and TV series to YouTube channels. Again, it depends on what you want to accomplish and in what context. According to the symbolic framework, however, what is true can always be questioned. There is also the argument that narrative logic can convey more and deeper truths than any logical system and extensive data can ever do (Bruner 1987). But, regardless of both the format used in the formulation of a vision and the degree of conformity that exists to some kind of truth, this moves us on to the next section as regards what characterizes symbolic leadership: telling a good story.

Telling compelling stories

The symbolic leader is a skilled rhetorician. Rhetoric as a scientific subject is intimately associated with Aristotle's rhetoric model, developed almost 2,500 years ago (Aristotle

Table 8.1   **Three cornerstones of rhetoric**

Objective	Means
Docere: to teach	Logos: reason, factual argument
Delectare: to entertain	Ethos: personality, charm
Movere: to move, touch	Pathos: strong emotional expression

Source: Aristotle (1991)

1991). For Aristotle, the truth was always stronger than the lie, but if the owner of the truth was not schooled in rhetoric, their message could still be forced out by the liar's, if the liar was skilled in rhetoric. It was therefore important that leaders, even the most knowledgeable and objective, were educated in the science of rhetoric. For Aristotle, facts and logic were the cornerstone of all convincing messages, but they were not enough. To be a really convincing storyteller, the symbolic leader therefore needs to complement his logical ability with an entertaining and charming personality and an emotional commitment. In accordance with Aristotle's model, a skilled storyteller needs to master the three pillars of rhetoric (see Table 8.1). By *teaching* with the help of logic and reason, *entertaining* with the help of charm, and *touching* with the help of strong emotional expression, the symbolic leader can create meaning and specific interpretations among her or his employees.

The importance of storytelling for leaders and leadership has received considerable attention, and 'storytelling' has become an established concept in leadership and leadership education. It is linked both to how 'mediatized' the organizing and leadership of companies and organizations have become, and to the increasingly highlighted importance of 'branding'.

Mediatization is itself a complex phenomenon, but it involves, among other things, the role of business life and leadership as entertainment in all kinds of media. Even outside of financial media, reporting on companies and managers has considerable information and entertainment value (Grafström 2006). Organizations and their managers get attention and are increasingly judged on the basis of how well they can entertain and tell interesting stories in various media, rather than on the basis of how well they organize and lead production systems (Petrelius Karlberg 2007).

Branding has a partially similar logic. If all organizations and companies comprise efficient production systems, the possibility of gaining competitive advantage through efficiency improvements is limited. Lifestyle, meaning, identity, brand loyalty and several more symbolic values then become a relatively more important area in which organizations and companies can compete. For business executives and managers, this means that it is at least as important to *present*, *represent* and *personify* a company as it is to *manage its technical production of products and services*.

For such symbolic leadership, skillful storytelling is crucial (Salzer-Mörling & Strannegård 2004). An analysis of a manager's or leader's symbolic leadership is thus about assessing how skillfully the manager/leader uses symbols, frames the experiences of others, formulates visions and tells stories. Such an analysis should include whether a leader, in competition with others, succeeds in gaining power over thought, that is, in manipulating their employees in a given situation.

Brunsson's model for decision rationality, action rationality and organizational hypocrisy

The last model described in this chapter, Brunsson's model for decision rationality, action rationality and organizational hypocrisy, is similar to Janis' theory of groupthink, originating from studies of decision theory. In this case, however, the normative and rationalist assumptions that both a lot of social psychological research and Janis' model rest on are abandoned to a greater extent. Brunsson's model can also be viewed as an extension of the symbolic leadership described above. It is not only leadership that can be 'symbolic', but also the most basic organizational activities such as designing formal structures and processes.

Decision versus action rationality

Brunsson (1985, 1989, 2003) believes that formal decisions made in organizations often do not lead to action, that is, the decisions are never implemented. Although companies and organizations spend extensive resources on problem-solving, goals and strategy formulation, extensive data collection, the formulation of alternative actions, risk assessments and evaluations of the alternatives, these decision-making processes usually do not lead to any subsequent implementation process – they often don't even lead to action.

Brunsson also notes that most of what happens in organizations, that is, the actions performed, are *not* preceded by any formal decision-making processes. Instead, the actions are governed by organizations' 'ideologies' or what, for example, Schein calls organizational culture (see the beginning of this chapter). The overwhelming majority of actions in organizations take place by routine, in the form of repetition, by following rules, conventions and habits. Brunsson also emphasizes social and economic psychology research that shows that individuals do not make rational decisions, as well as organizational research that shows that organizations do not make rational decisions either (Weick 1979, Feldman & March 1981). Compared with this research, however, Brunsson draws a more extreme conclusion: people and organizations cannot and *should not* make rational decisions, if they want to bring about action. In order to achieve action, the focus should rather be on avoiding rational decision-making processes as much as possible. This is because rational decision-making processes have a tendency to generate unmanageable amounts of information, create doubt and reduce the motivation to act, which together lead to paralysis. It is, therefore, according to Brunsson's model, completely logical and sensible to avoid rational decision-making processes if the goal is to achieve effective action in companies and organizations.

Companies and organizations must avoid rational decision-making processes to enable effective coordinated action. But there is also a deeply rooted idea that both individuals and organizations, as well as whole societies, should be characterized by rationality. An ideal about a rational society, rationally designed organizations and rational decision-making managers and leaders, is one of the most important basic assumptions in the structural framework, as well as a basic pillar of modern society, according to, for example, Weber (see Chapter 2 on rational bureaucracy). Companies are evaluated on the basis both of how rational they appear in the design of their production processes and of how efficient they are, that is, how efficiently they produce goods and services. Managers and leaders are evaluated on the basis of how rational the decisions they make are. Companies therefore need to both demonstrate rational decision-making processes and implement efficiently coordinated action.

The problem, however, is that these two processes disrupt rather than support each other. Brunsson therefore proposes that the loose connection between decision and action is a solution, rather than a problem. Organizations can design both efficient *decision-rational* processes and effective *action-rational* processes, as long as they are kept apart. By de-coupling the two types of process, efficient production of goods and services can continue without being disrupted by paralyzing rational decision-making processes. At the same time, demands for rational decisions and rationally designed structures and processes are satisfied via the de-coupled rational decision-making processes.

Decision-rational processes – talk

Decision-rational processes are characterized by talk. Business executives talk about which strategies are appropriate, which formalized processes are efficient and which alternative actions are optimal. Managers represent their organization in the media, they associate with other managers and they collaborate with strategy and management consultants. They investigate, formulate plans and, not least, make decisions. Decision-making processes and the resulting decisions, plans and strategies can be seen as talk, which, according to Brunsson, rarely leads to action. Equity market players put considerable resources into assessing the value of companies. Analysts, investors and potential investors have different views on the correct value of companies. In these assessments, great emphasis is placed on the talk and the decision-making

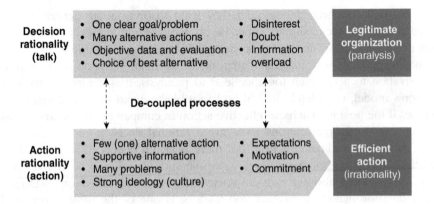

Figure 8.2   **Decision versus action rationality**

processes that companies and business leaders produce. A business will find it easier to finance itself if it produces large amounts of advanced decision-rational talk, regardless of how effective are its operations, that is, its actions. The same applies to the labor market. For example, newly graduated students from the world's top schools look for companies and organizations that produce large amounts of advanced decision-rational talk, regardless of how efficiently they operate (see Figure 8.2).

Organizations can thus attract important resources (for example, money and people, but also government permits, customers and suppliers) by producing decision-rational talk. The more rational, that is, the larger the factual basis, the more alternatives and the more advanced evaluations (for example, risk-assessment techniques), the more resources an organization can attract through its production of talk. The fact that this talk could lead to a paralyzed organization plays less of a role, if it is de-coupled from the action-rational activities.

Action-rational processes – action

Action-rational processes are characterized by coordinated repetitive action – do as has been done before – that is, by a more stable, continuous production of goods and services. Regardless of management trends, reorganizations and senior managers' decisions, the effective business grinds on. Products and processes are gradually refined and based on what is needed in the production and distribution system, and regardless of talk higher up in the organization. The business is governed by a strong ideology/culture and by established structures and processes. The strong ideology/culture means that there is no doubt about what is to be done, by whom or how.

If a more comprehensive change is required, a solution is chosen that people believe in, but care is taken *not* to investigate a large number of options to try to find the best one – it would risk getting caught up in a paralyzing, comprehensive, rational decision-making process. Often, other successful companies are mimicked or imitated instead, without knowing why or exactly what makes these companies successful (so-called benchmarking). External consultants may also deliver solutions that can be implemented without exactly understanding how they work. Primarily supportive information about the change that one wants to implement is also sought, as well as primarily negative information about any alternative options (for example, not doing anything). Experienced middle managers or other influential people (such as previously successful designers or consultants) state that they personally believe in and want to invest in the change, in order to create expectations among other employees that it will be implemented. It is also common to formulate several problems that the change might solve. By presenting the change as a solution to many different problems, the support of many different actors can be obtained for the change. Action rationality is thus almost a decision-rational process turned upside-down – instead of talking about many different solutions to a problem, a solution to many problems is implemented (see Figure 8.2).

Decoupling decision-rational talk from action-rational action

The de-coupling of decision-rational talk from action-rational action can take place in several ways. A common division between talk/decision and action/implementation is between hierarchical levels. Senior executives represent, speak and decide, but avoid directing the actual production of goods and services. Further down the hierarchy, the production of goods and services is attended to. Action on the lower levels is protected from talk and decisions at the higher levels by middle managers and intermediate hierarchical levels. It does not matter how many reorganizations, how many new management concepts, formal processes or new strategies are formulated by the organization's management, as long as they are not implemented at the lower levels. When senior managers make a large number of formal decisions, which, in many ways, collide with what is actually done lower down in the organization, middle managers often experience a conflict and are caught in between what the management wants to do and what is required for the business to proceed efficiently. However, this perceived problem is a solution rather than a real organizational problem: the middle managers and the hierarchical levels protect the production of goods and services from senior managers' talk and decision-rational decision-making. The hierarchical levels and the middle managers buffer the efficient production from top management's decision-rational talk.

Other organizational units, which seemingly only exist to control the business, also devote themselves to decision-rational talk rather than to the governance and control of operations. Administrative staff, strategy formulation units, risk-control departments, branding units, and reorganization projects with several 'technostructures' (see Figure 2.4 and Mintzberg's model in Chapter 2) produce decisions, strategies, visions and formal processes that are never implemented in action-rational operations. But all these units and all their action-rational talk are making the organization legitimate and thus gaining support from the environment. People will want to work there, investors want to invest and customers want to buy their products and services.

Organizational hypocrisy

Organizations and companies thus produce a lot of talk and decisions that are presented as something that the organization is to carry out. The making of a decision is often considered to increase the likelihood that a certain action will be carried out in the future. Boards, business executives, governments and other management functions often use decisions as a way of trying to control their organization and their members. The same actors, as well as their staff and support units, also produce talk in the form of visions, strategic goals, policies, formalized processes and structures, which they also consider will increase the likelihood of a certain type of organizational action. But, despite all these decisions and guidelines, it is often the case that the other members of the organization do not act according to them. Talk is one thing, decision another and action a third. Applied to an individual, this phenomenon is called hypocrisy – formulating a moral guideline that does not correspond to one's own actions. The fact that organizations formulate guidelines that do not correspond to their actions can thus be called organizational hypocrisy.

Organizations, unlike individuals, can blame the complexity of large systems and the fact that many people are involved. Complex processes lead to the occurrence of 'implementation problems'. There is therefore considerable acceptance of a more systematic organizational hypocrisy. The de-coupling of decisions from actions can be systematic and stable, but, for that reason, does not need to be conscious hypocrisy. Organizational hypocrisy can occur without anyone actually deciding that this should be the case; rather, it is a consequence of the many conflicting demands that organizations are exposed to.

In addition to the conflicting demands to produce both effective action and rational decisions, there are other conflicting demands on companies and organizations. For example, it is very difficult for a company to manufacture cars as cheaply as possible (which requires low inventory costs and thus frequent and long-distance haulage of components) and, at the same time, invest in environmentally sustainable enterprise (which, among other things, means as little and short-distance haulage of components as possible). Neither is investing in staff, their competence and development (compared to the HR framework) and, at the same time, rationalizing the business through automation, outsourcing and temporary employees and consultants (compared to the structural framework), an easy undertaking.

One way to deal with these conflicts is precisely through organizational hypocrisy. The HR department formulates responsible HR strategies, which are presented to employees and those parts of the labor market that the company wishes to recruit from. The IR (*investor relations*) department formulates staff-reducing rationalization strategies that are presented to the financial market. Banks' risk-control functions formulate risk-assessment models and capital adequacy levels that are reported to supervisory authorities. Organizations formulate guidelines for quality, environment, gender equality, ethics, core values and several other objectives that marry neither with each other nor with other parts of the business.

An additional way of de-coupling conflicting demands, that is, organizing hypocrisy, is to do so over time. What an organization cannot do today or in the short term can be put into plans, strategies and explicitly formulated objectives. Long-term goals reduce the demand for actions today. According to Brunsson's theory of organizational hypocrisy, formulated plans and goals may decrease rather than increase the likelihood of something being implemented (Brunsson 1989, 2003). Setting up the objective that an organization's managers will, in 10 years' time, consist of half women and half men, can reduce the demand for concrete measures, compared to no goal being formulated. Setting the goal of a steel plant reducing carbon dioxide emissions by 20 percent in five years, can make it easier to obtain new permits to release high levels of carbon dioxide for another year.

According to Brunsson (2003), organizational hypocrisy can be functional for organizations as it increases their room for maneuver. They can act forcefully even though opinions are divided regarding the action in question. This enables, for example, continued gender inequality in management, high carbon emissions, use of child labor by subcontractors in low-wage countries, but also powerful actions in the exact opposite direction. Riskier ventures on new (greener) technology, the recruitment and promotion of highly skilled and competent (female) managers, and improving working conditions in low-wage countries via several powerful actions, require action rationality to avoid paralysis. Organizational hypocrisy is also required to deal with conflicting demands from both internal and external stakeholders. Action rationality and organizational hypocrisy are thus a necessity and a reality, and their relation to morality is ambiguous.

Analyzing organizational hypocrisy

An analysis based on Brunsson's model for action rationality, decision rationality and organizational hypocrisy involves trying to identify loose connections and contradictions between what is said and what is done. Different people in an organization can express different and conflicting messages or perform inconsistent actions. Different parts of an organization can work in different and conflicting directions and/or have goals that are difficult to reconcile. There may also be contradictions in both actions and objectives over time.

One possible way to make an organizational analysis with the help of Brunsson's model is to start from a previous analysis based on Schein's three levels of culture and identified differences between artifacts, espoused values and basic assumptions. For example, can differences between observable behaviors (artifact level) and espoused values be seen as organizational hypocrisy? If so, it may well be a functional solution, rather than a problem. Another way to use Brunsson's model is to link it with an analysis of the political landscape (see Figures 6.4 and 6.5). Are actors with conflicting interests handled using organizational hypocrisy? Another possible analysis, with the help of Brunsson's model, is to analyze the implementation of organizational changes and projects with the help of action and decision rationality. Can a successful business project be explained by applied action rationality? Similarly, can difficulties in implementing a change project be explained by applied decision rationality?

There is also room for normative conclusions here. Given that the implementation of a certain change is desirable, action rationality should be applied. Or, more specifically, too many alternative actions may be examined and their consequences evaluated to too high a degree, to create action within a business project. But, at the same time, an analysis using Brunsson's model should highlight the fact that change projects may not at all be designed to actually lead to action, that is, to be implemented. A change project can be formulated based on a decision-rational logic, that is, to handle expectations and demands for rationality and change, but, at the same time, to protect the business from both paralysis and more extensive change. The exact same change project can also have different functions for different actors – again, the link to a power analysis becomes important.

Brunsson's model is also a variant of an organizational theory approach within the symbolic framework, which is called the 'institutional' or 'neo-institutional' organizational analysis. This theory is, to a large extent, a part of the symbolic framework, and a couple of 'neo-institutional' models will be described in the next chapter, where the symbolic framework is expanded on. Brunsson's model (like Schein's) focuses on the organizational level (meso). The neo-institutional analysis usually focuses on a more comprehensive macro level, either in the form of society at large or in the form of different organizational fields. In the next chapter, the symbolic framework will also be extended in the opposite direction. By analyzing meaning creation and identity work by and between individuals, analyses based on the symbolic framework can provide even more explanatory value.

Videos

Don't forget to watch the videos to discover more about the key concepts in this chapter: **https://study.sagepub.com/blomberg**

9

An In-Depth Symbolic Framework – Micro, Meso and Macro

In this second chapter on the symbolic framework, two theoretical in-depth descriptions will be given. Here, both an 'interactionist' or 'micro-sociologically' founded organizational theory, and a structural or 'macro-sociological' one, are described. Thus, the main part of this chapter consists of a description of two contemporary areas of organizational theory. In Weick's *sensemaking* perspective on organizing, people's meaning-making and action-creating processes are in focus (Weick 1995). In the so-called neo-institutional organizational analysis, on the other hand, meaning is treated less as an interpersonal process and more as something that exists in the 'institutional environment', at a collective or structural level. The norms and cultural elements of the institutional environment can explain why organizations and organizational fields look like they do (Powell & DiMaggio 1991, Scott 2008).

After these two extensive parts, project management, as seen from a symbolic framework, is presented. There then follows a final, in-depth examination of symbolic leadership. This can be said to complete the circle and combine a micro and a macro perspective on symbols, meaning and culture. In order to understand in depth what concepts such as authentic leadership and post-heroic leadership entail, an individual and group-focused analysis at the micro level needs to be tied in with a social analysis at the macro level. Such an analysis can also be quite personal. It can enable you to see yourself and your own leadership in more detail, and allow you to analyze how you influence and are influenced by organizational processes and society. Such an analysis of yourself and social identity leads to questions about what you really want, regarding the relationships, organizations and societies of which you are co-creator. One way to formulate answers to these question is to apply the concept of your own inner compass, which will also be discussed: How can you develop your own individual leadership theory and leadership practice?

Finally, the chapter concludes with the strengths and weaknesses of the symbolic framework, and with a number of generic questions that can serve as a starting point for an analysis of management, organization and leadership based on the symbolic framework.

Sensemaking and human action

A small elite unit was to perform a mission characterized by great complexity and high risks. The group members were well trained, experienced and meticulously prepared. They were to fly long and low, through the French Alps, to be dropped behind enemy lines. The commando group had trained every step of their mission in a simulated enemy environment.

When the small, specially equipped plane had come just over halfway, it was surprised by a heavy snowstorm. The storm threw the plane off course and knocked out most of its navigation system. However, the crew managed to estimate their position and were able to continue the mission. The commandos parachuted into the stormy winter weather, but the wind forced them to land high up on an alpine peak and not, as planned, down in a valley. Once gathered on the mountain, the captain and group leader realized that they were completely lost – they could not determine which mountain they were on or in which direction they should move in order to carry out their mission and not freeze to death on the mountain.

Then the captain discovered a map in his pocket. As the commandos had memorized the terrain through which they were going to navigate, the original plan did not require a map, but now it could save their lives. With the help of the map, the commandos found their way down to the valley, followed the river and found shelter in a nearby small village. With great relief and a simple but tasty dinner at the village inn, they went through the events and planned how to continue their mission. The map was unfolded again – and it was discovered that it was a map of the Pyrenees and not the French Alps.[1]

'Any old map will do'

The above story can be seen as an illustration of Brunsson's theory of decision and action rationality (see Chapter 8). Lost at the top of a mountain, the commando group virtually had an almost endless number of options. Stay where they were, go south, north, west, east or something in between? When they did not know which option was best, they risked becoming paralyzed, and both failing in their mission and freezing to death. However, the map made them stop researching alternatives and hesitating over what to do. They began to move in the direction which, according to the map, was the right way down the mountain. The map's function, however, was not to show which route was right – the map did not even describe the right mountain range and could have made them walk straight off a cliff. But it was the map that saved the group's life because it made them start walking at all. Once on their way, they could continuously adjust their journey. The map created action rationality, and it was exactly action that was required, not extensive decision-making processes.

The map can also be seen as an artifact or a symbol that helped the commando group create meaning. Without the map, the group had difficulty orienting themselves even at a deeper level. The map became a trigger that enabled the group to see its situation as meaningful, interpretable and actionable. Mountains have peaks, between the peaks there are valleys, in the valleys often rivers flow, on the rivers are often villages, in the villages there are houses with heat, and so on. The map did not just mean that the commandos actually moved physically, but also that they could interpret their situation as meaningful. Based on 'interactionist' and 'micro-sociological' theory, it is this *sensemaking*, interpretative and action-constructing process that is the basis for how we develop as individuals and for how we relate socially to each other and to the world.

Explanatory models for human action

Both physical and mental sensemaking processes can be compared to two other models for how people act. According to the *behavioral psychology model*, individuals react to stimuli. We respond to stimuli in the form of actions. We can say that the structural framework assumes such a model in that formalized structures (control or incentive) lead to predictable behaviors. Stimuli (structure) provide a given response (behavior) (see Figure 9.1).

The other model, which is both a little more complex and a little more realistic, as well as resembling the micro-sociological model (see below), is the *cognitive psychology model*. According to this model, the actions of individuals are not simple reactions to stimuli. Stimuli are interpreted selectively based on individuals' cognitive maps (see Figure 9.2). These cognitive maps are seen as products of both biological heritage and previous social experience. They are relatively stable and function as a kind of filter. The cognitive map at the individual level can be compared with the basic assumptions

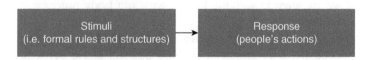

Figure 9.1   Stimuli–response as an explanatory model for human action

Figure 9.2   **Stimuli–filter–response as an explanatory model for human action**

in Schein's description of organizational culture (see Figure 8.1). We perceive certain stimuli at the expense of others. We do not perceive any stimuli 'as they are' but choose and interpret them based on our cognitive maps. Our actions are thus a consequence of both external stimuli and our inner cognitions.

The *micro-sociological model* differs from the cognitive model in that it gives the actor, that is, the human being, even more space and explanatory value. It sees people as more active and creative than passive and reactive. We are co-creators of the very stimuli that produce actions. We can only act based on the world we perceive. As the perceived world is as much a product of our own sensemaking processes, as of an external objective material world, and we are constantly active in our sensemaking, there is no given external objective stimuli that cause action. Neither is it filtered external stimuli that are the cause of the actor's actions. The actor is co-producer of the stimuli that the same actor acts upon. The actor's actions are largely caused by the actor (re)acting to themselves and their sensemaking. Sensemaking is thus a process in which the actor, in interaction with their environment, generates the stimuli that they then feel they are (re)acting to. This may sound both complicated and counterintuitive, but it will be explained further below.

Whether it's about communicating with another person, interacting with a smartphone or protecting themselves from a sudden summer rain shower, the actor is active in the creation of these 'stimuli'. When we react to another person, we both have an interpretation of what has just happened and an expectation of what will happen. The other person could be seen as a stimulus, but we must perceive them as meaningful to communicate with them, that is, it requires an active sensemaking process for the other person to be perceived as a stimulus. Similarly, we need to perceive a dinging smartphone as something meaningful. If we are concentrating on something else, we may not hear the ding, but if we are waiting for an important message or feel bored and alone, we are more likely to hear it. In other words, in order for the smartphone's ding to constitute a stimulus, we must actively participate in making it meaningful to us, just then. And if it starts to rain – if we have just fixed our hair, we may try to find shelter. But, if we are already wet due to the sweat our body produces when jogging, we may not even notice it.

Regardless of what we think we are reacting to, and no matter how, the 'reaction' is always preceded by a frequently unnoticed but still active sensemaking process (see Figure 9.3). It is the result of this process that we perceive as a stimulus, not

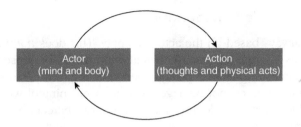

Figure 9.3   Sensemaking as an explanatory model for human action

Note: Both the actor, their thoughts and body, and their own and other actors' mental, linguistic and physical actions, constitute both 'stimuli' and 'responses'.

the stimulus 'in itself'. The same applies to ourselves. Besides making sense *for* ourselves, we also make sense *about* ourselves. Our constantly ongoing sensemaking also includes understanding ourselves. We are co-creators of ourselves as actors and thus 'react' to ourselves just as we 'react' to others. We can observe both our own actions, our thoughts, memories and expectations as if they were external 'stimuli'. According to the micro-sociological model, there is no real difference between making sense of ourselves, of others and of something else. The human, the actor, is an active co-producer of themselves, of their actions, of others and of artifacts.

Micro: Weick's seven properties of sensemaking

Weick (1995) argues that individuals' *sensemaking* has seven distinct properties. It is:

- based on identity
- retrospective
- *enacting*
- social
- constantly ongoing
- based on *cues*
- striving for plausibility over accuracy and precision.

The seven properties are described along with a discussion of how this sensemaking model might be applied in management analysis. Based on these properties, Weick constructed a more dynamic model for how organizing works: the 'pulsating' organizational model, which we describe later in the chapter. We thus begin with micro, that is, with a focus on individuals and their close relationships, and then move towards meso, that is, the organizational level.

Sensemaking is based on identity

Sensemaking is always based on the actor's identity. This does *not* mean that identity should be seen as a cause of or an explanatory variable for sensemaking. Instead, identity is a fundamental part of a person's sensemaking. If a person cannot create a meaningful identity, they cannot manage to create a meaningful world either. Sensemaking also includes creating identity, that is, the actor's perception of themselves.

As an individual, you can never create an objective, neutral, true image of yourself. When you reflect on yourself, it is always from a perspective, in a local, unique situation, with a specific temporal and spatial interest (Schütz 1962). This perspective, like the sensemaking and identity-creating process, is completely unnoticed, but this means that the self-image that emerges is always 'here and now'. In another situation, in a different context, quite a different identity may well be the result of the actor's sensemaking processes. If you consider yourself an 'A-student' and fail to pass an important exam, it may be more difficult to reproduce your identity as an A-student. If you see yourself as a good leader and manager but get low points in a leadership evaluation, it can put your sensemaking to the test. One way for the actor to keep their identity reasonably intact is then to give their environment a new meaning: the grading system is unfair, the grading faculty incompetent, the leader evaluation focuses on the wrong leadership qualities, and so on. In both the student and leader examples, the sensemaking of the situation is intimately associated with the sensemaking of the actor's identity.

Identity is often given 'priority' in our sensemaking. We strive to maintain a previously created stable identity. Most often, the actor, completely without paying attention, can reproduce their identity as a reasonably good, rational, normal individual and human being. However, in different contexts, quite different versions of such a person can be created: an A-student, an inspiring leader, a faithful partner, a trustworthy good friend, a good parent, a temperamental lover, a rational boss, an unfairly treated victim or someone else entirely. If a person fails to create an identity of a reasonably functional person, it also means that the person's surroundings will appear to be largely meaningless or confusing. If a person does not succeed in creating a meaningful identity, other aspects of sensemaking will also fail.

Sensemaking is retrospective

Sensemaking is retrospective. This applies both when we reflect on a specific aspect of our situation and the world around us, and when we consider ourselves more introspectively. Our sensemaking is retrospective, regardless of whether we think of something we have done, something that has happened before, something that is happening and being done right now or something that may happen in the future. For example, to be able to reflect on what we are doing in the present, we must first focus on that present and then reflect on it. Then the present is transformed into a 'just now' (Schütz 1962). This also means that our action has shifted from what we just did to now reflecting on what we just did. We can of course reflect on this reflection, but even then, it is a reflection that we just had, not now. This also means that we can never be fully aware of what we do when we actually do it.

To be able to reflect on the future, for example in the form of strategic planning, a future is needed to reflect on. Our sensemaking first constructs a picture of the future that we can then reflect on. Just as when it comes to sensemaking about what has happened and about what is happening now (just now), sensemaking about the future is thus retrospective. Studies of both court decision-making (Garfinkel 1967) and strategic planning (Rasche 2008) show that sensemaking is retrospective. The decision is created first, and then arguments and facts that support this decision are constructed. This, of course, does not mean that the formal decision must be made first. If we examine the steps in a rational decision-making process (see Figures 3.6 and 3.7 in Chapter 3), without taking into account the sensemaking of the interacting actors, the decision-making process can very well be described as a future-oriented process. In other words, we can describe a decision-making process as starting with a problem, continuing with an examination of alternative actions, and so on. But this does not exclude the notion that the sensemaking of the interacting actors is constantly retrospective, within the framework of all the steps of the decision-making process. When we 'identify' a problem, we first have to construct a problem to reflect on. The identification of the problem is thus retrospective. The problem does not exist before we have constructed it in a retrospective sensemaking process.

Sensemaking is enacting

The third property of sensemaking – *enact*, *enacting* or *enactment* – is formulated as a contrast to other concepts of human conduct. *Enact* should be seen as a contrast to *react*, but even if sensemaking is not *reactive*, neither is it *proactive* in the everyday sense of the word. It is not the case that sensemaking precedes action, or that the sensemaking of one actor precedes that of another. Sensemaking involves a more active view of the actor than, for example, cognitive psychology's view of how individuals filter external stimuli using their cognitive maps. If we describe stimuli as 'filtered', it implies that stimuli are 'out there' and that the actor's limited cognitive capacity can only perceive a small number of these. The concept of 'interpretation' also implies that there is something 'out there' to interpret. The concept of perspective can also be said to have this more passive meaning. Like the cognitive map, the perspective of the actor means that certain aspects of reality are perceived at the expense of other aspects.

Sensemaking is more of an active process. The example of the actor who identifies himself as an A-student and the grading faculty as incompetent, shows that sensemaking is based on and produces both 'stimuli' and action. It was the student who wrote the answers to the exam, and these answers are one reason why the student assesses the faculty as incompetent. The assessment of the faculty as incompetent is also the basis for the student's further action. The student's reading of literature prior to the exam retake, if and how they will appeal the grading and the student's course evaluation, are all actions that form part of ongoing sensemaking processes and that result in a large number of phenomena that can be perceived as stimuli. Sensemaking therefore does not imply a selection, filtering and interpretation of a number of external stimuli, but it is a creative and enacting process that creates identities, stimuli and actions.

Sensemaking is social

Sensemaking processes always involve several people. For example, the leader who received low scores in the leadership evaluation interacts with other leaders, with employees and with those who designed the evaluation tool used. The student interacts both with other students and with faculty. The interaction can be both direct (face to face) and indirect, mediated by various artifacts, technologies or media. The exam questions and the tools used in the leadership evaluation are examples of such media. From a sensemaking perspective, all physical objects, artifacts and nature are media for human interaction. The appearance and design of a building involve an influence on and interaction between the building's designer and its users. This book is part of the interaction between its author (yours truly) and its reader (that is, you). Even natural objects, such as rocks, mountains, forests and their trees, are social in the sense that we perceive, conceptualize and communicate these – that is, we create them as discernible meaningful objects – in and thanks to a social world.

An individual's sensemaking is social in all its forms. The identity and self-image you create are intimately associated with how you relate to others – how you may want to position, and succeed in positioning, yourself in relation to others (and to their identities). Even for the hermit, the lone forest ranger or anyone who spends long periods in solitude, sensemaking is social. In these actors' sensemaking, constant internal dialogues with other, imaginary people and with themselves take place. The imaginary actors are created by previous impressions of other people, both through direct contact and via media (we interact with all sorts of actors in, for example, fiction). But even internal dialogues between the ego, me and myself constitute a kind of social interaction between partly different identities. We also create more general images of 'the other' to have dialogues with, for example in the form of one or more gods.

Sensemaking is constantly ongoing

Sensemaking processes are ongoing all the time, but it is only in certain situations that they are noticed. In everyday life, sensemaking occurs more or less unnoticed. We do not reflect on whether we are rational, functional, ordinary people, whether we really understand each other when we communicate, and even less whether we understand our-selves. Despite this inattention, we make great cognitive, emotional and physical efforts to maintain our identities as sensible, functioning people and to maintain the feeling that we understand each other. Without these efforts, the world, our fellow human beings and our self-images would collapse in the form of existential anxiety, confusion and crisis.

In some situations, however, sensemaking becomes more visible, and that is when it doesn't really work, when our sensemaking is strongly contradicted. We may think that we have understood each other and have a common goal, only later to be sur-prised that we meant completely different things. We have a great ability to smooth over and repair such situations. A simple laugh or comment that 'I was just joking' can protect us from really starting to question whether we understand each other at all. But what may appear to be an exception in the form of a simple misunderstanding is, from a sensemaking perspective, nothing but a small glimpse of the constant work we are always doing to maintain an understandable, meaningful and common world. The examples of the A-student and the self-assured leader also show how well we can explain away and repair situations that are characterized by the fact that we cannot create a common meaning (intersubjectivity). We construct meaningful explanations for, for example, why I as a student and my teacher cannot see the world (my answers to the test) in the same way.

Sensemaking is based on cues

The fact that we become afraid and quickly jump away when we are about to step on a snake is a good example of how sensemaking is constantly shaped by small hints and fragmented sensory impressions or clues (*cues*). Despite the snake in fact being an old bicycle inner tube, we were able to create a meaningful 'stimulus' to 'react' to. Leadership, formalized processes and structures work in the same way. We do not need to know or understand what a particular rule means, or what leaders are trying to say when they talk about their visions. It is even the case that no rules or visions have an actual, true, stable and unambiguous meaning. It is sufficient that sensemaking processes fill in the gaps and create meaningful (effective or ineffective) structures and (inspirational or crazy) visions.

In everyday life, we translate small smiles, body language, critical looks, a weak smell of coffee, a barely noticeable sound from the printer into a logical and coher-ent meaning. Our inner thoughts and our impressions blend together into coherent impressions, explanations and perspectives. 'Culture' and 'norms' do not exist from a sensemaking perspective; they are constantly *made* by interacting actors, including their artifacts, in the form of technology, bodies and language. Our constantly ongoing but unnoticed sensemaking means we avoid having to doubt and process impressions on a more conscious, strenuous level.

Sensemaking is thus partly a consequence of the 'cognitive economy' (let's not waste mental energy on cognitive processes that are not absolutely necessary) that, according to cognitive psychology, we are striving for (Colman 2015). But it is also caused by more social and emotional aspects. If we do not contribute to each other's sensemaking processes, we will be subjected to sanctions by others. If we stop contributing and 'playing along', we will be exposed to negative emotional reactions.

Garfinkel (1967) instructed his students that the next time someone asked them how they were, they should ask the person asking to clarify the question. Instead of answering a little vaguely with some variant of 'good', the students were instructed to answer 'How do you mean?' When the person who asked the original question did not understand the response, the students were to continue to ask for clarification: 'Do you mean how I feel mentally? If I have a physical illness? If my finances are good? If I have been successful at work or in my studies?' No matter how the questioner answered these calls for clarification of this seemingly innocent question, students were to politely ask for further clarification: 'If it is my health that you are referring to, why do you ask about it? How should I judge whether I feel good or bad mentally? Should I compare with yesterday, with how others feel, with how I would like to feel?' The result of this exercise was always that the person who asked the student how they felt became increasingly emotionally irritated and eventually extremely angry. Even the students themselves felt uncomfortable in the situation early on and felt a strong need to discontinue the exercise.

Garfinkel (1967) believes that this and other similar experiments show that we are more or less aware that we will be emotionally punished if we do not contribute to creating a common (intersubjective), meaningful, logical and coherent world together with others. We neither can nor need to understand what the other person means in order to conduct a conversation that is meaningful for both of us. We neither can nor need to be checked meticulously to do our job. Based on small cues, we create meaningful impressions and actions. We are constantly and actively involved in social, 'responsive' action chains (Asplund 1987a, 1987b).

Sensemaking strives for plausibility over accuracy and precision

This last property overlaps in some ways with the previous one. Since we can never be absolutely sure of anything and never know anything exactly, striving for accurate, exact and precise impressions of how something is, including ourselves, will prevent us from creating a meaningful, common world. Striving for precise images and descriptions of the world, precise rules and complete instructions, in itself can lead us to become overloaded with an infinite amount of information that both confuses and paralyzes us (cf. Brunsson's concept of 'action rationality' in Chapter 8). When we are in doubt, the most important thing for us as humans is to be able to shake off this doubt. However, seeking extensive amounts of information tends to increase rather than reduce doubt. Had the soldiers navigating through the Alps using a map of the Pyrenees realized that it was a map of the wrong mountain range, it would have been much more difficult for them to start descending down the mountain. Their doubts about different alternative actions, as well as the likelihood that they would disagree, would increase and, in the worst case, lead them to freeze to death.

Instead of trying to create a more complete, accurate and correct image, we strive to create a sense of meaningful understanding of our situation. This happens constantly and usually unnoticed. We are constantly seeking supportive information. Or more correctly: the constantly ongoing sensemaking process – including the creation of 'stimuli' (based on cues, thoughts and our own actions) – strives to create perceived, coherent, understandable situations. Once we have achieved such a feeling, we can act, and sensemaking once again becomes an unnoticed process.

Therefore, when the neighbor's curious cat, Mimi passes by outside the kitchen window, we do not see a lot of physical matter moving at a different speed relative to the surrounding physical matter. We just need to see a quick glimpse of something small and black and white moving in the green vegetation in order for us to create a meaningful impression that it is a question of a four-footed animal, a cat, and a rather young and curious tomcat named Mimi. In the sensemaking process, we do not need to look carefully and for long to determine whether it really is Mimi or if it is another cat, maybe not even a cat but a black dog, or something completely different. Usually, this is both effective and successful, that is, it is not irrational or unreasonable to try to create meaning and actions based on vague cues and supporting information (cf. Brunsson's model for action and decision rationality in Chapter 8).

This model, or theory, developed by Weick and others, for how sensemaking occurs is critical of behavioral science's decision theory, according to which the human is systematically irrational (see, for example, Tversky & Kahneman 1974, 1981, Thaler 1993, Kahneman 2011). The micro-sociological theory and model for sensemaking are in line with decision research that does not categorize the human as rational or irrational in that manner (see, for example, Gigerenzer 1991, Gigerenzer & Brighton 2009). Or, expressed in Brunsson's terms: it is at least as rational to be action-rational as to be decision-rational. If business is about creating added value by dividing work and coordinating, organizing and leading *action*, action rationality is not only effective but also entirely necessary.

From a micro theory for individuals to a meso model for organization

The above model for how sensemaking occurs is fundamental and generic in the sense that it applies to all human activity. It is based on extensive behavioral and social science research areas which do not self-evidently form part of the subject of management and organization theory. It is, to a large extent, organizational theory, since it describes the human as a largely social and organizing creature, but it is not immediately obvious what implications it has for more applied analysis of business practice.

There is therefore reason to briefly develop how it can be applied in the analysis of management, organization and leadership.

Management of meaning and identities

A first implication is that management of and in organizations is intimately associated with people's identities. If you try to achieve a stable, efficient and long-term business, you should strive to create the conditions for managers and employees to create their identities in this business in a stable and long-term way. The organization should act as a domicile for the identity creation of its members. For a person who identifies themselves as a 'careerist', a clear hierarchy and career ladder are an important organizational component to attract and retain them. For an 'expert', educational initiatives, emphasis on knowledge development and challenging projects are more important. Because identities are products of sensemaking, they are never completely stable or given. Leadership and organizing are therefore not just about attracting and adapting to people's identities, but also about shaping and creating these identities. *Management of meaning* (Smircich & Morgan 1982), as well as the whole idea of symbolic leadership (see Chapter 8), involves influencing organizational members' identity creation so that it benefits the organization, or, reformulated according to the power framework, benefits certain actor groups.

Sense-giving and organizational solutions

Based on Weick's model for sensemaking, symbolic leadership is not only about framing experiences, formulating visions and telling stories. The cues that people use in their sensemaking (see above) can consist of much more than that. Companies can be described and discussed in all kinds of contexts: in informal conversations outside work, online and in news media. Leaders and representatives of organizations feature in all sorts of contexts and constitute material for people's sensemaking about their organizations. In company presentations, early stages of recruitment processes and, of course, in all possible internal processes, material is created that is incorporated into employees' sensemaking. Seeing and consciously designing all this is, from a sensemaking perspective, an extensive and resource-intensive activity. These activities have many names: marketing, brand building, *employee branding* and more. In addition, trying to optimize and formalize processes à la the structural framework has implications from a sensemaking perspective. Describing a well-planned activity within an organization as a 'carefully designed process', or even the organization as a 'bureaucracy' can cause that organization to be perceived as inefficient, rigid, outdated and unattractive to work in. It may be better to talk about the same organization's structural solutions as *lean-agile-hybrids*. It may be better to talk about a company's business as a new variant of 'circular-economic enterprise' than to describe it as 'leasing'.

But, even beyond language use, there are great opportunities for 'sense-giving'. As stated in Chapters 6 and 7 on the power framework, there are often reasons to deviate from what is optimal or right from the perspectives of the structural and HR frameworks. If less 'optimal' structural solutions can create employees whose identity is strongly associated with working hard and in the best interests of the company, then it can certainly compensate for sub-optimal organizational solutions, according to the other frameworks.

Motivation and meaningful work

Identity creation is not only an important part of symbolic leadership and manipulation (Lukes 1974), it is also related to motivation and different types of rewards. Based on the HR framework's view on motivation, understanding, social collaboration, self-realization and other 'motivators' are relatively more important than salary, physical work environment and other 'hygiene factors' (Herzberg 1964). In particular, for highly paid and highly educated employees and managers, intrinsic commitment is important, according to both the structural and HR frameworks. The fact that large, profit-driven companies start operations and invest resources in less profitable areas can be seen from a sensemaking perspective as a way to create such commitment. As a management consultant in a large, international consulting firm, the mere possibility of working on less profitable projects that are about helping vulnerable people, countries in crisis or similar humanitarian aid efforts, can create great commitment and identification with the consulting firm as a whole (including most of the rest of the business that has nothing to do with humanitarian aid initiatives). Seemingly relatively unprofitable projects can thus be highly profitable from a sensemaking perspective.

Meso: Weick's pulsating organizational model

Based on the seven properties of sensemaking, which were described earlier in the chapter, Weick (1995) has developed a dynamic – or, in Weick's own words, *pulsating* – model for how organizing works. The dynamics consist of the model 'collapsing' or at least reformulating the dichotomic relationship between a flexible and innovative business and a stable and efficient business. This dichotomic relationship is incorporated into a large volume of organizational and social theory. A clear example is Mintzberg's structural organizational model (see Chapter 2), in which a decision must be made to organize for either efficiency (machine bureaucracy) or flexibility (adhocracy). The same dichotomous relationship can be found in the lean model, which formulates a trade-off between resource efficiency and flow efficiency (see Chapter 3). For example, in Schein's model for organizational culture, which was described in the previous chapter, the corresponding contradiction can be identified: a 'strong' culture creates both effective coordination and an organization that is both slow and difficult to change. In Weick's pulsating organizational model, these contradictions are reformulated into a constant movement between a more change-inclined and a more static organization. This constantly ongoing pendulum movement, or pulse, can also be seen as a movement between the organizational ideal of the structural framework and of the HR framework.

Generic subjectivity versus intersubjectivity

Weick (1995) believes (with extensive support from other research) that all groups that work together gradually develop a certain degree of work division and specialization. Group members learn from each other and develop different complementary roles. The more this structure develops, the less the team members need to interact with each other. They know what the others can do and they can therefore solve tasks without having to explain, discuss and make joint decisions about how they should proceed. Especially where the sensemaking process creates situations reminiscent of those in the past, that is, when the 'environment is stable', the emerging work division can be more or less unproblematic (cf. the conditions for the structural framework's machine bureaucracy; see Chapter 2). The relatively stable situation created and the increasing specialization make the work of group members increasingly different from one another, and team members also interact less with each other and create increasingly different environments and contexts.

According to this dynamic model, organizations are thus *not* in either stable and homogeneous or turbulent and heterogeneous surroundings – it is rather their own internal processes that are (co)creators of different and changing surroundings. The identities of organizational members are also changing. Due to the diminishing interaction and the increasing distances between them, 'generic subjects' are being developed. Similar to Weber's formally rational bureaucracy (see Chapter 2), the scope for social interaction, community and friendship between the members of the original group or the organization decreases. They can continue to interact and feel affinity with others, but not in the original, gradually increasingly work-divided group. The members of the original group become increasingly abstract and generic for, and removed from, each other. According to Weick's model, this occurs regardless of whether the group is growing or not, and it doesn't require a conscious, formalized or hierarchically introduced structure for this to happen. Thus, Weick's model differs from both Mintzberg's and Greiner's structural models (see Chapters 2 and 3, respectively).

But the most important difference between Weick's model and the organizational models of both the structural and HR frameworks is that the former shows that the increasingly work-divided and heterogeneous group will also include increasingly different opinions and identities. Here we can see similarities with Pfeffer's conflict model (see Chapter 6): the increasing heterogeneity creates tension, friction and perhaps conflict. This can lead to the group splitting and their organization ceasing, or becoming an increasingly fragmented group. At this point, if the group don't split up, the cycle begins again when group members start to interact with each other again. Through new conversations and face-to-face interaction, people get closer to each other again, and the generic subjectivity is gradually replaced by a new intersubjectivity. However, the new community (or the organizational culture, according to Schein's terminology; see Chapter 8) can never be exactly the same as the original group's – on the contrary, it may have changed significantly. However, even this new intersubjectivity and the close interaction will meet the same fate as the original group. New roles, a new specialization and new generic subjects gradually take shape. Perhaps the organization will dissolve, perhaps it will come together again, but once again in a changed shape.

According to Weick's dynamic, pulsating organizational model, the organization can be said to be oscillating between the ideal of a HR framework and that of a structural framework. Community develops into a specialized system, in order to return to a new community. The model also means that organizations can never be completely stable and in an optimal state. Organizations are always changing, regardless of the complexity of core processes, turbulence in the surroundings, new organizational members or the strategic intentions of new leaders. Organizations are always changing because of their own internal dynamics.

Organizations don't exist; they are made

Weick's pulsating organizational model is a good example of an 'interactionist' and 'micro-sociological' perspective on management, organization and leadership. According to this perspective, organizations do not exist as stable, delimited objects – they *are* not something. Instead, meaning and organizing processes are constantly taking place that enact, construct and reconstruct, or *make*, organizations. In the unlikely event of the members of the organization and other stakeholders ceasing to interact, the organization would cease to exist. Artifacts (organizational charts, registers, machines, IT, cloud data, etc.) would continue to exist, as well as meaning in the form of people's knowledge and memories. But, if these artifacts and meanings are not enacted via human interaction, the organization ceases to exist.

The micro-sociological perspective also means that neither formal organizational structures, self-governing groups nor similar phenomena 'exist'. These, too, must be continuously enacted, constructed and reconstructed via actor interaction and sensemaking. Even if a management team decides to introduce a 'machine-bureaucratic' structure, it can, by virtue of all the interacting actors' sensemaking and organizing processes, be given completely different forms, and will never be completely stable. In an organization, the machine bureaucracy can constitute a 'hint' or 'clue' to organizing a rigid, hard and authoritatively controlled organization with unmotivated employees.

In another organization, machine bureaucracy may be a well-planned, effective, fair meritocracy where everyone knows what they are expected to do, but also, thanks to transparency and clear processes, what they can do beyond formal rules and frameworks. Two very similar machine bureaucracies on paper can thus be two completely different organizations. They don't have to be rigid or boring to work in, just like an adhocracy need not be innovative or stimulate all employees to take initiative. From a micro-sociological perspective, the formal organizational structures are merely one of many clues that affect the sensemaking of the interacting organizational members.

Leadership

Weick's dynamic model also provides a partially new picture of leadership. For an organization's survival, different leadership is required depending on where in the pulsating dynamic it finds itself. When work-divided roles and generic subjects have taken shape, a structurally competent leader is appropriate. It is about coordinating the efforts of organizational members – that is, task-oriented leadership. But, when the work division has progressed so much that the heterogeneity risks splitting and dissolving the organization, both politically skilled leadership and an ability to unite the organizational members are required, and then more HR-oriented, person-oriented and symbolic leadership is appropriate.

Applying Weick's pulsating model in analysis

Weick's organizational model can be used to analyze leaders, groups, companies and organizations with regard to where in the pulsating pendulum movement they find themselves, as well as with regard to the type of sensemaking leadership that could work. Is a situation being created in which the organization risks being fragmented? Is there a need for a new joint sensemaking process, or is it enough to focus on the system working without major disruptions? Since the members of the organization are co-producers of the organization and its processes, and the organization is a co-producer of its surroundings, core technology and the surroundings cannot be treated as independent variables as they are, according to, for example, Mintzberg's structural model. The surroundings cannot determine which structure is appropriate. In Weick's pulsating organizational model, all cause–effect relationships can be replaced by mutual influence.

Neo-institutional organizational theory – from micro and meso to macro

A careful analysis of management, organization and leadership using micro-sociological and interactionist organizational models à la Weick thus implies that different structural configurations cannot be taken for granted. Regardless of the number of hierarchical levels, the amount of rules and the degree of specialization, an organization can function in completely different ways. An analysis based on Weick's model therefore involves investigating the actors' sensemaking processes and what they result in. This, in turn, requires looking rather carefully at the organizational members and their interaction, including their verbal communication (cf. the analysis based on Schein's model in Chapter 8). However, it is not always possible to access this type of empirical material, or have enough resources to acquire it. Then, a pure thought construction and 'desktop study' may suffice, that is, you simply think through the situation based on what you already think you know and from a sensemaking perspective. You can simply go through how the seven properties of sensemaking find expression in the present case, and try to determine where this goes in terms of the pendulum movement between interaction and generic subjectivity.

Sometimes, however, you want to analyze more extensive segments of reality. But it is not always practically feasible to study how all actors, their media, technologies and other artifacts interact. Then you can tread a completely different path. Instead, starting from a macro perspective – or a helicopter perspective – you can create an understanding of entire societies, industries, sectors or organizational 'fields', without having to go into detail about all actors' sensemaking and organizing.

Below, we describe two established models that may be used for such a macro analysis. The neo-institutional organizational analysis virtually ignores the heterogeneity that always characterizes all groups of people and individuals. Instead, it produces powerful explanations for why all these basically different people and organizations still show great similarities. For example, how is it that companies and organizations, large and small, with completely different activities and contexts, introduce the same, or at least very similar, formal processes?

Norms, isomorphism and overall organizational trends

Why did all large manufacturing companies introduce quality control processes (*Total Quality Management*, TQM) in the late 1970s and the 1980s? Why did virtually all large companies buy so-called BPR (*business process reengineering*) projects during the 1990s? Is it really reasonable for a global retail chain, a small, relatively low-tech manufacturing company with 20 employees, and a large hospital, encompassing vastly different types of business, to all introduce the same *lean* processes? Why do all companies suddenly engage in *talent management*? Despite all the differences in size, type of business, markets, staff and local contexts, companies and organizations seem to be pursuing their operations in surprisingly similar ways. This is something that conflicts with the structural situational dependencies and Mintzberg's various structural configurations, described in Chapter 2, but also with many other models that prescribe situational solutions. There are a number of explanations for why organizations often resemble each other, despite different conditions. Here, we discuss two of them: institutional versus technical environments; and institutional isomorphism.

Institutional versus technical environments

In the neo-institutional theory of organization (Powell & DiMaggio 1991, Scott 2008), the basic idea that organizations' structures and processes can be clarified by what is most effective in a more objective, technical sense is criticized. This critique is primarily directed towards the structural framework, but also the HR framework. Instead of companies being structured to have the most technically efficient production of goods and services in demand, it is believed that the design of organizations can be better explained by the fact that they follow taken-for-granted expectations, cultural rules and norms. Organizations with completely different core processes and technologies are similar to each other because they are exposed to the same cultural expectations, the same 'institutional pressure'.

Scott (1998) divides organizational environments into technical and institutional ones. The technical environment is characterized by the fact that organizations are under high pressure to produce goods and services as efficiently as possible. This 'technical pressure' is due in part to the fact that there are relatively known causal relationships regarding how to design efficient processes. On the contrary, institutional environments are characterized by high uncertainty regarding how different production technologies, organizational solutions and strategies are related to efficient production. Expectations, culture and norms will then exert greater pressure on how organizational processes are designed. If organizations do not adapt to the normative pressure of the institutional environment, they will lose legitimacy, and without legitimacy they will not attract resources. It will be difficult to attract labor, customers, financing, permits, and so on, if you do not live up to the institutional environment's expectations of what constitutes a contemporary successful organization.

This neo-institutional organizational model also distinguishes (a technical) *efficient* organization and (an institutional) *legitimate* organization. All organizations must, in order to survive, try to obtain resources both from the technical environment, using efficiency, and from the institutional environment, using legitimacy.

According to Scott (1998), all organizations operate in both technical and institutional environments, but they are subjected to relatively different pressures from them. For some organizations, the technical environment is most crucial; for others, the institutional environment is most crucial. Scott believes that manufacturing companies operate in relatively strong technical environments, churches in strong institutional environments, while banks operate in both strong technical and institutional environments (see Figure 9.4). However, it is important to emphasize that all organizations, regardless of sector, operate in both institutional and technical environments. Even in the most competitive, toughly evaluated and optimized industrial system, organizations

Institutional environment			
Strong		Weak	
Public service		Manufacturing industry	
Banks	Pharmaceutical industry		
Hospitals			
Psychiatric clinics Schools		Restaurants	
Law firms		Health clubs	
Churches		Preschools	

(Left axis: Technical environment — Strong / Weak)

Figure 9.4   Combinations of technical and institutional environments

Source: Scott (1998: 139)

need to adapt to an institutional pressure that cannot be reduced to the requirement for a technically efficient production process.

The view that the environment consists of technical pressure on efficiency and institutional pressure on legitimacy fits very well with Brunsson's model for action and decision rationality and organizational hypocrisy (see Chapter 8). Decision rationality, and the production of talk, are appropriate methods for producing legitimacy in an institutional environment, as action rationality is appropriate in order to produce efficiently coordinated action in a technical environment. This means that de-coupling and organizational hypocrisy (see Chapter 8) can also be understood as a way of combining requirements from a technical and an institutional environment. In cases where the requirements for technical efficiency do not match the requirements for institutional legitimacy, both legitimate and effective structures and processes can be produced, provided they are kept separate from each other. If the prevailing organizational ideal advocates flat, decentralized organizations (an institutional pressure), while the production of goods and services requires extensive formalized processes, techno-structure and vertical control (a technical pressure), then the organization's core values and decentralized decision-making can be formally emphasized, while, at the same time, applying far-reaching formalization and top-down management. The formalized processes then become 'informal', while the more 'informal' decentralized organization is formally emphasized.

An organizational analysis using this neo-institutional model involves trying to determine whether there is technical and institutional pressure on organizations within

a specific area or 'field'. It will then be important for organizations in this field to create technically efficient coordination and legitimacy-creating structures and processes.
Regarding the latter, sometimes entire businesses can be better explained by the fact
that they create legitimacy rather than contribute to efficiency. For example, a profit-
driven consulting firm can start a non-profit help organization that does not make a
profit, but gets a lot of attention, provides great legitimacy gains and attracts resources
to the entire company.

An analysis based on this model may also include a connection to Schein's and
Brunsson's models (see Chapter 8). Are the loose connections and tensions between
the cultural levels (Schein) an expression of a successful de-coupling and organizational hypocrisy (Brunsson)? Are some artifacts and espoused values a function of a
specific institutional pressure? And can other artifacts, at the same time, indicate basic
assumptions and a cultural existence, which is rather a consequence of a tightly controlled and stable production and distribution system? Consider a successful, global IT
group's Stockholm office, which is characterized by airy premises with colorful carpets
and cushions, where employees get free fruit and lunch and together create a meaningful, creative and decentralized workplace, while everyone works long hours with
tightly structured saleswork.

Scott's model can explain why organizations are similar to each other, despite
different conditions regarding the technical environment. But it also allows for the
fact that different combinations of institutional and technical pressure entail different
organizational solutions.

Institutional isomorphism

Another important concept in the neo-institutional theory of organization is institutional isomorphism. DiMaggio and Powell (1983) coined the concept to explain why
organizations become and are so similar within the same 'organizational field'. This,
to an even greater extent than institutional and technical environments, focuses on
similarity and rectifying forces and thus offers a powerful explanation for why management, organization and leadership show such a comprehensive homogeneity, despite
there being so many powerful arguments saying they should be characterized by heterogeneity. In Sweden, for example, municipalities have very similar organizational structures and processes, despite them differing considerably from one another in terms of
size, population basis, tax revenue, and so on. When a national municipal reform was
implemented in order to decentralize decision-making and enable municipalities to
adapt to their respective local conditions to a greater extent than before, their organizations became even more similar (Fernler 1996). The formal work division among
securities traders and in investment banks has, over the past 30-plus years, become
increasingly similar, despite them perhaps having completely different strategies and
foci as regards traded instruments, markets and business deals (Blomberg et al. 2012).

According to DiMaggio and Powell (1983), there are constant rectifying processes, or isomorphism, within organizational fields. Isomorphism also takes place independently of the technical requirements derived from organizations' strategies, sizes, core processes and possible turbulence in their environment. The authors distinguish between three types of isomorphism:

- *Coercive isomorphism* occurs when organizations respond to external demands on a particular type of organization. All of the world's university business and economics programs have increasingly been adapted to fit an MBA format, just as all the world's MBA programs have becoming increasingly similar. The design of global banks' internal risk-management processes is largely driven by increasingly comprehensive and internationally coordinated legislation.
- *Mimetic isomorphism* occurs when organizations simply imitate each other – for example, a company that introduces the same processes as a successful competitor with the hope that they too will be successful. This type of benchmarking can also take place between organizations in completely different industries. For example, a hospital can introduce lean principles inspired by both a car factory and a large IT consulting firm. A small, unranked MBA program may copy a well-known prestigious school in the hope of gaining legitimacy and reputation.
- *Normative isomorphism* occurs when people with similar education and experience bring these to the various organizations they start work in. MBA-educated young 'professionals' bring with them a mindset and a set of tools from their education to the organizations they work in. Management consultants disseminate their organizational solutions to all sorts of customers. Doctors, lawyers and other professionals align the organizations they work with through their homogeneous education.

Institutional isomorphism can increase the legitimacy, attractiveness and success of organizations, whether or not it leads to more efficient production of goods and services. Organizations can be rewarded solely because of their similarity to other organizations. They become more predictable and thus easier to do business with. Employees can both be attracted to and see themselves in a company that is reminiscent of other successful companies. As an analyst or investor, it is easier to assess the risks of investing capital in a company that 'lives up to' how a modern, well-run company should be designed. As a licensing authority or as a large customer, it is easier to contribute resources to a quality, environmental and risk-certified organization, and so on.

An organizational analysis using the various types of isomorphism involves trying to identify isomorphism and its consequences. You can focus on a company and compare it with others, you can focus on groups of companies, but also on parts of companies as well as on entire industries. One can also relate the analysis of isomorphism to, for example, an analysis of organizational culture based on Schein's model (see Chapter 8). A company's culture can perhaps be explained by how things are in other companies, not just in its own. Is it primarily the artifacts that are the same, or is it the espoused values that are becoming increasingly similar? Can isomorphism be divided into different levels and perhaps even be seen as a kind of interorganizational hypocrisy? And, if so, can we do an interorganizational power analysis using Michel's oligarchy model (see Chapter 7, and in particular Figure 7.2)?

It is also possible to imagine a kind of inverted isomorphism, that is, an organization achieves benefits by being as *different* from other organizations as possible. In organizational fields that, for some reason, are perceived as outdated, inefficient or otherwise substandard, a newly started company can create legitimacy by being as different as possible from its competitors, and perhaps instead resembling companies in a field that is perceived to be innovative and modern. For example, when a previously heavily regulated sector is deregulated, the old organizations can be perceived as bureaucratic, rigid and inefficient. For a start-up company, there is then the opportunity to demonstrate completely different processes and organizational solutions. A very clear and well-known (but quite old) example of such inverted isomorphism is the deregulation of the American airline industry at the beginning of the 1980s and the birth of People Express. The deregulation fueled many start-up airline businesses, but the most successful of them all was People Express. People Express attracted financial recourses, got its flying permits in record time, attracted highly motivated staff and experienced record growth, thanks to its 'people strategy'. Instead of organizing its low-cost business as per most of the other airline companies – as a machine bureaucracy – it did exactly the opposite. People Express resembled an extraordinarily large adhocracy. This may explain its rapid success, but also why it could not work in the long run. The adhocratic organizational structure was perfect in the institutional environment, but was not sustainable in the technical.

Rational and normative grounds for organizing

The last model described in this chapter, which can be seen as part of the neo-institutional theory of organization, includes another variant of the contradiction between the 'rational' and the 'normative'. In this model, these two poles are put into a longitudinal historical perspective. Barley and Kunda (1992) state that management, organization and leadership, as described in practice, shift between expressing a rational and a normative ideology. They show how different management concepts and schools can be fitted into two partially contradictory ideologies that alternately succeed each other. In the same way as skirt length varies within fashion, models and concepts vary within management (between rational and normative). The rational ideology of Barley and Kunda's model implies extensive formalization, structuring and centralization, that is, developed hierarchical structures. Normative ideology, for its part, implies decentralized, flat organizations where employees cooperate and are driven by commitment and intrinsic motivation.

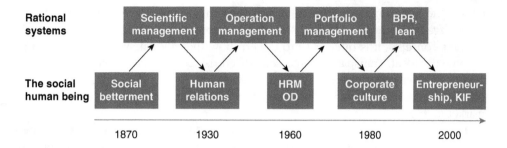

Figure 9.5   Rational systems versus the social human being as varying management ideals

Source: Based on Barley & Kunda (1992)

The model describes *managerial discourses*, that is, how management is described and perhaps perceived, but not necessarily how it is conducted. It is, therefore, like both the other neo-institutional and micro-sociological models (above), true to the basic assumption of the symbolic framework that there is always an uncertainty about what actually happens and that it is how things are perceived rather than how they really are that is important. Barley and Kunda's model thus describes the development of the subject of management as described in practice (not necessarily the same as in academic research), as a pendulum movement between two poles – rational systems and the social human being (see Figure 9.5). The pendulum movement can be seen as changes in organizational fashions or as a wheel that is constantly being reinvented, albeit in partially new guises. This Image is a criticism of management, as described in practice, as a growing mass of knowledge comprising the currently best-known methods of successful enterprise. On the contrary, it is the same thought material that is reused over and over again, disguised as the latest evidence-based and most superior management, organizational and leadership methods.

In Figure 9.5, we recognize some of the established models discussed in this book. *Scientific management* is one of the early models within the structural framework. We also recognize *human relations* from the focus of the early HR framework on human beings and their psychological and social needs. But the ideas of the HR movement were neither new nor unique. They were strongly reminiscent of the ideas of the *social betterment* movement, which, in the second half of the 19th century, was concerned with the very poor conditions of the new working class in emerging industrial cities (Cole 1948). We may also recognize the emergence of *corporate culture* in the early 1980s as an important factor in the advent of the symbolic framework. Then, *lean* gained increasing influence in the 1980s and 1990s, along with *business process reengineering* (BPR), the best-selling management consulting concept of the 1990s. Both lean and BPR can be said to have reintroduced the structural framework as an ideal, and the similarities with scientific management are striking. Then, once again, the focus fell on the normative end, this time described in the form of *entrepreneurship* and *knowledge intensive firms* (KIFs). Although entrepreneurship and KIFs are still highly relevant concepts, it is quite easy to discern how the rational system has once again become the ideal. Transparency and centralized risk control have become increasingly central to discussions about how organizations and companies should be designed, driven mainly by problems in the financial markets, beginning with the US mortgage market in 2008.

Possibly, we can now identify yet another pendulum movement. There are more and more tools being commonly used to measure and forecast the individual employee's performances. These ever more criticized *performance management* and *talent management* tools might be the beginning of a more general critique of so-called quantitative key performance indicators (KPIs). Additionally, old concepts expressing the more normative end in Barley and Kunda's model are re-emerging. 'Soft HR', 'agile HR', social entrepreneurship and sustainable leadership are currently becoming ever more popular concepts when describing successful management, organization and leadership.

Barley and Kunda's model constitutes a roughly simplified interpretation of how management ideals and fashions change over time between two different basic perspectives: rational systems and the social human. These perspectives are reminiscent of the structural framework and the HR framework presented in this book, that is, the two more 'modern' basic perspectives on management, organization and leadership (see Chapter 1). Barley and Kunda's longitudinal analysis moves at an overall macro level. It does not differentiate between industries, national or regional differences, and even less between individual firms and formal organizations and their different phases. That is why it is fruitful to use the model to analyze management, organization and leadership at both the micro and meso levels. By inserting individual leaders' actions or specific organizational changes into a larger institutional and historical context, our understanding of these phenomena increases significantly. Do you, consciously or unconsciously, follow the typical trends? Or do you go against strong ideological currents? Even purely normatively and practically, Barley and Kunda's model can be very useful. Instead of blindly following trends, you can get insights from the model into where the trends are heading and what will happen, and you may even get involved in consciously setting a new trend in the ever-changing management world. Instead of engaging in thoughtless imitation, one may pursue conscious innovation.

Projects based on a symbolic framework

According to a symbolic framework, projects (as organizations) don't exist, but are made. This means that any activity at all can, or could, be called a project. If an activity is called a project, it will affect the sensemaking of involved actors with regard to this activity, and also their actions, that is, the actual activity itself will change when it is re-named 'a project'. Based on the symbolic framework, a project can thus be any activity that, for whatever reason, is perceived as a project. If you name an activity, describe it using any established project methodology and start to divide work and coordinate using such a methodology, then it is highly likely that such an activity will begin to be perceived as a project. It is also likely that employees will begin to identify themselves as project members or not, and that they will start to draw boundaries between activities and resources that belong or do not belong to the project. Projects are not activities limited in time and space, but projects can become enacted with boundaries in time and space – projects are *enacted*, they are *made*, they can continuously be created and recreated.

A project, just like any other phenomenon, can be seen as consisting of talk or *words* (for example, the word 'project', but also words such as 'project phase', 'deliverables', 'waterfall', 'agile' and others associated with projects and project management), *thoughts and ideas* (about change, focus, development, impossible deadlines and more) as well as the actual *actions* of people and technology (Blomberg 2003, 2013; cf. the three levels in Schein's model in Chapter 8).

Just because an activity is described as 'a project', it doesn't necessarily mean it is very different from another activity not described as such. And, if two activities are described as 'projects', it doesn't necessarily mean they need to be very similar. A project in a construction company's department, whose business mostly consists of asphalting roads, will therefore have very little in common with a software development project that is part of the development of next-generation fighter aircraft, and even less with what the French philosopher Sartre refers to when he, time and again, uses the word project in his texts (see Sartre 1943/1983). Words and thought are thus loosely linked to each other. The fact that Swedish construction companies boasted about their activities in the mid-1960s (e.g. in their annual reports) without using the word project once, while the same boast included the word project everywhere 10 years later, shows that the same or very similar activities can be described using completely different words. What is perceived as a project and as a non-project varies from industry to industry, from situation to situation and over time. Thus, analyzing projects using a symbolic framework means that projects, like companies and organizations, should be analyzed at several different (ontological) levels. Projects can be analyzed as languages, ideas and actions. One can also take the help of any suitable model that divides phenomena into levels, such as Schein's cultural model (see Chapter 8).

Most of the definitions of project include the idea of time- and space-delimited activities, the aim of which is to achieve goals that are reasonably well defined in advance. Projects are often perceived as a tool used to implement some kind of development, adaptation or other form of change. This might be to develop a new product, or to adapt standard modules to the needs of a particular customer, a reorganization or competence development. Despite this, many projects are initiated that have the exact opposite effect. In particular, reorganization projects tend not to be implemented, at least not fully or according to plan. The consequence of such projects may then be that they stabilize rather than change the activities that the projects, in any case formally, were intended to change. Projects can thus be formulated and initiated to 'protect' organizations from real and potential demands for change.

Legitimacy-creating projects

Projects can be seen both as 'talk' and as 'action', according to Brunsson's concepts of decision rationality and action rationality (see Chapter 8), and as an expression of or response to pressure from an institutional and technical environment (Blomberg 2003). As a project manager or project employee, you should ask yourself what role a particular project has in an organization. Perhaps it is not the intention that it should ever be implemented, but that it is primarily a way of creating legitimacy in an institutional environment. If the institutional pressure consists of demands for rational, systematic and transparent management, the project management should be characterized by the most comprehensive project models in line with the structural framework (see Chapter 3). The more alternative actions that are examined, the more and more advanced risk-assessment techniques that are applied, the more extensively the facts are collected and evaluated, the more comprehensive and technically advanced project plans are drawn up, the more legitimacy the project can create. If institutional pressure instead consists of demands for an innovative, creative and rapid-response organization, then it is better for the project to be managed based on one of the fast and flexible 'agile' project models (see Chapter 5). With inspiration from fast and creative agile data programming, the project is driven forward by commitment and self-governing groups.

No matter what type of project organization the institutional environment prescribes, projects can create legitimacy without being implemented. The fact that the rational and structural project model (the waterfall model; see Chapter 3) leads to a paralysis of action, according to both Weick and Brunsson, is completely unproblematic. The fact that the normative and HR-like agile project model can result in virtually anything, including groupthink, need not be a problem either, as long as it fits into the institutional environment of organizations. When analyzing whether activities described as projects primarily fulfill the role of legitimizing (talk) or streamlining (action), it is often relevant to link the analysis to the power framework. One and the same activity, in this case the project, can be perceived completely differently by different actors. For one actor, the implementation of a project can be perceived as absolutely necessary, while another actor looks at the same project as a way of talking and creating legitimacy, but certainly not as a way of actually changing a business.

Dynamic change projects

If you want to achieve real change with the help of a project, you should not try to optimize it from a structural or a HR framework perspective, nor from a combination

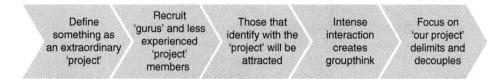

Figure 9.6 The advent of dynamic projects

Source: Blomberg (2003: 259)

of the two. Instead, Weick's micro-sociological model and the expression 'Any old map will do', as well as Brunsson's model for action rationality, can be applied. Figure 9.6 shows how a forceful 'real change' project can be created.

In an organization whose activities are usually not described as consisting of projects, it may be sufficient to call an activity a project in order for it to have meaning as something different and non-routine. In organizations where project work is more everyday, divergence needs to be emphasized by the activity being described as extraordinary, unique or otherwise something out of the ordinary. Clear, detailed goals should not be defined; instead, vague but beautiful and flexible goals should be formulated. This means that different players may input their respective agendas and identify with the project. When various stakeholders in the mid-1980s could not agree on how to design the Johanneshov area of Stockholm (in which an old worn-down sports arena was located), they could nevertheless agree on a project goal: 'to create a world-class arena'. What that meant in more concrete terms was very open to interpretation, but there was no doubt that it would be something extraordinary.

After that, it is necessary to recruit one or two people with a successful track record and with a high level of built-up confidence (gurus). The important thing is not their competence or even that they actually do something, but that they can absorb uncertainty and create expectations merely by their presence. This reduces the need for other methods that are perceived to reduce uncertainty, such as rational decision-making processes. These should be avoided at all costs as they, according to Brunsson's model, lead to a paralysis of decision. 'Gurus' can create confidence and reduce uncertainty, both internally within the project group and for external stakeholders. Recruiting gurus is also important in relation to other, less experienced project members. The larger the status difference between the guru and those who work on the project, the greater the symbolic significance of the guru. As a newly graduated architect, getting to work on the same project as one of the industry's great stars creates a great commitment and enthusiasm for work, compared to exactly the same project but without the star architect.

Once the activities, that is, the project, are defined as extraordinary, as well as there being one or two successful profiles included in the project group, the project will automatically attract people who want to make a difference and change the status quo. Therefore, a difference will emerge between those who identify with the project and those who identify themselves as being outside or even against it. Then, in accordance with Weick's pulsating organizational model (see above), a phase of intensive interaction will lead to the project group developing its own perspective and its own social identity. The conditions for groupthink will be the best possible, which is why risk-taking can be expected to increase and consideration for all kinds of circumstances outside the project can be expected to decrease. A dynamic change project has been created.

A final in-depth examination of symbolic leadership

Symbolic leadership is largely about creating meaning for yourself and for others: meaning with a certain direction. Inspiring leadership is often seen as something positive and almost noble, especially when compared to authoritarian leadership. In the many distinctions between manager and leader (see Table 5.1), inspirational leadership is usually described as something more positive than plain, boring and bureaucratic management. Symbolic leadership can, however, also be described as manipulation. The link to the power framework and the third dimension of power (power over thought) then becomes clearer, while the overlap with the ideal leader of the HR framework decreases. The power framework and the HR framework, however, share a common denominator in that both criticize the image of leadership as something consisting of managers who, with the help of a formal position, exercise vertical control. According to the HR framework, formal authority demotivates employees so leaders should instead decentralize and let everyone participate and decide.

The power framework can be said to support the HR framework in this criticism of the structural framework. Leadership that relies on formal position can demotivate employees. But instead of decentralizing, leaders should, according to the power framework, manipulate. Then their power will become hidden behind what is experienced as inspiring and motivational leadership.

Specifically, this means that one can decentralize at a formal level – or in terms of Schein's culture model: at the artifact level – while, at the same time, centralizing at an informal, symbolic or cultural level, using manipulation and inspiration. Symbolic leadership may therefore be seen as highly insidious, dishonest and manipulative.

Since leaders in themselves can be regarded as symbols, and artifacts as expressing and reproducing culture, as well as leadership being viewed as manipulative, we need to discuss symbolic leadership further. This is done below by (1) introducing the concept of post-heroic leadership, and (2) addressing the moral and ethical dimension of leadership and the need for leaders to develop their 'inner compass'.

Post-heroic leadership

As we saw in Chapter 7, Maccoby warns us that large, well-known, larger-than-life leaders often have clearly dysfunctional personality traits. This criticism is important, since these heroic leaders are often hailed for managing to make difficult strategic decisions and, against all odds, succeeding in carrying out heroic actions. At the same time, studies of managers show that they very rarely make this kind of decision or perform any heroic action. In fact, managers' work is quite unremarkable (Carlson 1951/1991, Kotter 1990b, Sveningsson et al. 2009). They talk to their employees, make formal decisions about things that others have investigated and have pretty much already decided on, as well as represent their organization externally in accordance with the communication department's strategies and instructions.

When journalists and researchers ask managers about what they do, they often refer to the heroic leadership image. They talk more about ideal leaders and about other, well-known leaders than about what they actually do on a regular working day. The image of the heroic leader thus fulfills an important function for the manager's self-image. Managers see themselves as heroic leaders, when much of their work could equally well be done (and is performed) by secretaries, assistants and other employees.

This heroic image of leadership is also important to the manager's subordinates. When a senior manager walks around and talks to and listens to their staff, visits them in their offices, on the shop floor or out in the shops, then that manager is perceived as a special and good leader. The usual everyday work that the manager performs is perceived based on the well-known descriptions of heroic leadership. That a manager who has something of that 'heroic' leadership image comes down to see 'ordinary' people, is perceived as a fantastic effort. If a colleague or secretary came by and did the same thing, the likelihood that we would think that they are just disturbing us is significantly higher (Alvesson & Sveningsson 2003, Sveningsson et al. 2009). It is almost paradoxical that the same actions are interpreted completely differently if they are performed by another employee, but this is explained by the fact that we have all been colored by the idea of managers as heroic leaders.

Post-heroic leadership (Sveningsson et al. 2009) means, in other words, that the manager does not actually exercise any extraordinary leadership, neither task-oriented nor people-oriented, any more than taking care of simple administrative tasks and walking around among their staff. But, because they are the manager, these everyday tasks are perceived to be remarkable, special and, to some extent, heroic (Alvesson, 2003). As a manager, they are thus part of a sensemaking process that involves the reproduction of a myth about heroic leadership. Again, almost paradoxically, this means that managers, together with their employees, create situations in which managers, despite everything, obtain more influence than others. Just because their everyday actions are perceived to be remarkable and special, they have more of a say. We are motivated by the fact that they brighten up our workplace with their presence, and we listen more to what they have to say. The managers themselves may be a little dissatisfied with their everyday tasks, but, on the other hand, they receive high prestige and standing. Even their economic and material situation is highly prioritized, and their identity is built on leadership myths rather than on leadership practice.

Authentic and ethical leadership – an inner compass

However, managers are not merely objects of admiration framed by a myth of heroic leadership; they can also take on the role of scapegoats. Regularly recurring scandals and financial crises are often explained by a lack of good leadership and by the fact that managers lack a proper ethical foundation on which to act. Since symbolic and inspirational leadership does not naturally have to do with extensive facts, logic and formalized processes, but at least as much with emotions, rhetoric and manipulation, the risk of unethical leadership is evident.

In response to the development and popularization of symbolic leadership, but also to many corporate scandals, discussions on ethical, responsible and authentic leadership have become increasingly prominent. As a leader, it is not enough to exercise influence by structuring, motivating and maneuvering in the political landscape and creating culture. As leaders, we should also see ourselves in a larger context. Although we do not have an inner stable self (an 'inner essence' or a 'preference function'), we should still try to create a meaningful self-image and identity that we can live with. Our actions and our leadership should not contradict this self-image too much. We should strive to see the consequences of our actions beyond the short term and the immediate here and now. Are these more long-term and indirect consequences something we can support? Are they leading to employees, organizations and a world which we can identify with? If not, perhaps we should re-examine our ongoing projects and more closely related efforts. Thus, it may be argued that authentic leadership is not just about knowing oneself, but also about basing this self on a moral, ethical and socially responsible position (Gardner et al. 2005).

Research on so-called authentic leadership (Gardner et al. 2011) shows that there is a correlation between whether the leader is perceived to be authentic and how the groups, employees and organizations they lead, perform. But perhaps the most important thing is not what exact level of innovation, productivity and efficiency the authentic leadership leads to, but in which direction you choose to go. In a world characterized by complexity, uncertainty and a furious pace, authentic leadership can be crucial to the mental and physical health of employees (Ilies et al. 2005, Shiry 2009, Wong & Cummings 2009). Since, from a symbolic framework perspective, we cannot be sure of what we really want or if we understand each other, and since some degree of organizational hypocrisy is a necessity to get something done at all, authenticity and ethically critical thinking are especially important.

As support both for developing a self-image and identity and for understanding the consequences of our own actions, analyses based on the four frameworks and their many models work excellently. When they are based on different basic assumptions, the different analyses will contradict each other. It is then not possible to 'hide' behind *one* analysis. These partly contradictory analyses must always be supplemented by a standpoint. Which organization do we want to create and reproduce? What kind of leader do we want to be? In what world do we want to live?

Many popular texts about authentic leadership and about the needs of leaders with an inner compass can be perceived as a return to a romanticism about individuals and heroes who discover themselves and then make the world good. But it is possible to stick to the idea of an authentic leadership and the importance of an inner compass without falling into such naive individualism. We cannot avoid creating our identities, we cannot avoid organizing and we cannot avoid influencing the world. By raising our ability to reflect, for example through theory-driven organizational analysis from different frameworks, we can both become more authentic and find a direction in the creation of ourselves and our common worlds.

The symbolic framework's generic questions, strengths and weaknesses

Just as with the concepts and models belonging to the other frameworks, those that belong to the symbolic framework can be used for the analysis of all kinds of activities, organizational processes, management and leadership practices. Even when there is no obvious problem or specific phenomenon to analyze, there might still be a lot to be learned from a theory-driven analysis. Trying to answer the symbolic framework's generic questions can then be a good way to get started.

Generic questions

Of the four frameworks, the symbolic framework is the one that is based on the least far-reaching assumptions about human essence and about the nature of the world. As in the more complex models of the power framework (see Chapter 7), it is therefore more difficult to formulate normative questions about how to organize and lead. The framework itself, however, is powerful in terms of producing analyses whose conclusions create new perspectives and descriptions. The symbolic framework has a high potential to enable us re-frame what we usually perceive as natural and self-evident to be viewed as something that is a product of processes that we can understand, influence and change. To initiate this type of analysis, a number of more descriptive questions can be formulated (see Table 9.1). When applying the models and concepts of the symbolic framework, however, we do not need to completely abandon the ambition to construct solid and clear normative and action-based conclusions. It is possible to formulate (and answer) a number of 'should questions' provided that more is taken for granted than the basic assumptions of the symbolic framework can be said to do in themselves. Given that we want to achieve a certain goal, given a particular actor's interests, given an interpretation of the institutional pressure in the environment, given which organization we want to create – how should we then organize and lead based on a symbolic analysis?

Table 9.1   Generic issues from a symbolic framework perspective

IS? (descriptive analysis)	Which culture characterizes the organization?
	Strengths/any subcultures
	Content of the culture's basic assumptions
	Tensions between levels and over time
	How is culture created, maintained and changed?
	Founder, influential leader
	Recruitment, socialization, environmental pressure
	Artifacts, ceremonies, stories, sensemaking processes
	Which functions?
	As a variable/coordination mechanism
	As inertia/an impediment to change
	For legitimizing and attracting resources
	Organizational hypocrisy
SHOULD? (prescriptive/ normative analysis)	Is the culture/s appropriate?
	Given the need for stability and change
	Given the interests of different actors
	Given the technical and institutional environment
	Given micro (who do I want to be?) and macro (what world do I want to live in?)
→ (conclusion)	To what extent does the symbolic analysis explain the phenomenon?
	What is unexplained? What new questions will be relevant?

Strengths of the symbolic framework

The relatively less far-reaching assumptions of the symbolic framework about the nature of human beings and the world make it more flexible than other frameworks. It can be used for a comprehensive analysis of a person's thoughts, statements and actions at a particular moment. It can also be used to analyze how our cultures and ways of thinking have evolved over several hundred years. It also has the ability to explain things that the other frameworks fail to do. The fact that the implementation of a formal process or structure, which, according to a structural analysis, should be optimal, nevertheless leads to both poorer quality and lower production rates, can be explained by how the new organizational form is interpreted and enacted by employees and other people concerned. In addition, why these particular interpretations are created can be explained on the basis of both the formal structures and other artifacts, including employees' constantly ongoing sensemaking, values and fundamental assumptions. What appears to be irrational when applying other frameworks can be given rational explanations when applying the symbolic framework.

Because of these less far-reaching assumptions, the symbolic framework also has the ability to break more with our everyday thinking and the assumptions that we are not aware we make. The very purpose of many models within the symbolic framework is to make us aware of our taken-for-granted assumptions. This also means that the symbolic framework has a high potential to increase the self-awareness of the person performing the analysis. Symbolic analyses therefore often have a greater effect on a personal level, compared to, for example, a structural analysis. The symbolic framework and its various analytical models thus often receive both very committed followers and emotionally affected opponents. The opposition can become so powerful that it is described as hatred. In particular, taking into account a recommendation already made in the section on critical thinking in Chapter 1: if you want to maximize your multi-frame analytical capability, if you want to excel in re-framing, you should put extra effort into analyses based on models that you find the most difficult. This means that precisely those who dislike the symbolic framework have the most to gain from using it.

Weaknesses of the symbolic framework

The focus of the symbolic framework on the more invisible aspects of management, organization and leadership, that is to say, thoughts, ideas, interpretations, sensemaking, norms and culture, can also lead to less precise analyses and conclusions. A symbolic analysis can be perceived as less scientific, since it is based more on theory and theory-driven interpretation of indirect expressions of mentalities and cultural content. It is not as easy to base a symbolic analysis on measurable data, which many analyses in the other frameworks can do. A symbolic analysis usually requires a more complex language than is enabled by quantitative data, tables and flowcharts. Both the analysis and its results often have to be developed in and by a more complex written language. This, in turn, places demands on a literary competence in terms of both writing and reading. The symbolic framework can therefore be perceived as being quite unscientific by the less knowledgeable.

The relatively less far-reaching assumptions of the symbolic framework on the human being and the nature of the world can also be seen as a shortcoming. Instead of assuming how things work, they have to be examined. This requires resources that are not always available. Even if these investigations are reduced to a kind of thought exercise or 'desktop research', that is, you simply think through the phenomenon in question based on theoretical models but without making any more extensive empirical examination, it can be difficult. Since the models of the symbolic framework are often based on less far-reaching assumptions, a larger mental effort is required when it comes to questioning and thinking through how things might work. It is, quite simply, cognitively and emotionally difficult to question both your own and others' assumptions.

Based on Brunsson's model for action and decision rationality, it could even be argued that the symbolic framework risks making the analyst more paralyzed than the other frameworks. The questioning character of the symbolic framework creates so much doubt that both the analyst and the analysis get stuck in a decision-rational process. There are strong arguments against this, however. In practice, we are so pressured to constantly decide and act, to agree and support, that the risk of paralysis due to an extensive organizational analysis, regardless of which models and frameworks are used, is nevertheless slim. And, on the contrary, it could be argued that it is precisely a little mental activity and the ability to slow down the pace that characterize successful and sustainable management and leadership. But, for sure, the symbolic framework is not an equally handy tool to lean on (or hide behind) as a solid structural or HR analysis. But that is precisely why all four frameworks have their given place, alongside each other. The potential of the four frameworks to create more knowledge and better understanding, leading to decisions and actions based on them, is that they complement each other. A good management, organizational and leadership analysis always includes models from all four frameworks.

Videos

Don't forget to watch the videos to discover more about the key concepts in this chapter: **https://study.sagepub.com/blomberg**

Note

1   The story is inspired by Weick's (1995) tale of a Hungarian unit that got lost in the Alps. In turn, Weick got the story from a poem by Miroslav Holub, which in turn is inspired by an anecdote that can be traced back to a Hungarian soldier who participated in the First World War (www.americanscientist.org/issues/pub/2013/4/a-fict-for-a-fact).

10

A Case Study in Theory-Driven Practical Analysis

Applying management, organizational and leadership models in analysis of real-life situations, events and problems is both simple and difficult. It is not difficult to increase one's knowledge of a situation by seeing it through a more structured perspective and using an analytical model. But, to really get to the bottom of a problem, to use theoretical frameworks and models to their full potential and, based on such analyses from both a large number of models and several conflicting frameworks, formulate concrete solutions and alternative actions, are things you never fully achieve. However, the difficulties in analyzing management, organization and leadership mean that there is always room for improvement. Through training, the absolute beginner, the highly experienced employee, the consultant, the manager and the successful leader can improve.

In this concluding chapter, the four basic theoretical frameworks and some of their key models will be applied to a small, but in many ways typical, real-world case. The case consists of a brief description of the introduction of digital 'knowledge management' systems in a Scandinavian management consulting firm. The short description is of course a simplified picture of reality. The complexity is thus extremely reduced compared with the situations and events that one as an employee, a consultant, manager or leader deals with on a daily basis. But, as the basis for a simple illustration of what insights some models and frameworks can produce, this case works well.

Knowledge management at RMCG

After you finalized your MBA two years ago, you immediately got hired as a junior consultant at the now international management consulting firm Research Management Consulting Group (RMCG). RMCG was founded in 1974 by an associate professor and a professor at the Stockholm School of Economics. In line with the funding clause of that school, the business concept was to promote 'Swedish business with the help of management science applied on individual company conditions'. By the early 1980s, the business had become Nordic, but it was not until the beginning of 2000 that the company took the step towards a global market. Today, there are over 1,200 employees, meaning that the company may be characterized as large, both compared to its Scandinavian competitors and to most of the international competitors operating in the Scandinavian market.

You like your work and are appreciated by your colleagues as well as by management. You have just been informed that shortly it will be suggested that you advance to associate level. Right now you are preparing for a meeting with Linn, one of the more experienced senior partners at Stockholm corporate headquarters. It is not a part of your current assignments and you have never worked with Linn on any project. All you know is that Linn has asked for you specifically to join a meeting about an important strategic matter for the whole firm.

When Linn started working at RMCG as a junior consultant in the mid-1990s, the company had just started using email. The Internet had barely been introduced. A few years later, when Linn advanced to associate and then senior associate, the simple email tool 'CCmail' was replaced with the Groupware tool 'Team Space'. Before Team Space was introduced, dissemination, storage and development of knowledge within the company was handled through long mailing lists and physical project binders that were placed in an archive after the completion of a project. With Team Space, project teams were able to meet virtually and communicate in real time. They were able to store specific information on an electronic project platform. This made the administrative work much smoother, which was appreciated by most consultants. In addition, since Team Space replaced CCmail, which was completely shut down, all consultants, regardless of seniority level, region or competence area, had to move to Team Space. The implementation was relatively hassle-free, and the various functions of the tool were increasingly exploited.

Project IntCom

In 2013, Linn was project manager on a project to phase out Team Space and make room for the web-based knowledge management system IntCom. IntCom was not just an internal meeting place where employees could communicate with each other and store specific project information. It was also fully integrated with the Internet, could be used on all possible platforms and had its own browser and tools corresponding to Microsoft Office. In addition, there was an advanced and automated database function, which was tailored to RMCG's needs as a growing, increasingly global management consultancy. Given that the data was recorded in the database, IntCom made it possible for all company consultants to search for information on all projects. The paths were many and designed to suit users with different needs. The system was able to combine information from different projects and repackage it into finished compilations in the form of checklists, tables, diagrams and other types of graphical representation. IntCom was therefore able to supplement and replace a large amount of manual work to produce materials that were used both internally within the project work and during presentations for clients.

The data stored in IntCom included three categories:

- basic data on the customer company and the industries the company was active in
- the process and the analytical models that had been used in the project, as well as lessons learned from that use, including any modifications to the models made during the project period
- qualitative assessments of the relational, organizational, cultural and relation/conflict-related characteristics of client companies which had affected the project's implementation, and how these aspects had been handled.

When Linn presented IntCom at RMCG's major partner meeting in the fall of 2013, she described the benefits of the system as follows:

> The investment in the extensive upgrade of our knowledge management system IntCom is motivated by the major gains that will be realized in terms of the system's large potential leverage. We partners will be able to communicate our most valuable industrial wisdom with each other across projects, continents and specialist areas. We will also be able to streamline and ensure quality in the competence development of our consultants with lower seniority and experience. In other words, with a working IntCom in place, we will be able to secure our present and future skills base, our most important competitive advantage, much more efficiently than ever before.

Reviewing IntCom's success

It is not without some panic that she now, just over four years later, goes through the user statistics since the launch of IntCom in spring 2014. The system has not been the success she had anticipated. In view of the cost of purchasing and development, it is rather a fiasco. There are two major problems. The first is the limited use of the system alongside pure email functions and communication within individual project groups. Among RMCG's senior partner consultants, the use of IntCom has been almost non-existent in all four years. For associates and senior associates (intermediate consultants), use has also been at a very low level, but with a marginal increase over time. Junior consultants used the system quite diligently when it was introduced but have, over time, reduced their use significantly.

The second but related problem is that relevant data are not recorded in the system. It is particularly serious that the senior partner consultants have largely not contributed any data at all. Since the senior partner consultants, who have by far the most industry and specialist knowledge and experience of project implementation, do not use the system, it will be impossible to achieve the leverage and learning that IntCom was meant to realize.

When Linn reviews the catastrophic figures, she immediately calls together her old project group, which together with her was responsible for launching IntCom. You are also called to the meeting. You have been employed at RMCG for a year, joining when you received your master's degree in management and organization theory. Linn's idea is that since you are new to the company, you see the problem with fresh eyes, compared to those in the project group who have invested much in developing and introducing IntCom.

At the meeting, Eric (a senior associate) shares the results from a qualitative evaluation of why different groups of consultants do not use IntCom. The evaluation shows that the most junior consultants find that it is at least as efficient to seek information via Internet search engines as by using IntCom. Since there are hardly any company-specific data stored on IntCom, there is even more information available online.

You recognize yourself in this description. During your first year at RMCG, you've mainly searched for information via your favorite Internet routes, much more than you have on IntCom. If there has been anything project- or client-specific you needed to know, which you couldn't find online, you have simply asked a more senior colleague. Associates and senior associates (the intermediate consultants) use IntCom more, mainly to seek general information. But they are, at the same time, frustrated at not having access to the more specific knowledge they need in order to streamline the work of specific client projects. As one of the consultants says in the evaluation:

> We are a bit in the hands of our senior partners. They are helpful in projects, but they rarely have the time or inclination to share their experiences on other projects or with those who do not usually work with them.

This view is also recognized not from your own experience but from a knowledge management module that you studied at business school. There it was described how a leading management consulting company (BCG) worked to create a learning culture to eliminate the 'mini pyramids' created by the senior partner consultants.

The partners who have been interviewed as part of the evaluation have explained that their little use of the system and their reluctance to record data are down to three reasons. First, their relationships with clients are based on personal trust. Although client and specific knowledge is anonymized before it is added to IntCom, there is a concern among clients that their competitive advantage could be made more transparent and benefit their competitors. This is not something partners are willing to compromise on. Second, several partners believe that there is a risk that less experienced consultants will start using the standardized knowledge that exists on IntCom in a less reflective and more mechanical way, instead of building on knowledge of the actual conditions in the specific client project. If this happens, and several partners argue that they can see a tendency towards this, RMCG's high brand value as the only Scandinavian-based consultancy at the top among international management consulting firms, could be hurt. Third, many partners note that it takes too much valuable time to input data from each project into the system. As partner, they have ultimate client responsibility for the implementation and results of projects. To sit and enter data into a system rather than prioritize maximizing the quality of delivery is wasting precious time.

On Eric's presentation of the assessment, Linn comments that all doubts that the partner consultants have expressed were carefully handled in the development of IntCom. All client and specific data that may be perceived as competitive or sensitive are filtered out from the data entered into the system. IntCom is also benchmarked with other major consultancy agencies' systems, and these agencies have no problem with clients distrusting them because they use this type of database. As for the risk of more standardized products, it is one of the system's benefits. If parts of the consultancy work can be done quickly and efficiently with the help of previous project experience, there will be more time to adapt, and for client interaction and deep analysis of the specific conditions. There is no risk that RMCG's consultants would produce some half-baked standard solutions, says Linn. On the contrary, IntCom can ensure that each client is able to benefit from the full RMCG knowledge base. Finally, partners do not have to input the necessary data. Each project has a team consisting of different-level consultants. If each project's reconciliation, which is always done at the end of a project, is entered into the system, it would be a good start. In addition to the existence of funds earmarked for this in each project budget, junior and semi-senior consultants have incentives to perform this function. The lower ranked consultants have the opportunity to learn from the knowledge of partners and, second, the use of IntCom is one of several grounds for their evaluation, salary and promotion (something that, however, several senior partners are very critical of).

When you listen to Eric's, Linn's and the others' discussion, you remind yourself of the content of the courses you read in 'Management' during your master's – how important it is to conduct a thorough analysis, applying several theoretical frameworks, and to systematically analyze the problem by using different models. You think that the partners, Linn and their team, despite all their experience, don't really understand the complexity of the problem.

Just then, Linn turns to you and says, 'OK, we have all grappled with this problem before, but I have called here one of our young, promising junior consultants with the hope of getting a fresh look at the problem.'

Linn looks right into your eyes and continues, 'Can you explain why IntCom has not been used as intended?'

Formulating an introductory question

In the above description, a rather clear question is formulated: why is the new system not used as it was intended? Often, a clear problem is defined, but at least as often there is confusion and there are different opinions about what problems are to be solved. This is why we should always devote a certain amount of energy to an initial problem definition. If there is already a problem definition, we should be open to the possibility that it is merely a description of a symptom and that there might exist an underlying but less apparent problem.

Before you start applying the theory, it is often beneficial to try to formulate a more analytical 'why' question. Once the analytical work is in progress, different analyses may well result in new problem formulations being possible. Perhaps the initial question seems increasingly irrelevant. Moreover, what previously appeared to be a problem could not only appear to be irrelevant, but it may even increasingly appear as a solution. However, this depends on what the analyses reveal. A further reason to devote some time to formulating an initial purpose for subsequent analyses is that there is every reason to analyze a situation that seems to lack all kinds of problems. For example, trying to understand what led to an organization being extremely successful is at least as important as understanding adversity and problems.

A major support in situations where it is difficult to formulate a clear initial problem definition are the 'generic questions' of the different frameworks. Even though, as in the case above, you have a clear question, you can benefit greatly from initially structuring the analytical work based on the generic questions of each framework. Based on these, you can almost always come up with a good analytical process. And, as Weick's expression 'Any old map will do' (see Chapter 9) indicates, it is important to get started with the analytical work. Then you can adjust and change along the way, as you learn about the elements analyzed.

A short structural framework analysis

In this analysis based on the structural framework, we make use of Mintzberg's structural configurations and the six structural situational dependencies (see Chapter 2).

Why is IntCom not used as intended? Could it be due to the design of RMCG's formal processes and formal organizational structure? One way to find out is to decide which of Mintzberg's structural configurations RMCG's processes and structures resemble, and to compare these with the structural configurations that it should have, according to the six structural situational dependencies. An important part of such a structural analysis is to describe what IntCom means structurally, i.e. what IntCom *is*, and whether it is something that RMCG *should* be.

What structure does RMCG have?

Although the case study gives us very limited information, compared to what we would have if we really worked at RMCG or perhaps performed a consulting assignment there, the case study does provide a lot of useful facts. There are obviously a number of hierarchical levels. You start as a junior consultant, and we know that there are associates and senior associates, as well as partners and senior partners. This adds up to five hierarchical levels. We may also assume that the management team is a further level, that is to say, a sixth. We know less about division of labor and specialization, but the consultants' various specialist areas and different continents are talked about (see Linn's quote above), as are projects and customer-specific knowledge. We do not know what the formal division of labor looks like, but we can assume that there is a division of labor at either industry competence, geographical location or type of customer. We do know, however, that the consultants work on projects, so we could assume that RMCG has some sort of matrix structure.

As for formalized processes, both wage-setting and promotion seem to be at least partially formalized, as Linn mentions that how much one uses IntCom is a criterion for both salary and advancement. We can also see that IntCom itself is a formalization, or an attempt at formalization, of the dissemination of knowledge within RMCG. Whether IntCom is a horizontal support structure or a more vertical steering technostructure (see Mintzberg's model in Chapter 2) is not obvious. It is largely presented as a support structure by Linn, but, at the same time, it also guides the work of the consultants. Either way, IntCom is an (attempted) increased formalization of RMCG. In sum, we can see that RMCG seems to have a rather expanded and extensive structure and a lot of formalized processes.

As for which of Mintzberg's structural configurations RMCG resembles, we can exclude both adhocratic and simple structure, at least at the corporate level. So machine bureaucracy and professional bureaucracy remain. It appears that at least one junior consultant got their first job after their master's degree at a business school, and that RMCG was founded by two senior researchers from Stockholm School of Economics. In addition, RMCG's basic strategy was formulated with reference to a central section of the funding clause of the School of Economics and also with reference to a scientific foundation. It is therefore not too wild a guess to make that a lot of RMCG's consultants come from the Stockholm School of Economics and can be said to constitute a profession.

Together with the relatively extensive formal structure, we might therefore dare to say that RMCG resembles a professional bureaucracy with relatively extensive machine-bureaucratic elements.

We might also add that, at project level, there is likely to be a proliferation of more adhocratic and simple structures. In any case, we know that there are more senior partners who are likely to exert a great deal of vertical control over the individual projects. Already, by describing RMCG as a sort of mixture between professional bureaucracy and machine bureaucracy, we can draw some interesting conclusions. A disadvantage of professional bureaucracy is precisely the difficulty of implementing substantial changes from above. The profession can contradict such changes if, for some reason, they do not like them, something that seems relevant to how RMCG's senior partners feel. But, let us do a little more thorough analysis of the 'should' issue.

What structure should RMCG have, and is the introduction of IntCom in line with it?

The very simplest way to carry out a reasonably proper analysis of the structure RMCG should take, is to go through the six dimensions of Mintzberg's model of structural situational dependencies (see Chapter 2, in particular Table 2.1). By analyzing what IntCom means from the perspective of each of these dimensions, we should be able to arrive at an idea of whether the structural framework can explain the problems with IntCom's uptake. Since the different dimensions and situational dependencies are often relevant to varying degrees in a given situation, one might choose to focus on those with the most explanatory value. However, in order to arrive at the most relevant, an analysis is required on the basis of all. Below, we go through all six dimensions, although some have significantly higher relevance than others in the analysis of RMCG's problems with IntCom.

Size and age

It is clear that RMCG has existed for more than 40 years. Given that the management consulting industry is fairly young, 40 years can be seen as relatively old. In terms of size, the case is even clearer. It has grown significantly during this time – from two to 1,200 employees. The company has also become larger than several of its competitors. Although the major, internationally well-known consultancy agencies are many times larger, RMCG is among the largest in the Scandinavian market. Both size and age therefore point towards RMCG having a relatively developed structure, and that it will likely increase in scope. Thus, based on the firm's dimension size and age, the introduction of a formalized knowledge dissemination process, a support or technostructure, is absolutely right!

Central processes and core technology

We do not know much about the complexity of projects that RMCG takes on, but perhaps we can rely on a more general knowledge of management consulting and knowledge work. The 'common picture' of this type of activity is that it is largely complex. Companies turn to management consultants when they are unable to manage their problems themselves, or, in any case, feel that they need outside assistance. Based on this description of RMCG's activities as relatively complex processes, the machine-bureaucratic elements should be smaller and the professional-bureaucratic elements all the more appropriate. In the same way, the more governing, technostructural elements of IntCom can be seen as more dubious, while the more supportive elements are more sensible. In other words, the idea that senior consultants should devote time to entering data into the system rather than solving complex problems for their customers is not sensible. It is also doubtful whether it is appropriate to use pay and promotion to steer less experienced consultants to devote time to the system, rather than by making the system (and its content) so supportive that it becomes attractive without that kind of vertical control.

But, at the same time, one might question whether all the activities of a company such as RMCG are as complex as the 'standard image' of management consulting appears. Most projects cover quite a few relatively simple tasks. Reading, collecting data, writing reports and giving attractive presentations are not the same as carrying out complex analyses and solving undefined problems. There should therefore be scope for a great deal of specialization and vertical coordination. We may also assume that it is the most junior consultants who perform the least complex tasks. This would explain why it is the seniors who use IntCom the least and are most critical of it; however, it does not explain why the junior consultants hardly use it, nor why the intermediate consultants use it only a little more. Thus, to unequivocally dismiss IntCom as inappropriate according to this dimension is wrong. Rather, it should be possible to get more people to use it, especially if you relieve the more senior consultants of the boring elements of the task, through a more structured process of inputting their experience into the system. It cannot be unequivocally said that IntCom is right or wrong based on this dimension. It should be able to increase horizontal coordination and dissemination of knowledge, even if it requires elements of vertical control.

Environment

There are very few concrete facts regarding RMCG's environment in the case study, but we can draw some conclusions. The growth of RMCG and, moreover, its becoming increasingly international, as well as its larger competitors at home being made up of a number of large international consultancy agencies, suggest that this is an industry that is being consolidated. That is, fewer and larger consultancy companies cover an increasingly large part of the market. There don't appear to be any major legal or technological shifts that could shake the market. There is a legal degree of convergence between countries and continents, even though issues like Brexit can entail some turbulence. However, this level of turbulence leads to increased demand for consultancy services rather than shaking and threatening the activities of RMCG. Technological development – including cloud services, digitalization, artificial intelligence and the increasingly intertwined nature of technology – is a growing need for consultants rather than a more cumbersome uncertainty for the consultancy industry. It provides scope for planned product development rather than threatening the core competencies of management consultants. The environment can therefore be said to be relatively predictable, which speaks both for a gradual increase in structuring and for the introduction of systems such as IntCom.

Strategy

As far as strategy is concerned, we can only interpret RMCG indirectly. In a real situation, you could easily complete the information by way of a few simple conversations with managers and consultants. The fact that RMCG is growing can be assumed to be an expression of a growth strategy. Regardless of whether you grow organically or through acquisitions, both can be said to constitute an argument for increased structuring and therefore for IntCom to have a place in it. If growth is a strategy, then this dimension will largely be a repetition of the size and age dimension. Linn refers, among other things, to the firm's large international competitors' unproblematic use of systems similar to IntCom. This can be interpreted as meaning that RMCG is aiming high, both in terms of growth and in terms of types of projects taken on. If you deal with really complex projects, the reasoning is similar to that used in the dimension of core processes and technology. In a really large project, a pure adhocracy or simple structure is not preferable, regardless of complexity, because the size itself (the number of people involved – both consultants and representatives of customers) means that a certain structuring becomes necessary. In these very large projects, there should be scope for exploiting the experience of previous major projects, primarily in the form of formalized processes for organizing and implementing the project. This would suggest that systems such as IntCom have an important function. Again, the less complex data need to be implemented and controlled by more standardized process models, while the more complex problem-solving can only, to some extent, be facilitated by IntCom.

Information technology

IntCom consists largely of an IT system. It is therefore a bit tricky to manage this dimension as an independent variable that affects how RMCG should be organized. The information technology dimension means that IT systems can coordinate more extensive activities without having to use other mechanisms. If there are extensive IT systems, less developed structures and other formalized processes are needed. A comparison with the major international consultancy companies shows that RMCG does not have the latter's IT-supported processes in place, but is, at the same time, not as large and dispersed as these international competitors with their global reach. The safest route here is thus to not put too much emphasis on this dimension in the analysis.

Labor

A management consultant is, as a rule, educated to university level, and at RMCG we have dared to assume that a considerable number of staff are educated at the Stockholm School of Economics, that is to say, at a so-called elite school with an international reputation. A quick conclusion would therefore be that RMCG's activities should not be structured with vertical control and an elaborate technostructure. That would explain the problems in getting consultants to use IntCom. At the same time, it is possible to identify differences between employees in terms of experience. The most experienced consultants use IntCom the least and are most critical of it. The labor force dimension thus, to some extent, explains why the most experienced consultants are the most negative about IntCom.

Summary of the structural analysis

If we summarize the analysis of RMCG and IntCom based on the six situational dependencies, we can conclude that one of them, size and age, clearly indicates that IntCom is a suitable type of mechanism for RMCG. In addition, we may interpret that the environment dimension provides weak support for the same conclusion. We can also see that the labor force dimension clearly indicates that IntCom, as well as the machine-bureaucratic elements of the RMCG, are inappropriate. Other dimensions are more ambiguous and serve to nuance the analysis. The less complex parts, carried out by the least experienced consultants, should be structured with the help of vertical control and technostructure, while the more complex elements should be taken care of by the more experienced consultants, without vertical control.

A result of the above analysis is thus that we have discovered a 'tension', 'friction' or 'contradiction' between the different situational dependencies. Some speak for increased structuring, others against. One way to deal with this 'contradiction' is to return to the basic assumptions of the structural perspective. According to these, one should always specialize and develop hierarchical structures as far as possible. Different degrees and types of uncertainty, in the form of different situational dependencies (the six dimensions), sometimes limit how far you can drive specialization and structuring, but the ambition is always to push it as far as possible. In our present case, if this basic structural reasoning is valid, it implies that we should rely more on the size

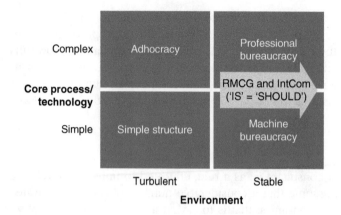

Figure 10.1   IntCom and increased vertical and horizontal coordination are, in principle, appropriate, according to an analysis based on two key dimensions

and age dimension and try to adapt and manage the labor dimension accordingly. In this case, despite very scarce data and contradictory results, our analysis points to the conclusion that RMCG *should* be structured better, and that IntCom is an *appropriate* tool for this endeavor.

Our analysis, as illustrated in Figure 10.1, shows that RMCG should be in the professional and machine-bureaucratic half of the model.

The introduction of IntCom can be seen as moving further from the adhocratic and the simple structures, which justifies the direction of the arrow in the figure. This movement towards increased structuring is also appropriate, according to our earlier analysis. A part of the reason why increased structuring is appropriate is that the environment seems to be stable, with an ongoing consolidation of the relatively young management consulting industry. However, the decisive reason for the appropriateness of increased structuring is neither the degree of complexity of the core technology nor the stabilization of the environment, but the increasing size and age of RMCG.

An in-depth analysis using Greiner

We can deepen the above analysis of RMCG's increasing size and age by using Greiner's model (see Chapter 3). According to Greiner's model, RMCG can be said to be in a phase characterized by *delegation* (see Figure 10.2). In the case of continued growth, RMCG may thus risk falling into a *control crisis*. The introduction of a new coordination mechanism such as IntCom would therefore constitute an appropriate measure to avoid a crisis of control and instead enable RMCG to enter a phase characterized by *coordination*. IntCom is therefore an appropriate solution, as coordination with the help of *delegation* does not work in such large organizations. Supplementing the

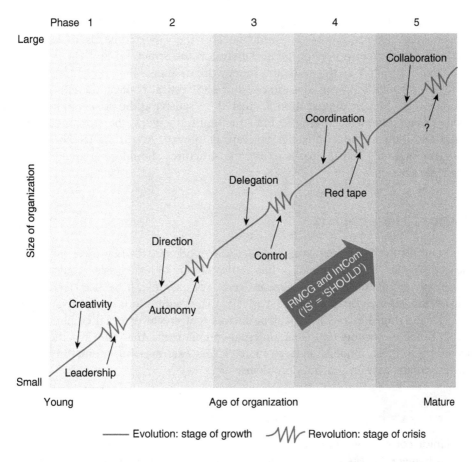

Figure 10.2 **An in-depth 'Greiner analysis' of RMCG's growth and IntCom as an appropriate mechanism**

structural analysis using the six situational dependencies with the Greiner model thus strengthens the conclusion that RMCG *should* be structured better and that IntCom is an *appropriate* tool for this endeavor.

In summary, a structural analysis using Mintzberg's model, supplemented by Greiner's, has resulted in assessing the introduction of IntCom as a structurally appropriate measure. Our structural analysis has thus not been able to offer a reasonable explanation for the consultants' minimal or non-existent use of IntCom. We should therefore look for explanations in the other frameworks. The structural analysis has given us a clue, however, that there may be a problem with IntCom regarding the labor dimension. Since the workforce is relatively highly educated, there could be a problem with increased structuring.

One way of considering the partly contradictory analysis, with conflict mainly between the dimensions of size and age and the labor force, is to see it as a special case of a more general conflict between the structural and HR frameworks (see Figure 4.7). Just as the structural framework assumes that efficient organization is created through long-run division of labor and vertical control, the HR framework assumes that efficient organization is created by satisfying the social and individual needs of employees. According to the structural framework, the structures are optimized and then the appropriate people are employed. According to the HR framework, the opposite is true, that is to say, the structures should be adapted according to people's needs.

A short HR analysis

According to the HR framework, organizations work best if they meet the needs of their employees. In addition, according to the slightly older, 'classic' motivation models, people are characterized by similar needs. For example, if we use Herzberg's and Argyris' models (see Chapter 4), we may state that organizations can motivate employees by satisfying the so-called hygiene factors that create external commitment and the so-called motivators that create internal commitment. Analyzing whether IntCom, according to these models, leads to more or less external and internal involvement, might perhaps explain IntCom's problems.

IntCom as a hygiene factor and a motivator

For junior consultants, IntCom does not imply any major improvement or deterioration in hygiene factors or motivators (see Figure 4.3). Since junior consultants prefer to search for information using Internet search engines over using IntCom, the use of IntCom would rather imply additional regulation and thus reduced freedom with reduced internal involvement (see Table 4.1). But there is one aspect that could favour IntCom increasing both external and internal commitment. Since the use of a fully developed IntCom both affects promotion and pay (hygiene factors) and serves as a means of obtaining information and facilitating personal skills development (motivators), IntCom could, in this way, increase the involvement of both junior and experienced consultants. If IntCom were to contain important and useful information, junior and intermediate consultants would be less dependent on the willingness of senior partners to share their experience.

For the senior partner consultants, however, it is exactly the opposite. They feel no need to either input data into or retrieve information from IntCom. For them, IntCom is a formalized structure that reduces both internal and external engagement.

Models 1 and 2

The key to getting IntCom to work is thus to get information into the system and to somehow get the senior consultants to look beyond their own situation, and to ensure the incentive and efficiency gains that IntCom could provide for RMCG as a company. One possible way forward would be to engage in dialogue with the senior consultants to really understand their reasoning and try to create a common goal with IntCom. When Linn hears what Eric is saying about the senior consultants' attitudes, she rejects them with logical arguments and facts. This may be seen as the expression of communication, according to Argyris' model 1 (see Table 4.2), which does not lead to a productive conversation and probably does not lead to mutual understanding and consensus. According to the HR framework, instead of dismissing the senior consultants' perspective, it would be more appropriate to communicate according to model 2, and in this way try to create a common strategy for IntCom and RMCG's knowledge diffusion.

But is it only up to the perspective and goodwill of the senior partners? Or are there more inherent problems with a so-called knowledge management system like IntCom?

IntCom as a knowledge management system

According to Nonaka and Takeuchi (1995), so-called tacit knowledge cannot be fed into and taken out of a system such as IntCom. A large part of the experience that senior partners share with colleagues, customers and others during their assignments, is gained implicitly. Tacit knowledge is created, according to Nonaka and Takeuchi's model, through 'socialization'. To 'externalize' this type of knowledge in the form of models, written instructions and other, more formalized tools is difficult, energy-intensive and perhaps, to some extent, impossible (see Figure 5.2).

Based on this model, the senior consultants' resistance to IntCom is not primarily about unwillingness or some such, but, rather, these consultants may not be aware of their own knowledge and therefore would find it extremely difficult to externalize this kind of tacit knowledge. To create high-quality input at IntCom, it is not enough to 'write it down'; it requires a more well-thoughtout process. One way to get some sort of information might involve IntCom setting a number of standardized questions for each project. This would require less effort than entering project experience completely freely. On the other hand, such questions would scarcely cover all the tacit knowledge created over the course of a project. Another method is the junior consultants on the project having a structured way to externalize their (and, above all, the experienced consultants') experience. They can record their own experience using a standardized template, and they can both observe and interview the more experienced consultants. By writing down, and interviewing, the junior consultants will be able to reflect on and formulate their experience, which should include an externalization of tacit knowledge. Regardless of the method, an important conclusion from an analysis based on Nonaka and Takeuchi's model is that it is not that simple, and perhaps not even possible, to externalize and disseminate all tacit knowledge into a system like IntCom.

Summary of the HR analysis

This very short HR analysis has resulted in the conclusion that IntCom does not directly hinder or support the involvement of the more junior consultants, but that IntCom would, if it contained more useful information, be able to contribute to increased motivation. However, for the experienced partner consultants it is quite clear that IntCom might impair their internal engagement. If those responsible for IntCom's implementation communicated with the experienced consultants in accordance with model 2, they would probably both be able to improve IntCom and get more people to use it.

At the same time, it may not be possible to spread all the lessons learned through a system such as IntCom. It is not entirely obvious that so-called tacit knowledge can be externalized and forwarded in a formalized knowledge system. Perhaps expectations are unrealistic in terms of what function IntCom can serve?

A short power analysis

According to the power framework, the idea that it is possible to optimize an organization's structures and processes so that it leads to an efficient organization, is not realistic. Also, the idea that it is possible to create common objectives with the right kind of communication, is naïve, according to the same framework. According to the power framework, the introduction of IntCom, the resistance to it and the resulting consequences, are due to the different interests and agendas of various actors. What is happening at RMCG is the result of how these actors play their cards in an ongoing power game.

Analysing the political landscape

The important actors in this case are the junior consultants, the intermediate consultants (associates and senior associates), the experienced partner consultants, Linn and her team (those responsible for IntCom) and the company's management. If you list these actors and try to formulate their agendas, and partly determine how much power they have and of which type, you can create a description of the political landscape, as shown in Figure 10.3. Here we have chosen not to include external actors (such as owners, customers and competitors), which risks giving a misleading picture. But these

Goals and power sources	Actor Management group	Linn's team	Junior consultants	Intermediate consultants	Partner consultants
Goal	Pro	Pro!	(Pro)?	?	Against!
Position	XX	X		X	XX
Knowledge	XX	XX	(X)	X	XX
Control of rewards	XX				XX
Coercive power	X				X
Alliances and networks	XX	X		X	XX
Control over agendas	X	X			
Control over symbols	X				XX
Charisma	?			?	X?
Total power	11? X	5 X	(1) X	3? X	12? X

Figure 10.3   RMCG's political landscape regarding the introduction of IntCom

can instead be dealt with in the analysis of the alliances and networks of the various internal actors. Which actors are included, and which not, in the analysis is partly a matter of taste. The fewer players, the more transparent the analysis; the more players, the more nuanced and informative the analysis. In doing this kind of analysis, one should always try to identify as many players as possible at the start, and assess their objectives and influence. Once that maximum list is constructed, one can reduce the number of actors to the most important ones, and structure the analysis to the specific case.

Another important consideration when analyzing the political landscape is to remember that it has been designed specifically to address the current problem, i.e. the introduction of IntCom. Linn and her team have great knowledge of and good control over the agenda for IntCom, but this is a unique situation. In another situation, the political landscape could therefore look quite different. It is also important to point out that the markings for the actors' influence points – 'X', 'XX', and so on (in Figure 10.3), only represent rough estimates. With more information and with the opportunity to study how the different actors reason, one could produce a much more accurate estimate. For example, we have no idea whether any partner consultants are really perceived to be charismatic, but since they have extensive experience and exert a great deal of influence over day-to-day operations, we can assume that they are generally perceived to have more charisma than the other actors at RMCG.

The above description of the political landscape shows that Linn and her team have much less influence than the experienced partner consultants (5X and 12X respectively). If we limit ourselves to these two stakeholders, it is no wonder that IntCom is difficult to implement. That the company's partner consultants are against IntCom is, from a power framework perspective, very obvious. Several of the partner consultants' strong power bases would probably decrease if IntCom were to be used in full. Their knowledge monopoly would be broken because their knowledge would be turned into structural capital, accessible to all. Both junior and intermediate consultants would be less dependent on partners and could even gain a knowledge advantage over their senior colleagues, if they could use IntCom more. As the use of IntCom also affects promotion and wage-setting, IntCom would reduce partner consultants' control over positions and rewards, given that they currently have quite a lot to say about this.

Developing a power strategy

Linn can thus expect strong resistance from RMCG's partners. The obvious actor for Linn and her team to form an alliance with is RMCG's management. We do not have any information about how management think and what their agenda is. Since the management team is likely to consist of experienced partners, it is likely to have a slightly ambivalent approach to this conflict. However, they are not only partners but also responsible for the entire company, so it is not too daring to assume that they, to some extent, are behind Linn and her quest. It could also be argued that the management team, as well as Linn indirectly, has an indirect alliance with RMCG's international competitors on this issue, in that the latter already have systems similar to IntCom in place, and hence they have a kind of support to lean on.

The question, however, is how far management is willing to go to influence RMCG's partners to, above all, contribute their information and experience to IntCom. And even more problematic for the introduction of IntCom is that, although Linn and her team receive strong support from the company management team, power is still widespread. The company management team perceives IntCom as a sufficiently important strategy to implement, yet, even together with Linn's team, it does not have much more power on this issue than the partner consultants. Linn's team and management's total power is estimated at 16X in the above matrix, while the partner consultants' power is estimated at 12X. The power is thus spread, and, as we can see in Pfeffer's model in Chapter 6 (Figure 6.2), the distribution of power is a decisive factor in whether a conflict will result in an open power struggle. With regard to the second decisive factor, the importance of the decision, we might imagine that the partner consultants attach great importance to the issue. Since partner consultants have a lot to lose, they are likely to fight hard for their cause. The question then remains whether management and Linn, and perhaps other actors, also deem it an important issue to fight for.

From Figure 10.4, we are also able to deduce that the partner consultants have a strong powerbase in the control of symbols. This means that the experienced partner consultants can be said to be role models for other employees in the company. For a long time, the senior partners have been generating large revenues and have extensive,

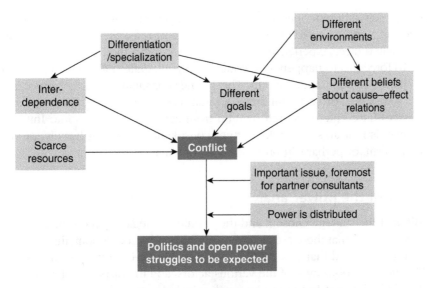

Figure 10.4   According to Pfeffer's (1983) model, there are conditions for an open power struggle for IntCom's future

sought-after skills. It is likely that our junior and intermediate consultants would like to have a future as an experienced partner and they are therefore probably inspired and influenced by them. One possible conclusion of this is that power over symbols and their interpretation (or the third dimension of power, according to Lukes, 1974) is crucial to whether and how IntCom will be implemented. This is linked to which actors it is possible to influence – if not the senior consultants, the junior and less experienced consultants should be easier to get onboard. Their agenda will be more ambiguous, and they can choose to support IntCom and thus stand on the side of management and Linn, and become less dependent on the possible arbitrariness and power of the partner consultants. On the other hand, they might instead choose to ally themselves with their role models, the partner consultants, against IntCom.

A possible power strategy would thus be to try to win over the junior and less experienced consultants with skillfully exerted symbolic leadership. Part of such a strategy would be to emphasize the specific advantages of the system for the less experienced consultants. Another strategy would be to try to win over those partners with extra influence at RMCG. One might be able to coopt some influential partners by adding a group of experts who, alongside management and Linn's team, will be responsible for RMCG's long-term development and knowledge management systems. One could also contact and form an alliance with some of RMCG's large clients and emphasize the benefits of IntCom for them, thereby weakening partner consultants' alliance with clients and, at the same time, avoiding getting into direct conflict with the partner consultants.

A completely different option is to try a harder power strategy (the first and second dimension of power, according to Lukes, 1974), and force the partner consultants to 'debrief' their project experience to junior partners who then encode them into the system. To force this to happen, one could simply integrate IntCom with, for example, the company's remuneration system. The partner consultants simply cannot get their salary or start a new project until they (or junior consultants, based on the information they receive) have entered all information from completed projects into IntCom. But, as our analysis indicates, this risks partner consultants protesting heavily, perhaps by leaving the firm, or perhaps in other ways detrimental to the company.

Summary of the power analysis

Regardless of the strategy chosen, and the counter strategies of the senior consultants, the analysis shows that there are clear indications that IntCom is something that creates extensive conflict and that this conflict may possibly develop into open power struggles. The different objectives of the various actors, and the dispersal of power, explain why it is difficult to get IntCom to be used to its full potential.

The third dimension of power – the power over symbols – seems to be a power-base that Linn and the management team lacks. A partially unanswered question is how the various actors really perceive IntCom. Increased knowledge of the perspectives and assumptions, or cultures, that can be said to exist at RMCG may therefore be a key to solving the riddle of the almost non-existent use of IntCom. Our conclusions so far are crying out for a proper symbolic analysis!

A short symbolic analysis

According to a symbolic framework, actors do not have given goals (or preferences) – they are created and recreated through social interaction. They can be relatively stable, but they are never completely static. The agenda of RMCG's partners is thus not carved in stone but something that is always changing and can be influenced. We have already theorized about whether cooptation of a number of partners could change their attitude, but perhaps there are more underlying explanations for their resistance and more tools to use, given a proper symbolic analysis? Perhaps one can see the conflict between proponents and opponents of IntCom as a clash of two subcultures? Perhaps there is a more general corporate culture that could explain both IntCom's genesis and the resistance to it?

RMCG's three levels of culture

From the case study, we can identify a number of artifacts that may act as clues to identifying some kind of essence within RMCG's corporate culture. An obvious artifact is the name 'Research Management Consulting Group'. What stands out in this name is 'Research'. It is not apparent from the description above, but none of RMCG's competitors has anything similar in their name. Something that is also not apparent from the case study is that, more than 10 years ago, the company management proposed to remove 'Research' from the name, but the more experienced consultants objected. That both founders of RMCG were senior researchers at the Stockholm School of Economics also has relevance and becomes even more relevant if one adds that management, organizational and leadership research at the School of Economics is generally based on qualitative studies. Their researchers also have a close relationship with the objects of their study since both management teams and boards within large Swedish companies are largely staffed by former students from SSE. Both the name RMCG and the founders' background could thus be seen as an expression, at the artifact level, of a basic assumption that knowledge of management is best created through personal interaction with the managers and staff of corporations, and not by the collection of 'data' or formal analyses thereof.

Another telling artifact is RMCG's formal structure. We have already noted in the structural analysis that it consists of several hierarchical levels and probably some sort of matrix structure. This is more or less a standard model for all major international consultancy companies. We can thus see how much the company resembles its major international competitors. However, as we saw in the case study, 40 years ago RMCG only had a handful of employees and has since then grown to over 1,200 employees. Although we have no information on how the company has been organized over the years, we can assume that it didn't have as many levels or equally developed divisions a couple of decades ago as it does today. This in turn means that the senior partner consultants both forged their individual careers and contributed to RMCG's success in a much less structured and formalized RMCG than that which the new, junior consultants experience today.

Even in terms of education, major changes have been made over the years, which means that the junior consultants and RMCG's founders and senior consultants have not really gone to the 'same' school. Today, the education programs at the Stockholm School of Economics have four grading levels; 40 years ago, they had three. Today, the finance programs at bachelor and master's level have more students than the corresponding management programs. If we add the programs in economics and accounting, we see how education at the SSE has become increasingly quantitative in terms of the content that students learn and how it is taught. Today, grading requirements for clear criteria for what produces high scores, as well as choice of focus for what leads to the highest paid jobs, are much more present at most top schools within business education than 40 years ago, not least at the SSE.

Even in terms of espoused values, there is a great deal of material in the case study. Linn explains how effectively IntCom should be able to function as a diffuser of important information. It could make RMCG equipped for future growth. The senior consultants express a concern that IntCom will result in poor service to customers, as less experienced consultants will have incentives and opportunities to settle for giving more standardized and undeveloped advice and solutions to their clients. Linn does not really agree with this and believes that the very point of IntCom is precisely to streamline the more standardized parts of projects to simultaneously free up time for the consultants to develop even better advice and solutions. It is therefore agreed that IntCom can help streamline parts of the activities of RMCG, but there is disagreement about what this will mean in consequence: worse products or more time to develop better products? The diversity of IntCom's consequences may be an expression of the same differences in perspective, as discussed above. How is knowledge of management, organization and leadership best created? Through close and social interaction between consultants and managers, or through the compilation of large amounts of formalized data?

The conflict identified in the power analysis can now be seen from a new perspective. It is not about two different groups of actors with different interests, but a clash of cultures. Established corporate culture that emphasizes social interaction, qualitative tacit knowledge and experience stands against an emerging culture that emphasizes systems, large amounts of data and knowledge in the form of formalized models. The two cultures are about much more than just IntCom, which is rather an artifact that is seen as a solution or a threat, depending on which culture's perspective it is considered from. The partner consultants, junior consultants and Linn can also be seen as artifacts who express the different sides of the cultural clash. However, the clash is much larger than and extends far beyond RMCG's premises. Perhaps it is naive to believe that this collision can be dealt with by new structural solutions, open communication or smart political moves. If the conflict is about two different basic perspectives on how knowledge is created and how consultancy companies and their customers are best organized, then perhaps much more extensive and long-term processes are needed to somehow deal with the problem.

Figure 10.5 shows that RMCG has changed at the artifact level. The once small consultancy firm with its founders and a handful of consultants has been transformed into a large, growing and increasingly international consultancy company. The small group has grown into an increasingly structured and formalized system. On the level of espoused values, however, the change is not as clear-cut. Values created in the small company remain, alongside new values. In the case study, we can therefore find values that express both the old and the emerging cultures.

At the level of basic assumptions, which, according to Schein, is the essence of culture, there is a cultural clash. The assumptions of the old culture about who constitutes 'we', about what constitutes human nature, and how to conduct both consultancy and business in general, are in stark contrast to the new, emerging culture's assumptions. These conflicting assumptions are not limited to RMCG's corporate culture, but are found in the consultancy industry in general, throughout the business world, in

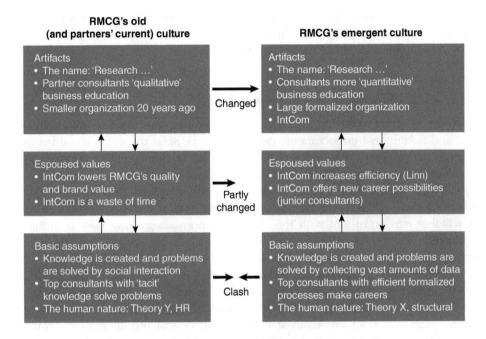

Figure 10.5   RMCG's cultural clash, described using Schein (2004)

educational institutions, in society and even in the deepest academic and scientific philosophical discussions. The two cultures can also be said to be represented by the structural framework (and to some degree by the power framework), on the one hand, and the HR framework (and the symbolic), on the other. It is therefore a conflict on a fundamental and almost all-inclusive level.

One model that helps us understand the above-identified conflicting perspectives in a wider context is that of Barley and Kunda (1992) (see Chapter 9). They describe how management ideals oscillate over time between two basic perspectives: the social human being and rational systems (see Figure 9.5). One might also describe the situation at RMCG as the link between the artifact level and the underlying levels becoming increasingly weak. In other words, in the current situation, there is a loose connection between the substantially altered artifacts and the rigid and partly unchanged basic level of culture.

Is there no possibility that these two basic organizational ideals and subcultures can be integrated or combined within the framework of RMCG's activities? Can one find an optimal balance between the two, as some of the structural models suggest? Or, as the power framework indicates, do you have to fight one of them to reach the other? Based on the symbolic framework, there is an additional opportunity that does not see the problem either as a 'trade-off' or as a struggle that only one side can win. Instead, one could try to maximize both cultures' ideals and thus transform RMCG into both a social community and a lean, mean consulting machine.

RMCG's legitimacy and institutional environment

According to Scott (1998), all organizations need to adapt to pressure from both technical and institutional environments (see Figure 9.4). Scott mentions law firms as an example of companies that find themselves in weak technological and strong institutional environments. It is difficult to measure and evaluate whether a complex consulting service is technically effective, productive or efficient. What difference do RMCG's services actually make for its clients? Instead, this type of activity is evaluated based on whether it is consistent with the ideals and norms regarding how it should be conducted. Do you have the structures and processes considered to characterize a successful organization in the field in question? Such structures and processes, which are perceived to be good, modern and trendy, mean that organizations like RMCG can obtain support by showing off these legitimate structures and processes, regardless of whether they really contribute to their business. It is clear from the case study that systems such as IntCom already exist at RMCG's successful and international competitors. It is therefore important that RMCG also has such a system, regardless of whether it helps in the actual production of consultancy assignments. IntCom makes RMCG a more attractive supplier of consultancy services in the eyes of its potential clients, and makes it a more attractive employer among newly graduated business students. We can therefore explain the advent of IntCom from the perspective that it creates legitimacy rather than efficiency. IntCom is a product of institutional mimetic and normative isomorphism (DiMaggio & Powell 1983), rather than of a quest for effective knowledge dissemination in accordance with the structural or HR frameworks.

IntCom as organizational hypocrisy

We can supplement this view of the role of the institutional environment at RMCG by analysing IntCom using Brunsson's model for organizational hypocrisy (see Chapter 8). The clash between the two cultures or, somewhat reformulated, the loose connection between the changes at the artifact level and in basic assumptions, need not be seen as a problem. On the contrary, the clash, or the loose connection, can be seen as a solution. In Brunsson's terms, IntCom is an example of organizational talk. This talk creates legitimacy by following a 'decision rational' logic (Brunsson 1985; see also Figure 8.2). The more RMCG's management, Linn's team and various project groups and experts are studying the conditions, developing alternative solutions and implementing a 'state of the art' knowledge management system, the greater the legitimacy RMCG will receive. Whether IntCom is then actually used within RMCG's client projects might

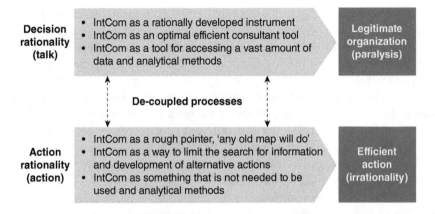

Figure 10.6   IntCom as decoupling decision from action rationality

not be all that important. Chances are that if IntCom is put to use, the projects will be characterized by paralysis. Given that conversations between experienced consultants and customers are replaced by junior consultants' extensive theoretical analysis based on large amounts of data, it can be difficult to find concrete and useful solutions to customers' problems. According to Brunsson's model, the solution is therefore to decouple IntCom from the more practically oriented work in the client projects. In the latter, it is better to act according to 'action rationality' than it is to perform actions based on personal commitment, experience and social interaction.

IntCom can also be put to use in an 'action rational' context. Given that the models and information contained therein are limiting, rather than an opportunity for, more options and more comprehensive evaluations, IntCom can support action rationality. But then it is important that you do not take the rational and structural aspects of the system too seriously. The decision-rational aspects of IntCom need to be de-coupled from the action-rational, as illustrated by Figure 10.6. To foster action rationality, IntCom should be used as a way to set a direction and get under way, but then consultants should not hesitate to depart from all process plans and formalized procedures. In other words, IntCom can be used as 'any old map', in accordance with Weick's model for sensemaking (see Chapter 9). However, in the case of experienced consultants it is hardly necessary to have a map, since they already have procedures and methods for getting through in partly unknown terrain.

Summary of the symbolic analysis

Based on the above analysis of IntCom from a symbolic framework perspective, three important conclusions can be drawn:

1. The advent of IntCom, as well as its role for RMCG, need not have much to do with how the consultants work at RMCG, or any special need for more efficient production. IntCom can instead be seen as an expression of a profound and extensive cultural clash between two basic approaches to how knowledge is created, how people work and how they are best organized.

2. The specific problem with implementing IntCom can also be seen as a solution rather than a problem. The problem contains a formal and an informal side that expresses but also handles the two different subcultures or perspectives. Instead of viewing the two subcultures and their clash as a problem, it can be re-framed and viewed as a solution. It mirrors two major societal cultures and thus creates external legitimacy and support for RMCG.

3. In order for IntCom to contribute to RMCG's future success, it should decouple its (IntCom's) formal, *decision-rational* and legitimizing function in an institutional environment from its *action-rational* and informal function in a technological environment. If you can keep these apart, RMCG can benefit a lot from a system like IntCom. If the two functions are mixed together, IntCom may produce lower levels of legitimacy, less efficient production of consultancy services, fundamental cultural clashes and open power struggles between different groups within the company.

A concluding integrated analysis

Each framework has resulted in a number of interpretations and conclusions. In this final part of the analysis of RMCG's implementation of IntCom, these partial conclusions will be seen in the light of each other, and the analysis will be pushed one more step. Based on the structural analysis, IntCom is a fairly appropriate tool for structuring the growing business. However, the HR framework adds that if you implement IntCom, it risks reducing the motivation of the experienced partner consultants. However, from a power framework perspective, the efforts of the structural and HR analyses to find the optimal combination of coordinated and motivated consultants are naïve. It is rather that the different interests of different groups are in stark conflict with each other and that the risk of open power struggle is palpable.

According to the symbolic framework, however, this conflict does not need to consist of actors and groups that fight each other to achieve their specific goals. According to a symbolic analysis, it is more a question of a fundamental clash of cultures, which, moreover, cannot be delimited to IntCom or RMCG. The experienced partner consultants need not at all be seen as struggling for power, but instead as having strong beliefs about how consultancy assignments are carried out and how knowledge about business development is created in the best way. While the partner consultants are artifacts for a perspective on knowledge and knowledge work, Linn and her team are artifacts for a different perspective. Nor can it be argued that any of these approaches is more correct than the others. We cannot therefore say that the normative conclusion of the structural analysis – that the introduction of IntCom is broadly good – is in line with the conclusion of the symbolic analysis.

However, the symbolic analysis opens up a solution which is neither a balanced optimized structure, a collaborative strategy, nor an open power struggle. Since members of the two subcultures have valid opinions (based on their respective basic assumptions), and these cultures and assumptions are also found outside RMCG, the smartest option is to reflect both these different norms or institutional environments fully. By introducing IntCom at a formal level, and thus mimicking its large, successful competitors, it obtains legitimacy both among clients and among young consultants and potential consultants in the top business schools. By letting senior partners completely ignore IntCom and work as they best please, motivation and high quality customized projects may be produced. The problem of implementing IntCom is then reformulated into a solution. Instead of balancing the recommendations of the structural and HR frameworks, one follows the other. RMCG could do so by developing an advanced system in accordance with the structural framework (and Brunsson's concept decision rationality), while, at the same time, allowing experienced partners to determine their own business in accordance with the HR framework (and Brunsson's concept of action rationality). As IntCom and work on individual projects then become more or less decoupled processes, open power struggles are avoided. In the pinch are those who are unable to see that a partially implemented system can be a solution rather than a problem. It can be a small price to pay for a growing, successful organization. What a good thing it is that all partners do not act in accordance with the decision-rational talk that IntCom encompasses!

Choice of models and reasonable applications

All of the above analyses based on the four frameworks contribute to an increased understanding of IntCom and how little the system is used. It is important to emphasize that the analytical possibilities are far from exhausted in terms of the models used, and in addition there are more models and theories. In other words, the above analyses are only examples of possible analyses. The theory-driven analyses above are not the best or only possible answer, either in terms of choice of models or in how they are applied. However, the choice of analytical models is motivated by the fact that they are all relatively central in their respective framework and that they generate relevant new knowledge of this particular case, that is, the issue of IntCom. The different interpretations made are not the only ones imaginable, or those that are obviously the most logical consequences of the empirical material and the models applied, but they are reasonable. There are limits on how to interpret the empirical material from a given theory. The more rigorously you apply one or more models in an analysis, the more you can reinterpret the material. Consistently conducted theory-driven analysis means that you can go far beyond the seemingly obvious first interpretation without speculation and guesswork.

The reflective practitioner and the good leader

With the help of theory-driven analysis from different organizational theoretical frameworks, reflection has two very positive consequences. On the one hand, the increased understanding creates an increased number of possible actions for how to solve problems and influence events. The increased understanding also creates a self-awareness of the direction in which you want to change the current phenomenon and, by extension, both yourself and the world. A possible negative consequence is that the increased insights and the discovery of more alternative actions lead to paralysis. In accordance with Brunsson's theory of action and decision rationality (see Chapter 9), an increased ability to reflect and apply critical thinking could also reduce the ability to lead, act and interact in a decisive way. Two arguments, however, speak against the suggestion that increased analytical capacity would lead to a worsening of leadership – the need to slow down, and the strong demands on action. It is not difficult to argue that just a dash of paralysis is needed, at the individual, organizational and societal levels. On the other hand, it is unlikely that an increase in analytical capacity will lead to a radically increased level of paralysis in our daily work.

The need to slow down

Our espoused values and our models and theories have evolved over the past century towards increasing focus and rewarding rapid and continuous improvement, over predictability and optimization of resource efficiency (for example, compare the lean model with the classic model of bureaucracy, or the agile methods for project management with the waterfall project methods). At the same time, we measure and evaluate increasingly smaller units, in both time and space. Managers, employees, customers, financiers – all are measured and evaluated more and more often in order to deliver measurable results. In practice, this is translated into an ever-increasing pressure, at all levels and for everyone involved. Today, there is less breathing space and time for more rigorous analyses and for human interaction, without the demand for immediate, measurable results.

Here there is no space to lay out more than a crude and very brief sketch of this development, and even less possibility to develop any kind of solution. But, precisely in the light of our time's almost hysterical focus on ever faster and increasingly measurable results, the ability to see and act beyond this nearsightedness is particularly important. Being able to judge the consequences that a defined project has within a larger context is more important than ever. Being able to stop, albeit just for a second, and devote oneself to reflecting on and critically examining a phenomenon, has even greater value in a world where time really is out of step. Taking the time to talk to and see each other, beyond the task, beyond the deliverables, scorecards, key performance indicators and evaluations, is crucial to our psycho-social health.

It follows that if the creation of both a more rational and human world requires a higher level of analysis and critical thinking, then a dash of paralysis is not just a small price to pay, it is also part of the solution. We need a certain amount of paralysis. It is part of a reflective, fact- and reason-based democratic society, as well as inherent in sustainable organizations, employees and leaders. The academy in general, and the business schools and their various efforts in particular, must have integrity enough to not only run with but also work for a slightly more reflective and critically scrutinizing business and society. A book on organizational theory, used in various academic education contexts, must do the same. And, dear readers, it is also your responsibility as a student, fellow human, coworker and leader, with help from organizational analysis, re-framing and critical ethical thinking, to promote a sustainable working life, sustainable organizations and a sustainable society.

Demands for reflective action

However, slowing down is not the same as stopping. A more rational, reflective and humane working life still requires us to solve fundamental problems through coordinated and effective action. However, it is extremely difficult to imagine how an increase in reflective re-framing and organizational analysis could, in practice, make coordinated action break down. The requirements to perform as individual, group and organization (and entire chains and networks of organizations) are so great that we urgently need to fight for time for reflection, rather than to just continue to perform. The goal of management, organizational and leadership analysis is also not to stop, but rather to choose better roads. If we choose a smarter path, we can get more done, even at a slower pace.

A meaningful metaphor can be gleaned from the world of sailing where a successful regatta can be said to be won by two factors: (1) a high boat speed, which can be accomplished by trimming sails, hulls and crew based on constantly changing wind, wave and current, and (2) choosing the right (shortest) path, which is accomplished by navigating after how the wind shifts and using the help of rips and waves. However, it does not matter if you have the fastest boat speed if you are sailing in the wrong direction. Rather, the sailor who sails the right path wins over the highest speed. The goal of increased reflection and analytical ability is thus to choose the right path and in this way reach goals, without having to keep to an unnecessarily high tempo. Choosing the right path requires that you can see, understand and choose between the different routes available.

Last word: There is so much more!

The content of this book consists of a careful selection of management, organizational and leadership theoretical models. Together, they form an effective package, a compact toolbox containing the most important tools, which can be used to analyze organizational phenomena and create new, actionable knowledge. However, this content only scratches the surface of all the knowledge created in this still relatively young scientific field. Thus, there is much more knowledge to be gained from academic research on management, organization and leadership. The hope is that this book not only constitutes a first journey into this amazing theoretical, analytical and practically relevant world, but that it also sparks your interest to continue the search for knowledge that might help you with your projects and with the responsibility that you have to make companies and organizations even better, in the widest possible sense. Do not, however, see this responsibility as something I, the author of this book, and my colleagues just hope you will take, or require you to take. See it instead as a standing invitation from me, my colleagues and all the research papers and introductory texts on the subject that you can find in databases and libraries. There is nothing wrong with the ongoing popular conversation about organization and leadership, but why not supplement it by reading a book, written by some established researchers on the subject? Why not search the web for the latest developments in motivation theory, based on robust scientific studies? To conclude, I would therefore like to make you more than welcome to look into this academic open house every now and then!

References

Acker, J. (1990), Hierarchies, jobs, bodies: A theory of gendered organizations. *Gender & Society*, *4*(2), pp. 139–58.

Acker, J. (2006), Inequality regimes: Gender, class, and race in organizations. *Gender & Society*, *20*, pp. 441–64.

Acker, J. & Van Houten, D.R. (1974), Differential recruitment and control: The six structuring of organizations. *Administrative Science Quarterly*, *19*(2), pp. 152–63.

Allen, T.J. (1984), *Managing the flow of technology: Technological transfer and the dissemination of technological information within the R&D organization*. Cambridge, MA: MIT Press.

Alvesson, M. (2003), Critical organization theory. In B. Czarniawska & G. Sevón (eds), *The Northern Lights: Organization theory in Scandinavia*. Malmö: Liber ekonomi, pp. 151–74.

Alvesson, M. & Sveningsson, S. (2003), Managers doing leadership: The extra-ordinarization of the mundane. *Human Relations*, *15*, pp. 1–25.

Argyris, C. (1991), Teaching smart people how to learn. *Harvard Business Review*, *69*(3), pp. 99–109.

Argyris, C. (1998), Empowerment: The emperor's new clothes. *Harvard Business Review*, May–June, pp. 98–105.

Argyris, C. & Schön, D.A. (1978), *Organizational learning: A theory of action perspective*. Reading, MA: Addison-Wesley.

Argyris, C. & Schön, D.A. (1996), *Organizational learning II: Theory, method, and practice*. Reading, MA: Addison-Wesley.

Argyris, C., Putnam, R. & Smith, D.M. (1985), *Action science: Concepts, methods, and skills for research and intervention*. San Francisco, CA: Jossey-Bass.

Aristotle (1991), *On rhetoric: A theory of civic discourse* (2nd edn). Trans. G.A. Kennedy. Oxford: Oxford University Press.

Asplund, J. (1983), *About the wonder of society* (new edn). Lund: Argos.

Asplund, J. (1987a), *About greeting ceremonies, micropowers and antisocial talkativeness*. Gothenburg: The Raven.

Asplund, J. (1987b), *The elemental forms of social life*. Gothenburg: The Raven.

Barley, S.R. & Kunda, G. (1992), Design and devotion: Surges of rational and normative ideologies of control in managerial discourse. *Administrative Science Quarterly*, *37*, pp. 363–99.

Barnard, C. (1938), *The functions of the executive*. Cambridge, MA: Harvard University Press.

Bass, B.M. (1985), *Leadership beyond expectations*. New York, NY: Free Press.

Bass, B.M. (1998), *Transformational leadership: Industrial, military, and educational impact*. Mahwah, NJ: Lawrence Erlbaum Associates.

Beck, K. et al. (2001), *Manifesto for agile software development*. Available at: http://agilemanifesto.org.

Blake, R.R. & Mouton, J.S. (1964), *The managerial grid*. Houston, TX: Gulf Publishing.

Blanchard, K.H., Zigarmi, P. & Zigarmi, D. (1985), *Leadership and the one minute manager: Increasing effectiveness through situational leadership*. New York, NY: Morrow.

Blomberg, J. (2003), *Project organisation: Critical analyses of project talk and practice*. Stockholm: Liber.

Blomberg, J. (2005), *Financial market players: An organizational finance perspective*. Malmö: Liber.

Blomberg, J. (2013), *Project myths* (2nd edn). Lund: Student Literature.

Blomberg, J., Kjellberg, H. & Winroth, K. (2012), *Marketing shares, sharing markets: Experts in investment banking*. Basingstoke: Palgrave-Macmillan.

Bolman, L.G. & Deal, E.G. (2013), *Reframing organizations: Artistry, choice, and leadership* (5th edn). Hoboken, NJ: Wiley.

Bruner, J. (1987), *Actual minds, possible worlds*. Cambridge, MA: Harvard University Press.

Brunsson, N. (1985), *The irrational organization: Irrationality as a basis for organizational action and change*. Chichester, NY: Wiley.

Brunsson, N. (1989), *The organization of hypocrisy: Talk, decisions and actions in organizations*. Chichester, NY: Wiley.

Brunsson, N. (2003), Organized hypocrisy. In B. Czarniawska & G. Sevón (eds), *The Northern Lights: Organization theory in Scandinavia*. Malmö: Liber Economics, pp. 201–24.

Burawoy, M. (1979), *Manufacturing consent: Changes in the labor process under monopoly capitalism*. Chicago, IL: University of Chicago Press.

Burns, J.M. (1978), *Leadership*. New York, NY: Harper & Row.

Carlson, S. (1951/1991), *Executive behaviour* (new edn). Uppsala: Acta universitatis Upsaliensis.

Chemers, M.M. (2001), Leadership effectiveness: An integrative review. In M.A. Hogg & R.S. Tindale (eds), *Blackwell handbook of social psychology: Group processes*. Oxford: Blackwell, pp. 376–99.

Chomsky, N. (1988), *Language and politics*. Montreal: Black Rose Books.

Cialdini, R.B. (2009), *Influence science and practice* (5th edn). Boston, MA: Pearson.

Cialdini, R.B., Wissler, R.L. & Schweitzer, N.J. (2002), The science of influence: Basic principles media and negotiators can use. *Dispute Resolution*, 9, pp. 20–2.

Cole, G.D.H. (1948), *Short history of the British working class movement, 1787–1947*. London: George Allen & Unwin.

Colman, A.M. (2015), *A dictionary of psychology*. Oxford: Oxford University Press.

Czarniawska-Joerges, B. (1997), *Narrating the organization: Dramas of institutional identity*. Chicago, IL: University of Chicago Press.

Daft, L.R., Murphy, J. & Willmott, H. (2014), *Organization theory and design: An international perspective* (2nd edn). Andover, Hants: Cengage Learning.

Dahl, R.A. (1957), The concept of power. *Behavioral Science*, 2(3), pp. 201–15.

Deal, E.G. & Kennedy, A.A. (1982), *Corporate cultures: The rites and rituals of corporate life*. New York, NY: Perseus/Addison-Wesley.

DiMaggio, P.J. & Powell, W. (1983), The iron cage revisited: Institutional isomorphism and collective rationality in organizational fields. *American Sociological Review*, 48, pp. 147–60.

Duncan, R. (1979), What is the right organizational structure? Decision Tree Analysis provides the answer. *Organizational Dynamics*, 7(3), pp. 59–70.

Fayol, H. (1916/2008), *Industrial and general administration*. Trans. K. Holmblad Brunsson. Stockholm: Santérus.

Feldman, M.S. & March, J.G. (1981), Information in organizations as signal and symbol. *Administrative Science Quarterly, 26*(2), pp. 171–86.

Fernler, K. (1996), *Diversity or uniformity? Effects of deregulation*. Stockholm: Nerenius & Santérus.

Fielding, K.S. & Hogg, M.A. (1997), Social identity, self-categorization, and leadership: A field study of small interactive groups. *Group Dynamics: Theory, Research, and Practice, 1*, pp. 39–51.

Follett, M.P. (1924), *Creative experience*. New York, NY: Peter Smith.

Follett, M.P. (1927), *Dynamic administration*. New York, NY: Harper & Brothers.

Forssell, A. & Ivarsson Westerberg, A. (2007), *Organization from the ground up*. Malmö: Liber.

Foucault, M. (1969/2002), *The archaeology of knowledge*. London & New York, NY: Routledge.

Foucault, M. (1977), *Discipline and punishment*. London: Tavistock.

Foucault, M. (1980), *Power/knowledge: Selected interviews and other writings, 1972–1977*. New York, NY: Pantheon.

Gagné, M. & Deci, E.L. (2005), Self-determination theory and work motivation. *Journal of Organizational Behavior, 26*, pp. 331–62.

Galbraith, J. (1971), Matrix organization designs: How to combine functional and project forms. *Business Horizons, 7*(3), pp. 29–40.

Gardner, W.L., Avolio, B.J., Luthans, F., May, D.R. & Walumbwa, F.O. (2005), Can you see the real me? A self-based model of authentic leader and follower development. *Leadership Quarterly, 16*, pp. 343–72.

Gardner, W.L., Cogliser, C.C., Davis, K.M. & Dickens, M.P. (2011), Authentic leadership: A review of the literature and research agenda. *Leadership Quarterly, 22*, pp. 1120–45.

Garfinkel, H. (1967), *Studies in ethnomethodology*. Englewood Cliffs, NJ: Prentice-Hall.

Gartner (2015), *Gartner says bimodal IT projects require new project management styles*. Press release, 23 April. Available at: www.gartner.com/newsroom/id/3036017.

Gigerenzer, G. (1991), How to make cognitive illusions disappear: Beyond heuristicising and biases. *European Review of Social Psychology, 2*(1), pp. 83–115.

Gigerenzer, G. & Brighton, H. (2009), Homo Heuristicus: Why biased minds make better inference. *Topics in Cognitive Science, 1*(1), pp. 107–43.

Goleman, D. (1995), *Emotional intelligence: Why it can matter more than IQ*. New York, NY: Bantham Books.

Goleman, D. (1998), *Working with emotional intelligence*. New York, NY: Bantham Books.

Grafström, M. (2006), *The development of Swedish business journalism: Historical roots of an organizational field*. Uppsala: Department of Business Studies.

Greiner, L.E. (1972), Evolution and revolution as organizations grow. *Harvard Business Review, 50*(4), pp. 37–46.

Greiner, L.E. (1998), Evolution and revolution as organizations grow. *Harvard Business Review, 76*(3), pp. 55–67.

Gustafsson, C. (1994), *Production of gravity: On the metaphysics of economic reason*. Stockholm: Nerenius & Santérus.

Habermas, J. (1984), *The rational conviction: An anthology of legitimacy, crisis and politics*. Trans. R. Matz. Stockholm: Academy Literature.

Hackman, J.R. & Oldham, G.R. (1976), Motivation through the design of work: Test of a theory. *Organizational Behavior and Human Performance, 16*, pp. 250–79.

Hackman, J.R. & Oldham, G.R. (1980), *Work redesign*. Reading, MA: Addison-Wesley.

Hägg, I. & Johanson, J. (eds) (1982), *Företag i nätverk [Companies in networks]*. Stockholm: SNS.

Hansson, J. (2005), *Competence as a competitive advantage*. Stockholm: Norstedts.

Hersey, P. & Blanchard, K.H. (1969a), Life cycle theory of leadership. *Training and Development Journal, 23*(5), pp. 26–34.

Hersey, P. & Blanchard, K.H. (1969b), *Management of organizational behavior: Utilizing human resources*. Englewood Cliffs, NJ: Prentice-Hall.

Herzberg, F. (1964), The motivation-hygiene concept and problems of manpower. *Personnel Administrator, 27*, pp. 3–7.

Hofstede, G. (1980), *Culture's consequences: International differences in work-related values*. Beverly Hills, CA: Sage.

Hofstede, G., Hofstede, J. & Minkov, M. (2010), *Cultures and organizations: Software of the mind* (3rd edn). New York, NY: McGraw-Hill.

Hogg, M.A. (2001), A social identity theory of leadership. *Personality and Social Psychology Review, 5*(3), pp. 184–200.

Ilies, R., Morgenson, F.P. & Nahrgang, J.D. (2005), Authentic leadership and eudaemonic well-being: Understanding leader–follower outcomes. *The Leadership Quarterly, 16*, pp. 373–94.

Janis, I. (1971), Reprint of 'Groupthink'. *Psychology Today Magazine*, Nov., pp. 183–91.

Johanson, J. & Mattsson, L.-G. (1987), Interorganizational relations in industrial systems: A network approach compared with the transaction-cost approach. *International Studies of Management & Organization, 17*(1), pp. 34–48.

Johanson, J. & Mattsson, L.-G. (1988), Internationalisation in industrial systems: A network approach. In N. Hood & J.-E. Vahlne (eds), *Strategies in global competition*. London: Croom Helm.

Kahneman, D. (2011), *Thinking, fast and slow*. New York, NY: Farrar Straus Giroux.

Kanter, R.M. (1977), *Men and women of the corporation*. New York, NY: Basic Books.

Kotter, J.P. (1987), *The leadership factor*. New York, NY: Free Press.

Kotter, J.P. (1990a), *A force for change: How leadership differs from management*. New York, NY: Free Press.

Kotter, J.P. (1990b), What leaders really do. *Harvard Business Review, 68*(3), pp. 103–11.

Losada, M. & Heapy, E. (2004), The role of positivity and connectivity in the performance of business teams: A nonlinear dynamic model. *American Behavioral Scientist, 47*(Feb.), pp. 740–65.

Lukes, S.M. (1974), *Power: A radical view*. London: Macmillan.

Lunenburg, F.C. (2011), Leadership versus management: A key distinction – at least in theory. *International Journal of Management, Business, and Administration, 14*(1), pp. 1–4.

Maccoby, M. (2004), Narcissistic leaders: The incredible pros and the inevitable cons. *Harvard Business Review, 82*(1), pp. 92–101.

Malcolm X (1963), Interview by Louis Lomax. Available at: http://teachingamericanhistory.org/library/document/a-summing-up-louis-lomax-interviews-malcolm-x.

Maslow, A. (1943), A theory of human motivation. *Psychological Review, 50*, pp. 370–96.

Mayo, E. (1924), Recovery and industrial fatigue. *The Journal of Personnel Research, 3*, pp. 273–81.

Mayo, E. (1933), *The human problems of an industrial civilization*. New York, NY: Macmillan.

Mayo, E. (1945), *The social problems of an industrial civilization*. Boston: Division of Research, Graduate School of Business Administration, Harvard University.

McGregor, D. (1960), *The human side of enterprise*. New York, NY: McGraw-Hill.

Michels, R. (1915/1968), *Political parties: A sociological study of the oligarchical tendencies of modern democracy*. New York, NY: Free Press.

Mintzberg, H. (1983), *Structures in five: Designing effective organizations*. Englewood Cliffs, NJ: Prentice-Hall.

Modig, N. & Åhlström, P. (2013), *This is lean? Resolving the efficiency paradox* (Ericsson edn). Stockholm: Rheologica Publishing.

Morgan, G. (1986), *Images of organization*. Beverly Hills, CA: Sage.

Nonaka, I. & Takeuchi, H. (1995), *The knowledge creating company: How Japanese companies create the dynamics of innovation*. New York, NY: Oxford University Press.

Northouse, P.G. (2019), *Leadership: Theory and practice* (8th edn). Thousand Oaks, CA: Sage.

Ott, E.M. (1989), Effect of the male–female ratio at work. *Psychology of Women Quarterly*, *13*(1), pp. 41–57.

Peters, T. & Waterman, R.H. (1982), *In search of excellence: Lessons from America's best companies*. New York, NY: HarperCollins.

Petrelius Karlberg, P. (2007), *The media director*. Stockholm: Economic Research Institute at the Stockholm School of Economics, EFI.

Pettigrew, A.M. (1973), *The politics of organizational decision-making*. London: Tavistock.

Pfeffer, J. (1983), *Power in organizations*. Cambridge, MA: Bollinger.

Powell, W.W. & DiMaggio, P.J. (1991), *The new institutionalism in organizational analysis*. Chicago, IL: University of Chicago Press.

Rasche, A. (2008), *The paradoxical foundations of strategic management*. Heidelberg: Physica/Springer.

Roethlisberger, F.J. & Dickson, W.J. (1939), *Management and the worker*. Cambridge, MA: Harvard University Press.

Ryan, R.M. & Deci, E.L. (2000), Self-determining theory and the facilitation of intrinsic motivation, social development, and well-being. *American Psychologist, 55*, pp. 68–78.

Salovey, P. & Mayer, J. (1990), Emotional intelligence. *Imagination, cognition, and personality*, *9*(3), pp. 185–211.

Salzer-Mörling, M. & Strannegård, L. (2004), Leadership in a branded world. In S. Chowdhury (ed.), *Next generation business handbook*. New York, NY: Wiley & Sons, pp. 174–85.

Sapolsky, H. (1972), *The Polaris system development*. Cambridge, MA: Harvard University Press.

Sartre, J.-P. (1943/1983), *Varat och intet [Being and nothing]*. Trans. R. Matz and S. Almqvist. Gothenburg: The Raven.

Schein, E. (1996), Culture: The missing concept in organization studies. *Administrative Science Quarterly*, *41*(2), pp. 229–40.

Schein, E. (2004), *Culture and leadership* (3rd edn). San Francisco, CA: Jossey-Bass.

Schütz, A. (1962), *Collected papers I: The problem of social reality*. (Originally published from 1940–59.) The Hague, Netherlands: Martinus Nijhoff.

Schön, D.A. (1983), *The reflective practitioner: How practitioners think in action*. New York, NY: Basic Books.

Scott, R.W. (1998), *Organizations: Rational, natural, and open systems* (4th edn). Englewood Cliffs, NJ: Prentice-Hall.

Scott, R.W. (2008), *Institutions and organizations: Ideas and interests* (3rd edn). New York, NY: Sage.

Shiry, M.R. (2009), Authentic leadership, organizational culture, and healthy work environments. *Critical Care Nursing Quarterly, 32*(3), pp. 189–98.

Simpson, R. (2004), Masculinity at work: The experience of men in female dominated occupations. *Work, Employment & Society, 18*, pp. 349–68.

Smircich, L. & Morgan, G. (1982), Leadership: The management of meaning. *The Journal of Applied Behavioral Science, 18*(3), pp. 257–73.

Stogdill, R.M. (1974), *Handbook of leadership: A survey of the literature*. New York, NY: Free Press.

Sun, Z. (approx. 500 BC/2015) *Sun Zis Art of War*. Trans. B. Pettersson, K.B. Ooi & H. Friman. Stockholm: Santérus.

Sveningsson, S., Alvesson, M. & Kärreman, D. (2009), Leadership in knowledge-intensive activities: Heroism and everyday magic. In S. Jönsson & L. Samantha (eds), *The leadership book*. Malmö: Liber.

Taylor, F.W. (1911), *The principles of scientific management*. New York, NY: Harper & Brothers.

Thaler, R.H. (ed.) (1993), *Advances in behavioral finance*. New York, NY: Russell Sage Foundation.

Thompson, J.D. (1967), *Organizations in action: Social science bases of administrative theory*. New York, NY: McGraw-Hill.

Tuckman, B.W. (1965), Developmental sequence in small groups. *Psychological Bulletin, 63*(6), pp. 384–99.

Tversky, A. & Kahneman, D. (1974), Judgment under uncertainty: Heuristics and biases. *Science, 185*(4157), pp. 1124–31.

Tversky, A. & Kahneman, D. (1981), The framing of decisions and the psychology of choice. *Science, 211*, pp. 453–8.

Ury, W.L., Fisher, R. & Patton, B.M. (1992), *Getting to yes: Negotiating agreement without giving in*. New York, NY: Houghton Mifflin.

Walker, G. & Weber, D. (1984), A transaction cost approach to make or buy decisions. *Administrative Science Quarterly, 29*, pp. 373–91.

Warming, K. & Ussing, P. (2005), *When this is a man: Joint base analysis*. Roskilde, DK: Roskilde University, Research Center on Gender Equality.

Weber, M. (1905/2003), *The Protestant ethic and the spirit of capitalism*. Trans. T. Parsons. New York, NY: Dover Publications.

Weber, M. (1924/1983), *Ekonomi och Samhälle 1 Förståendesociologins grunder Sociologiska begrepp och definitioner [Economy and society 1: Sociological concepts and definitions]*. Trans. A. Lundquist. Lund: Argos.

Weber, M. (1924/1987), *Ekonomi och Samhälle 3 Förståendesociologins grunder Politisk Sociologi [Economy and society 3: Political sociology]*. Trans. A. Lundquist & J. Retzlaff. Lund: Argos.

Weick, K.E. (1979), *The social psychology of organizing* (2nd edn). New York, NY: McGraw-Hill.

Weick, K.E. (1995), *Sensemaking in organizations*. Thousand Oaks, CA: Sage.

Wheelan, S.A. (2015), *Creating effective teams: A guide for members and leaders*. Thousand Oaks, CA: Sage.

Whyte, W.H. (1952), Groupthink. *Fortune* (March), pp. 114–17, 142, 146.

Williams, C. (ed.) (1993), *Doing 'women's work': But in nontraditional occupations*. Newbury Park, CA: Sage.

Williamson, O.E. (1973), Markets and hierarchies: Some elementary considerations. *Economic Review, 63*(2), p. 316–25.

Williamson, O.E. (1975), *Markets and hierarchies: Analysis and antitrust implications*. New York, NY: Free Press.

Williamson, O.E. (1981), The economics of organization: The transaction cost approach. *American Journal of Sociology*, *87*(3), pp. 548–77.

Wong, C.A. & Cummings, G. (2009), The influence of authentic leadership behaviours on trust and work outcomes in health care staff. *Journal of Leadership Studies*, *3*(2), pp. 6–23.

Yukl, G.A. (2002), *Leadership in organizations*. Englewood Cliffs, NJ: Prentice-Hall.

Zaleznik, A. (1977), Managers and leaders: Are they different? *Harvard Business Review*, *55*, pp. 67–78.

Index

Page numbers in *italics* refer to figures; page numbers in **bold** refer to tables.

legitimate authority, 184, 226
liking principle, 170–171
long-term orientation, 220
Losada, M., 131
Lukes, S.M., 154–156, 173, 228

Maccoby, M., 195–199, 228, 266–267
Machiavelli, N., 149
machine bureaucracy, 37–38, 39–41, *40*, 71, 78, 93, 134, 135
management, 136–139, **137**
management of meaning, 250
managerial discourses, 261
managerial grid, 137–139, *138*
manipulation, 155–156, 167, 173, 228
marketing personality, 198–199
Marx, K., 27
Marxist theorists, 186, 189
masculinity, 219
Maslow, A., 97–99, *98*
matching strategy, 112–113
matrix organizations, 33, 54–58, *55–56*, **58**
Mayo, E., 95–96
McGregor, D., 104–105, *104*, 215
meaningful work, 251
mediatization, 231
Michels, R., 183–185, *184*, 189, 191–192, 225
micro-sociological model, 242–243. *See also* sensemaking
middle management, 38, *38*
mimetic isomorphism, 259
minorities, 176–181
Mintzberg, H. *See* structural configurations
Model 1 and 2 communication, 102–104, **103**, 131
Modig, N., 69, 70
molding strategy, 112
Morgan, G., 24n3
motivation, 106, 118–122, *119*, 251, 260, 286–287
Mouton, J.S., 137–139, *138*
multi-frame analysis, 4–5, 8–9, 13–14, *13*, 18
mutual dependencies, 64–65

narcissistic leaders, 195, 196–198
narcissistic leadership, 228
negotiation, 167–173, 188

neo-institutional organizational theory, 254–263, *257, 261*
networking and alliance building, 166
networks, 75–76. *See also* industrial network approach
Nonaka, I., 117, 123–127, *125*, 287–288
normative ideology, 260–262
normative isomorphism, 259
norming phase, 130
norms, 208–209. *See also* symbolic framework

obsessive leaders, 195, 196, 197–198
Oldham, G.R., 107–108, *109*
oligarchy. *See* iron law of oligarchy
operation management, 21–22
operational core, 38–39, *38*
operations management, 68
organization of work, 107–115, *109–111*
organization theory
    analytical devices for, 20–22
    concept of, 1–2
    critical thinking and, 5–14, *10–13*
    empirical material of, 2–5, *3–4*
    functions of, 8–9
    overview of theoretical frameworks on, 14–20, *15, 17–18, 20*
    See also Research Management Consulting Group (RMCG): case study; *specific frameworks*
organizational behavior (OB), 93
organizational culture
    definition of, 210
    Schein's three levels of culture and, 209–218, *210*, 221, 237–238, 241–242, 251–252, 258, 259–260
organizational development (OD), 93
organizational hypocrisy, 236–238, 257, 258, 296–297
other focus, 131–132, *132*
outsourcing, 75

panopticon, 190–191, *190*
partially controlled motivation, 120–121
perceived autonomy, 119
perfect state, 72
performance-based individual compensation, 187–188

CPSIA information can be obtained
at www.ICGtesting.com
Printed in the USA
JSHW080305211122
33416JS00002B/42